OXFORD HISTORICAL MONOGRAPHS

Duke Richard of York
1411–1460

P. A. JOHNSON

CLARENDON PRESS · OXFORD
1988

Oxford University Press, Walton Street, Oxford OX2 6DP
Oxford New York Toronto
Delhi Bombay Calcutta Madras Karachi
Petaling Jaya Singapore Hong Kong Tokyo
Nairobi Dar es Salaam Cape Town
Melbourne Auckland
and associated companies in
Berlin Ibadan

Oxford is a trade mark of Oxford University Press

Published in the United States
by Oxford University Press, New York

British Library Cataloguing in Publication Data
Johnson, P. A.
Duke Richard of York 1411–1460.—
(Oxford historical monographs).
1. England. Richard Duke of York, 1411–1460.
Biographies
I. Title
942.04'092'4
ISBN 0–19–822946–1

Library of Congress Cataloging in Publication Data
Johnson, P. A.
Duke Richard of York, 1411–1460 / P. A. Johnson.
p. cm. — (Oxford historical monographs)
Bibliography: p.
Includes index.
1. Richard, Duke of York, 1411–1460. 2. York, House of. 3. Great
Britain—History—Henry VI, 1422–1461. 4. Great Britain—History—
Wars of the Roses, 1455–1485. 5. Great Britain—Kings and rulers—
Succession—History. 6. Great Britain—Nobility—Biography.
I. Title. II. Series.
DA247.R47J64 1988 942.04'3'0924—dc19 88–1059
ISBN 0–19–822946–1

Set by Hope Services, Abingdon

Printed in Great Britain
at the University Printing House, Oxford
by David Stanford
Printer to the University

For Margaret Mary

PREFACE

Richard, third duke of York, was a very wealthy peer, and, in the middle years of the fifteenth century, a very important one, but, despite his wealth and his eminence, it is not possible to develop a complete biographical portrait of him, for the sources to permit such a study have not survived. Duke Richard as a landowner, as a patron of the Church, as a man of taste and leisure, does not figure much in these pages and is, anyway, an elusive subject under such headings. Rather, it is Duke Richard as a political peer who is the principal focus of investigation. The work of Griffiths and Wolffe has brought fresh understanding to the problems of government in the reign of Henry VI. It is my hope that this study may offer a preliminary understanding of the most vociferous of the regime's critics.

My interest in the fifteenth century was first aroused in the excellent seminars held by Miss Ann Kettle at the University of St Andrews. The book itself started life some years ago as a doctoral thesis and profited much from the early guidance of Dr J. R. L. Highfield, and the comments of the examiners, Professor Charles Ross and Dr Maurice Keen, but had it not been for the encouragement and painstaking guidance of Dr Gerald Harriss it would have floundered at that stage, and such merit as it may possess ought properly to be ascribed to his generosity of time and critical effort. My departmental colleagues, Clive Carter, Colin Davies, and Hugh Gammell, have been very tolerant of my sundry derelictions of duty while preparing this book, and I am grateful for the assistance of another colleague, Robert Noble, in the deciphering of various manuscript idiosyncrasies. The time to complete this work was allowed me by the Warden and Fellows of Keble College, Oxford, who generously elected me to an education fellowship for the Hilary Term of 1986, and by the support and encouragement of the headmaster of Charterhouse, Peter Attenborough, who made possible my absence from the classroom.

P.A.J.

Charterhouse
April, 1987

CONTENTS

Annales	'Annales Rerum Anglicarum' in *Letters and Papers Illustrative of the Wars of the English in France During the Reign of Henry the Sixth*, ed. J. Stevenson, 2 vols. in 3, Rolls Series (1864), ii/2. 743–93.
Anstis, *Order of the Garter*	J. Anstis, *Register of the Most Noble Order of the Garter*, 2 vols. (1724).
Bale's Chronicle	in *Six Town Chronicles of England*, ed. R. Flenley (Oxford, 1911).
Benet's Chronicle	'John Benet's Chronicle for the Years 1400 to 1462', ed. G. L. and M. A. Harriss, in *Camden Miscellany*, 21, Camden Society, 4th ser. 9 (1972), 151–233.
Berry, *Statutes of Ireland*	*Statute Rolls of the Parliament of Ireland*, ii. *Reign of Henry VI* ed. H. F. Berry (Dublin, 1910).
Bib. Nat. MS Fr.	Paris, Bibliothèque Nationale, Manuscrit Français.
Bib. Nat. MS Fr. nouv. acq.	Paris, Bibliothèque Nationale, Manuscrit Français, Nouvelle Acquisition.
BIHR	*Bulletin of the Institute of Historical Research.*
BJRL	*Bulletin of the John Rylands Library.*
BL Add. Ch.	British Library, Additional Charter.
Brut	*The Brut, or the Chronicles of England*, ed. F. W. Brie, Early English Text Society (1906–8).
CCR	*Calendar of Close Rolls.*
CFR	*Calendar of Fine Rolls.*
Chronicles of London	*Chronicles of London*, ed. C. L. Kingsford (Oxford, 1905).
Complete Peerage	G. E. Cockayne, *The Complete Peerage of England, Scotland, Ireland*, ed. Vicary Gibbs, H. A. Doubleday, G. H. White, and R. S. Lea, 12 vols. in 13 (1910–59).
CPR	*Calendar of Patent Rolls.*
Croyland Chronicle	'Historiae Croylandensis Continuatio', in *Rerum Anglicarum Scriptores Veterum*, ed. W. Fulman (Oxford, 1648).

Davies, *English Chronicle*	*An English Chronicle*, ed. J. S. Davies, Camden Society, 1st ser., 64 (1856).
Davis (ed.), *Paston Letters*	*Paston Letters and Papers of the Fifteenth Century*, ed. N. Davis, 2 vols. (Oxford, 1971–6).
DKR	*Report of the Deputy Keeper of the Public Records.*
EHR	*English Historical Review.*
Emden, *Cambridge*	A. B. Emden, *A Biographical Register of the University of Cambridge to 1500* (Cambridge, 1963).
Emden, *Oxford*	A. B. Emden, *A Biographical Register of the University of Oxford*, 3 vols. (Oxford, 1957–9).
English Historical Literature	C. L. Kingsford, *English Historical Literature in the Fifteenth Century* (Oxford, 1913).
Fabyan's Chronicle	R. Fabyan, *The New Chronicles of England and France*, ed. H. Ellis (1811).
Gairdner (ed.), *Paston Letters*	*The Paston Letters 1422–1509*, ed. James Gairdner, 6 vols. (1904).
Giles, *Chronicon Angliae*	*Incerti Scriptoris Chronicon Angliae de regnis . . . Henrici IV, Henrici V, et Henrici VI*, ed. J. A Giles (1848).
Great Chronicle	*Great Chronicle of London* ed. A. H. Thomas and I. D. Thornley (1938).
Gregory's Chronicle	in *Collections of a London Citizen*, ed. J. Gairdner, Camden Society, 2nd ser., 17 (1876).
Hist. Mss. Comm.	*Historical Manuscripts Commission.*
Nicolas, *Chronicle of London*	N. H. Nicolas and E. Tyrell (eds.), *A Chronicle of London 1189–1483* (1827).
PPC	*Proceedings and Ordinances of the Privy Council of England*, ed. N. H. Nicolas, 6 vols., Record Commission (1834–7).
Reg. Whethamstede	*Registrum Abbatiae Johannis Whethamstede*, ed. H. T. Riley, Rolls Series (1872).
Report on the Dignity of a Peer	*Reports from the Lords Committees Touching the Dignity of a Peer of the Realm (to 1483)*, 5 vols. (1829).
Rot. Parl.	*Rotuli Parliamentorum*, ed. J. Strachey, 6 vols. (1767–77).
Rot. Pat. et Claus. Hib.	*Rotulorum Patentium et Clausorum Cancellariae Hiberniae Calendarium*, i/1. ed. E. Tresham, Irish Record Commission (Dublin, 1828).

Rymer, *Foedera*	T. Rymer, *Foedera, Conventiones, Litterae, et Cuiuscunque Generis Acta Publica*, 20 vols. (1704–35).
Short English Chronicle	'A Short English Chronicle (Lambeth MS 306)', in *Three Fifteenth-Century Chronicles*, ed. J. Gairdner, Camden Society, 2nd ser., 28 (1880).
Six Town Chronicles	*Six Town Chronicles of England*, ed. R. Flenley (Oxford, 1911).
Stevenson, *Letters and Papers*	*Letters and Papers Illustrative of the Wars of the English in France During the Reign of Henry the Sixth*, ed. J. Stevenson, 2 vols. in 3, Rolls Series (1864).
Stow, *Annales*	John Stow, *Annales, or a General Chronicle of England*, ed. E. Howes (1631).
TRHS	*Transactions of the Royal Historical Society*
WAM	London, Westminster Abbey Muniments
Waurin, *Croniques*	J. de Waurin, *Receuil des Croniques et Anchiennes istories de la Grant Bretaigne*, ed. W. and E. L. C. P. Hardy, 5 vols., Rolls Series (1864–91).
Wedgwood, *Biographies*	J. C. Wedgwood, *History of Parliament: Biographies of the Members of the House of Commons, 1439–1509* (1936).

All manuscript citations are of records housed in the Public Record Office, London, unless otherwise stated. Manuscripts housed in the Public Record Office are cited by their class number only, details of which are given in the bibliography. Modern punctuation and accents have been introduced only where necessary to preserve the sense of the original. All books are published in London unless otherwise stated. Figures in accounts are given to the nearest penny. The mark, a unit of account, is two-thirds of a pound, that is, 13s. 4d. A pound was worth approximately nine francs, or nine *livres tournois*.

I

INHERITANCE

Born on 22 September 1411[1] Richard of York was early orphaned. His mother Anne, sister of Edmund Mortimer, earl of March, died soon after his birth. His father, Richard earl of Cambridge, died on the scaffold at Southampton, the penalty for the failure of his plot against Henry V. The child's future was precarious. The one great lord who had an interest in his prospects, his uncle, the childless Edward duke of York, fell at Agincourt, and in November 1415 Richard's father was posthumously attainted.[2] To the great credit of Henry V this act was in no way extended to the young and helpless heir. Henry's motives can only be guessed, but Duke Edward's death had somewhat redeemed the house of York, and there was no reason to suppose that the boy would not grow to be a useful peer of the realm. There was the further consideration that Cardinal Beaufort had an interest in the duchy estates.[3] The 4-year-old Richard succeeded, therefore, to the duchy of York.

On 10 October 1417 he was placed in the guardianship of Sir Robert Waterton, under whose tutelage he remained until 1423.[4] His wardship and marriage were then sold to Ralph Neville, earl of Westmorland for 3,000 marks.[5] On his death, in October 1425, he bequeathed these to Joan Beaufort, already, as his executrix, guardian of the duke.[6] The bequest was now a very valuable one, for the death of his maternal uncle Edmund earl of March, on 19 January 1425, had left Richard sole heir to the vast Mortimer inheritance.

Little can be established of these early years. He was knighted at

---

[1] *Complete Peerage*, xii/2, citing BL Cotton MS Vespasian E VII fo. 58ᵛ (new foliation), gives 21 Sept. (feast of St Matthew) but the source says 'feast of St Maurice' (i.e. 22 Sept.).

[2] *Rot. Parl.* iv. 65–7.   [3] *CPR 1413–16*, p. 349.

[4] J. H. Wylie and W. T. Waugh, *The Reign of Henry V*, 3 vols. (Cambridge, 1914–29), i. 535 n. 1; R. A. Griffiths, *The Reign of King Henry VI: The Exercise of Royal Authority 1422–61* (1981), 666.

[5] *CFR 1422–30*, p. 64. Custody was granted on 13 Dec. 1423. 200 marks were to be paid to the earl for Duke Richard's maintenance (E404/43/341).

[6] *PPC* iii. 194; *CPR 1422–9*, p. 343.

Leicester by the duke of Bedford in May 1426,[7] but he did not appear again on the public scene until 6 November 1429, when he attended the king's coronation in Westminster abbey,[8] and then in January 1430, when he acted as constable of England at a duel in the presence of the king at Smithfield.[9] Having discharged this office, he accompanied the young king on his journey to Paris for coronation, with a small personal retinue of twelve lances and thirty-six archers.[10] Meanwhile, some time before 18 October 1424, Joan Beaufort had betrothed her 9-year-old daughter Cecily to the young Richard,[11] and the marriage had taken place before October 1429,[12] probably in the early summer of that year when Cecily would have reached the canonical age.[13] The first child, Anne, was not born until ten years later and although eleven more children were to be born to the couple only six survived infancy.[14]

Other details of the family and private life of the duke and duchess are entirely wanting. Even so trivial a matter as a portrait is difficult. In the parish church of Cirencester (Glos.) a stained-glass window contains only the head of what was originally a full-length figure which may have been commissioned during York's lifetime.[15]

[7] Rymer, *Foedera*, x. 356. The council added a further 100 marks to his allowance in recognition of this (*CPR 1422–9*, p. 343).

[8] Griffiths, *Reign of Henry VI*, p. 667.

[9] *CPR 1429–36*, p. 38; Griffiths, *Reign of Henry VI*, p. 667. This appointment may have been made in part at least to thwart the aspirations of the Staffords to this office (C. Rawcliffe, *The Staffords, Earls of Stafford and Dukes of Buckingham 1394–1521* (Cambridge, 1978) 37).

[10] *PPC* iv. 28. For this he was paid 500 marks in cash on 12 Apr. 1430 (E403/693). On 3 Aug. 1431 he was further rewarded for service on this expedition with an assignment of 600 marks paid by the hands of John Simmonds (E401/698).

[11] The date is given by her father's will, in which she is mentioned as duchess of York (*Wills and Inventories Illustrative of the History, Manners, Language, Statistics, etc., of the Northern Counties of England, from the Eleventh Century Downwards*, ed. J. Raine, pt. i Surtees Society (1835), 72).

[12] *Calendar of Papal Letters*, viii. *1427–47*, p. 132; but cf. Griffiths, *Reign of Henry VI*, p. 700 n. 4.

[13] Cecily Neville was born on 3 May 1415 (J. R. Lander, 'Marriage and Politics in the Fifteenth Century: The Nevilles and the Wydevilles', *BIHR* 36 (1963), 121). The council allowed an additional 200 marks for his maintenance on 25 Nov. 1429 (*CPR 1429–36*, p. 35).

[14] W. Dugdale, *Monasticon Anglicanum*, ed J. Caley, H. Ellis, and B. Bandinel, 6 vols. in 8, vol. vi (1830), 1602. This metrical chronicle, probably composed for the Austin Friars at Clare (*Victoria County History: Suffolk*, ii. 28), mentions all the children except Richard (b. 2 Oct. 1452). *Annales*, pp. 762 ff., records only ten children. Those not mentioned, William and John, died in infancy.

[15] R. Atkyns, *Ancient Gloucestershire*, 2nd edn. (1768), 179. The surviving glass is reproduced in S. Lysons, *A Collection of Gloucestershire Antiquities* (1804), pl. XV.

Another likeness, also in stained glass, small but full length, is a figure described as 'Ricardus Dux' in the north east oriel window of the hall of Trinity College, Cambridge; though the identification is not without difficulties. Yet if contemporaries were little interested in the young duke, they were very interested in his estates, and a considerable body of written record has survived to reflect this interest, records best presented in the chronology of inheritance.

The attainder of his father deprived Richard of the endowment of the earldom of Cambridge,[16] but in fact he lost little thereby, as his father had no landed interest, being entirely dependent on two exchequer annuities granted him for life by Richard II, and subsequently confirmed by Henry IV.[17] When the first Parliament of Edward IV's reign reversed the attainder, it was indulging solely in an attack on the legitimacy of the Lancastrian regime. No lands or other interests were at stake; no one during the reign of Henry VI felt his interests threatened by the possibility of a revival of the earldom, and such a possibility was at all times remote.

It was as heir to his paternal uncle, Edward duke of York, that Richard first became a landed magnate. Duke Edward had been a very considerable landowner, but held many of his estates for life only, principally those belonging to the Despenser family, and at his death they reverted, by prior agreement, to Richard Beauchamp, earl of Worcester and Isabelle his wife, sole heiress of Thomas Lord Despenser.[18] Another estate, the lordship of the Isle of Wight, together with the castle of Carisbrooke, had been granted to Edward

There is a conventional representation in an illustrated manuscript of the pedigree of Henry VI, the duke being supporter of the English part, but the coat of arms alone distinguishes the figures (BL Royal MS 15 E VI, fo. 3, reproduced in C. D. Ross, *The Wars of the Roses* (1976), 27).

[16] *Rot. Parl.* iv. 65–7.

[17] *CPR* 1399–1401, p. 108. The suggestion that there were entailed lands to be claimed is incorrect, as is the suggestion that he had a reversionary interest in the dower lands of Maud, countess of Cambridge (E. F. Jacob, *The Fifteenth Century* (Oxford, 1961), 465; H. L. Gray, 'Incomes from Land in 1436', *EHR* 49 (1934), 614). The Countess Maud's lands were not dower of the earldom but the jointure of John Lord Latimer on his marriage with the then Maud Clifford, a jointure settlement which the feoffees refused to reverse when the couple were divorced. Maud died seized of these estates, which then by royal licence reverted to Lord Latimer (*Complete Peerage*, vii. 477; *Calendarium Inquisitionum Post Mortem sive Excaetarum*, ed. J. Bayley and J. Caley, 4 vols. Record Commission (1806–28), iv. 232, 348; *CPR* 1446–52, p. 28). Maud retained no ties with her stepson (*Testamenta Eboracensia*, ed. J. Raine, Surtees Society (1855), 118–24).

[18] *CPR* 1413–16, p. 286. Isabelle was the daughter of Constance, sister to Duke Edward (*Complete Peerage*, iv. 282).

and the heirs male of his body,[19] and it, therefore, reverted to the Crown, but was regranted, for life only, to the dowager Duchess Philippa on 10 December 1415, a reversion in favour of the duke of Gloucester being agreed before July 1418.[20] At Philippa's death the Isle of Wight accordingly passed into the hands of Duke Humphrey, but Richard was not to forget the earlier interest of the duchy of York.[21]

The returns of the inquisitions *post mortem* show that Edward died seised of very few of his estates.[22] He had obtained a royal licence on 5 August 1415 permitting him to enfeoff Henry Beaufort bishop of Winchester, Thomas Langley bishop of Durham, Sir Walter Hungerford, Roger Flore of Oakham, Peter Mavan, John Lawrence, John Russell of Hereford, Henry Bracy of Fotheringhay, and John Wykes and their heirs of all his lands in Wiltshire (except Somerford Keynes), Northamptonshire, and Yorkshire (except Wakefield and Sowerby), which were not of the Despenser inheritance, together with Stamford and Grantham (Lincs.), Anstey (Herts.), and Doughton (Glos.).[23] The preamble to the licence states that it was given because Edward had incurred many costs both in preparations for the king's journey to France and in the endowment of the college of Fotheringhay.[24] Edward took advantage of the licence[25] and transferred the estates on 12 August 1415 (except for Doughton, which was transferred only on the eve of Agincourt).

The feoffees retained control of the duchy estates until Duke

---

[19] *CPR* 1408–13, p. 152. A. Crawford, 'The King's Burden?: The Consequences of a Royal Marriage in Fifteenth Century England', in R. A. Griffiths (ed.), *Patronage, the Crown, and the Provinces in Later Medieval England* (Gloucester, 1981), 43, notes the forfeit of the Isle of Wight in 1405. The property was restored to Duke Edward in 1409.

[20] *CPR* 1416–22, p. 129.

[21] Duchess Philippa had been a party to the contest for the Mohun inheritance, which was eventually settled on the Luttrell family. Fear of a reversion of this settlement may well have shaped the political attitudes of James Luttrell. In 1460 he killed the duke of York (*CPR*, 1401–5, p. 506; H. C. Maxwell Lyte, *A History of Dunster*, 2 vols. (1909), i. 83–6).

[22] C138/14/16 n. 45.

[23] BL Campbell Charter X 5; *CPR* 1413–16, p. 349.

[24] Edward pledged jewels to raise cash for the French expedition and the enfeoffment was probably also a pledge for a loan (*The Register of Henry Chichele, archbishop of Canterbury, 1414–1443*, ed. E. F. Jacob, Canterbury and York Society, 4 vols. (1937–47), iii. 63).

[25] *CCR* 1413–19, p. 294.

Richard came of age,[26] partly for financial reasons, but also to permit the endowment of Fotheringhay College. What steps they took themselves, if any, to further this foundation are unknown, but when, on 1 July 1433, the duke of York entered into recognizances with Cardinal Beaufort in the sum of £2,000 it was agreed that a maximum of £1,000 would be applied in ten equal instalments to the endowment of the college. It was also agreed that, having fulfilled various obligations to annuitants of the late duke, and discharged diverse debts within two years, York would be re-enfeoffed with the duchy estates.[27]

A modest group of properties was not part of this enfeoffment, and their administration, therefore, reverted to the Crown during Richard's minority. The manor of Somerford Keynes was committed to the keeping of Sir Walter Beauchamp and the Essex estates to Joan countess of Hereford.[28] The duchy manor of Barton Bristol brought problems of a different kind. Originally a life grant to Duke Edward, when earl of Cambridge,[29] it was confirmed to him in tail male on 15 October 1402,[30] and though the Gloucestershire inquisition *post mortem* recorded that it had been enfeoffed on a group of persons headed by the bishop of Durham and Sir John Pelham,[31] the same manor was, on 12 December 1415, settled on Humphrey duke of Gloucester, again in tail male, and it remained with him until his death.[32] In itself, there was nothing difficult about

[26] In 1428 and again in 1430 they presented to the duchy living of Anstey (J. E. Cussans, *History of Hertfordshire*, 3 vols. (1870–81), ii. 62.

[27] *CCR* 1429–35, p. 260. Dugdale erroneously interpreted the enfeoffment licence of 5 Aug. 1415 as a licence to endow the college, citing in support an indenture of 24 Sept. 1434 whereby a mason, William Horwood, was granted a total payment of £300 for building the college, Duke Richard providing the materials. Thompson suspected the error, but Dugdale has been supported by Rosenthal (W. Dugdale, *The Baronage of England*, 2 vols. (1675–6), ii. 157, id., *Monasticon Anglicanum*, viii. 1414; A. H. Thompson, 'The Statutes of the College of St Mary and All Saints Fotheringhay', *Archaeological Journal*, 75 (1918), 247; J. T. Rosenthal, 'Richard, Duke of York: A Fifteenth-Century Layman and the Church', *Catholic History Review*, 50 (1964–5), 176.) The visitation records of 1438 and 1442 report the college as modestly endowed. An undated *valor* of the college estates shows gross income of £268. 4s. 4d. (SC11/519; cf. *CPR* 1446–52, p. 113). In 1447/8 York was paying £425 to the college in 28-mark instalments (WAM 12165). He retained an interest in the college thereafter (*Calendar of Papal Letters*, x. *1447–55*, p. 93).

[28] *CPR* 1413–16, p. 380; *CPR* 1416–22, p. 172.

[29] *CPR* 1377–81, p. 578.

[30] *CPR* 1401–5, p. 168.

[31] C138/14 n. 45(1). This is probably to be identified with the enfeoffment of 26 May 1412 (*CPR* 1408–13, p. 406).

[32] *CPR* 1413–16, p. 397.

this, but the loss of Barton Bristol did have implications for one of the two exchequer annuities which Richard inherited from Duke Edward.

At the original creation of Edmund of Langley as earl of Cambridge a thousand-mark annuity was granted him until suitable landed provision could be made for this support.[33] Successive grants, including Barton Bristol, whittled down this annuity and at the death of his son, Duke Edward, only £283. 6s. 8d. was still paid at the exchequer, £94. 8s. 10d. of this being paid to the Duchess Joan in dower. The value of Barton Bristol, £83. 18s. 5d. in October 1402, had been deducted in 1402 from the duke's exchequer entitlement, as was correct, and so the loss of the manor in 1415 should have brought a compensatory addition to the annuity payable to Duke Richard. Not only was no such compensation to be attempted in 1430s and 1440s, but the warrants for issue actually rubbed salt into the injury by reciting that Duke Richard was entitled to £188. 17s. 9d., less the value of Barton Bristol, and duly ordered payment of £101. 19s. 4d.[34] The warrants were not, of course, intended to be malicious, simply to clarify the dower entitlement of the Duchess Joan,[35] who enjoyed no dower portion in Barton Bristol, but they did serve as a constant reminder that the loss of the manor to the duke of Gloucester was costing York £83. 18s. 5d. in annuity entitlement, and when Duke Humphrey died York was quick to secure confirmation of his full rights.[36]

Edmund of Langley, on creation as first duke of York, had been assigned a second annuity of £1,000 — £500 coming from the wool subsidy at London, £400 from the wool subsidy at Hull, and £100 from the issues of Yorkshire. At Duke Edward's death £239. 6s. 8d. was due from London, the balance having been settled in land, £400 from Hull and £100 from Yorkshire. These annuities were inherited by Duke Richard, the dowager duchesses Joan and Philippa having appropriate portions.

York was unable to realize the full value of these annuities. In the years 1432–60 he received from the London customs £6,369. 2s. 9d. and from the Hull customs £5,447. 12s. 8d.; a total of

---

[33] *CPR* 1374–7, pp. 347, 367.

[34] For example, E404/52/309. Many warrants for York's annuities survive.

[35] On her death York retained the dower portion of her annuity, but had payment of this thereafter by separate warrant, presumably because of the Barton Bristol complication (E404/55/93).

[36] *CPR* 1446–52, p. 117.

£11,816. 15s. 5d.[37] In theory he was due £17,901. 6s. 8d., so a total of £6,084. 11s. 3d. was outstanding.[38] For this, his agents sought assignment at the exchequer. In addition they sought payment there of the £101. 19s. 4d. due from the thousand-mark annuity, and also, after the death of Duchess Joan, of the dower portion of the same annuity, £86. 6s. 8d., which amounted to a total of £5,188. 8s. 0d. Over the twenty-eight-year period the sum due to York was £11,272. 19s. 3d., and, given the many pressures on the exchequer, York's agents were to be remarkably successful in obtaining payment, securing assignments totalling £4,600. 16s. 8d.[39] Usually, the success of assignments is difficult to determine, but it is possible to have confidence in many of these. Frequently, York's agents contrived to secure them against payments due from the duke to the exchequer. The fee farms of Builth and Montgomery were regularly used until remitted and, when resumed, they were promptly used again for the purpose.[40] Friendly sources were also employed, especially the escheators' revenues and the fee farms of sheriffs in the marcher counties. In July 1454 annuity arrears were assigned against fines due in Derbyshire, where York was to act as principal commissioner of oyer and terminer.

In total, York received approximately £16,000 of the £29,000 due to him, an average annual income of £600. Although entitled to much more, he did not, given the general financial circumstances, do badly out of his annuities, and, in defence of the exchequer's failure to meet its full obligations, it might be urged that the original intention of the grants had been to enable the estate of a duke to be maintained. By the time he came of age, York was well able to do this on landed income alone.

It was the earldom of March which changed Richard of York from a substantial landowner to a great one,[41] but, like the duchy estates, the transmission of the Mortimer estates is complicated, this time by a fine levied in the King's Bench in Trinity Term 1415. By this fine,

[37] J. M. W. Bean, 'The Financial Position of Richard, Duke of York', in J. Gillingham and J. C. Holt (eds.), *War and Government in the Middle Ages* (Cambridge, 1984), tab. i.

[38] These, and subsequent, calculations are taken from the issue and receipt rolls of the exchequer (E401, E403) except where otherwise acknowledged. They ignore the assignment made on the fee farm of Yorkshire and the sums due in lieu of Barton Bristol.

[39] Bean, 'Financial Position' tab. ii., gives £4,297. 19s. 1d.

[40] £310 in Jan. 1454, £406. 13s. 4d. in July 1458 (E403/795, 814).

[41] The returns of the inquisition *post mortem* are C138/18, 19.

the earl quitclaimed all his right in a large number of properties to
Richard Courtney bishop of Norwich, Thomas earl of Arundel,
Richard earl of Warwick, Sir Henry Scrope, Sir Thomas Berkeley,
Sir Edward Cherleton, Joan Lady Bergavenny, Sir John Pelham,
Robert Corbet, Sir John Greyndour, Sir Walter Lucy, Thomas
Chaucer, William Walwyn, Thomas Holcote, and Richard Wigmore,
in consideration of £100,000, Thomas Berkeley being given a
reversionary interest in Orleton, Farlow, Clifton, Docklington, and
Finmere.[42] The whole picture is then complicated further by a debt
of £6,046. 13s. 4d., owed as part of the 10,000 marks which the late
earl had agreed as his marriage fine with the king.[43]

On the death of the earl, the exchequer set about the recovery of
the money owed for the fine. Initially it sought to seize the goods and
chattels of the late earl, but the executors were uncooperative,[44] and
the exchequer turned instead to the profits of his estates. The actions
of Maurice Bruyn, sheriff of Hampshire, illustrate the technique. He
was ordered, on 12 April 1425, to hold an inquiry into the earl's
lands and seize them for the liquidation of the debt. Eight days later
he returned, correctly, that the late earl held no land, it all being
enfeoffed, but, none the less, he seized the three enfeoffed
properties, Hooke Mortimer, Worthy Mortimer, and Stratfield
Mortimer, and accounted for them for a quarter of a year and
seventy-two days. This arrangement continued to hold for the next
two years, until 7 November 1428 when the first two manors were
farmed to William Knight.[45] In Buckinghamshire the sheriff acted
similarly, again entering enfeoffed lands.[46] In Essex the sheriff
seized the only manor not enfeoffed, North Fambridge, on 9 July

---

[42] CP25(1) 291/63; copy in Winchester College Muniments (Hants) n. 19811. It is
possible that both this enfeoffment and that of Duke Edward were, in part, an attempt
to keep lands out of royal hands in the event of sudden death on campaign. For earlier
examples of this practice in the earldom of March see G. A. Holmes, *The Estates of
the Higher Nobility in XIV Century England* (Cambridge, 1957), 45.

[43] Edmund's will directed that his feoffees, in default of issue, should pay his
debts, then give seisin to Isabelle his niece, wife of Sir Thomas Gray, of lands to the
value of 300 marks p.a. in tail to her right heirs and, after the death of Anne his
consort, of lands to a total value of 500 marks p.a. In Mar. 1462 this had not been
done, but Edward IV evidently believed that some residual title to part of his
inheritance remained, and so he granted Henry earl of Essex, Isabelle's husband, a
total of fifteen manors in East Anglia together with the reversion of the manor of
Newhall (*CPR* 1461–7, p. 145).

[44] SC8/26/1296.

[45] E199/16/22, 23.

[46] E199/2/11.

1426.[47] In Kent the manor of Kingsdown was seized, and subsequently farmed to Thomas Tonbridge esq.[48] The exchequer's plodding labour in pursuit of its dues was, however, already profoundly handicapped by the decision, on 1 May 1425, to grant to the duke of Exeter the keeping of all lands of the earldom of March in East Anglia and Hertfordshire, to hold until the majority of Duke Richard, rendering their full value.[49] On 23 June 1425 the duke of Gloucester was committed with the care of the remainder of the earldom, excepting the manors of Marshwood and Gussage Bohun, again rendering their full value.[50] Such powerful interests hindered further exchequer efforts,[51] but it retained control of some estates until York came of age, when he was initially obliged to undertake to pay the remainder of the debt to the Crown. In August 1433 he petitioned for the cancellation of the whole debt,[52] and by June 1434 he had obtained a general pardon, as heir of the earl of March, which he successfully pleaded thereafter.[53]

The commitment of most of the earldom to the dukes of Exeter and Gloucester cut across not only the claims of the exchequer but also the legal rights of the feoffees. Not all the earldom had been enfeoffed (the earl dying seised of most of his Welsh estates but not those in the marcher counties), but this made no difference to the effect of the grants to the two dukes. Riding roughshod over the rights of the feoffees, they took up the farm of the estates. Publicly the action may have been justified on the grounds that the returns of the inquisitions *post mortem* were insufficient.[54] The real reasons are unknown, but they can only have been grave. Much the most probable was the fear of a Mortimer insurrection, for Sir John Mortimer had recently admitted to a wide-ranging plot in the Welsh

[47] E199/11/27 mm. 5, 6. The sheriff, John Doreward, was an official of the earldom.

[48] *CFR* 1422–30, p. 300.

[49] Ibid. 85; *CPR* 1422–9, p. 518.

[50] *CFR* 1422–30, p. 103. Marshwood and Gussage Bohun were committed on 6 Mar. 1425 to John Warren, John Jordan, and John Hilary (ibid. 98) and on 28 Feb. 1426 to Sir Richard Stafford (ibid. 119).

[51] On 15 July 1427 £701. 3s. 0d. in tallies assigned against the fine were cancelled, and reassigned against the issues of the earldom (E404/43/354).

[52] SC8/26/1289. This was allowed on condition that such assignments against the fine as had been paid should be allowed to stand.

[53] E159/214 Easter Term 16 m. 10. He was thereby also relieved of a debt of £435. 4s. 4d. owed by the earl of March to Henry Lord Scrope, which the Crown claimed.

[54] *CPR* 1422–9, p. 290.

march, which had floundered, he claimed, only because of the late earl's indifference; 'a draw', to quote Sir John.[55]

When Exeter died, on 31 December 1426, the administration of the estates again reverted to the Crown, where they remained for the next three years, to be committed, on 5 December 1429, to Henry earl of Northumberland, Sir John Tiptoft, Sir Maurice Bruyn, John Simmonds, and John Gargrave, at a yearly farm of their full value.[56] Meanwhile, on 4 November 1428, the particulars of the grant to the duke of Gloucester had been clarified, it being agreed that he render £1,764. 4s. 5d. per annum over and above the £361. 17s. 8d. paid as fees and wages to office-holders.[57] Provision was also made for the dower of the countess Anne. The terms, as regards allowable charges, were further clarified on 15 February 1429,[58] with a view to Gloucester surrendering custody the following day. The estates farmed to him were immediately regranted to Duke Richard, William Alnwick bishop of Norwich, and the earl of Northumberland, on identical terms.[59]

The intention underlying this grant was presumably to allow Duke Richard to acquire some familiarity with his estates and their management, and perhaps to allow him an opportunity to recruit a modest retinue to accompany the young King Henry on the proposed journey to France for coronation. It is not known where he was at this time, but the two settlements of his estates both include Henry earl of Northumberland as custodian. Joan Beaufort may well have committed Richard to the care of the earl, her son-in-law, his wife Eleanor being Duchess Cecily's sister.

The duke of York gained livery of his estates on 12 May 1432, a complicating factor being the various statements of his age returned at the inquisitions on Duke Edward and Earl Edmund. For this, an act of grace was required.[60] It was the first, and most trivial, of the legal problems now facing him. The Crown was in a position to restore his March estates, but had held them for the most part in defiance of the rights of the feoffees. These had now to be disentangled, and there were also the interests of dowagers to be considered.

The duchy of York was restored to him without undue difficulty,

[55] *Great Chronicle*, p. 131. John Tiptoft was created steward of all lands of the earldom five days after the earl's death (*CPR 1422–9*, p. 266).
[56] *CFR 1422–30*, p. 286.   [57] Ibid. 249.   [58] *CFR 1422–30*, p. 260.
[59] Ibid. 262.   [60] *CCR 1429–35*, p. 150.

as was a part of the earldom of March. The enfeoffed portion of the earldom was more taxing. It can be shown that in 1436 these estates were in the hands of Duke Richard, Sir Walter Lucy, and Richard Wigmore,[61] so by that date the original feoffees had evidently surrendered their interest, but probably not without some sort of financial settlement. This is suggested by a draft indenture, cancelled and undated, between the feoffees and the duke alone, restoring the estates to the duke for a term of twenty years, he to pay 2,000 marks per annum.[62] That there might be some sort of challenge to his right in these estates had been in part anticipated by York (or more probably his advisers), for on 20 February 1429—in person, in the King's Bench—he laid claim to the south-western manors and Bromsgrove by right of inheritance.[63] The cases were deferred to his majority, but the possibility cannot be ruled out that the duke was obliged to come to some sort of financial arrangement with the feoffees before his legal title in the estates could be clearly established.

If this is so, and it can only be surmised, York in his early years faced considerable financial outgoings relating to the minority administration of his estates. He was committed to clearing Duke Edward's debts and endowing Fotheringay, and was bound to the duke of Gloucester for £969. 7s. 2d., and to the king for 1,000 marks.[64] The money due to Gloucester was almost certainly arrears from the three years in which he had had custody of the estates, and arrangements were made on 18 July 1432 to repay him over the next five years.[65]

On 18 July recognizances were entered into in Chancery for half-yearly instalments of 100 marks for livery of the estates.[66] He incurred a further livery fine of 1,000 marks for the lands of the dowager countess of March, on 26 November 1432, but he was pardoned this in August 1433.[67] The death of the countess also relieved him of the burden of dower. Duke Edward's wife, Philippa, had died during his minority, but the dowager duchess Joan was still

---

[61] CP25(1) 292/68 n. 186. P. H. Reaney and M. Fitch, *Feet of Fines for Essex*, 4 vols. (Colchester, 1964), iv. 23.

[62] BL Harleian Charter 53 H 17.   [63] BL Egerton Roll 8758, 8759.

[64] *CCR 1429–35*, pp. 260, 190; *CPR 1429–36*, p. 207. The order that he be given livery speaks of great waste (*CCR 1429–35*, p. 159).

[65] The conditions of repayment are added in a hand different from that of the original parliamentary petition for livery (SC8/26/1260; cf. *Rot. Parl.*, iv. 397).

[66] *CCR 1429–35*, p. 190.   [67] *CFR 1430–7*, p. 122; SC8/26/1289.

enjoying her dower portion when he came of age. She, however, died on 12 April 1434,[68] so the third duke enjoyed all his estates before he was 23; a very fortunate circumstance. Thereafter, his landed holdings were only marginally augmented.

As one of the sisters of Edmund earl of Kent, Duchess Joan was an heiress in her own right, from which, in a complicated manner, York benefited. Earl Edmund had died in 1408, but the estate was still disputed nearly twenty years later, when the heirs lodged a joint petition to Parliament, requesting that John Lord Audley's claim to the whole earldom, in the right of his wife Eleanor as sole child of a purported marriage between Edmund and Constance (a daughter of Edmund of Langley), be disallowed.[69] The petition was successful, and so, on the death of Joan, childless despite her four marriages, her estates were partitioned amongst her sisters and their heirs.[70] York's mother Anne was one of the three daughters and co-heirs of Eleanor, one of the five sisters, Anne being the child of Eleanor's first marriage to Roger Mortimer earl of March, and Joyce and Joan the daughters of her second marriage to Edward Lord Cherleton.[71] Richard, therefore, inherited one third of a fifth portion, valued by the exchequer at £36. 1s. 3d.[72] He also inherited an enemy in Lord Audley. The other addition was equally modest, if less contentious. Cressage (Salop) escheated to him on the failure of right heirs to Thomas Foulehurst.[73] Attempts to buy Canford (Dorset) in 1445 and Caister (Norfolk) in 1456 both failed.[74]

Two royal grants brought York advantages from estates he already held. The fee farm for Builth, 170 marks, was remitted to him,[75] as

[68] Order to give seisin of her lands, 25 June 1434 (*CFR* 1430–7, p. 207). For the inquisition *post mortem* see C139/66.

[69] *Rot. Parl.* iv. 375.

[70] C47/9/35. The duke of York received lands in Cottingham (Yorks. ER) valued at £26, other small properties in the same area (£2. 4s. 4d., the hundred of Berstaple (Essex) (£5. 0s. 8d.), and a moiety of the fee farm of Droitwich (£2. 16s. 3d.).

[71] *Rot. Parl.* iv. 375; *Complete Peerage*, xii, 1 746–9. T. B. Pugh, 'Richard Plantagenet (1411–60), Duke of York, as the King's Lieutenant in France and Ireland', in J. G. Rowe (ed.), *Aspects of Late Medieval Government and Society* (1986), 111 and 133 n. 19, overlooks Joyce and Joan and so overestimates the value of the Holland inheritance descending to the Mortimer line.

[72] *CFR* 1437–45, p. 270.

[73] *CCR* 1435–41, p. 401.

[74] BL Egerton Roll 8782; Davis (ed.), *Paston Letters*, ii. 166.

[75] *CPR* 1436–41, p. 168. A condition of the grant was that York should pay Sir John Popham the 100-mark annuity which he had hitherto drawn at the exchequer by assignment on the Builth fee farm. In 1459 it was believed that the value of the lordship scarcely exceeded the fee farm (*CPR* 1452–61, p. 550).

were the eighty-five marks due for Montgomery,[76] and there was some advantage in having his Home-Counties estates exempted from purveyance.[77] A fourth grant, to act as a custodian of the lands of Isabelle countess of Warwick, brought nothing but trouble, the bishop of Durham taking umbrage at the infringement of his rights and forcibly occupying Barnard Castle.[78]

The duke himself made only two gifts of land, a close, a cottage, and six acres in Great Walsingham (Norfolk) to the convent of the Friars Minor there,[79] and to William Oldhall a life grant of the manors of Standon, Plesshy (Herts.), Swanscombe (Kent), and Hambledon (Bucks.), in May 1441.[80] The manor of Arley, the subject of a legal action in York's minority, had to be defended when he came of age from the claims of John Harpur. York won the action in the Hilary Term of 1438,[81] but seems to have felt the title less secure than others, and he parted with the manor later, probably by sale, to his councillor Sir William Burley, along with another less assured manor, Cressage.[82] Another legal action, of considerable complexity, was fought with the Pauncefoot family over the lordship of Crickhowell, but, despite a licence to sue for recovery obtained in Parliament in March 1445, York chose not to prosecute the action further.[83]

In March 1441 he made provision for the Duchess Cecily, granting her nine properties in East Anglia, together with Marshwood, Bisley, and Pirbright.[84] This was almost certainly part of a much more comprehensive arrangement, as it was possible for a large number of properties to be mortgaged by the duke and duchess jointly in 1448–9, and when, in 1460, provision was made for her husband's attainder, a much longer list of manors (worth at least

---

[76] *CPR* 1436–41, p. 167. The fee farm had been assigned in 1422 to Catherine of Valois, and the reversion was probably negotiated after her death (*CCR* 1422–9, p. 26).

[77] *CPR* 1436–41, p. 473.

[78] Ibid. 279, 408; E40/15049. [79] *CPR* 1436–41, p. 544.

[80] Ibid. 541. This grant was substantially amended in the late 1440s.

[81] *CPR* 1429–36, p. 186; C44/27/25; S. Shaw, *The History and Antiquities of Staffordshire*, 2 vols. (1798–1801), ii. 257.

[82] J. S. Roskell, 'William Burley of Broncroft, Speaker for the Commons in 1437 and 1445–6', *Transactions of the Shropshire Archaeological Society*. 56 (1960), 264, 270, repr. in J. S. Roskell, *Parliament and Politics in Late Medieval England*, 3 vols. (1983), iii. 343–53. Burley's wife already held the dower portion of Cressage (*CCR* 1468–76 n. 624; *Victoria County History: Shropshire*, viii. 75). For other properties granted as life interests at this time see below p. 62.

[83] *CPR* 1441–6, pp. 320, 334. [84] *PPC* v. 136–8.

1,000 marks per annum) was assigned to her.[85] In June 1461 Edward IV sought to recompense his mother in full for her jointure lands with a grant of property worth 5,000 marks per annum,[86] an interesting indirect pointer to contemporary opinion of the value of the duchy. It was his father's intention that Edward should inherit all his estates,[87] as indeed he did, and that Edmund of Rutland should become a French landowner. This project collapsed in 1450, and York devised no other settlement for Edmund, nor for his younger brothers. For the two daughters he managed to marry he found dowries in cash. Essentially, York sought, with success, to preserve his inheritance intact.

The estates of the duchy and the earldom had long since been let to farm, and York, therefore, like most of his contemporary magnate landowners, was essentially a rent-collector. For this purpose, his estates were grouped in receiverships founded for the most part on geographic convenience. There were nineteen receiverships in all. Eleven lay in Wales and the Welsh march, of which one, Ewyas Lacy, was formerly a duchy receivership, and another, Builth, was farmed from the Crown. A reasonably compact group of estates, their administration could be readily conducted from Ludlow and Montgomery, the Pembrokeshire lordship of Narberth excepted. This latter was, administratively, a most inconvenient group of estates, and it is not surprising that it was farmed separately during the duke's minority, and in 1449 was to be the only Welsh property to be mortgaged. Of the eight English receiverships, five were reasonably well grouped. The honour of Clare included outlying lands in Surrey, Sussex, Cambridgeshire, and Huntingdonshire, but was essentially a compact block on the Norfolk–Suffolk border. A Mortimer honour, Duke Richard found it administratively convenient to add to it the duchy lands at Rayleigh and elsewhere in Essex. Other Surrey and Sussex properties were grouped together with the north Kent manors into a small and diffuse receivership. There was a good case for placing the former Mortimer manors in Berkshire into this receivership, but, instead, they were united with the duchy manors in Wiltshire. The two Oxfordshire and three

[85] *CPR* 1452–61, p. 542.

[86] *CPR* 1461–7, p. 131.

[87] The only indication that York took any steps in this direction in his lifetime is the presentation by the earl of March of William Sherry to the living of Stanton Lacy on 22 Sept. 1456 (*Registrum Johannis Stanbury, episcopi Herefordensis 1453–74*, ed. A. T. Bannister, Canterbury and York Society, 25 (1919), 174).

Buckinghamshire manors comprised another small, cumbersome receivership. Altogether more coherent were the receiverships of Hertfordshire (centred on Hitchin), of Somerset and Dorset, Northamptonshire and Lincolnshire, and of the Yorkshire lands in the West Riding. If locally manageable, these receiverships were, none the less, inconveniently dispersed for more general administrative purposes.

The problem was partly overcome by creating administrative centres at Fotheringhay, which controlled the Yorkshire, Midlands, East Anglian, and south-eastern receiverships, and at Ludlow, which controlled the marcher and Welsh estates. Duke Richard was to spend most of his time at one or other of these centres, and the consequent necessity for regular movement led to the formation of an itinerant household.[88] The south-western shires defied any sustained regional control, probably because no prestigious centre was available. A manor-house was maintained at Cranborne, but there is no record of York staying there.[89] On two occasions he stayed at Fasterne,[90] and cash may occasionally have been deposited there,[91] but neither it nor Cranborne became established centres. In 1438 York held a council-meeting in Cirencester,[92] and the 1450 audit was also held there.[93]

Central administration was conducted by a small group of permanent staff, aided by councillors nominated by the duke. When he came of age, York had difficulties with both categories. Estate officials usually made their careers in the service of a great house, continuing bureaucratic traditions from the old lord to the young heir, and often, in their own families, from father to son. Duke Richard's father had no estates. His uncle of York had been dead some seventeen years when Richard came of age, and most of Duke Edward's friends and servants had moved on.

In Duke Edward's will mementoes were given to three companions, Thomas and Philip Beauchamp, and John Popham, and his closest councillors were nominated as supervisors and executors.[94] Of these, York inherited only the services of Sir John Popham. Two other families, the Mulsos and the Fitzwilliams, gradually found their way

[88] BL Egerton Roll 8774.   [89] SC6/1113/9.

[90] 10 June 1439, 3 Sept. 1453 (SC6/1113/11; SC6/1114/2).

[91] BL Egerton Roll 8364.   [92] BL Egerton Roll 8783.

[93] SC6/850/27.

[94] Peter Loege, Robert de Morton, Edmund Fitzwilliam, John Skelton, Baldwin Vere (*Reg. Chichele*, ed. Jacob, ii. 65).

back into duchy service, but most of Duke Edward's men found service with the king's brother, Humphrey.[95]

Duke Richard gained more servants from his uncle of March, probably because only four years elapsed between his uncle's death and his own involvement with estate administration. Sir John Tiptoft,[96] Sir William Lucy,[97] and the lawyers William Burley and John Doreward the elder[98] continued in the service of the earldom, although the last earl's English receiver, Nicholas West,[99] played no further part in the affairs of the earldom, and other recipients of Mortimer bounty likewise fell away.[100]

In many ways, therefore, the new duke had to start afresh. Coincidentally there were others in the same position, the servants of John duke of Bedford. It is difficult to overemphasize the importance of this coincidence. Bedford's men were, heart and soul, committed to the Lancastrian supremacy in France. Their estates, their positions, very often their titles, were French. When York went to France in 1436 he had little by way of a council. To have the services of men such as Fastolf and Oldhall was no less flattering than it was essential, if Normandy were to be governed. Many, not all, of Bedford's leading men attached themselves to the service of Duke Richard, who was not only lieutenant in France but a great landowner, disposer of much patronage in England.[101] Richard needed good councillors; they needed good lordship. What started as a marriage of convenience in Rouen rapidly grew into a binding union.

---

[95] *CPR 1452–61*, p. 71; J. S. Roskell, *The Commons in the Parliament of 1422* (Manchester, 1954), 206, 215. See also R. Somerville, *A History of the Duchy of Lancaster* (1953), 419, 463.

[96] *CPR 1422–9*, p. 266.   [97] Ibid. 342; SC6/1113/1.

[98] Burley accounted with the exchequer in 1425/6 for Ludlow, and Doreward for three of the Essex manors of the earldom (£364/60).

[99] SC6/1113/1.

[100] Hugh Fraunceys received Claret in Ashen for life but died in 1428 (*CFR 1422–30*, p. 211). Thomas Whitgreve, Thomas Lygon, and Sir John Phelip enjoyed life grants from the earl and M. Thomas Dunkan enjoyed £40 p.a. from Marshwood (*CPR 1422–9*, p. 442). Whitgreve became a Stafford servant (Rawcliffe, *The Staffords*, p. 213). Of the others nothing is known. Some Mortimer annuitants may not have been such by the earl's choice, e.g. Sir Roland Lenthale, 'a retainer by appointment of Henry V' (*CPR 1422–9*, p. 380), or were appointed during Duke Richard's minority (e.g. Sir Terry Robsart, ibid. 13).

[101] A. J. Pollard, *John Talbot and the War in France, 1427–1453*, Royal Historical Society (1983), 82; A. E. Marshall, 'The Role of English War Captains in England and Normandy, 1436–1461', (University of Wales, Swansea, MA thesis, 1975); Griffiths, *Reign of Henry VI*, p. 670.

Paucity of evidence makes it difficult to reconstruct the ducal council in the 1430s, as no one is explicitly described as a councillor before the 1440s. John Wigmore and Richard Wimbush, his attorneys-general during his first lieutenancy in France,[102] may safely be considered councillors in this period. Sir John Tyrell, receiver-general until his death in 1437, and Richard Dixton, who succeeded him,[103] should also be included, together with Thomas Newnham and Thomas Willoughby, the auditors, and Richard Wigmore, the steward of the household.[104] There were certainly others. There is, however, no evidence to suppose that York had on his council in the 1430s any other than estate or legal officials.

This changed in the 1440s. By 1445 York had secured the service of Ralph Lord Cromwell, Thomas Lord Scales, Sir John Fastolf, Sir Andrew Ogard, Sir William ap Thomas, and Sir William Oldhall.[105] There was also a new receiver-general, John Milewater.[106] The council was further augmented on York's return from France. Viscount Bourchier is first recorded as a councillor in 1448, although he may have served for some years previously.[107] John Lord Dudley and Reginald Lord de la Ware also appear in 1448, together with the lawyers Robert Darcy, John Stork, Richard Quatremains, and William Tresham.[108] Thomas Willoughby became auditor of the earldom of March estates in 1449.[109] There is good reason to believe that James Ormond earl of Wiltshire, Sir Edmund Mulso, and William Browning were also councillors.

In the 1450s Wiltshire and Scales fell away,[110] de la Ware, Mulso, and Oldhall died, and Tresham was murdered. John Stanlow, who may not have returned to England with York in 1445, was described as a councillor in 1448,[111] but his connections with York lapsed after 1450. There is no direct evidence as to who replaced these men. Simon Reyham, cofferer of the household from 1448 to 1450, became receiver of the earldom of March the following year, and he had been replaced in the household by Thomas Willoughby some

---

[102] C76/118 m. 4.   [103] BL Egerton Roll 8781; C76/124 m. 12.
[104] BL Egerton Roll 8781, 8774; Wigmore, together with John Sutton, Lord Dudley, and John Wynnersbury of Glasbury esq. was a mainpernor for York in 1432 (*CCR* 1429–35, p. 190).
[105] BL Egerton Roll 8783, 8364; WAM 12165.
[106] BL Egerton Roll 8737.
[107] Loc. cit.   [108] SC6/1113/9, 10.   [109] BL Egerton Roll 8783.
[110] The evidence for Wiltshire is circumstantial, for Scales see A. R. Myers, 'The Household of Queen Margaret of Anjou, 1452–3', *BJRL* 40 (1957–8), 226.
[111] SC6/1113/9.

time before 1454.[112] Some, at least, of those who stood surety for the marriage settlement of Elizabeth to John de la Pole, in 1458, must have been of conciliar status.[113]

Bound to him by oath,[114] the ducal council was responsible for the financial and legal elements of estate administration. As circumstances required, they contracted debts in the duke's name,[115] and considered the possible acquisition or disposal of property[116] and other administrative issues which were bound to develop from time to time on any great estate, to which end they had control of a ducal seal of arms.[117] When the duke was overseas, their responsibilities expanded accordingly. William Burley was entrusted in the 1440s with authority not only in estate matters but also in the initiation of other matters of ducal concern.[118] John Wigmore, initially appointed as the duke's financial agent at the exchequer to collect his various annuities,[119] expanded his responsibilities during York's French lieutenancies, to act as his agent in London for all aspects of Norman finance.[120] This arrangement was repeated while York was in Ireland.[121]

In the 1430s the upper echelons of the ducal household were probably not to be distinguished from the ducal councillors, although lack of evidence prevents any certainty on this point. Once in Rouen, his household had, of necessity, to be distinguished from his council, and this distinction was retained on his return to England in 1445. The administrative link between the two was the cofferer of the household, an official known to other fifteenth-century lords, even if his functions are uncertain.[122] In York's case, the idea almost certainly derived from his Norman experience and it is from his Rouen household that his first known cofferer, John Stanlow, was recruited. Stanlow was followed by another servant from Rouen days, Simon Reyham. William Oldhall, chamberlain to the duke in Normandy, continued in that office in England,[123] and

---

[112] BL Egerton Roll 8783; SC6/1113/11; E403/798.
[113] *Descriptive Catalogue of Ancient Deeds*, i. ser. A 6337–43.
[114] BL Egerton Roll 8708.
[115] BL Egerton Roll 8783, 8364.   [116] BL Egerton Roll 8782.
[117] *CCR* 1461–7, p. 115.   [118] SC11/818.
[119] E101/335/24; *The Antient Kalendars and Inventories of the Treasury of His Majesty's Exchequer*, ed. F. Palgrave, 3 vols., Record Commission (1836) ii. 170–2; E159/214 m. 2ᵛ Trinity term 1438.
[120] C76/118 m. 4; E403/750; E403/781.
[121] *CPR* 1446–52, p. 245.
[122] Rawcliffe, *The Staffords*, p. 69.   [123] SC6/1113/10.

Edmund Mulso also continued as a member of the duke's household.[124] The physical proximity of the 'Normans' to the duke no doubt explains their influence over him. The relationship between the long-standing servants of the duchy and earldom and the later officials whom York acquired in Normandy is difficult to probe satisfactorily. The latter were no more numerous than the former, but seem to have exerted much greater influence on their lord. Lacking any documentation of the ducal council's discussions, evidence for this must, perforce, be indirect; but France and its problems are the dominant theme of York's political criticisms in the decade after 1445, and, by contrast, it is very noticeable in 1459–60 that the duke's senior estate servants for the most part co-operated with the Lancastrians, and that Edward IV was to give them little by way of reward.

Infirmity and death whittled away the Norman group, and by the late 1450s they played no part in York's domestic affairs; but, with no unequivocal evidence surviving from these later years, it is difficult to construct any clear indication of the composition of the household, or its functioning. For the most part, after 1455 York did not attract the services of high-calibre men, and it is likely that he was dependent on minor gentry for his household staff; men such as Roger Ree.[125] Passing into the service of Edward IV, they were to do well in the 1460s and 1470s, but they had started as men of little social consequence in the 1450s, and it is worth noting that Duke Richard was not able to place his sons for training in other baronial households, as was customary. They stayed at home and were bullied by the Croft children.[126]

Estate servants in the localities were drawn from their local communities, with positions appropriate to their social status. John Eyleriche, York's receiver in Shropshire,[127] was a well-established member of the local community, as was William Browning in Dorset,[128] and William Prelatte in Gloucestershire.[129] Sir Roger Chamberlain was seneschal of the Kent manors,[130] Thomas Bernard esq. acted likewise in the Cambridgeshire and Huntingdonshire

[124] Bib. Nat. MS Fr. Nouv. Acq. 2320 n. 265. There is no specific authority to support his status in England, but the cumulative impression of the details of his career is that he was very close to Duke Richard.
[125] Yeoman of the chamber 1439, valet of the chamber 1440, usher of the chamber 1451 (*CCR 1435–41*, p. 272; WAM 12165; *CPR 1467–77*, p. 62).
[126] C. D. Ross, *Edward IV* (1974), 436.   [127] SC11/818.
[128] SC6/1113/11.   [129] SC6/850/26, 27.   [130] KB9/265/109.

estates,[131] and Sir John Montgomery was for many years seneschal of Clare and Thaxted.[132] The instances can be readily multiplied, for York employed many in his service. Exactly how many is impossible to say, but surviving records show him filling 190 posts at fees varying from a penny a day to £10 or more per annum. In addition to feed servants, York had annuitants. This was also typical, and there is, at least until 1460, nothing to excite suspicion that his intentions differed much from his contemporaries' in negotiating indentures of retainer. The one surviving annuity indenture contracted before 1460, with George Darell esq. on 30 January 1458,[133] has some interesting features, but none that are unusual in documents of this type. York sanctioned at Fotheringhay an arrangement negotiated earlier on his behalf, probably by a receiver or other local official. The arrangement, £10 in cash in equal portions, until an office to the value of 20 marks per annum could be provided, would seem to imply that Darell was expected to discharge the responsibilities of whatever office he was to receive, as well as those of an annuitant. Unfortunately, it is difficult to generalize on the basis of this one document. There were certainly many others.

In all, there are forty-two traceable annuitants.[134] Four of the women, Emma Bailey, 'Clarementine', Agnes Lenche, and Alice Mortimer, look to be recipients of charity, as do William Barrow, John Colston, Robert Doughton, Hugh ap Meredith, and Roger Norton. Of the large annuities paid, he inherited the obligations for four of them from the earl of March, those to M. Thomas Dunkan, Sir Edmund Hull, Sir Roland Lenthale, and Sir John Popham. He inherited, too, an obligation to pay a £100 annuity to the earl of Shrewsbury, which, of his own accord, he doubled.[135]

Talbot's services were intended to be political, as, in part at least, were James Ormond's. Other annuitants recruited for political services must include Sir John Wenlock, Edward Bourchier esq., and John Lord Clinton. Local politics probably suggested the recruitment of the Brugge brothers in Gloucestershire, of Sir William Skipwith, in Lincolshire and of Sir John Barre in the marches. Of the office-holders, some, no doubt, especially those of lower social status, were, indeed, appointed to discharge the duties

[131] WAM 12166.
[132] SC2/173/90 m. 1; SC2/171/51 m. 9; SC6/1113/10.
[133] C146/6400: Printed as App. I.
[134] See App. III.   [135] Cf. Pollard, *Talbot*, p. 81.

of their post, but most lords, and York was no exception, used posts such as seneschal as a means of currying local favour. The appointment of men such as Sir John Montgomery and Sir Leonard Hastings ought to be viewed in this way.

York had several advowsons at his disposal, but his appointments tended, by and large, to the mediocre. James Hamelin, his chaplain[136] and Richard Sherbourne, his almoner,[137] were credited with degrees, although of what university is unknown. His proctor in Rome, Thomas Candover, was much the best qualified; a papal chamberlain and doctor of civil law. For his benefit, York procured the amalgamation of the two livings of Pimperne and Tarrant Gunville (Dorset).[138] The other livings in his gift he filled with candidates of no obvious quality. Only two other graduates were presented to benefices by York, M. John Taptone, who held, successively, Winterborne Steepleton (1453) and Neen Sollars (1456), before gaining a canonry at Lincoln[139] in the period of Yorkist control, and the distinguished musician M. Thomas St Just, for whom, in 1455, York found the benefice of Anstey, and, in 1460, of Trim.[140]

The maintenance of his household and of his estates required a considerable income. Just how much Duke Richard enjoyed is, however, very difficult to establish. There has been one extended study of York's income,[141] and several authorities have attempted estimates.[142] The attraction of Professor Rosenthal's study is that it seeks to draw together surviving estate records to build up a picture of receipts, receivership by receivership. The problem is that records do not survive in sufficient quantities to provide adequate information on such crucial issues as arrears, and, in several

---

[136] *Calendar of Papal Letters*, ii. *1431–7*, p. 463.
[137] Ibid. 237.   [138] Emden, *Oxford*, iii. 2158.
[139] Emden, *Cambridge*, p. 576; *Reg. Stanbury*, ed. Bannister, p. 174.
[140] Emden, *Cambridge*, p. 503; Berry, *Statutes of Ireland*, p. 794.
[141] J. T. Rosenthal, 'The Estates and Finances of Richard, Duke of York (1411–60)', in W. M. Bowsky (ed.), *Studies in Medieval and Renaissance History*, ii (Nebraska, 1965). A summary of the article's conclusions is given by the same author in 'Fifteenth-century Baronial Incomes and Richard, Duke of York', *BIHR* 37 (1964), 233–40.
[142] £2,874 (H. L. Gray, 'Incomes from Land in 1436', *EHR* 49 (1934), 614; *c.* £6,500 gross (C. D. Ross and T. B. Pugh, 'The English Baronage and the Income Tax of 1436', *BIHR* 25 (1953), 14, followed by Jacob, *Fifteenth Century*, p. 465); £6,500–£7,000, gross (K. B. McFarlane, *The Nobility of Later Medieval England* (1973), 177); £3,500–£4,500, net (J. R. Lander, *Conflict and Stability in Fifteenth-Century England* (1969), 34, following Rosenthal).

receiverships, it is necessary to employ estate records more than half a century apart.[143] Of the various estimates that have been offered, some seem to be little more than figures conjured from the air, but others have been advanced on the basis of a serious attempt to tease something from the documentation available. In the absence of new evidence, the best that can be attempted is a similar exercise, based as far as possible on surviving accounts, and covering as short a time-span as possible. The documentation for the earldom of March is just about sufficient for this purpose. The duchy of York is altogether more nebulous.

For the earldom, an account survives, drawn up in consequence of the grants of parts of the earldom to the dukes of Exeter and Gloucester.[144] The heading on the roll describes it as revenue anticipated from the earldom for those lands now in the custody of the two dukes, which implies a date for the roll between June 1425, when the grant was made, and December 1426, when Exeter died.

The accounts give totals for each manor or accounting unit, arranged not by receivership but by shire. For the estates in the hands of Exeter the total given is £357. 16s. 1d., for those in the hands of Gloucester, £3,092. 7s. 10d. From these totals a dower portion was then deducted for the Countess Anne (£1,150. 1s. 3d.). Some estates are absent from these totals, principally the Oxford-shire and Buckinghamshire estates, the Kent manors of Swans-combe, Erith and Tonge, Wokefield and Stratfield Mortimer (Berks.), and the manor of Plesshy (Herts.), all of which were in the hands of feoffees, and estates in Essex farmed to the countess of Hereford and valued at £156. 13s. 4d.[145] Also in the hands of feoffees were the Gloucestershire manors, which the inquisition *post mortem* on the earl valued at £94. 3s. 4d.[146] The lordship of Narberth was at farm, as were Marshwood and Gussage Bohun. The accuracy of valuations recorded in inquisitions may be doubted, and the exchequer valuations may also have been on a different basis to the valuation established for the two dukes. The exercise of adding one to another must, therefore, be somewhat crude, but if it is attempted, without any allowance for supposed undervaluation, and

[143] For criticisms of Rosenthal's study see R. R. Davies, 'Baronial Accounts, Incomes and Arrears in the Later Middle Ages', *Economic History Review*, 2nd ser., 2 (1968), 211–29, and C. D. Ross, 'The Estates and Finances of Richard, Duke of York', *Welsh History Review*, 3 (1967), 299–302.

[144] C47/9/33.   [145] *CPR 1416–22*, p. 172.   [146] C139/19/4.

excluding all manors for which no figure is available, the value of the lands of the earldom of March, given by adding the various figures, was £3,701. 0s. 7d., after fixed costs and fees had been met.

The duchy of York lands had been granted to the first two dukes piecemeal, and with each grant deduction was made from the annuity due at the exchequer. When Duke Richard succeeded, it was the exchequer's belief that land to the value of £645 had been settled on the duchy.[147] This included £83. 18s. 5d. allowed for Barton Bristol, which York did not, in fact, receive. The theoretical value of the duchy of York therefore stood at £561. 1s. 7d.

Few historians have placed much confidence in exchequer valuations, although they have not been tested in any sustained fashion. One study has suggested that the exchequer was cautious in its estimates, substantially undervaluing properties.[148] It is possible to check the exchequer valuation in three instances. Compton Bassett was valued at £50 per annum in 1377, a figure repeated in 1395.[149] Ministers' accounts for the fifteenth century give a value (that year's receipts less that year's costs) of £37 to £39.[150] Somerford Keynes, valued in 1387 at £26. 16s. 8d.,[151] yielded £35 in 1415 and £22 in 1450.[152] Although it would be unwise to suppose that these figures in any way confirm the accuracy of exchequer estimates, they must be a caution against a presumption that the value of the estates granted to the duchy of York was consistently and substantially underestimated. The exchequer's figure of £561. 1s. 7d. is the best available, despite its many weaknesses.

The net landed income to be derived from the estates in the 1420s was probably, therefore, in the order of £4,000 per annum.[153] It was likely to have been a struggle to maintain his income at this level. He was absent from the country three times, once for four years. Of the nineteen receiverships, eleven were in Wales and the marches. Most lords found that the proceeds of their Welsh estates declined in the fifteenth century, because they were heavily dependent on the

---

[147] See above p. 6.
[148] B. P. Wolffe, *The Royal Demesne in English History* (1971), 100–5.
[149] *CPR* 1374–7, p. 474; *CPR* 1391–6, p. 656.
[150] These figures are taken from Rosenthal, 'Estates and Finances', p. 150.
[151] *CPR* 1385–9, p. 403.   [152] Rosenthal, loc. cit. n. 150 above.
[153] Pugh, 'Richard Plantagenet as King's Lieutenant', pp. 110–13, points to a rather higher figure, though he does not offer a total income. His endorsement of Monstrelet's 'le riche duc d'Yorck' is certainly justified.

collection of legal dues; dues which were increasingly difficult to exact.[154] When regularly resident in the march, York may have been more successful in collecting his dues, but it would be unsafe to presume this.

On the positive side, there is a revenue source which does not appear in the accounts; livestock. In 1450 York brought with him into London 80 cattle and 999 sheep.[155] In the same year, the household accounted for livestock brought from Bewdley, but whether these had been purchased there or handed over to the household by estate officials is unclear.[156] There are records of the lord's cattle pastured at Blakedon in 1453 and at Brimpsfield in 1461, and there is a strong suspicion that these are not isolated instances.[157] The account roll for Somerset–Dorset for 1452–3 records the sale of 100 head of cattle and 300 sheep, raising £90. 6s. 8d.[158] York may well have been a significant cattle baron, deriving revenues from this trade which are not normally revealed in the receiver's accounts. Mention of horse-breeding at Fotheringhay raises the possibility of another significant source of income.[159]

The most difficult administrative operation was the collection of arrears. Part of the problem lay in obsolete valuations, principally for the duchy of York lands, Grantham having last been valued in 1379 and the West Riding estates in 1396.[160] Other difficulties arose through mishap rather than incompetence,[161] but it is difficult to explain why in 1461 the receiver of Babwell was expected to account for revenues assigned in 1447 to the Franciscan convent there.[162] In some instances arrears were deliberately allowed to accumulate. The earl of Salisbury never paid rent for the Grange estate in Cottingham. Richard Hanson had, by 1461, run up arrears of £118.

---

[154] T. B. Pugh (ed.), *Glamorgan County History*, 3 (Cardiff, 1971), 318–31; W. R. B. Robinson, 'An Analysis of a Minister's Accounts for the Borough of Swansea for 1449', *Bulletin of the Board of Celtic Studies*, 22 (1966), 182. A rough indication of the contribution of the Welsh estates is given by the order of 1 Mar. 1430 to pay the dowager countess £349. 0s. 9d. as dower of the Welsh lands (E404/47/180).

[155] Hants County Record Office 23M58/57b.

[156] BL Egerton Roll 7360.   [157] BL Egerton Roll 8784; SC6/850/29.

[158] A stock sale from Swanscombe, Erith, and Tonge recorded on an undated bill yielded £270 (BL Egerton Roll 8413).

[159] SC6/1115/6. The Deptford stables were extensively repaired in 1455 (SC6/1113/13).

[160] SC6/1115/6; DL29/8899/560.

[161] For example, in 1450 the bailiff's accounts were not presented, as not only had the bailiff died but also his executor (BL Egerton Roll 8364).

[162] SC6/1114/2.

6*s*. 8*d*., also in Cottingham.[163] Lord Botreaux settled his £40 rent for Exmoor every two years.[164] When the earl of Devon took over the rental, at the lower rate of £33. 6*s*. 8*d*., he never managed to pay a penny.[165] Social or political circumstances may have led to similar tolerance locally, albeit at a more modest level.[166] When pushed, the administration showed itself capable of collecting arrears very effectively. The appointment of a receiver for arrears in 1447–8 brought in £70. 18*s*. 1*d*. of the total arrears of £121. 0*s*. 1*d*. accumulated at Bisley.[167] The following year, Gussage Bohun paid £38. 1*s*. 0*d*. to the receiver of arrears.[168] The operation was continued that year in Gloucestershire[169] and was shortly to be extended, first to the Northampton, and then to the Somerset and Dorset receivership, where the account for 1452–3 records no arrears but a surplus on the previous year's account.[170]

This calling in of arrears no doubt relates to York's financial difficulties in the late 1440s,[171] but there are signs that the related problem of decayed rents had been an administrative concern for some years previously. On 10 November 1439 the duke remitted all arrears due from Andover, and instructed Thomas Willoughby to agree new rentals. Just when this was completed for Andover is unknown, but the process was completed by Willoughby at Stratfield Mortimer, part of the same receivership, by 15 March 1440.[172] New rentals were negotiated throughout the 1440s at Standon, Bisley, Winstone, and Compton, and in 1451 at Nassington and Yarwell.[173] Had political circumstances permitted, the (necessarily slow) process would probably have continued. Accusations that York was a negligent, even incompetent, landlord seem unduly harsh.[174]

---

[163] DL29/8899/560.

[164] SC6/1113/9.   [165] SC6/1113/11, 14.

[166] The duke was himself not always the promptest of payers, and there are instances of both annuities and wages falling into arrears (e.g. SC6/870/4; SC6/1113/10).   [167] SC6/850/26.

[168] SC6/1113/9. As these stood at £19. 15*s*. 4*d*. the previous Michaelmas, the total paid presumably included sums due for the accounting year.

[169] SC6/850/27.   [170] SC6/1115/6; BL Egerton Roll 8784.

[171] See below, p. 62.   [172] SC6/1115/1, 6.

[173] SC6/870/5, 26; SC6/1115/1, 6.

[174] Lander, *Conflict and Stability*, p. 34, following E. M. Carus-Wilson, 'Evidences of Industrial Growth on Some Fifteenth-Century Manors', *Economic History Review*, 2nd ser., 12 (1959–60), 194, though the latter article points to attempts by York to improve his income from Bisley. In the 1450s he appears to have turned to the problem of Welsh arrears (*CPR* 1452–61, p. 570).

As a great landowner, York had many men economically dependent on him to varying degrees, but there were, of course, other, social, contacts. Friendship leaves few traces in medieval records but there is a hint of warmth in the choice of Thomas Lord Scales as godfather for Edward of Rouen,[175] and in Sir Theobald Georges's choice of Duke Richard as godfather to his infant daughter.[176] A certain camaraderie is to be detected between these Norman soldiers and their royal lieutenant.

There were also relatives. Ties of kinship linked York with several other baronial houses. On his mother's side there were plenty of cadet Mortimers, but only one of these, Alice, had any active connection with Duke Richard.[177] Sir Leonard Hastings married another Alice, granddaughter of Edmund earl of March, by Elizabeth, wife to Lord Camoys.[178] On his father's side the connections were, at least in title, more impressive. Henry Broomflete, fourth husband of the dowager duchess Philippa, and created Lord Vesci in 1449, had remarried (as her third husband) Eleanor, a daughter of Lord FitzHugh.[179] Duke Richard's stepmother Maud received her annuity until death, but had otherwise retained no connection with him. His sister Isabelle had been pledged to Thomas Gray of Wark, but was now the wife of Henry Viscount Bourchier, and links with the viscount were well established.[180] Edmund of Langley's daughter had three children—Richard the last Lord Despenser; Isabelle, successively the wife of both Richard Beauchamps, earls of Worcester and Warwick; and Eleanor, her illegitimate daughter by Edmund earl of Kent, who married James Lord Audley. Isabelle's children by both marriages acquired Neville husbands, so it is impossible to gauge what their relationships owed to direct kinship with York, and what to their closer relation to Cecily Neville; if anything, more the former, as the Nevilles were a quarrelsome family from whom York seems to have kept studiously distant before the 1450s.

---

[175] *Annales*, p. 773.   [176] BL Add. Ch. 26043.

[177] *CPR* 1452–61, p. 551; SC6/1113/10. Alice is not to be found in any Mortimer family pedigree. Fastolf had a Mortimer connection, his mother's first marriage having been to Thomas Mortimer (*Complete Peerage*, ix. 250).

[178] Hist. MSS. Comm. *Hastings MSS*, i. 273 seems to imply this, as do Hastings's many ties with the earldom. But cf. *Complete Peerage*, ii. 508.

[179] *Complete Peerage*, xii/2,. 205–8.

[180] L. S. Woodger, 'Henry Bourchier, Earl of Essex and His Family', (Univ. of Oxford D.Phil. thesis, 1974), and *Complete Peerage*, ii. 247–8. Isabelle received a £100 annuity from her brother (SC6/1113/10).

As an only child, York was relieved of the common tendency for young brothers to cause their titled seniors acute political embarrassment by their irresponsible, even illegal, public behaviour,[181] but, being the only child of such a politically sensitive union, there were from the outset more than enough political pressures on him. He was inescapably heir not only to the earldom of March but to the whole Mortimer inheritance, with its claim to the English throne. This Mortimer legacy was a real one, alive throughout Richard's minority,[182] and it could not be readily swept under the carpet. The Crown did its best to ignore York's position, and he himself seems to have concurred readily enough at first. Personal grievances were eventually to throw him into conflict with the Beaufort family, and in his attempts to outflank his rival he emphasized, increasingly, his closeness of blood to the throne, but as right heir of Henry VI, not through Mortimer as right heir to Richard II. Others, anxious to overthrow successive administrations, saw in York a focus for their hopes, and came to see in his blood a guarantee of legitimacy and stability for their various causes. As a political inheritance it was a mixed blessing, an embarrassment in times of loyal service to the Crown, a potent escalator of political stakes in times of opposition. York was not obliged to oppose Henry VI. When he did, he did not have to claim the throne, but if sustained opposition were to prove persistently unproductive then the possibility of that claim could not be ignored, by him or anyone else. For Henry VI York could never be just another critic, and those other critics knew it.

---

[181] R. A. Griffiths, 'Public and Private Bureaucracies in England and Wales in the Fifteenth Century', *TRHS*, 5th ser., 30 (1980), 129.

[182] *Brut*, ii. 452.

2

FRANCE

On 2 July 1440 Duke Richard sealed indentures as Lieutenant of France.[1] He was to serve for five years, drawing £20,000 per annum from the English exchequer so long as Normandy was in danger, together with suitable ordnance, an adequate provision for his own maintenance, agreed councillors, and provision for shipping and other more detailed eventualities.

This was not to be York's first term of service, as he had already served in the same office for eighteen months after the death of the regent, John duke of Bedford. The intention of the council in appointing York on that occasion is made clear from the terms of his commission, sealed on 8 May 1436.[2] In it, the council stated explicitly that Henry, who was to come of age in eighteen months' time, proposed shortly to come to France, and that York's appointment, which was for an indeterminate period, was necessary only to provide good government in the interim. There was no mention of military, financial, or similar matters. It was a stop-gap appointment, designed to avoid a decision about a most important office, until the king's majority could provide the necessary political will for a more permanent arrangement.

The commission does not, however, give a clear picture of the council's hopes in 1436. Since Bedford's death, on 14 September 1435, the English had suffered a series of sharp reverses. Paris was threatened, Dieppe had been lost in October, and a major uprising in the Pays de Caux left only Caudebec and Arques secure. Normandy needed not only a governor but a fresh army, if authority

---

[1] C76/122/10; Stevenson, *Letters and Papers*, ii/2 585.
[2] Bib. Nat. MS Fr. 5330 fo. 137ᵛ, printed as App. II. He was indented to serve on 22 Feb. 1436 (E404/52/28). Two chronicles claim that his appointment was made in Parliament, though there is no record of Parliament being in session at this time (*Gregory's Chronicle*, p. 178; *Chronicles of London*, p. 141). In appointing York with powers substantially less than those of Bedford, the English council reasserted its control over French affairs (A. E. Curry, 'The First English Standing Army? Military Organisation in Lancastrian Normandy, 1420–50' in C. D. Ross, (ed.) *Patronage, Pedigree, and Power in Later Medieval England*, (Gloucester, 1979), 205).

was to be restored. York's willingness to undertake the recruitment of a sizeable force prompted his appointment. On 20 February 1436 he received payment of a quarter's wages for himself, a baron and a banneret, seven knights, 490 men-at-arms, and 2,200 archers.[3] This force was to muster at Winchester on 3 May, when a second quarter's wages would be paid.[4] Loans to this end were duly negotiated.[5] The army did not in fact arrive in Normandy until 7 June, landing at Honfleur,[6] its muster presumably delayed. The first six months having elapsed, the payment of the army became the obligation of the Norman exchequer, as was customary.[7]

He arrived too late to save Paris, but his troops did much to re-establish the English military position in Normandy, control over the Pays de Caux being restored and Fécamp recovered, though not Dieppe.[8] In the circumstances, this was a creditable performance, though to whom the credit should be assigned is less clear. The earl of Suffolk had accompanied York, and had gone directly to Caen[9] to take control of Lower Normandy.[10] York himself went to Rouen,[11] as was correct, but the extent of his influence immediately on arrival

---

[3] E403/722 (cash payment of £8,056. 7s. 6d.).

[4] *CPR* 1429–36, p. 535; R. R. Sharpe, *Calendar of Letter Books Preserved among the Archives of the Corporation of the City of London: Letter Book K* (1911), 204. Shipping had been arrested for 1 Apr. (*CPR* 1429–36), p. 533).

[5] Hist. MSS. Comm., *Various Collections*, iv. 198; G. A. Holmes, 'The "Libel of English Policy"', *EHR* 76 (1961), 203.

[6] BL Add. Chs. 1162, 3790. York may have been kept waiting for last-minute instructions and a copy of his commission (Stevenson, *Letters and Papers*, ii/1, p. lxxii. The reference to secretary Calot implies a date of 1436, rather than 1441 as suggested by Stevenson). The commission to take muster of his force on arrival in France was issued on 22 May (*CPR* 1429–36, p. 608). This delay may explain why, in Nov. 1436, York ordered indentures for garrisons should run only to June 1437 (R. A. Newhall, *Muster and Review* (Cambridge, Mass., 1940), 137).

[7] It has been suggested that York was expecting payment for his army while in France, from the English exchequer, to a total of £18,000 (Jacobs, *Fifteenth Century*, p. 465, followed by Griffiths, *Reign of Henry VI*, p. 455). For the source of this figure, properly relating to Warwick's lieutenancy, see Pugh, 'Richard Plantagenet as King's Lieutenant', p. 138 n. 28.

[8] For a résumé of military events see Pollard, *Talbot*, pp. 22–5.

[9] *Brut*, ii. 469; *Chronicles of London*, p. 141; BL Add. Ch. 11919; Bib. Nat. MS. Fr. 26062 n. 3006; R. Jouet, *La Résistance à l'occupation anglaise en Basse-Normandie (1418–1450)* (Caen, 1969), 134–40.

[10] Suffolk was to claim, in 1450, that in 1436 he had 'put the Countre in reule', though this was disputed (Hist. MSS. Comm. *Third Report*, p. 279). For problems in the Caen area see C. T. Allmand, *Lancastrian Normandy, 1415–1450: The History of a Medieval Occupation* (Oxford, 1983), 38, and references there.

[11] He spent most of his first lieutenancy there (Stevenson, *Letters and Papers*, ii/2, 289–93), except for a brief visit to Honfleur in Oct. 1436 (BL Add. Ch. 3790).

is unclear. There are indications that Talbot enjoyed direct authority over York's army,[12] and the influence of Louis of Luxemburg at the council-table must have been considerable.[13]

Several of the initiatives of this period look to be the work of more experienced heads, and it was under their guidance that York learnt something of Anglo-French diplomacy, of Church–State relations, and of the subtleties necessary to draw into the English fold an old campaigner like the count of Luxemburg; but if he was initially hesitant, as was only prudent, he did not remain a figure-head for long. When Montereau fell, in October 1437, he could only be restrained from an impulsive attempt at recovery by the Norman council's refusal to co-operate with the scheme, on the grounds that his commission had expired.[14]

As his one-year term came to an end, York professed himself anxious to depart, but it transpired that he was to stay for several more months, initially to 1 July,[15] to allow time for a successor to be nominated. The post went to Richard Beauchamp, earl of Warwick, probably at the earl's own request, but he was delayed in England by the need to attend Queen Joan's funeral, to which York was not summoned,[16] and then by contrary winds. He had hoped to sail on 29 August, but did not do so until 6 November, York leaving France (in all probability) on the eighth.[17]

By the end of this time York could take some of the credit for the restoration of English authority in Normandy, which Bedford's illness and death had so seriously weakened; but the economic distress brought about by bad harvests, and the economic dislocation consequent on the rebellion, were problems beyond anyone's powers to solve.[18] Where he achieved most was in the simultaneous mustering of the major garrisons, probably the result of prompting at a meeting at Honfleur in October,[19] and his measured response to

[12] Bib. Nat. MS. Fr. 26062 n. 3106; Pollard, *Talbot*, p. 40; G. du Fresne de Beaucourt, *Histoire de Charles VII*, 6 vols. (Paris, 1881–91), iii. 9 n. 4. In Jan. 1437 York had, at Pontoise, a small but independent force of 6 knights, 44 men-at-arms, and 200 archers (Bib. Nat. MS. Fr. 26062 n. 3164).

[13] During the regency he had enjoyed full powers in Bedford's absence (B. J. H. Rowe, 'The *Grand Conseil* under the Duke of Bedford, 1422–35', in F. M. Powicke (ed.), *Oxford Essays in Medieval History Presented to H. E. Salter*, (Oxford, 1934), 222.

[14] *Chronicles of London*, p. 143.

[15] *PPC* v. 8. York was in Rouen on 25 July (Bib. Nat. MS Fr. 26063 n. 3256).

[16] *PPC* v. 56.   [17] *Chronicles of London*, p. 144.

[18] Allmand, *Lancastrian Normandy*, pp. 163–4.   [19] Ibid., p. 183.

the local problems which rebellion had brought.[20] This was a worthy achievement,[21] but it did not touch on the major difficulty which had arisen within seven days of Bedford's death, at the Congress of Arras. There, the Burgundians and the French had established a diplomatic understanding which left Burgundy a disinterested spectator of the Anglo-French war. The French might still have difficulties with the Burgundians but, after Arras, England had, for a time, to face active Burgundian hostility. After the successful defence of Calais, this hostility faded, but the Anglo-Burgundian alliance was in ruins and with it English prospects in France; for, without some help from Philip the Good, England would be hard put to retain what it held, the more so as the duchy of Brittany was unlikely to overlook the attractions of a similar *rapprochement* with the French. It was a diplomatic problem which dominated English policy-discussions in the late 1430s, and which lay behind the five-year term offered to the duke of York in 1440.

The hopes of the young Henry VI, born of deep personal conviction, were for a lasting peace. Cardinal Beaufort agreed with this policy for a variety of reasons, not the least being that a successful war without Burgundian support would be impossible. Their main critic was Humphrey duke of Gloucester, who saw peace as an unacceptable repudiation of Henry V's achievements, and as wrong in principle, being contrary to the Treaty of Troyes. As has been pointed out, this was not mindless warmongering.[22] Much blood and treasure had been expended, and much glory gained, in the winning of French lands, and the war was the Lancastrian success which legitimized the dynasty. If the French war was abandoned, what was to replace it? A total withdrawal from France was unthinkable, as the Cardinal also realized, but the question was

---

[20] Bib. Nat. MS Fr. 26062 nn. 3010–13; Newhall, *Muster and Review*, p. 133. The monthly muster arrangements, negotiated *ad hoc* until Warwick's arrival, created some financial confusion for his successor (BL Add. Chs. 3808–9, 3812–5; Newhall, *Muster and Review*, p. 143).

[21] A French chronicler records the good justice which he brought (A. Hellot, *Les Croniques de Normandie 1223–1453* (Rouen, 1881), 82). Two contemporary English sources are critical, in very similar language, of York's conduct, but this seems to be with the intention of setting the earl of Somerset's achievements in a more glorious context (Giles, *Chronicon Angliae*, p. 18; *English Historical Literature*, p. 399). For a more muted criticism see *Chronicles of London*, p. 141, but cf. p. 143. Marshall, 'English War Captains', p. 14, and Pugh, 'Richard Plantagenet as King's Lieutenant', p. 114, agree that York's first lieutenancy did see improvements.

[22] Griffiths, *Reign of Henry VI*, p. 450.

whether the French would be satisfied with anything less? It took
two to stop a war and, as Gloucester was not slow to point out, the
French showed no sign of wanting to do so. Admittedly, neither did
he.

The debate focused on the proposal to release Charles duke of
Orleans, it being urged that his release would be a substantial
gesture of good will, and a stabilizing influence on the peers of
France, who might, thereby, be encouraged to restrain Charles VII.
The duke of Gloucester publicly doubted that Orleans could be
trusted, and he urged, with increasing vehemence, that the
Armagnac–Burgundian split was the source of Henry V's original
victories, and the most likely diplomatic opportunity for future
military success. At the core of the debate was the vital political issue
as to whether the king was bound by the wishes of his father, or was
free to make his own policy.

Despite Gloucester's best efforts to draw him into it, York took no
part in this debate, which rumbled on for most of 1439 and 1440. In
his attempts to weaken the Beaufort position, Duke Humphrey went
so far as to allege that Cardinal Beaufort had deliberately excluded
the duke of York from the king's council, as well as the new
lieutenant of Gascony, John Holland earl of Huntingdon.[23] Evidence
exists only to test the allegations concerning Huntingdon, and they
prove groundless. In York's case it is true that he was not one of the
king's inner councillors, but there is no evidence to suggest that he
wanted to be. The impression is that Gloucester, in his growing
political isolation, was claiming allies he did not, in fact, possess.[24]
The only source to link them is Waurin, but the passage in which he
does so is unusually garbled and confused.[25] A small piece of
evidence which points away from a York–Gloucester alliance is a
royal commission, appointed in the summer of 1440 to judge a claim
made by Edmund earl of Dorset on the estates of the hapless James
Berkeley.[26] Gloucester evidently enjoyed some influence in the
composition of this commission, for he headed it himself. The duke
of York and earl of Stafford, together with the judges, John Hody

[23] Stevenson, *Letters and Papers*, ii/2, 442.
[24] When he stormed out of Westminster Abbey on the occasion of Orleans's
liberation, 'in the presence of the Kyng and all the lordes', he did so alone (Davis,
Paston Letters, ii. 22).
[25] Waurin, *Croniques*, iv. 352–3. The context appears to relate more properly
to the disputes of the mid-1440s.
[26] C76/122 m. 9; *CCR* 1435–41, p. 325.

and Richard Fenton, were the other members. Stafford was usually pro-Beaufort. York looks to have been the 'indifferent' member, not a Gloucester partisan.

Neither do his activities in England since coming of age give support to any theory of partisanship. Most of his time had been spent in visiting his estates,[27] and it was as a marcher lord that the council approached him, soon after his return from France, to seek his co-operation in a campaign of law enforcement.[28] Although nothing came of this, there is no reason to suppose that York did not intend to co-operate, and he was to pick up the threads of this programme when he returned from his second lieutenancy.

York was drawn into the problems of French policy because the earl of Warwick had died, on 30 April 1439, and a successor had to be found who would be sensitive to the hopes which Orleans's release had been intended to foster, but sufficiently firm of purpose to reassure the Gloucester faction that France was not to be abandoned overnight. The new lieutenant needed to be of sufficient social status, and, of the modest number of possible candidates, York was, in the eyes of the council, the most promising. The duke of Gloucester was anxious to secure the post, but this the Beaufort group successfully resisted. The only other available duke was the inexperienced Norfolk. John Beaufort, earl of Somerset, who was acting as temporary governor in 1439–40,[29] was obviously anathema to Gloucester. Salisbury was Joan Beaufort's son and had served as lieutenant to York in 1437;[30] Huntingdon was already lieutenant in Gascony; and Suffolk had also been a subordinate of York in his first lieutenancy. The remaining available earls were either of little political significance or, like Stafford, were too closely identified with Beaufort interests. On the positive side, York had a little experience, had the landed resources from which to raise fresh troops, and in 1436–7 had shown himself willing to listen to advice, and to let the professionals get on with the task in hand. He was the only serious candidate remotely acceptable to all interested parties.[31]

---

[27] His movements are summarized in Rosenthal, 'Estates and Finances', p. 197.

[28] *PPC* v. 81, 86, 92, 95.

[29] E. M. Burney, 'The English Rule of Normandy, 1435–50' (Univ. of Oxford B.Litt. thesis, 1958), 132.   [30] Pollard, *Talbot*, p. 39.

[31] For a contrary opinion of York's relations with Gloucester see K. H. Vickers, *Humphrey Duke of Gloucester* (1907), 269; C. L. Scofield, *The Life and Reign of Edward IV*, 2 vols. (1923), i. 7; S. B. Chrimes, *English Constitutional Ideas in the Fifteenth Century* (1936), 26.

This gave him some negotiating strength, and his position was
further bolstered by the fact that the detailed negotiations he
undertook with the council were going on at the same time as the
negotiations for the release of Orleans, and the council could not
afford to risk further criticism by inadequate support of its new
lieutenant.

The duke's choice of a council to represent him in England had to
be sensitive to the tensions at court. The men he selected were of
stature in domestic politics as well as experienced in the affairs of
France. Of the bishops, Brown of Norwich was a diplomat who had
spent much of his time at Basle before attending the peace
negotiations of 1439,[32] and had been a feoffee in several settlements
of York's estates. Alnwick of Lincoln was a curialist who had held a
canonry at Bayeux in the 1420s, had been a councillor for York in
1437, and also enjoyed York's confidence as a feoffee.[33] The bishop
of Salisbury, Aiscough, was the quintessential curialist and, at that
time, the king's confessor.[34] All the laymen had had some experience
of French affairs. Lord Sudeley had been chamberlain to the duke of
Bedford, but had subsequently made his way in the royal household.[35]
Beaumont, a recently promoted viscount, had followed a similar
path to fortune.[36] Stourton was custodian of the duke of Orleans;[37]
Popham was a relative of the Beaufort family by marriage, stepfather
to Huntingdon, the new lieutenant in Gascony, and a man most
closely involved in recent negotiations.[38] In all, York had requested
seasoned administrators, diplomats and friends, none of whom were
closely associated with Gloucester or too closely identified with
Beaufort.

The military terms on which York accepted the appointment
reflect both the personal wishes of the lieutenant and the policy
disputes in the council. Five years' service substantially funded from
England would display the determination of the English Crown to
retain its lands for the foreseeable future, and give York sufficient
resources to discharge his commission without further recourse to

[32] *Dictionary of National Biography*, iii. 29.

[33] Emden, *Cambridge*, p. 11; *PPC* v. 6.   [34] Emden, *Oxford*, i. p. 16.

[35] *Complete Peerage*, xii/1, 419–21.   [36] Ibid. ii. 62.

[37] Ibid. v. 254.

[38] J. S. Roskell, 'Sir John Popham, Knight Banneret of Charlford, Speaker-elect in
the Parliament of 1449–50', *Proceedings of the Hampshire Field Club and
Archaeological Society*, 21 (1958), 38–52, repr. in Roskell, *Parliament and Politics*,
iii. 353–68; Stevenson, *Letters and Papers*, ii/1, pp. lxxv–lxxx.

England. However, the indentures were careful to allow for the possibility of a sustained truce and eventual peace, and the general expectation was that York should hold Normandy with English support until peace could be arranged. In this York evidently concurred.

Peace was, essentially, the diplomat's problem. York's obligation was to defend English possessions in France. Because Normandy was under some pressure, it was intended that an advanced contingent of 200 men-at-arms, together with archers, should be dispatched in September 1440, and that York should follow with 700 men-at-arms and archers, mustering at Portsmouth, Southampton, or Poole on 1 April 1441.[39] To this end, payment of the second quarter of his wages was brought forward by fourteen days.[40] The advance force did indeed set sail, and, confident of the main force assembling, commissions were issued on 8 February 1441 to gather shipping at Portsmouth before 1 March or, at latest, 25 March.[41] It was hoped to start taking the muster on 20 March,[42] and letters were sent to Rouen announcing, somewhat optimistically, that York's departure-date had been brought forward by a month. In fact, it was postponed to 24 April, but York was not to leave London until 16 May,[43] and the muster could not be taken until 26 and 27 May,[44] although continual pressure was exerted on York to be quick.[45] By 31 May the muster was complete, except for that of Henry Husee,[46] but York had still not arrived in Normandy three weeks later.[47] He probably did not set sail until about 25 June, when prayers were ordered for the success of the expedition.[48]

There may be some truth in the charge that York was unreasonably dilatory,[49] and it has to be said that he was prone to dally before all

---

[39] E404/57/130 (warrant dated 30 Nov. 1440).
[40] E404/57/127.
[41] *CPR 1436–41*, p. 538.
[42] Ibid. 539.
[43] Stevenson, *Letters and Papers*, ii/2, 605.
[44] *CPR 1436–41*, p. 539.
[45] *PPC* v. 146.
[46] *CPR 1436–41*, p. 571.
[47] Stevenson, *Letters and Papers*, ii/2, 605.
[48] Hist. MSS. Comm. *Eighth Report*, i/3, 634.
[49] Griffiths, *Reign of Henry VI*, p. 459; cf. *Rot. Parl.* v. 61. Allmand's suggestion that he delayed in order further to improve his terms of service is difficult to substantiate, as is that of Pugh, that the exchequer was having difficulty in finding the cash for his wages (Allmand, *Lancastrian Normandy*, p. 45; Pugh, 'Richard Plantagenet as King's Lieutenant', p. 117).

his expeditions. He may in this instance, however, have been delayed by personal problems,[50] at least initially, and when he failed to muster in April the shipping dispersed. Fresh arrangements had to be made to muster the earls of Oxford and Ormond and Lord Clinton at Dover,[51] York parting company from them *en route* for Portsmouth.[52] He had, however, managed, against the general trend,[53] to raise a sufficient gentry-contingent, mostly from his own retainers and local gentry-circle,[54] and to ensure an adequate balance of men-at-arms and archers. One contemporary blamed the delays on his subordinates, and there may be some truth in this, as the muster roll records Oldhall as missing nearly a third of his archers, and it is a reasonable guess that manpower problems explain why Henry Husee mustered after the main party.[55]

The duke may also have delayed in the hope of last-minute efforts to meet his requests for ordnance. He had sought, on well-informed advice, six 'grete gonnes of divers sortis' and twelve 'grete Foulers', with appropriate powder and shot.[56] Siege warfare was a virtual certainly, but, despite the evident reasonableness of his request,[57] he was to be completely disappointed. Some powder was forthcoming, but of the 1,000 lances, 4,000 bows, and 1,200 quires of arrows requested he received only half the desired lances and bows and a third of the arrows.[58] His request for license to ship wheat and other

[50] York's first son, Henry, was born at Hatfield on 10 February 1441. He may not have survived more than a few hours, but if he lived for a few weeks York may have felt it necessary to make provision for his heir before his departure. It was thought in Westminster on 14 Feb. that the child was still alive. (*Annales*, p. 763; E404/57/172).

[51] E101/54/9. The muster was taken at Dover.

[52] *Gregory's Chronicle*, p. 183: *Brut*, ii. 477. A draft muster roll survives which evidently anticipates that all these contingents will be mustering together (E101/53/33; cf. *Antient Kalendars*, ed. Palgrave, ii. 191).

[53] M. R. Powicke, 'Lancastrian Captains', in T. A. Sandquist and M. R. Powicke (eds.), *Essays in Medieval History Presented to Bertie Wilkinson* (Toronto, 1969), 371–81.

[54] Of the nineteen captains in his own retinue seven were already his feed men, and four others, John Scudamore, Henry Mulso, John ap Howell, and Hugh Mortimer, were noted members of gentry-circles in the areas in which York was a great lord.

[55] *English Historical Literature*, p. 339; E101/53/33; *CPR* 1436–41, p. 571.

[56] Stevenson, *Letters and Papers*, ii/2, 87–8.

[57] For the substantial developments in French artillery at this time see M. G. A. Vale, *War and Chivalry* (1981), 130–44.

[58] E404/57/264; *PPC* v. 132–3, 164. The balance should have been made up in cash, but there is no sign that this happened (E404/57/263). It is possible that the smaller weapons could be purchased more cheaply in Normandy (Stevenson, *Letters and Papers*, ii/1, p. lxviii).

victuals from England for military purposes was, in all probability, conceded.[59]

His powers in France were clearly specified in his commission of 2 July 1440.[60] This gave him authority to appoint to all offices, including those of constable and chancellor,[61] and to all benefices. He could also dispose of all lands which might come to the Crown either for life or in tail male. York had also requested, and now received, the right which Somerset had enjoyed, of appointing captains to castles where absentee custodians had failed to make provision,[62] a sensible precaution against the trend to let castles to farm without adequate provision for their safety.

Although personally responsible for his actions in office, York was anxious to obtain the discharge of his heirs from any obligations arising from his lieutenancy, together with a guarantee that in the event of a serious set-back neither he nor his heirs would be legally responsible, given that he had been conscientious in his duties. He requested, as was customary, a general pardon for offences to date, which was duly granted.[63]

Thus far, York's terms of service were unexceptional,[64] and the army which resulted, if a little late and somewhat underprovisioned, was much the same as any other such force. What made York's expedition different was its political context, both international and domestic. Prudence suggested that Burgundy be presumed hostile. In consequence, York was anxious to obtain, before departing, sanction for direct contacts between Rouen and Brittany, in order to encourage Breton loyalty to the English alliance.

At home there was the problem of money. For his own expenses Duke Richard was allowed 36,000 francs from the Rouen exchequer, 6,000 francs more than Warwick, or he himself, in 1436–7.[65] In addition, he had control of all Norman revenues, but these alone could not provide the funds necessary to recover castles lost in the last decade, and hold what yet remained. It was, therefore, allowed

---

[59] There had been severe grain shortages in England, 1437–9 (*English Historical Literature*, p. 352).

[60] Rymer, *Foedera*, x. 786–7.

[61] These had been specifically excluded in Warwick's letters of appointment (ibid. 674).

[62] Stevenson, *Letters and Papers*, ii/2, 590.   [63] *CPR* 1436–41, p. 433.

[64] Cf. the earl of Warwick's terms (Stevenson, *Letters and Papers*, ii/2, p. lxvi).

[65] Other sources suggest that Warwick drew only 20,000 francs (ibid., p. lxvii). For a receipt for York's Norman allowance in 1436 see BL Add. Ch. 1162; for an order to pay his salary in Oct. 1442, BL Add. Ch. 11153.

that York should have, in the second and subsequent years, £20,000 from the English exchequer by secure assignment. This was a remarkable financial commitment, as the only serious guarantee of such sums would be votes of a subsidy every other year by Parliament and Convocation, all other sources being already overassigned. Apart from the fact that this left policy in Normandy vulnerable to intermittent Parliamentary review, it presumed a goodwill towards the French war which had in fact been dwindling since 1429. Tax demands had risen in the 1430s, and had needed increasing efforts to secure them.[66] If York's finances were to be guaranteed, then the king's councillors in England would have to be persistently eloquent on his behalf, and Parliament readily sympathetic. In particular, Henry's support could not be allowed to waver, a concern which may underlie York's otherwise puzzling request that a significant number of household men of substance should serve for a period in the duchy.[67] None did. Nor was Parliament to manage the necessary votes. No doubt the financial arrangements had some political value in 1440 in muting criticisms from Gloucester, but, as Cromwell and his financial colleagues must have appreciated, it was a precarious financial guarantee. York, however, was seemingly content.

He landed in Normandy in late June 1441. In his absence Somerset, as lieutenant for war, had maintained a measure of military control, and the council in Rouen had sustained the administration since Warwick's death. A warrant of 4 June 1440 is endorsed 'Par le Rey a larelacion du gents [du] conseil tenu par messieurs les commissaires ordonnez au gouvernement de France et Normandie', and an identical formula is found on warrants for 22 June and 8 September 1440.[68] On 20 December, and again three days later, the warranty is 'a la Relacion du grant conseil', which continues until 19 June 1441. The first warrant on York's authority is dated 6 July 1441 'Par le Roy a la relacion de monsieur le duc de york'.[69]

In his capacity as civilian governor of Normandy, the most

[66] Griffiths, *Reign of Henry VI*, pp. 117–18, 378–9.

[67] Stevenson, *Letters and Papers*, ii/2, 589.

[68] Bib. Nat. MS Fr. 26067 nos. 4055, 4069, 4109. The powers of this council were set out in its commission of 22 May 1439 (BL Add. MS 11542 fo. 78, printed in Burney, 'English Rule of Normandy', App. pp. iv–vi).

[69] Bib. Nat. MS Fr. 26067, nos. 4182, 41864; MS Fr. 26068, nos. 4309, 4224, 4243, 4320.

important decision he made was to reduce French representation on the Norman council from a majority presence, as it had been under Bedford and through the 1430s, to a minority of just two.[70] As has been pointed out, this made the council very much a government of an occupying power, but York did make an attempt to identify the major grievances of his Norman subjects, actively soliciting their complaints[71] and, for three months in the summer of 1443, touring the provinces.[72] When, in 1446, a tax was sought from the Norman estates, the claim was made that much had been done in the name of good justice, a claim not made since 1430.[73] Under the terms of his indenture the duke enjoyed wide powers of patronage, particularly in the disposal of land, but it is doubtful whether there was much of value to grant, the only substantial estate being that of the duke of Alençon, formerly in Bedford's hands. His most effective power was the appointment of captains, which he was to use to the advantage of his supporters, if not always to the military advantage of Normandy.[74]

His powers of ecclesiastical patronage were considerable, but he did not exploit them, only one of his promotions, William Estoby, having had previous links with him.[75] Much more important was the frustration of French attempts to infiltrate their influence through episcopal appointments. Three bishoprics and the metropolitan see were at risk between 1440 and 1445. Avranches, Lisieux, and Rouen he managed to keep in sympathetic hands, but Évreux passed, in January 1443, to a Poitevin clergyman, John Balne.[76]

Much his most pressing difficulties, however, were military. In October 1440, before York's arrival, the security of cross-channel links and of the lower Seine had been much improved by the recovery of Harfleur, thanks to a very thorough land and sea

---

[70] Pollard, *Talbot*, pp. 29–30, 42–3. It has been suggested, probably correctly, that the royal council in France is to be identified with the body which organized the 1442 truce (Marshall, 'English War Captains', p. 53, citing Rymer, *Foedera*, xi. 13. Sir William Oldhall ought perhaps to be added to the list).

[71] BL Egerton Charter 190. His first lieutenancy had been noted for its attention to good justice (Hellot, *Croniques de Normandie*, p. 82).

[72] Stevenson, *Letters and Papers*, ii/2, 371–3; Allmand, *Lancastrian Normandy*, p. 172.

[73] Jouet, *Résistance à l'occupation anglaise*, p. 86.

[74] Marshall, 'English War Captains', pp. 100–1.

[75] C. T. Allmand, 'Some Effects of the Last Phase of the Hundred Years War upon the Maintenance of the Clergy', in G. J. Cuming (ed.), *Studies in Church History*, 3 (1966), 181.

[76] C. Eubel, *Hierarchica Catholica Medii Aevi* (Regensburg, 1901), 87, 150, 164, 195, 248.

blockade.[77] Conscious of this, York had sought in his terms of
appointment a guarantee of a 2,000-man, naval task force, in the
event of further coastal sieges, and his explicit reference to Dieppe,
in this context, implies that its recovery was high on his list of
priorities. In April, York persuaded the Estates-General in Rouen to
vote sufficient funds to keep an army in the field for the campaigning
year, a major development in Norman taxation, although the results
did not quite match expectations.[78] With these funds, York could
put a sizeable force into the field, but the navy, which was vital, was
not forthcoming. Then the attack was delayed until November
1442,[79] when Talbot moved a modest force to a vantage point above
the town, only for the dauphin to wipe it out the following summer.

With Normandy dependent on England for men and money, the
failure to take Dieppe was a major set-back. By the autumn of 1443,
sailors from Dieppe, Boulogne, and Brittany were raiding English
shipping,[80] and it would only be a matter of time before East Anglia,
the Thames estuary, and the south coast felt the pressure of
privateering raids.[81] The reputation of the duke cannot have stood
very high in south-east England.[82]

It was not his fault. The demands were too many, the resources
too few. When he landed, he marched immediately, with a force of
150 men-at-arms and 450 archers, to help the relief effort at
Pontoise.[83] These fresh forces made a difference, and for a time
Pontoise was saved, only to fall to a major French assault in
September.[84] Beaumont-le-Roger, Évreux, and Creil fell in the same

[77] Pollard, *Talbot*, p. 53.

[78] Allmand, *Lancastrian Normandy*, p. 181.

[79] The delay may have been the result of slow recruitment of an English naval task
force (C. F. Richmond, 'The War at Sea', in K. Fowler (ed.), *The Hundred Years
War* (1971), 116–17).

[80] *Chronicles of London*, p. 152.

[81] C. F. Richmond, 'Royal Administration and the Keeping of the Seas, 1422–85'
(Univ. of Oxford D.Phil. thesis, 1963), 131–8; Allmand, *Lancastrian Normandy*,
p. 74 n. 2.

[82] Cf. *Rot. Parl.* v. 52.

[83] E404/57/168, 260 and *CPR* 1436–41, p. 571. The issue-roll entry records a
payment for this force on 8 July of £3,180. 12*s*. 8*d*. to Walter Colles, Lewis John, and
William Browning, each having different keys to the chest, the chest to be opened on
arrival (E403/742). For arrangements to provision York's force see C. P. Cooper,
Report on Rymer's Foedera; Appendix D: Archives of France; Record Commission
(1836), 497.

[84] For York's part in these events—not especially distinguished—see Pollard,
Talbot, pp. 56–8. Allmand points to the limited forces available (*Lancastrian
Normandy*, p. 45).

year, despite the syphoning-off of other garrisons to assist in their defence.[85] What most annoyed York and Talbot, whom York had sensibly made captain of the army,[86] was that such resources as were available were directed towards an expedition to be led from England by John Beaufort, earl, (soon to be duke) of Somerset.[87]

Although the expedition was eventually to prove disastrous to English fortunes, there was a certain logic behind it. As Lord Cromwell pointed out to the council on 6 February 1443,[88] money spent in Normandy was showing little return; domestic opinion would not accept that only one of the duchies be saved, an effort must be made for both; and immediate action must be taken to relieve the more hard pressed. The council followed this analysis, Kemp underlining the financial impossibility of providing relief for both. The duke of Gloucester and Cardinal Beaufort supported the venture, but by 2 March Kemp's financial reservations had been confirmed,[89] and Somerset was, therefore, approached to discover his preference.[90] Maine Herald had already been despatched to Rouen on 25 February, returning by 2 March.[91] Before 4 March it had been decided that Gascony should be the objective of the expedition, and Somerset its leader, but the writs for the arrest of shipping, of 7 March, recite not only the threat to Gascony but also the threat to Normandy from an army under the dauphin.[92]

During March, discussions took place over the final terms of Somerset's service,[93] and they were concluded by 2 April, when Somerset, on being paid £100, was described as lieutenant and captain-general in the duchy of Aquitaine, and in those parts of France not under the authority of the duke of York.[94] When Garter was sent, on 5 April, to the duke, it was to advise him that the

---

[85] Cooper, *Report on Rymer's Foedera: Appendix D*, pp. 470–4.

[86] Pollard, *Talbot*, p. 58.

[87] For the most recent study of this expedition see M. D. Jones, 'John Beaufort Duke of Somerset and the French Expedition of 1443', in Griffiths (ed.), *Patronage, the Crown, and the Provinces*, pp. 79–102.

[88] *PPC* v. 223.

[89] *PPC* v. 229. For the financial details see K. B. McFarlane 'At the Deathbed of Cardinal Beaufort', in R. W. Hunt, W. A. Pantin, and R. W. Southern (eds.), *Studies in Medieval History presented to Frederick M. Powicke* (Oxford, 1948), 424, repr. in McFarlane, *England in the Fifteenth Century* (1981).

[90] *PPC* v. 227.   [91] Ibid. 232–3, 236.

[92] Rymer, *Foedera*, xi. 21. For the French plan of campaign see Beaucourt, *Charles VII*, iii. 251.

[93] *PPC* v. 231.

[94] E403/748. For an identical statement dated 6 April see E404/59/161.

council, aware of the threat to both Normandy and Gascony, had commissioned Somerset to lead any army via Cherbourg,[95] and thence south to cross the Loire, give battle to the French, and relieve Gascony.[96] The observations of Cromwell, on 6 February, had clearly borne fruit. Somerset was expected with one army to relieve the pressure on Normandy and on Gascony. The emphasis on the report to York was, therefore, on mobility. Within the context of such a strategy, independence of command was essential, and it was emphasized, at Somerset's request, that there was no detriment intended to York's authority.[97] This was again stated in the formal commission, of 4 June, appointing Somerset captain-general of the duchy of Gascony, and of France,[98] and was subsequently recited in all official documents.[99] The command in France was to be kept distinct from that in Gascony, which Somerset would enjoy in the same fashion as any previous lieutenant. All arrangements in France, excluding Gascony, were to pass under the seal of France, those for Gascony under the seal of England.[100]

Just what York made of all this is very difficult to establish. Somerset's military record in recent years was adequate, and the plan itself was, logistically, very similar to the duke of Clarence's expedition of 1412.[101] If it were to succeed, it might put York's own position in some jeopardy, and York was probably conscious of Beaufort resentment at his appointment. In military terms, it represented a shift from the defensive policy which York had hitherto pursued. On this, York had already faced criticism in the English council at the end of his first campaigning season, it being noted that he had both field and garrison armies of some strength, together with an estimated disposable income of 508,000 *li. t.*,[102] and, although not explicitly mentioned, had called the *arrière-ban*

[95] Certainly decided on as the landing point before 3 April (*PPC* v. 257).

[96] Ibid. 259–64. Garter may have been sent in response to a request for information from York. On 6 April John St John was rewarded for bringing a request from the duke and for 'his retorne with answer etc.' (ibid. 264).

[97] Ibid. 251.

[98] The title of captain-general implied a degree of subordination. Talbot had been so described in 1435 (Cooper, *Report on Rymer's Foedera: Appendix D*, p. 423).

[99] C76/125 m. 1; cf. *CPR* 1441–6, p. 199.

[100] This reflects the traditional English standpoint over the feudal relations of Gascony to the French Crown (*PPC* v. 225; and see P. Chaplais, 'The Chancery of Guyenne, 1289–1453', in J. Conway Davies (ed.), *Studies Presented to Sir Hilary Jenkinson* (1957), 61–89).

[101] Cf. Allmand, *Lancastrian Normandy*, p. 2.

[102] *PPC* v. 178.

three times.[103] He had achieved little with this by November 1441, and precious little since. One source states explicitly that Somerset was set into France because York was such a mediocrity,[104] and in April 1443 Garter was instructed to inform York 'it is seemed ful behoveful and necessaire that the maner and conduit of the werre be chaunged'.[105] At court, the independence of command,[106] the decision to cross the Loire, and the determination to go on the offensive all made sense. In a more cautious Rouen it was less clear. While in Normandy, Somerset was bound to draw on Norman resources, and, as captain of several castles, he was at liberty to command their garrisons to reinforce him.[107] His brother, now earl of Dorset, was governor of Anjou and Maine and also at liberty to divert resources without reference to Rouen.[108] Lastly, there was the question of where the expedition was leading. Any success would have to be followed up and consolidated, and, as the council itself had pointed out, funds were insufficient.

York, oblivious of the speed of decisions in England, left Rouen for a three-month tour on 27 March, with the intention of identifying and remedying grievances, and it may have taken some time for a full account of Somerset's intentions to catch up with him.[109] When a Norman deputation of key figures[110] finally arrived in London, on 21 June, it was on the problems of authority and resources that they addressed the council.[111] They were given little comfort on either count. Stanlow, the Norman treasurer, was able to raise only 2,500 marks to further the siege of Dieppe, despite the fact that 6,000 marks was the agreed minimum for success.[112]

---

[103] I am indebted to Dr Anne Curry for this information.
[104] Giles, *Chronicon Angliae*, p. 31.   [105] *PPC* v. 260.
[106] Occasionally, Westminster had given direct orders to Norman garrisons and instructed York to co-operate, e.g. the panic caused by a report from Garter in 1441. (Stevenson, *Letters and Papers*, i. 187–9; *PPC* v. 162). York, following Bedford, had brought the principal commanders back into the governor's household in order to unify command structures (Pollard, *Talbot*, p. 35).
[107] Cooper, *Report on Rymer's Foedera: Appendix D*, p. 506; Jones, 'John Beaufort's Expedition', p. 93.
[108] Ibid. 90.
[109] Stevenson, *Letters and Papers*, ii/2, 371–3; BL Egerton Ch. 190. He was back in Rouen by 23 July, but was expected in Caudebec by 14 Aug. (Bib. Nat. MS Fr. 23189 fo. 20; Stevenson, *Letters and Papers*, ii/1, 346).
[110] Louis of Luxemburg, John earl of Shrewsbury, Lord Fauconberg, Sir Andrew Ogard, John Stanlow, and Jean Rinel.
[111] *PPC* v. 306; *Chronicles of London*, p. 151. They stayed until at least 13 July.
[112] £1,666. 13s. 4d. paid in cash on 22 July. It was agreed, on 13 July, that 6,000 marks were necessary but half would have to be raised by commercial ventures. On

Somerset's expedition proved a political and military disaster. Henry VI was by all accounts outraged. In Rouen, York's attitude can only be guessed. Two points were clear. It had made a diplomatic nonsense of his own initiatives over the last two years to exploit the internal stress in France following the release of the duke of Orleans. The duke, thanks to his marriage to Mary of Cleves, had, by 1442, been showing distinctly pro-Burgundian tendencies. Meanwhile, Philip the Good had drawn John V of Brittany and the duke of Alençon into a defensive alliance by incorporating them into the order of the Golden Fleece, which action, in the aftermath of the *Pragurie*, appeared particularly hostile to Charles VII.[113] Repudiating the diplomatic advances of Charles of Orleans, Charles VII effectively sundered relations with Burgundy by disavowing the latter's status at the Laons conference.[114] The princes then sought an alliance with the English. The duchess of Burgundy sent embassies to London and Rouen,[115] representatives of the dukes of Brittany and Alençon came to Rouen shortly after York arrived, in September 1441,[116] and arrangements were made for a meeting of the princes in or near Calais,[117] York to guarantee Breton security in the duke's absence.[118]

By offering a daughter in marriage to Henry VI, in 1442,[119] the count of Armagnac, with another daughter already married to the duke of Alençon, was proposing a widening of this tentative alliance. The enterprise had been weakened with John of Brittany's death and the collapse of the Armagnac marriage negotiations, but it had pointed to a possible avenue of foreign policy which might keep the English in Gascony and Normandy.[120] Negotiations with the

---

the same day a further £1,000 was authorized but never paid, and on 7 Aug. 2,000 marks, similarly disregarded (E403/750; *PPC* v. p. 306; E101/193/7; E404/59/284).

[113] R. Vaughan, *Philip the Good* (1970), 98–127.

[114] Cooper, *Report on Rymer's Foedera: Appendix D*, p. 81; Beaucourt, *Charles VII*, iii. 199 ff. For a brief analysis, see J. Ferguson, *English Diplomacy 1422–61* (Oxford, 1972), 25–6.   [115] Loc. cit*; *PPC* v. 165.

[116] Cooper, *Report on Rymer's Foedera: Appendix D*, p. 475.

[117] H. Morice, *Memoires pour servir de preuves à la histoire ecclesiastique et civile de Bretagne*, 3 vols. (Paris, 1742–6), ii. 1349.

[118] G. A. Knowlson, *Jean V. duc de Bretagne et l'Angleterre (1399–1442)* (Cambridge/Rennes, 1964), 174.

[119] *Brut*, ii. 511 describes the arrangement in terms which imply a contract. If a pre-contract of marriage could be claimed, this might provide the foundation for the later propaganda claims that the prince of Wales was illegitimate.

[120] York spent most of 1442 in Rouen sustaining these negotiations (Stevenson, *Letters and Papers*, ii/1, 325.

duchess of Burgundy were sufficiently advanced for York to conclude a truce with her in April 1443, effective throughout King Henry's English and French domains from 16 July.[121] Somerset, by attacking Brittany, and La Guerche in particular, a property of Alençon, made any further developments impossible.[122]

On the military side, Basin, who provides an informed indication of Norman sentiment, makes the point that if Somerset had assisted in the siege of Dieppe it would certainly have fallen.[123] This seems a somewhat inadequate criticism. The expedition had prevented Charles renewing the attack on Gascony, as was intended, and it is noticeable that this part of the Norman frontier was to prove more stable than most in the next few years.[124] These benefits are more evident with hindsight. Basin's pithy and personal criticism shows clearly the attitude in Normandy, the professional soldiers sharing the opinion of the administration that if Somerset had behaved with crass stupidity then the first folly lay with those who had appointed him.[125] Anti-Beaufort feeling must have been strong on both sides of the Channel, but with John Beaufort's death and the virtual retirement of the Cardinal it had, for the moment, no obvious target. That York shared the general resentment against Somerset there is no reason to doubt, but whether this extended, on a personal basis, to anyone else on the council is uncertain. In sanctioning the expedition, the council evidently felt that York was making insufficient military impact, a judgement which York may well have resented. It is, however, impossible to demonstrate any breach between York and the English council arising from Somerset's expedition, still less any rift between York and John Beaufort's heir, his brother Edmund.

The earl of Suffolk now had an unenviable diplomatic task. He

[121] C76/125 m. 8; BL Add. Ch. 75749; Rymer, *Foedera*, xi. 24. The scope of the truce may have exceeded York's remit (*PPC* v. 212).

[122] B. P. Wolffe, *Henry VI* (1981), 179. Duke Francis eventually did homage to Charles VII on 14 March 1445.

[123] T. Basin, *Histoire de Charles VII*, ed. C. Samaran, 2 vols, (Paris, 1933–44), bk. iii. ch. 18. For the loss of Dieppe see also Pollard, *Talbot*, pp. 60–1. Soldiers of York's retinue took part in the siege but without the duke (BL Add. Ch. 12193).

[124] Somerset's capture of Beaumont-le-Vicomte, for which York sent reinforcements, was certainly of strategic significance (Jones, 'John Beaufort's Expedition', p. 96). York had himself tried to relieve the pressure on Gascony in 1442, ordering Talbot to attack Conches (A. Bossuat, *Perrinet Gressart et François de Surienne, agents d'Angleterre* (Paris, 1936), 278).

[125] Scales lost most of his property from a French attack on Granville at this time (BL Add. Ch. 3976; *Chronicles of London*, p. 151).

had to try to secure a stable settlement for Normandy and Gascony without the military resources to put pressure on the French. Moreover, as he pointed out in February 1444, there was popular opposition to the idea of peace, and the attitude of Parliament to peace negotiations was unpredictable.[126] Hoping to find a bargaining position in the final French peace-offer at Arras,[127] it was soon evident to him that further concessions would have to made to the French, concessions which would undoubtedly prove unacceptable to a section of English public opinion.

The immediate outcome of the Tours negotiations was a two-year truce and the possibility of a marriage-agreement. While in France, Suffolk advised York[128] to use the truce to strengthen and revictual the garrisons of Normandy, and in June he urged Parliament to vote funds to allow military commanders to take advantage of the lull, but Parliament was uncooperative.[129] In Normandy, York was much more helpful. In the summer, as part of a wider campaign to rid Normandy of wageless soldiers,[130] he sent Matthew Gogh with a motley collection of *écorchuers* to help the dauphin in Alsace,[131] and he sustained diplomatic contacts with interested French parties.[132] When Gogh's men returned, he did his best to push them out of the province.[133]

The truce left York with little to do beyond routine administration.[134] He spent from 19 February to 12 March 1445 on a progress via Pont-Audemer to Lisieux,[135] and then returned to greet Margaret of Anjou at Pontoise on 18 March,[136] entertained her entourage at Rouen for a fortnight over Easter, and then

---

[126] *PPC* vi. 33.

[127] Stevenson, *Letters and Papers*, i. 56–64; Palgrave, *Antient Kalendars*, ii. 195.

[128] While Suffolk's mission was in France, York moved to Caen, presumably to facilitate communications between London and Tours (V. Hunger, *Le Siège et prise de Caen* (Paris, 1912), pp. 31 and lxi–lxii). He held a council meeting in May; in Sept. he was expected in Caudebec (BL Add. Ch. 8020; Stevenson, *Letters and Papers*, ii/1, 355).

[129] *Rot. Parl.* v. 74.

[130] Jouet, *Résistance à l'occupation anglaise*, p. 136.

[131] J. H. Ramsay, *Lancaster and York*, 2 vols. (Oxford, 1892), ii. 62, n. 4.

[132] Stevenson, *Letters and Papers* ii/2, 468.

[133] Allmand, *Lancastrian Normandy*, p.209.

[134] It was safe for his cellarer to buy wine in Paris (P. Le Cacheux, *Rouen au temps de Jeanne d'Arc et pendant l'occupation anglaise 1419–1449*, Société d'Histoire de Normandie (Paris, 1931), 373).

[135] BL Add. Ch. 12244.

[136] Stevenson, *Letters and Papers*, i. 448.

accompanied the bridal party to Honfleur.[137] In these last months of his lieutenancy his concerns seem to have been mostly personal.

Duchess Cecily had accompanied York to Normandy,[138] and on 28 April 1442 gave birth to a son, Edward, at Rouen. A second son, Edmund, was born on 17 May 1443, and a daughter, Elizabeth, on 22 April 1444.[139] Duke Richard's first concern was with Edmund, styled earl of Rutland, and it seems to have been his intention to set the boy up as a Norman landowner, allowing his inherited estates to pass intact to his elder son.

In the circumstances, this was remarkably optimistic, the more so as the estates in question, Orbec,[140] Beaumont-le-Roger, Arques, Breteuil, Évreux, Conches, and St-Sauveur-Lendelin,[141] were particularly vulnerable to enemy action; Évreux and Beaumont-le-Roger being already in French hands, and Orbec being for a time lost to the French in May 1445.[142] But by 20 October 1445 a receiver-general, Nicholas Molyneux,[143] had been appointed, and a council was established to administer the estates in York's absence.[144]

What profit York gained from these estates is uncertain. Orbec provides the only direct indication of income, an account-roll for 1444/5 which shows income almost entirely dependent on confiscated lands.[145] The mills required, and received, expenditure in 1446 and

[137] *Brut*, ii. 488.

[138] Ibid. 477.

[139] *Annales*, p. 763.

[140] Acquired before 28 Jan. 1445 (H. de Frondeville, *La Vicomté d'Orbec pendant l'occupation anglaise 1417–49* (Paris, 1936), 5).

[141] Acquired before 9 Feb. 1445, with William Oldhall appointed their governor-general on 30 April (Bib. Nat. MS Fr. 14882 n. 186; MS Fr. 26074 n. 5390; BL Add. Ch. 12332; M. Nortier, *Sources de l'histoire de Normandie: fonds latines* (Nogent-sur-Marne, 1959) p. 128 n. 613. For Rutland's involvement see also BL Add. Ch. 1230 and Bib. Nat. MS Fr. 3624 n. 367). The most secure of the properties, St-Sauveur-Lendelin, had previously belonged to John duke of Somerset (Allmand, *Lancastrian Normandy*, p. 62).

[142] BL Add. Ch. 1219; Pollard, *Talbot*, p. 58. Beaumont was the subject of dispute in 1446 (Cooper, *Report on Rymer's Foedera: Appendix D*, p. 85).

[143] Stevenson, *Letters and Papers*, i. 79. He was still acting on 17 Feb. 1447 but by 21 April had been replaced by John Profoot (Bib. Nat. MS Fr. 26076 nn. 5674, 5720).

[144] BL Add. Ch. 1030; Bib. Nat. MS Fr. 1482 n. 186. The council met in Rouen and had a seal bearing his arms: (ibid. n. 189). The actions of this council have given rise to the belief that York was in France 1446–7 but this was not so. (Griffiths, *Reign of Henry VI*, p. 541 n. 132, dates Stevenson, *Letters and Papers*, incorrectly.)

[145] Bib. Nat. MS Fr. 8769. The total income due was 1,081. 16. 8. *li. t.* Rents in Rouen, collected January–March 1445, amounted to 125. *li. t.* (Bib. Nat. MS Fr. 26074 n. 5436).

again in 1447,[146] which suggests some confidence, but in October 1447 it was necessary to warn Orbec, and York's other lands, that Roger Lord Camoys intended to descend on them and live off them.[147] Whether he did is unknown, but in an atmosphere of such uncertainty longer-term plans and hopes for these estates cannot have been considered, and an allowance in 1447 for a reduction in the fee farm for Clairefontaine, due from Lawrence de la Hay,[148] reinforces the impression of economic gloom. However, on 12 August 1448, using the facilities of the comptroller-general of the Norman exchequer, York paid into Rouen £600, and corn and wine were shipped to London to the same value, presumably for resale for York's benefit.[149] As Oldhall and Ogard had also transferred sums by this means earlier in the year,[150] the transaction was probably private, and may represent, in part at least, the proceeds in kind of the Norman estates. York, in his own name, was also captain of Lisieux, Orbec, Avranches, Bernay, Conches, and Beaumont-le-Roger, but, as he was responsible for the payment of the garrisons, it is not clear whether these offices were a source of profit.[151]

A second initiative, partly family-orientated but essentially political in intent, surfaces at this time, the possibility of the betrothal of York's son, Edward, to a daughter of Charles VII.[152] This was not an independent initiative by the duke, as the possibility had first been broached by the duke of Suffolk during the

[146] Bib. Nat. MS Fr. 26076 n. 5730.

[147] Bib. Nat. MS Fr. Nouv. Acq. 7629 (Fontainieu MSS) fos. 407ᵛ–408ᵛ (an 18th-c. copy).

[148] Bib. Nat. MS Fr. 26076 n. 5780.

[149] C76/25/9/18. The export of grain from Normandy had been forbidden, by York's council, on 17 June 1446 (BL Add. Ch. 12289). The cash was probably paid to Rouen in order to meet commitments to men serving there; e.g. in 1447 Shrewsbury was paid £100 by John Profoot (part of his annuity), by assignment (BL Add. Ch. 12328).

[150] C47/25/9/20 and 21.

[151] BL Add. Chs. 1030, 1233, 12310, 12386; Bib. Nat. MS Fr. 26075 n. 5539; Stevenson, *Letters and Papers*, ii/2, 619, 621, 623. His costs as captain of Rouen were met by the Norman exchequer (Cooper, *Report on Rymer's Foedera: Appendix D*, p. 536; for a payment to his lieutenant in Rouen, Theobald Georges, see Bib. Nat. MS Fr. 26075 n. 5499).

[152] Pugh, 'Richard Plantagenet as King's Lieutenant', p. 123, draws attention to the titles acquired by the young Edward and Edmund, and suggests that they were the creation of Henry VI, partly to recognize York's services, partly to further the marriage. However, no patent of creation survives and the title 'earl' was insufficient for a son-in-law of the king of France, especially as the duchy of Aumale could readily have been resurrected. The titles were probably after York's devising, as courtesy titles, though very possibly with the marriage in mind.

course of his second embassy to the French, and must have enjoyed the blessing of the English court. York wrote enthusiastically to Charles on 18 April 1445, he replying with the suggestion that the Princess Madeleine might be suitable. York respectfully proposed the second daughter, Joanne, in a letter of 10 June which he sent via a fairly high-powered delegation. Charles declined this proposal, but continued to express interest in the possibility of a marriage for Madeleine.[153] By this time, York's term of office had technically expired, although he omitted to mention this in his letter of 21 September to the king of France, preferring, instead to explain his imminent departure as a response to a summons to Parliament.[154] His enthusiasm for the marriage was undiminished, and he was expecting to discuss the matter further with Henry VI while in England.

There is no hint in the correspondence as to the motives of the English and French courts in supporting this venture. Clearly, with the principals so very young the discussions would have no immediate consequences, and it may be reasonably supposed that Charles VII entertained the idea as part of the general goodwill which it suited his diplomacy to disseminate. From an English point of view, the proposal was more complex.[155] Margaret of Anjou was of child-bearing age, but was only a niece of Charles VII and was without a dowry. Any child of a union of Madeleine and Edward would be that bit closer to the French throne, and, were the negotiations to advance, a dowry would presumably have to be postulated. This would make little sense if it was intended that Richard of York should simply be a great English magnate. It would make more sense if Henry VI's intention was to give Duke Richard a second term as lieutenant in France. Even if this was not Henry's intention, it may well have been where Duke Richard believed the king's intentions to lie for, when he left France in late September

---

[153] Stevenson, *Letters and Papers*, i. 79–86.

[154] Ibid. i. 160–3.

[155] For an alternative view, that Suffolk was using the marriage-idea to lure the duke of York away from Burgundy, see Ferguson, *English Diplomacy*, p. 26. For York's negotiations with Burgundy see M-R. Thielemans, *Bourgogne et Angleterre: relations politiques et économiques entre les Pays-Bas Bourguignons et l'Angleterre, 1435–1467* (Brussels, 1966), 149. The council in Normandy still described itself as empowered in York's absence on 11 and 20 Dec. 1446 (Bib. Nat. MS Fr. 26076 nn. 5625, 5628).

1445,[156] there is good reason to believe that he expected to return by early November.[157]

York left Normandy very much as he found it. In a rough-and-ready way it could be defended, in a rough-and-ready way it was governable.[158] It still needed the military consolidation of its frontiers followed by a sustained period of peace to reconstruct its economy, but, given these, it had prospects. Contemporary judgements of York varied. One believed him an armchair governor, impressionable and ineffectual.[159] By contrast, Jean de Waurin, writing some years after the duke's death, saw him as an effective governor, determined to discharge the responsibilities of his office to the honour of the English crown.[160] The truth lies somewhere between the two. Brisker organization in 1441 would have done much to stabilize the military situation, and military reorganization during the truce would have made Normandy more defensible, but the resources promised were not forthcoming. York had established, however, that the French would have to fight to take Normandy,[161] and it was on this that Henry sought to construct his peace policy. How hard the French would have to fight, and for how long, was less clear, but it was Henry's policy, with its attendant confusions, which weakened resolve, not some legacy of military inadequacy bequeathed by his lieutenant. In domestic matters, York restored effective authority in a province all but lost to rebellion, and sustained business confidence in a continued English presence. This was an honourable achievement, and Duke Richard had good reason to expect that his appointment would be renewed.

[156] He was at Argentan on 16 Aug. and at Honfleur on 21 Sept. (BL Harleian Ch. 43 E 50; Stevenson, *Letters and Papers*, i. 163).

[157] In two letters, dated from Woodstock 17 Sept., but without a regnal year, Henry VI wrote to Normandy to say that the ambassadors of France were in England and that he needed the advice of his lords, for which purpose he expected them to assemble on 21 Oct. The duke of York would, therefore, be delayed, but would be back in Rouen on 6 Nov., along with the chancellor of France and others (Bib. Nat. MS Fr. 26067 nn. 4116, 4117). The only year appropriate to this correspondence when the king was in Woodstock is 1445, when Parliament was due to reassemble on 20 Oct.

[158] The major difficulties with unemployed soldiers broke out after York left (Jouet, *Résistance à l'occupation anglaise*, pp. 152–4).

[159] *English Historical Literature*, p. 339.

[160] Waurin, *Croniques*, iv. 349.

[161] The credit for this has been rightly assigned to Talbot (Pollard, *Talbot*, p. 27).

3

IRELAND

York had received a summons to the Parliament of 1445 as a matter of course,[1] but he was at Honfleur on 21 September,[2] and it was not until the opening of the third session, on 20 October, that he arrived in England. He had some private business to pursue concerning the lordship of Crickhowell,[3] but this could have been left to proctors. His presence was necessitated by Henry VI's determination to have a peace with the French. In pursuit of this, it was Henry's intention to go to France in person, an intention which was already public knowledge before the session began. As the session advanced, the king's confidence grew, and on 19 December he arranged an extension of the truce until April 1447, and on 22 December set in motion the voluntary surrender of Le Mans.

Given the importance of these decisons for York, it is unlikely that he left London while Parliament was in session.[4] Where he went over the Christmas recess is unknown. Not until 24 March are his whereabouts certain—he was again in London[5]—but it is likely that he had been in the capital throughout this session also. It was a difficult session, ending on 9 April on a very strained note. The clause of the Treaty of Troyes which required parliamentary ratification of any subsequent Anglo-French treaty was nullified, thereby giving diplomatic *carte blanche* to Henry, but the chancellor was also clear, in his declaration on behalf of all the lords, on the very last day of the session, that this policy was the king's alone.[6]

Henry's determination to press ahead with his policy placed York in considerable political difficulty. The policy was unpopular in Normandy, and was to be actively resisted. York's own council in Normandy was uncooperative,[7] and his councillors in England,

---

[1] *CCR* 1441–7, p. 279. [2] Stevenson, *Letters and Papers*, i. 160.
[3] Proceedings had been initiated the previous March. The final outcome is nowhere stated, but York apparently lost his case (SC8/85/4247; *PPC* vi. 37; *CPR* 1441–6, 320–1 and 334).
[4] He was in London on 21 Dec. (Stevenson, *Letters and Papers*, i. 171).
[5] BL Egerton Roll 8783. [6] *Rot. Parl.* v. 102.
[7] Stevenson, *Letters and Papers*, i. 179.

notably Oldhall, were highly critical. York himself may not have
been so hostile to the proposals, although his attitude can only be
guessed, but he certainly could not afford the luxury of public
opposition if he wished to return to France as the king's lieutenant.
If Henry did go in person to France, this would be expensive and
would delay the appointment of a lieutenant until he set sail again for
England.

On 15 July, the duke's council sought to test the water, asking
what forces the Crown expected York to assemble for the king's
journey,[8] and were answered, on 20 July, that he should raise 200
men-at-arms and archers, to indent at Michaelmas for three months,
and thereafter on a monthly basis.[9] He was evidently expected to
accompany the king to France, but, beyond that, York's council
could discern nothing of the king's intentions.

This uncertainty required that York adopt a flexible attitude to his
other problem, payment. He had returned from France expecting an
audit, and had brought with him not only the necessary documentation
but also one of the treasurers of Normandy and two exchequer
chamberlains.[10] As Stanlow, the Norman treasurer, left England on
8 December 1445,[11] it must be supposed that their audit was
concluded, but it does not seem to have commanded complete
satisfaction, and York, almost certainly during the final session of
Parliament, was obliged to petition the king:[12]

To the King oure souverain lord

Besecheth lowly youre humble subget Richard duc of york whiche to his
power hath evere bee ready and is to doo the service to him possible to your
hignesse and where as he hath been divers tymys in your service in your
Royaume of France he hath understande to his greet hevynesse that certain
sclaindereux langaige hath bee saide and reported in this your royaume of
his demenyng on the tother side of the see durying the tyme that he hadde
now last the charge and gouvernance there by your noble lettres of

---

[8] E28/76/26. Pugh, 'Duke Richard of York as King's Lieutenant', pp. 124, 138
n. 26, and Griffiths, *Reign of Henry VI*, pp. 505, 541 n. 132, citing independent
sources, suggest that he had been given a commission as lieutenant in France for a
further year in autumn 1445, but it is more likely that the Norman council,
anticipating York's return as Henry had originally advised them, continued to use the
title in anticipation of its formal confirmation.

[9] *PPC* vi. 52.

[10] BL Harleian 'MS 543 fos. 161ᵛ–3ᵛ, printed in A. C. Reeves, *Lancastrian
Englishmen* (Washington, 1981), App.

[11] E159/222 *Brevia Directa* Easter Term m. 5ᵛ; Bib. Nat. MS Fr. 26074 n. 5300.

[12] SC8/336/15877.

commission. Plese hit therfore to youre ecellence to commande that if any personne wol saye or susteyne any thing to the charge of your saide subget or of any of his touching the gouvernance that he hadde of your saide Royaume of France that whiles youre parlement is here assembled he may knowe hit and answere thereto for his excus and his in suche wise as he trusteth to god your highnesse shal be plesed and content.

One set of complaints, that of Adam Moleyns, has survived, included with the duke of York's replies and Moleyns's final replications.[13] It can safely be said that they were not presented while Parliament was assembled, as York had requested, but a more precise dating is difficult. The best that can be offered is a date some time between mid-April and late July 1446.[14] But, if the dating is uncertain, the charges themselves are clear; favouritism in the payment of some soldiers, non-payment of others, and general mismanagement to the detriment of the duchy. Moleyns specifically named Oldhall, Ogard, and Scales as having received preferential treatment, and sufficient evidence survives to test the charges. In Oldhall's case it can be shown that he was paid for himself and his retinue coming to England,[15] and it can also be shown that Scales was receiving pension payments at this time,[16] but Ogard, in December 1443, had had to seek a privy-seal letter from England to cajole the Norman exchequer into payment.[17] Unfortunately, there is no further evidence of his financial dealing with Rouen, but York's answer is evasive and, despite the Ogard evidence, the suspicion is that Moleyns was right; York had shown favouritism.[18] On the subject of a general non-payment of wages the duke's answer was straightforward. He had paid what he could from the resources available. Moleyns did not seek to contest this answer.[19]

The most dangerous charge was mismanagement. York claimed that Moleyns had, while in France, recruited men to testify against him. Moleyns, in a cleverly-worded reply, denied that he had ever

---

[13] BL Harleian MS 543, in Reeves, *Lancastrian Englishmen*, App.

[14] See Note A, p. 77 below.

[15] Bib. Nat. MS Fr. 26074 n. 5298.

[16] Bib. Nat. MS Fr. 26075 nn. 5451, 5577.

[17] Bib. Nat. MS Fr. Nouv. Acq. 3565 n. 55.

[18] York not only ensured full payment of Lord Bourchier's wages, but also a gift of 3,000 *li. t.* when he left for England in 1442 (Cooper, *Report on Rymer's Foedera: Appendix D*, p. 495).

[19] In Aug. 1445 he was voted money by the local estates at Argentan, in repayment of money lent by him for the payment of soldiers (Allmand, *Lancastrian Normandy*, pp. 184–5).

criticized York. The criticisms, he said, were already widespread in England before the duke returned. Moleyns was clearly frightened that this issue might escalate, and, as the duke of York had already received public recognition of his services in an act of Parliament, the privy seal was well aware that he was on precarious ground.

Although, therefore, apparently vindicated, York was, neverthe-less, politically much damaged by the exchange. Public charges of mismanagement were obviously unwelcome from any source, but it was especially disconcerting that they had been pressed by a royal councillor very close to the duke of Suffolk and, therefore, to the king. Although the record ceases at this point, it cannot be presumed that the debate itself ceased. The one point which Moleyns did not contest was that York had done his best to pay wages as resources would allow, but, as everyone was aware, many soldiers were unpaid, and York himself was owed money by the English exchequer. Determining the precise amount due was a complicated matter, not settled until 2 June.[20]

While in France, Duke Richard had had the disposal of two sources of income, the revenues of Normandy and an annual payment of £20,000 per annum from the English exchequer. Part of the Norman revenues, 30000 *li. t.*, was to be paid for his household expenses, and he drew this, without apparent difficulty, for the whole of his term.[21] This represented a considerable profit to York, as he was no longer meeting his ordinary household costs from his own pocket.[22]

Provided significant sums could be raised in tax, a sizeable force could be retained from Norman resources alone. In 1441, York had sought a vote of 600,000 *li. t.*, but he had to settle for 340,000 *li. t.*, the largest sum he was to be voted. In practice, it was difficult to collect the full amount, and the votes of subsequent estates-general diminished relentlessly.[23] In consequence, the sums due from England, at least until the truce of 1444, assumed an even greater significance.

[20] E404/62/188.

[21] BL Add. Ch. 12153; Nortier, *Fonds Latin*, p. 127 n. 609; Bib. Nat. MS Fr. Nouv. Acq. 7629 fo. 410.

[22] His own pay in the field of 14s. 4d. per day, would yield £261. 1s. 8d. p.a. In the 1440s ransoms, plunder, and other accidents of war were unlikely to have brought him much profit.

[23] *PPC* v. 171. For details of Norman taxation see Allmand, *Lancastrian Normandy*, p. 180.

Under the terms of York's indenture of 1440 he was due to receive £20,000 per annum once he had arrived in Normandy. All costs prior to his arrival would be met by the English exchequer, whether for ordnance or wages, without any upper limit.[24] On 22 July 1440 £2,859. 12s. 0d. was paid as wages, for 170 men-at-arms and 300 archers for half a year at the wages of France, and £1,771. 6s. 8d. for thirty men-at-arms and 300 archers at the wages of England.[25] An advance payment of £9,898. 13s. 0d. was made to York on 16 January 1441, and this was followed on 24 February by the payment of a further £2,457. 2s. 0d.[26] On the completion of York's musters, £7,115. 16s. 11d. was paid out, on 1 June 1441, with a further £570 being paid on that day for ordnance. On 8 July a total of £3,180. 12s. 8d. was committed to Walter Colles, Lewis John, and William Browning, for payment of 150 men-at-arms and 450 archers on landing in Normandy.[27] All these sums were paid in cash.[28]

First payment of the annual allowance, for 1441–2, came on 27 November 1441, when £5,000 was paid in cash to Peter Bowman,[29] who, on 21 January 1442, paid it into the Norman exchequer at Rouen, returning with the receipt on 11 May,[30] on which day a further £500. 0s. 2d. was paid in cash for various military supplies.[31] This last sum, it was stipulated, should be deducted from the £15,000 still due to York for that year. On 18 May 1442, £13,551. 13s. 4d. was assigned to York by the hands of Thomas Hoo and John Stanlow,[32] who, on 1 June, delivered an acquittance for £15,000,

---

[24] It has been claimed, erroneously, that York was to be paid £20,000 in his first year (Bean, 'Financial Position', p. 187).

[25] E403/739. A warrant of 15 July instructed that they be paid for one half-year, the second half falling due on 15 Aug.; both payments at the wages of France.

[26] E403/740.   [27] E403/742.

[28] The total sum was £27,850. 3s. 3d., spread over two financial years. Bean, 'Financial Position' (tab. ii.) gives £20,254. 8s. 0d. paid in cash, £165. 7s. 11d. in tallies, in 1440–1. (*Recte* £23,220. 4s. 7d. in cash, no tallies). He does not record any cash payments 1439–40.

[29] E403/743.

[30] Palgrave, *Antient Kalendars*, p. 193. The costs of this operation were born by the English exchequer (*PPC* v. 162, 178).

[31] E403/745. During Bowman's absence £6,614. 4s. 10d. was paid in cash, nominally to York, through the agency of Laurence Surrey. The money was intended as advanced wages for the earl of Shrewsbury's army, but, as York had indented for this army with the king, the payments were nominally to him, though they did not form part of the £20,000 p.a. entitlement (E404/58/131).

[32] E403/745; Stevenson, *Letters and Papers*, i. 431. The assignments were principally on the second part of the tenth and fifteenth due from the Parliament of 1440–1. (E401/778; BL Add. Ch. 8425). Four items totalling £57. 4s. 10d. failed.

under York's seal, into the exchequer.[33] Even making allowance for the payments for military supplies on 11 May, the duke would appear to have been underpaid by £948. 6s. 6d., but the acquittance of Hoo and Stanlow states that £1,448. 6s. 8d. had been paid in kind.[34] This additional payment in kind may have taken the form of supplies, or it may have been received in jewellery, as the warrant for Bowman's payment of 27 November 1441 also states that York was to receive jewels to the value of £1,000.[35] Whichever occurred, York was evidently fully satisfied.[36]

The first problems arise for the financial year Michaelmas 1442 to Michaelmas 1443, the third year of the lieutenancy, during which only one payment was made to York, of 2,000 marks, on 22 July 1443.[37] The payment was made in cash, but was specifically earmarked for the siege of Dieppe. Arrears of £18,333. 6s. 8d. were, therefore, due to York for this year, and there appears to have been some negotiation over payment. On 7 December 1443 the receipt roll credits York with a loan of £11,666. 13s. 4d.,[38] but the issue roll, in describing its repayment on 21 February 1444, states that the sum was wages for soldiers.[39] It would appear, therefore, that no attempt was made to pay the whole of York's annual allowance in that financial year (the third), but simply to reimburse him with an agreed sum for the wages of the soldiers for that year, and to pay an allowance for Dieppe. He was, therefore, due 10,000 marks, which he voluntarily surrendered. Confirmation of this comes in the exchequer warrant detailing the financial settlement of York's

This was entirely discharged by April 1448 (E401/806). The tallies themselves were probably delivered over several days. On 19 May, York's agents received £4,451. 13s. 4d. in tallies (E101/193/7).

[33] Palgrave, *Antient Kalendars*, ii. 193.

[34] E101/193/7.

[35] E101/193/7.

[36] Bean, 'Financial Position', tab. ii., records cash payments of £18,256. 12s. 11d. and assignments of £13,572. 6s. 4d. The cash figure seems improbable.

[37] E403/750. It had been intended that York should receive 6,000 marks for the siege, 3,000 marks to be paid in wool, tin, lead, etc. (*PPC* v. 306). An indenture of 30 July 1443 between the treasurer and John Wigmore says that £668. 13s. 4d. has been paid, a sum which presumably relates to the 2,000 marks already paid. Warrants for payments for this 6,000 marks survive for 19 July and 21 Aug., but without any recorded effect (E404/59/273, 284).

[38] E401/785.

[39] E403/752. Bean, 'Financial Position', p. 188, and tab. ii., treats this as a genuine loan. The repayment was on a wide variety of sources, £3,593. 10s. 0d. being subsequently reassigned.

account in June 1446.[40] It is there acknowledged that York was owed £18,666. 13s. 4d. for the fourth year and £20,000 for the fifth, but there is no mention of any sum outstanding for the third year (i.e. 1442–3). There is no trace of any payment to York in the fourth year in the exchequer's records, though the figure of £18,666. 13s. 4d. is mutually agreed. Presumably, the warrant of 7 August 1443, ordering a payment of £1,333. 6s. 8d., was given effect some time in the Michaelmas Term.[41] It was with the repayment of this total of £38,666. 13s. 4d. for the fourth and fifth years that York, in June 1446, had to grapple.

Whether York seriously expected to be paid this amount in full cannot now be established. His original indenture permitted a revision of his annual allowance in the event of a truce, and the exchequer could reasonably point out that about a third of the penultimate, and all of the final, year had been served under these circumstances. For his part, York could point to the fact that it was only a truce, that the garrisons had to be maintained, and, indeed, that he had been instructed to strengthen them. Contemporary figures put garrison strengths at 11,000 men in 1444 and 8,000 in 1445,[42] and, unlikely though they are to be precise, they do suggest that York's military costs were declining, thanks to the truce. York, anxious to be reappointed to Normandy, had good reason for not pushing his case too hard, and by 20 July it had been agreed that he would waive £12,666. 13s. 4d., and that the Crown would regard the balance, £26,000, not as wages due, but as a loan, thereby giving York greater security.[43]

The whole of the exchequer's business for 20 and 21 July was

---

[40] E404/62/188. On 4 Feb. 1446 the exchequer had been ordered 'to make paiement or sufficiant assignement unto oure said cousyn of all that shal befounden due unto hym by his said accompt' (E159/222, *Brevia Directa* Michaelmas Term m. 16d). Probably to delay settlement, the exchequer initiated a review of all York's obligations to the Crown (ibid. Easter term m. 2ᵛ; cf. G. L. Harriss, 'Marmaduke Lumley and the Exchequer Crisis of 1446–9', in J. G. Rowe (ed.), *Aspects of Late Medieval Government*, p. 150).

[41] E404/59/284.

[42] Hist. MSS. Comm., *Third Report*, p. 279.

[43] A tentative attempt to pay York £10,000 was made on 16 July, without any reference to a loan. The expression 'as for money lened to us' occurs on the warrant of 20 July and on all the Rolls entries thereafter (E404/62/224). The payment to York was part of a larger exchequer programme to repay all its major creditors, a programme which led to the overassignment of the customs revenues (Harriss, 'Marmaduke Lumley', pp. 150–1).

taken up with the assigning of the sum,[44] the principal assignments being made against the customs revenues. There is no need to suppose that these assignments were made in anything other than good faith. It was York's misfortune that the attempt to repay him coincided with, and, of course, partially caused, an acute financial crisis. Nearly £5,560 was needed to pay the costs of the retinue bringing Margaret of Anjou from France,[45] and Parliament had assigned her an income of a further 10,000 marks. With customs revenue running at an average of £24,000 per annum in the 1440s,[46] York's repayment might well take several years, but that was not entirely unexpected. In fact, York was fortunate, in as much as London, Boston, Hull, and Ipswich had a large export trade in 1447–8.[47] Had the attempts to raise a loan for Henry's projected visit to France necessitated more vigorous prosecution, the system would have been thrown into further disarray, but, fortunately for York, nothing came of it. The duke appears to have taken no personal interest in the assignment, making no request for the appointment of specific customs officers, or for letters of preferment.[48]

Of the £26,000 assigned, a sum in the order of £11,000 to £12,000 had to be reassigned.[49] Unfortunately, this does not necessarily imply that the balance of approximately £14,000 was assigned successfully, because the exchequer regarded an assignment as a total discharge of its obligations, and only resumed an interest in unsuccessful tallies as an act of grace. Silence on the fate of 'successful' tallies need not imply successful redemption. This silence makes it impossible to delve much further into their fate, but reassigned tallies do reveal something of what was going on.

It is clear that York was using tallies to pay wages. Moleyns

---

[44] Tallies were still in the exchequer's hands on 16 Aug., presumably awaiting collection by York's creditors (E404/62/230).

[45] BL Add. MS. 23938.

[46] E. M. Carus-Wilson and O. Coleman, *England's Export Trade: 1275–1547* (1963), p. 30.

[47] Ibid. 61. The position was somewhat eased by the parliamentary grant of one and a half subsidies. William Burley was the speaker.

[48] *CPR* 1446–52, p. 172.

[49] An accurate figure for reassignments is impossible, as reassigned tallies were not always cancelled on both rolls, the original sums separately assigned are not always consistent, and a whole sum assigned on one roll (e.g. for £100) may be discretely assigned on another (e.g. as two £50 tallies) and partially fail. A total of £11,062 reassigned is here suggested; Bean, 'Financial Position', tab. ii., gives £11,164, A. Steel, *The Receipt of the Exchequer, 1377–1485* (Cambridge, 1954), 227, gives £11,636, and Harriss, 'Marmaduke Lumley', p. 151, £12,023.

alleged, and York did not deny, that money for wages was owed,[50] and a warrant to the exchequer of 2 June stated that York had permitted captains to pay wages, but that he could not provide the money without payment from the exchequer,[51] implying clearly that York needed exchequer support to clear his obligations.

Two clear instances can be demonstrated where tallies were used to discharge, or partially discharge, current liabilities for wages. William Peyto on 8 May 1447[52] had a warrant in his favour directed to the exchequer, stating explicitly that York had given him two tallies for wages outstanding,[53] for 100 marks and £200, and that these should be cancelled, and fresh tallies issued to Peyto—not, however, in his name, but in the name of the duke of York.[54] This warrant was ineffective and another one was issued in like vein on 26 September 1450.[55] The second recipient was John Talbot, earl of Shrewsbury. He had received £1,500 for wages from York, by tallies against the Boston and Chichester customs, and it was agreed in a warrant of 4 June 1451 that these be surrendered, and that he have, instead, the issues of the lands of Cecily, late duchess of Warwick (*ob.* 28 July 1450); but the Warwick arrangement was rescinded, and Talbot never saw any of the wages due to him.[56] There is no further direct evidence that York was using tallies to pay wages, but there are a few suggestions in the reassignments made on occasion by the hands of soldiers, the destiny no doubt of the earlier, unsuccessful tally.[57]

York passed on some tallies in commercial and other transactions. Tallies for £100, issued to him on 14 November 1448, a reassignment of earlier tallies of 21 February 1444 and 20 July 1446, were paid over to the bishop of Worcester in settlement of a debt.[58] A Lucchese

---

[50] Cf. M. H. Keen and M. J. Daniel, 'English Diplomacy and the Sack of Fougères in 1449', *History*, 59 (1974), 379.

[51] E404/62/188.

[52] On 4 May Peyto had taken service under the earl of Dorset (C76/129 m. 10).

[53] 'The which taillies the said oure cousin hath delivered unto the said William for such paiement as he shulde have for his wages of werre' (E404/67/37).

[54] E404/63/93.

[55] E404/67/37. He was not paid until 5 Dec. 1455 (E401/848).

[56] E404/67/172; Pollard, *Talbot*, pp. 111–12. Talbot had a close family interest in the fate of these estates.

[57] William Burton kt., Robert Mansfield esq., Thomas Fulman esq., John Hert. For evidence that tallies for wages could be held other than by the nominee with a view to recovery see E404/67/175.

[58] The bishop 'hath take for dette due unto him' (PSO1/17/888, 889). The payment of 14 Nov. 1448 is described as being for a tally of 26 Oct. 1446 (E403/774), though

merchant with the anglicized name of Nicholas Giles was paid off by York with £1,200 in tallies on the Southampton customs; which tallies, it was arranged with the Crown, would be returned and cancelled, Giles to receive instead a licence to export wool.[59] Felix Fagman and Alex Palastrell, Milanese merchants, were credited with seven tallies of the duke totalling £250, on 16 January 1449,[60] though the original purpose of assignment of these tallies is uncertain. Home merchants were also paid by tally.[61]

There is, therefore, a very strong suspicion that many of the tallies issued nominally to York were in fact handed over to former soldiers and others. But a considerable number had to be changed by York himself. To this end, exchequer officials were employed to smooth the path for tally redemption, principally Sir Thomas Brown, under-treasurer of England, although the operation only emerges after it has broken down, precipitating a squabble between Brown and the duke.[62] This was put to the arbitration of the bishops of Winchester and Ely, Lord Cromwell, William Oldhall, and Richard Quatremains, who declared their award on 5 February 1452.[63]

From its terms, it would appear that York had handed over to Brown a substantial sum in tallies, presumably for Brown to clear, and, as an inducement, had made over his manors of Erith and Swanscombe.[64] Given the rigidity of exchequer procedures, the recruitment of a 'fixer' seems a sensible way round the morass of exchequer legalism, but York, at some time unspecified, lost

the issue roll records only a payment of £44. 6s. 8d. for this day (E403/766). It is clear, however, that the tallies had their original source in the settlements of 1444 and 1446. The reassignment was not allowed until 12 July 1448, when it was paid by the hands of M. Thomas Hawkins, a protégé of the bishop.

   [59] E28/79/59 (3 Dec. 1449). The council warrant speaks of payment for service in Ireland, a note which was then cancelled. Although the tallies were not issued until 11 Dec., it is probable that Irish, rather than Norman, service was the reason for payment (E403/777). A warrant of 13 Feb. 1451 says that a letter patent to this effect had been issued on 12 Dec. 1449, but this is no longer extant (E404/67/113).

   [60] E404/65/94. Palastrell was to have business dealings with York in 1457–8. (SC6/850/28).

   [61] Richard Drax of London, fishmonger, Robert Butler of London, goldsmith, Henry Wever of London, draper, John Snow of London, broker.

   [62] Brown lost office on 22 Sept. 1449, when Lumley ceased to be treasurer (J. L. Kirby, 'The Rise of the Under-Treasurer of the Exchequer (1412–83)', *EHR*, 72 (1957), 666.

   [63] *CCR* 1447–54, p. 326. They were commissioned by the duke on 20 Dec. 1451. For a slightly different interpretation of these events see Bean, 'Financial Position', pp. 194–5.

   [64] Feet of Fine, Trinity Term (CP25(i)293/71/343, 344 and CP25(i)116/322/715).

confidence in this agent, recovered the tallies, and harassed Brown in the enjoyment of the two manors, most probably in the winter of 1450–1.[65] At least 5,500 marks in tallies were at issue, which indicates the scale of York's involvement with the under-treasurer, but, as the duke was displeased with Brown's performance, it is difficult to be sure of the outcome of this arrangement. The award, incidentally, demonstrates that one advantageous method of employing tallies was to use them to smooth the path to a patent, York expending 1,300 marks in tallies for this purpose, according to the terms of the award.[66] Someone, somewhere, had confidence in their redemption.

York used other exchequer officials, apart from Brown. William Beaufitz, an exchequer clerk, frequently employed as a customs officer, had license to ship wool to the customs value of £1,200, having surrendered to the exchequer tallies to the same value. Five of these, totalling £253. 6s. 8d., had originally been issued in favour of the duke of York,[67] and, though it was explicitly stated that Beaufitz had cashed them at their full value,[68] the suspicion lingers that he had, in fact, cashed them at a discount. Reassignments show that the exchequer officials most used by York, apart from Brown, were Stephen Kirkby (tallies totalling £1,130), Robert Turnour (£780. 6s. 7d.), and Richard Simson (£420), but there were several others[69]

Exchequer officials, therefore, did much to help York, probably helping themselves in the process. Whether York did much to help former soldiers with the clearance of tallies is less certain but his indifference was more likely to cost him political support than hard cash. What is striking is how few tallies are reassigned in the periods when York's political influence was substantial; in particular, the two protectorates. It is unlikely that he had lost interest in them,

---

[65] The account roll for 28–9 Henry VI records the revenues of these manors as being alienated to Brown, but they were paid to York the following year (WAM 12166, 12167).

[66] The only patent sought by York in this period was for license to enfeoff (in effect, mortgage) some of his estates (see below p. 62). He also had license to have tallies to a total of £100 against the Newcastle customs reassigned on Sandwich, where John Profoot, his Norman receiver, was able to recover £12 (E159/226 *Brevia Directa* Michaelmas Term m. 12ᵛ. There is no mention of this transfer in the account rolls.)

[67] E404/65/93. [68] *CPR* 1446–52, p. 206.

[69] Some e.g. John Breknok, acquired tallies nominally issued to the duke, and had them reassigned to sources under their control, in this case the duchy of Cornwall. Simson was to be a mainpernor for Thomas Colt in 1458 (C237/44/91).

more probable that by then he held few outstanding tallies. The impression is confirmed in the earliest years of his son's reign, when tallies for his father were being presented to the exchequer, but for very modest amounts. It would be wrong to say that the duke of York had been fully paid the £80,000 to which his four years' service in France entitled him. If in this sum there was an element of profit, it accrued to him only in the second year of his lieutenancy. In the third year, the wages of his soldiers were paid, and honourable attempts were made by the exchequer to do so for the fourth and fifth years.

York was to claim, in 1454, that these subsequent financial arrangements had put him to very considerable distress, principally in pawning plate and jewels and in the sale of his 'lyvelood'.[70] There were, indeed, problems, but the first signs do not appear until late 1448, and, although it is impossible to be precise about rates of tally-clearance, the evidence seems to point to a fairly satisfactory redemption-rate over the two years from 1446 to 1448. York did, certainly, seek to raise money prior to going to Ireland, but whether to cover his costs, or for the payment of past debts, or both, is impossible to say.[71] In all, he raised £3,166 in a series of land-transactions in the financial year 1448–9, a considerable sum of cash, given the notorious difficulties that any medieval landowner had in the substantial liquidation of fixed assets. Initially, he intended to mortgage land, so far as one can tell, but on occasion he had to sell.

The clearest example of a mortgage is that of the lordship of Narberth and the associated properties of St Cleare and Traean, which passed, on 6–13 May 1449,[72] to John bishop of St Davids and Gruffydd ap Nicholas, in a transaction later to be explicitly described as a mortgage, for 1,000 marks, repayable at Hereford by the duke on 1 May 1454.[73] It seems likely that other transactions

---

[70] *Rot. Parl.* v. 255.

[71] Ireland is specifically cited in one instance: 'the costes that he hath . . . for thys your voyage into your lande of Ireland' (E28/79/3).   [72] *CPR* 1446–52, p. 235.

[73] *Calendar of Letters and Papers, Foreign and Domestic, Henry VIII*, ii/1, n. 557. This source is not above suspicion, as it was claimed that the mortgage had not been recovered, the property therefore defaulting to Gruffydd and his heirs. Since Narberth was forfeited in 1459, this cannot be entirely true, and it would appear from an enfeoffment of 15 May 1453 that the bishop of St Davids intended that the property should revert to York (*CPR* 1452–61, p. 71). For an alternative interpretation, that the 1449 transaction was an outright grant, subsequently changed to an enfeoffment, see R. A. Griffiths, 'Gruffydd ap Nicholas and the Fall of the House of Lancaster', *Welsh History Review*, 2 (1965), 217.

were of a similar nature. £1,000 was raised on Holwell (Dorset), North Fambridge (Essex), Finmere (Oxon,) and Clifton (Worcs.) from York's councillors, principally Thomas Buxhale.[74] Thomas Willoughby advanced £100 against Woodcotsworthy (Dorset),[75] and the same group of councillors (except Buxhale), advanced 1,000 marks for Odcombe (Som.), Marshwood and Portland (Dorset), and Charlton and Winstone (Glos.).[76] John Fortescue, the Chief Justice, found 100 marks for Easton in Gordano (Glos.).[77] The grant of Hambledon (Rutland), on 23 February 1449, probably had similar financial motives.[78] A further petition was put up to the king's council, in York's absence from England, on 8 September 1449, requesting license not only for some fines already negotiated, but also to alienate the forests of Narberth (Pembs.), Mendip and Petherton (Som.), and Exmoor (Devon), together with Hinton (Hereford) and Barton (Bucks.), again to a combination of royal and ducal councillors, but whether these transactions were ever finalized is unknown.[79] The accounts for Gussage Bohun at this time show a group of feoffees in possession, very similar in composition to that administering Holwell and, possibly, other properties in this receivership.[80] This too may relate to a mortgage.

In some instances mortgages turned into outright sales. Cressage and Arley were granted on 20 December 1448 to a group of councillors headed by Lord Cromwell, possibly as a mortgage, but they were eventually sold outright to York's legal councillor, William Burley.[81] At some point, the mortgage of Easton in Gordano to Sir John Fortescue turned into a life interest to Thomas Young,[82] and it is possible that John and Agatha Flegge bought a life interest in

---

[74] CP25(1)293/71/346; E. A. and G. S. Fry, *Full Abstracts of the Feet of Fines Relating to the County of Dorset* (Dorset Records, 9 (1896), 327).

[75] Ibid. 368.   [76] CP25(1)293/71/347.

[77] He was firmly associated in this grant with York's council, together with Maurice Bruyn kt., John Bleuet, William Vernour, John Burton, William Cannings, John Young, and John Gargrave. Accounts for 1449–50 record no payment to the duke (E. Green, Pedes Finium *for the County of Somerset: Fourth Series: Henry IV to Henry VI* Somerset Record Society, 22, (1906), 113; BL Egerton Roll 8783).

[78] *CPR 1446–52*, p. 218. For this, and the licence to enfeoff (*sic*) Narberth, he was liable for a total of £2 in payments of queen's gold. He did not pay (Myers, 'Household of Margaret of Anjou', *BJRL* 40 (1957–8), 398).

[79] E28/79/3.   [80] SC6/1113/9.

[81] Hist. MSS. Comm., *Second Report*, p. 38; *CCR 1468–76*, p. 165. The sale of Arley took place on 21 Oct. 1449 (Birmingham Public Library: Hagley Hall MS 25/351405).

[82] Young farmed the manor in 1461 (SC6/1113/15).

North Fambridge and Latchley Hall.[83] Lord Lovell certainly purchased lands in Oxfordshire from the duke around this time.[84]

Prominent in these transactions are York's councillors. While in France, he had left the conduct of affairs in their hands. On his return, he sought both to reconstruct this council and to come to grips with those problems of estate management common to every lord, but made more pressing by his financial circumstances, and by the need to give an English landed interest to several of his new councillors whose careers had hitherto been in France.

Much of October 1446[85] seems to have been spent at Bewdley on estate affairs, particularly those of the south and west, and the results of these deliberations reveal themselves in the account rolls of the next four years. In the south west, James Butler, earl of Wiltshire in 1449, had already been made seneschal for life on 24 March 1446, and by 22 June was farming the manors of Tarrant Gunville, Wareham, Steeple, and Creech.[86] On 27 May 1447, William Browning was appointed supervisor for life and overseer and principal bailiff in the south west.[87] In Gloucestershire, Thomas Young was created seneschal of Easton in Gordano,[88] and new rentals were introduced in Bisley[89] In the following year, John Vampage was working throughout the south west as receiver of arrears, and in Compton and Andover new rentals appeared.[90] Nearer home, John Milewater was given further responsibilities in the lordship of Clifford,[91] and attempts were made to encourage Welshmen to buy out various legal rights which York enjoyed over them.[92] In East Anglia, Thomas Bernard esq. was appointed seneschal of Cambridgeshire and Huntingdonshire for life.[93]

York seems to have been particularly anxious to give landed security to two of his erstwhile Norman councillors, Edmund Mulso and William Oldhall. By 1449 Mulso had acquired a tenement in Thaxted for life, and he rented land in Rochford together with a tenement, 'Skertes', in Gussage Bohun. It had also been intended to

---

[83] *CPR* 1461–7, p. 44.   [84] *CCR* 1476–85, nn. 255, 284.

[85] York was in London on 16 Sept., arriving at Bewdley on or before 1 Oct. and staying there until 12 Nov. (WAM 12165; *CPR* 1452–61, p. 588; *CPR* 1461–7, p. 44).

[86] BL Egerton Roll 8783. This grant may also have had political motives. By 1451 Ormond had been excused the rent (SC6/1113/1).

[87] SC6/1113/11.   [88] SC6/1113/9.

[89] SC6/850/26; Carus Wilson, 'Evidences of Industrial Growth', p. 197.

[90] SC6/1113/9; SC6/1115/1.   [91] *CPR* 1452–61, p. 588.

[92] WAM 12167.   [93] WAM 12166.

settle Finmere and Barton on him, but these were amongst the properties alienated in 1449, and so in 1450 he was granted Erbury and Clarethall.[94] Oldhall did rather better. Already, in 1441, he had been given a life grant of four manors.[95] By 1448 he enjoyed a one-fifth share in the returns of five Gloucestershire manors,[96] had the farm of Erbury,[97] which he was shortly to lose to Mulso, and was in the process of acquiring Hunsdon, a manor which York had begun to improve in 1446.[98] Oldhall was to spend considerable sums on this manor, but it does not appear to have been anything other than a gift for life.[99] York also appears to have spent appreciable sums restoring the lodges at Thaxted, Miserden, and Stratfield Mortimer.[100]

With estate reorganization in hand, York had returned to London by 30 November 1446, where he attended a council-meeting on 7 December, and similar meetings at Sheen, on the ninth and the fourteenth.[101] This last meeting agreed to the summons of Parliament to Cambridge, a venue subsequently changed to Winchester,[102] then, on 10 February, to Bury St Edmunds. York was summoned,[103] but, uneasy perhaps at what was afoot, stayed at Fotheringhay until 26 January at least.[104] On 18 February, the duke of Gloucester arrived at Bury, was arrested, and five days later was dead.[105] York is not recorded as present at these events, and his presence at Bury cannot be proved before 26 February.[106]

---

[94] WAM 12165–7; SC6/1113/14.   [95] *CPR 1436–41*, p. 531.

[96] SC6/850/27. These included the Cotswold wool manor of Bisley. Possibly Oldhall was hoping to emulate the business success of Sir John Fastolf at Castle Combe.

[97] SC6/850/28.

[98] C81/1445/13, 14; *CPR 1441–6*, p. 402; *CPR 1446–52*, p. 77. York was at Hunsdon on 28 July 1446 (Griffiths, *Reign of Henry VI*, p. 541, n. 132).

[99] *CCR 1468–76*, n. 705.

[100] SC6/850/26; SC6/1115/1; WAM 12165.

[101] Stow, *Annales*, p. 385; BL Add. Ch. 30050; C81/1546/17, 18. But cf. R. Virgoe, 'The Composition of the King's Council 1437–61', *BIHR* 43 (1970), 144, where it is incorrectly stated that York attended only one council meeting in the period 1445–9. The Sheen meeting was concerned with the problems facing the exchequer through overassignments against the customs, in which York had a considerable interest (Harriss, 'Marmaduke Lumley', pp. 151–2). He sent the queen a New-Year gift, his servant receiving the largest reward (A. R. Myers, 'The Jewels of Queen Margaret of Anjou' *BJRL* 42, (1959–60), 124).

[102] C81/1370/41; E101/409/16 fo. 10.

[103] *Report on the Dignity of a Peer*, ii. 912.

[104] BL Add. Ch. 8031; sign manual letter to John Profoot dated 26 Jan. 1447 (i.e without the regnal year). He had been there since at least 6 Jan. (Griffiths, *Reign of Henry VI*, p. 541 n. 132).

[105] Davies, *English Chronicle*, p. 116.   [106] SC6/1113/9.

His attitude to Gloucester's death is uncertain. A petition was submitted to the king on 25 February, and enrolled the following day, licensing York to give twenty acres of land to the Friars Minor at Babwell.[107] It may just be coincidence that Gloucester's body lay that day at Babwell.[108] York, however, had already been granted the reversion of the manor of Hadleigh at Gloucester's death, on 18 October 1446,[109] but it seems reasonable to suppose that then York was anticipating Duke Humphrey's death from natural causes in the due fullness of time. None of the reversions which cluster so thickly, and so suspiciously, in the patent rolls in late January and early February were in his favour, which seems to exonerate him of complicity in subsequent events. Indeed, in 1460 he was to claim that those who had murdered Gloucester proposed to murder him,[110] a claim he could scarcely have advanced had he been a party to the deed. At the time he, and especially his councillors, must have been dismayed by the circumstances surrounding the death of the man who had so epitomized their cause. Such considerations did not, however, restrain York from a determination to share the spoils. The lordship of the Isle of Wight, lost at Duke Edward's death, was now recovered,[111] as was the manor and advowson of Great Wratting (Suffolk), on petition.[112] Hadleigh was confirmed to the duke, despite a request from Queen Margaret,[113] and Baynards Inn was restored to him, again on petition.[114] It seems that York even had hopes of regaining Barton Bristol, but these must have fallen through, as on 28 October 1447 he was granted its original cash equivalent of £83. 6s. 8d.[115] On 14 July he was confirmed in the

---

[107] C81/1443/18; *CPR* 1446–52, p. 17.

[108] Davies, *English Chronicle*, p. 117.

[109] *CPR* 1446–52, p. 79.

[110] Davies, *English Chronicle*, p. 88.

[111] Wolffe, *Royal Demesne*, pp. 258–9.

[112] C81/1443/15: 'the whiche manoir advowson of the chirch with the appertaunences been of the old enheritance of the saide Duk of York' (cf. *CPR* 1446–52, p. 43). The manor had escheated to the Crown on the attainder of Edmund Mortimer in 1403 (*CPR* 1401–5, p. 256). That the Chancery should accept a petition with wording so prejudicial to the Crown is puzzling. In July 1446 York was also seeking recovery of the Mortimer estates of Cleeton and Farlow (E199/18/37).

[113] C81/1443/12, 13.

[114] C81/1443/17 (petition dated 25 Feb.). For a grant of Baynards Inn to Eton College on 23 Feb. see *Rot. Parl.* v. 132. York was certainly in possession of the premises in 1448, when a thief broke in and stole harness belonging to him (KB9/260 m. 55).

[115] *CPR* 1446–52, p. 117; *Report on the Dignity of a Peer*, v. 260.

offices of Steward, Justice, and Master of the king's forests south of the Trent.[116]

By then, Gloucester's stall in the Garter chapel had been filled, everyone at the election, including York, nominating the king of Portugal.[117] After this election, he remained in the London area until late July, and then retired to his Welsh estates, probably in time for the harvest.[118]

There can be little doubt that he did so disappointed. Since his departure from France, the government of Normandy had continued in his name, and Henry's failure to cross the Channel in autumn 1446 must have revived his hopes of reappointment, but, at a council-meeting on 24 December 1446, a meeting he did not attend,[119] the earl of Dorset was appointed to the lieutenancy for three years.[120] Recent Beaufort enterprises in Normandy could scarcely generate confidence in the new appointment amongst York's councillors, for the most part Norman veterans, and they might reasonably assume that Dorset had been appointed to further a peace policy, aspects of which did not command their respect, nor that of their military colleagues in Normandy. In France, York's council continued to govern in his name, at least until 23 April, probably in defiance of Dorset's commissioners,[121] but at home their lord seems to have accepted the decision, albeit reluctantly.

On 30 July 1447 York, at his own request, was made guardian of his son-in-law, the young Henry Holland, soon to be duke of Exeter.[122] For some time Henry VI, following government practice since the days of Edward III, had been encouraging the consolidation and social elevation of the families of the blood. When, in 1445, York

---

[116] *CPR* 1446–52, p. 66.

[117] Anstis, *Order of the Garter*, ii. 132. He also nominated the duke of Norfolk, the earl of Oxford, Viscount Bourchier, Lords Audley and Carew, Oldhall, Ogard, and Sir William Bonville.

[118] He was at London on 24 May (SC6/1113/9) and 27 May (BL Egerton Roll 8783, at a council meeting on 17 June (C81/1546/19), and in London on 20 July (WAM 12167). He was at Montgomery Castle on 31 Aug. (*CPR* 1495–1502, p. 523).

[119] He was in Westminster on 30 Nov., and at council meetings on 14 Dec. (Stow, *Annales*, p. 385; E28/77/14; C81/1546/18).

[120] E404/63/11. The appointment was effective from 1 Mar. 1447. Dorset was the only man who could, and would, steer through the surrender of Maine (Wolffe, *Henry VI*, p. 195).

[121] BL Add Ch. 12328; Basin, *Histoire*, ed. Samaran, bk. iv. ch. xi. Isabelle of Burgundy continued to sustain contact with York throughout the winter of 1447 (Thielemans, *Bourgogne et l'Angleterre*, pp. 152–3).

[122] *CPR* 1446–52, p. 86.

had sought a French wife for his eldest son, the royal council had played its part, only for the idea to flounder once it was obvious in Paris that York would not be returning to France for some time, if at all. In August 1445, when York had agreed with John Holland, duke of Exeter that his daughter Ann (b. 1439) should marry the young Henry Holland,[123] the king had put up no objections to the match, and now, with Duke John dying, King Henry was content to see Duke Richard as the guardian of the young couple. Duke Richard's motives behind this match in 1445 had been partly the desire to win over an important political ally in his efforts to procure reappointment in France, and partly dynastic, John Holland being Henry VI's closest legitimate male relative after the childless duke of Gloucester. He had thought this well worth a dowry of 4,500 marks, and had already paid off 1,500 marks, despite other pressing claims.[124]

A second royal patent, also dated 30 July, was altogether more contentious. By it, Richard duke of York was created lieutenant of Ireland.[125] Seemingly, there was much to commend the appointment. There had been trouble in Ireland throughout the 1440s, principally between the families of Talbot and Ormond, and, although the principals were at least partially reconciled by 1444,[126] the feud was continued by lesser figures until the death of Richard Talbot, archbishop of Dublin, in 1449.[127] Pleas for help from the archbishop of Cashel and the bishop of Kilkenny, in January 1447,[128] reinforced the more biased complaints of the Irish

---

[123] DL41/2/8.
[124] *Testamenta Vetusta*, ed. N. H. Nicolas, 2 vols. (1826), i. 283. John Holland's wife was a bastard daughter of the king of Portugal. There was also a Castilian interest, of importance both in Paris and for the duke of Exeter as lieutenant of Gascony (A. Goodman and D. Morgan, 'The Yorkist Claim to the Throne of Castile', *Journal of Medieval History*, 11 (1985), 61–71. The evidence of York's interest in a possible Castilian claim is here misdated to 1444.) For an interpretation of this wedding contract which strongly emphasizes the English dynastic implications see R. A. Griffiths, 'The Sense of Dynasy in the Reign of Henry VI', in Ross (ed.), *Patronage, Pedigree, and Power*, pp. 23–5. Pugh, 'Richard Plantagenet as King's Lieutenant', p. 123, believes the Castilian dimension to have been of concern not for this marriage but for the marriage negotiations with Charles VII.
[125] E101/71/4/920, 921; E28/79/61.
[126] H. G. Richardson and G. O. Sayles, *The Irish Parliament in the Middle Ages* (Phila. 1952), 502.
[127] M. C. Griffith, 'The Talbot–Ormond Struggle for the Control of Anglo–Irish Government, 1441–7' *Irish Historical Studies*, 2 (1941), 389.
[128] E101/248/15/1, 2.

treasurer, Giles Thornton.[129] York, who retained both John Talbot and James Ormond at this time, was an obvious, possibly the only, choice.[130]

There were some advantages in the appointment for Duke Richard, but more for the king and the duke of Suffolk. The appointment offered York an opportunity to consolidate his Irish estates, and perhaps recover those lands lost to the Gaelic Irish, at a cost to be born at least in part by the English exchequer. This was not, however, much of an inducement. His Irish estates were separately administered through an Irish council based at Trim, where complete audit and chancery departments were maintained,[131] but, despite the elaborate administrative structure, it is difficult to believe that York derived much income from these lands. Estimates in the order of £1,000 per annum seem much too high,[132] although they must have yielded something.[133] In July 1446, when York was seeking to expand his landed revenues, he was also attempting for the first time to defend his interests in Ireland.[134]

His terms of appointment were not unreasonable. He was to hold office from 29 September 1447[135] for ten years, with a salary of 4,000 marks for the first year and thereafter £2,000 per annum.[136] In addition, all surplus revenues of the Irish exchequer were to be his,[137] all Irish offices were in his gift, providing such appointments

[129] *PPC* v. 327; Griffiths, *Reign of Henry VI*, pp. 415–8.
[130] See also J. F. Lydon, *The Lordship of Ireland in the Middle Ages* (Dublin, 1972), 266–7.
[131] Berry, *Statutes of Ireland*, pp. 796–9.
[132] Rosenthal, 'Estates and Finances' p. 201.
[133] Ratouth in 1479 was estimated to be worth £18 p.a. (*CPR* 1476–85, p. 152).
[134] E28/76/26.
[135] On the strength of a patent of 9 Dec. 1447, his term of office is customarily, and probably correctly, believed to have started then (F. M. Powicke and E. B. Fryde (eds.), *Handbook of British Chronology*, Royal Historical Society (1961), 154, and A. J. Otway-Ruthven, *A History of Medieval Ireland* (1968), 378). The Michaelmas date was probably intended for exchequer convenience.
[136] The salary for the subsequent years is variously reported as 2,000 marks (*PPC* vi. 89; E28/71/6) or as £2,000 (E404/65/59, 104; *PPC* vi. 92). As Shrewsbury had indented for £2,000 (E404/61/138), it is unlikely that York would have accepted less.
[137] No accounts for the Irish exchequer for this period have survived, but accounts for 18–20 Henry VI and for 22–24 Henry VI show, in both instances, that fees were paid to the lieutenant. However, as only the total of all fees paid is recorded, this information is of little value. For the earlier period the fees totalled £1,882. 14s. 4d., for the later £1,169. 11s. 2d. (E101/248/13; E101/540/18). Taxation would probably have added no more than about 1,000 marks p.a. to this (*Calendar of the Carew Manuscripts Preserved in the Archiepiscopal Library at Lambeth: Book of Howth*, ed J. S. Brewer and W. Bullen 6 vols. (1867–73), v. 377–9). Squabbles over customs

passed under the great seal of England, and the costs of his shipping were to be borne by the English exchequer.

Contemporary opinion saw his appointment differently. He was 'exsylde into Irlonde for hys rebellyon as thoo a boute the kynge informyde hym',[138] 'banished for certain years';[139] 'exciled from our soveraigne lordes presens'.[140] They were almost certainly correct. Three days previously, York had taken part in discussions over the surrender of Maine.[141] No record of his contribution to the debate survives, but all his subsequent actions point to his outright hostility to the king's policy and to the financial settlement made on the Beauforts.[142] The furore surrounding Gloucester's recent death was such that direct action against Duke Richard was out of the question even if the king was contemplating it. In royal eyes, the Irish lieutenancy had much, therefore, to commend it.

The point has been made that York, in his terms of appointment, was empowered to nominate a deputy, a power apparently at odds with any intention of banishment.[143] Furthermore, York exercised this power, appointing Richard Nugent, Baron Devlin,[144] but, as has been pointed out,[145] this was solely for the purpose of holding a Parliament, and Devlin appears to have been anxious to keep Westminster informed of his actions.[146]

---

officers at Dublin and Drogheda in 1448–9 may relate to this, as York was specifically forbidden to intervene (*CPR* 1441–6, p. 419; *CPR* 1446–52, pp. 147, 168).

[138] *Gregory's Chronicle*, p. 189.

[139] Ibid. p. 195; cf. *Benet's Chronicle*, p. 195.

[140] *English Historical Literature*, p. 360. 'The Fawkoun fleyth, and hath no rest, / Tille he witte where to bigge his nest' (T. Wright, *A Collection of Political Poems and Songs Relating to English History*, 2 vols. Rolls Series (1859–61), ii. 223). Wolffe, *Henry VI*, p. 220, follows these contemporary opinions.

[141] Jones, 'The Beaufort Family' p. 199.

[142] York was present in council on 13 Nov. 1447 when the settlement was made (loc. cit.).

[143] E. Matthew, 'The Financing of the Lordship of Ireland under Henry V and Henry VI', in A. J. Pollard (ed.), *Property and Politics: Essays in Later Medieval English History* (Gloucester, 1984), 104. In 1414, John Lord Talbot had been appointed lieutenant of Ireland. He, too, was empowered to appoint a deputy, but his service in person was clearly required (*CPR* 1413–16, p. 164, and E. Powell, 'The Restoration of Law and Order', in G. L. Harriss (ed.), *Henry V*, (Oxford 1985), 71; Pollard, *Talbot*, p. 10).

[144] Berry, *Statutes of Ireland*, p. 110.

[145] E. Curtis, 'Richard Duke of York as Viceroy of Ireland, 1447–60', *Journal of the Royal Society of Antiquaries of Ireland*, 62 (1932), 164.

[146] Berry, *Statutes of Ireland*, p. 130. York may originally have intended to be present at this Parliament, as the first arrangements for shipping were made on 11 Dec. 1448.

In July 1447 it had been sufficient that it be known that in due course Duke Richard would be going to Ireland, and that his ten-year term of office would effectively exclude him from consideration for office in France when Somerset's three year term expired. Other critics of the king's policy would no doubt appreciate the isolation, political and (potentially) actual, of their leading spokesman, and so stay silent.[147] There was no immediate urgency to be rid of York, and he might reasonably argue that he could not seriously be expected to depart before the spring of 1448.

As it so happened, his short-term presence in England might be advantageous, as he was engaged, at the time of his appointment to Ireland, as the king's commissioner, to seize, by force if need be, the castle of Abergavenny from the claimant, his young brother-in-law, Edward Neville, and hold it on behalf of the Crown until the problem of tenure could be settled.[148]

By the spring if 1448 York was no nearer departure. He had been in London in November 1447, and had attended a Garter Chapter.[149] On 13 January 1448 he was at Fotheringhay.[150] Not until October, when he was again in London,[151] can his movements be identified. Over the summer months circumstances arose, such that in October he made public his intention to sail to Ireland.[152]

Two minor matters may have done something to persuade Henry to push his reluctant lieutenant. In May 1448 there had been violent disorders in central Wales, York's men from Maelienydd and Powys attacking the lands and livestock of Buckingham's men in Cantref Selyf. Instructed by the royal council to restrain his men, he does not appear to have been especially prompt to respond, as he had, subsequently, to be ordered to report on his actions to the council. He may well have ignored this instruction. Certainly, by December 1448 his men in Maelienydd, Cydewain, and Ceri were once more engaged in widespread disorder, and rustling in Carmarthen and Powys.[153] However, in fairness to the duke, it must be pointed out that the Welsh were notoriously difficult to control, and his failure to

---

[147] Despite his obvious experience, York was excluded from all negotiations with the French in the period 1446–9.

[148] *Excerpta Historica*, ed. S. Bentley (1831), 7.

[149] *Reg. Whethamstede*, i. 45; SC6/1113/9; Anstis, *Order of the Garter*, ii. 133.

[150] SC6/850/27.

[151] BL Cotton Ch. V n. 23. He attended council meetings on 12 and 18 Nov. (E28/79/9, 14).

[152] *CPR* 1446–52, p. 227.   [153] E28/77/45, 47, 48; E28/78/33.

intervene effectively may have had more to do with the limitations of his authority in Wales than with deliberate obstruction of the king's wishes.

More obviously political was his involvement in a dispute in East Anglia. This concerned a property known as 'Clements' in the village of Hawkswell near Rochford (Essex). On 25 April 1448 John Bayhous and others forcibly dispossessed John and Agnes Ingowe, and then enfeoffed the manor jointly on the dukes of York and Somerset.[154] The operation evidently failed, for the Ingowes were once again in possession when, on 10 July, a party led by Alice Arnold of Moulton (Lincs.), of different composition from that of Bayhous, again forcibly dispossessed the Ingowes, and again enfeoffed York and Somerset.[155] The Ingowes responded by enfeoffing the manor on the duke of Suffolk and his council. Somerset was in France, but York took up the challenge, and on 3 August 1448 a large force, headed by an usher of his chamber, Roger Ree, and composed of his Essex tenants, principally from Rayleigh, once more dispossessed the Ingowes.[156] The outcome of all this is unknown. York, despite the queen's support,[157] probably lost, but his hostility to Suffolk had been clearly signalled.

These, however, were modest considerations. The surrender of Maine had finally, if scrappily, been effected on 15 March, to much criticism. Partly in an attempt to retrieve its credibility, partly to secure the Norman border with Brittany, the council now pushed along a scheme which was intended to pressurize the duke of Brittany into reverting to the Anglo-Breton alliance of his father's days. The intention was to seize the Breton border town of Fougères. Just how many were privy to this plan is unclear. Talbot knew of it, but was probably discreet. Fastolf knew at least some of it, and may have revealed something to his old colleagues in arms, who also happened to be fellow ducal councillors.[158]

Initially, they may well have thought the scheme promising, but the aim of the operation shifted. Originally intended to persuade

---

[154] 'pro maintenencia habendi' (KB9/259/48).

[155] KB9/260/91.　　　　　　　　　　[156] KB9/260/88.

[157] *Letters of Queen Margaret of Anjou*, ed. C. Munro, Camden Society, os 86 (1863), 145.

[158] Stevenson, *Letters and Papers*, i. 283. Somerset was at pains to preserve secrecy (p. 285). On 14 Jan. 1449 Somerset sent a pursuivant from Rouen to Dieppe to meet the men of the duke of York waiting to carry news to the duke (Jones, 'The Beaufort Family', p. 198, citing BL Add MS. 11509 fo. 130).

Duke Francis to release his anglophile brother Gilles, it was redirected, during August, towards persuading Charles VII that Duke Francis was not his vassal, but a vassal of Henry VI. This made the surrender of Maine an absurdity. In March 1448 the purpose of English diplomacy was to secure lasting peace. By the summer, it was to coerce Charles VII into abandoning sovereignty over the duchy of Brittany. Anyone versed in French affairs could see the manifest inconsistency of such a policy. It is not surprising that Henry wanted York out of the way.

On 11 December 1448 warrants were issued for the arrest of shipping, the recipient, Henry Wyhom, acting on them on 9 February.[159] On 12 March, York appointed Thomas Young and John Wigmore as his attorneys.[160] Clearly, it was hoped to have York in Dublin before the next session of Parliament. He had, as was correct, been summoned on 2 January to the first session, but there is no evidence to suggest that he attended.[161]

Initially, it was the shipping arrangements which forced a delay, and the council was obliged to issue a new commission, on 16 April, to have ships arrested for his passage with all speed.[162] By this time, the capture of Fougères was public knowledge, and, seemingly, a very effective enterprise, which for a time silenced the administration's critics. If York could now be pushed out of England, a renewal of Somerset's term of office, to be determined by the end of the year, would be that much easier. Despite the pressure, he lingered, but towards the end of May, at the latest, he had left Fotheringhay and, journeying through his lordship of Denbigh, was at Beaumaris by 22 June.[163]

The duke sailed from Beaumaris in a modest fleet accompanied by the Duchess Cecily, an indication that he expected to stay for some

---

[159] E404/65/86; E404/66/116. On 7 Nov., at a time of acute shortage of ready cash, he was paid 2,000 marks in cash, as salary as lieutenant. A writ of 30 July 1447 ordering payment had been disregarded (E404/65/59; E404/63/160).

[160] *CPR* 1446–52, p. 23.

[161] *Report on the Dignity of a Peer*, ii. 918. He was at Fotheringhay on 20 Jan., 17 Feb., and 5 March (BL Egerton Roll 8783; SC6/1115/1; WAM 12166). He was absent from the St George's Day chapter of the Garter in 1448, and again in 1449 (Anstis, *Order of the Garter*, ii. 135–7). For the very restricted representation of York's servants in this Parliament see Griffiths, *Reign of Henry VI*, p. 676.

[162] *CPR* 1446–52, p. 238. On 3 Apr., the exchequer was ordered to stop immediately all processes against him, as he was going to Ireland (E159/225 *Brevia Directa* Easter Term m. 5ᵛ).

[163] He was at Denbigh on 6 and 15 June (Birmingham Public Library Hagley Hall MSS 25/351404; SC6/1115/6) and at Beaumaris by 22 June (loc. cit.).

time.[164] Although Irish sources speak of him as coming to Ireland 'with great glory and pompe',[165] it is unlikely that he had with him above 600 men.[166] Once in Ireland, his first concern was to establish his military authority, which he achieved, with a promptness which should have cautioned him, in the submission of Eoghan O'Neill. This he paraded to the English council as a great triumph, though, in fact, it was nothing of the sort.[167] The first report to the king's council, compiled after 15 August 1449, stated that York had received the submissions of MacMahon, MacOrbin, and both the O'Reillys.[168] Together, these four leaders of septs in theory brought in 3,000 men, and some may have been forthcoming when York led an army for the restoration of order into Kilkenny and Tipperary. The success of this campaign was announced in a second letter to England,[169] and the submission of O'Brien was reported along with that of forty-two Irish leaders, an impressive list as, indeed, it was intended to be. The winter months York intended to spend preparing for a major campaign against the Gaelic Irish in the following spring, and to this end he adopted a studied neutrality in his relations with the Anglo-Irish. The earl of Desmond had been one of the forty-two who had submitted to York. No further action was taken against him. Instead, he and the earl of Ormond were co-sponsors at the baptism of George, the future duke of Clarence.[170] The death of archbishop Talbot greatly eased this process, and York lost no time in procuring the election of Michael Tregurry, a distinguished scholar who had spent much time in Normandy, and who had been, in recent years, like the other former Norman councillors, Scales and Ogard, closely connected with Margaret of

---

[164] E364/90. He was in Ireland by 24 July (*Registrum Iohannis Mey*, ed. W. G. H. Quigley and E. F. D. Roberts (Belfast, 1972), 176–8.

[165] *Annals of the Four Masters*, ed. J. O'Donovan, 6 vols. (Dublin, 1851), iv. 964 n. s.

[166] There were only two large ships, the *Edward* and the *Julian* of Fowey. A barge, called the *Mary* of Dublin, had a complement of twenty, the remaining sixteen ships carrying only a handful of sailors each, together with non-combatants, household staff, and horses.

[167] E. Curtis, 'The Bonnaght of Ulster', *Hermathena*, 46 (1931), 87–91. cf. Curtis, 'Duke of York as Viceroy', p. 170; A. Cosgrove, *Late Medieval Ireland, 1370–1541*, (Dublin, 1981), 48; K. Simms, 'The King's Friend: O'Neill', in J. Lydon (ed.), *England and Ireland in the Later Middle Ages* (Dublin, 1981).

[168] J. T. Gilbert, *Facsimiles of the National Manuscripts of Ireland* (Southampton, 1874), iii. pl. xl.

[169] Loc. cit.

[170] Curtis, 'Duke of York as Viceroy', p. 172.

Anjou.[171] York also procured the bishopric of Meath for William Oldhall's brother,[172] and may have exercised some control over the timing of the consecration of Geoffrey Hereford OP as bishop of Kildare.[173]

York had potentially achieved a great deal in his first few months, especially against the two O'Reilly groups who had hitherto been fighting for control of their sept, one supported by O'Neill, the other by Ormond.[174] Of the forty-two who submitted to York, fifteen belonged to the septs of O'Neill, MacMahon, Magennis, and O'Hanlan, some members of which were operating in a loose political alliance under O'Neill leadership;[175] and the MacMurroughs, also mentioned by York, were relatives of the O'Neills. He needed now to consolidate this, and to find a reliable way of binding the slippery O'Neills, although it is very doubtful whether he fully grasped the subtle interplay of sept politics with the aspirations of the Anglo-Irish and of archbishop Mey.

On 17 October 1449 a great council assembled.[176] York was probably satisfied that it had assembled at his behest, and such business as was transacted was of a relatively trivial nature, the most important item being the preliminaries to the political rehabilitation of the earl of Ormond.[177] This process was completed at the second, and more significant, assembly, summoned by York for 28 February 1450.[178] This Parliament granted York permission to levy royal

---

[171] License to elect was granted by York seven days after Talbot's death (*Report of the Deputy Keeper of the Public Records of Ireland: Appendix viii: Calendar of Christ Church Deeds*, p. 90. Tregurry was subsequently a councillor in Ireland. (Rymer, *Foedera*, xi. 325).

[172] *Registrum I. Mey*, ed. Quigley and Roberts, pp. 287–8; *Calendar of Papal Registers x. 1447–55*, p. 72. For the background to Oldhall's provision see J. A. Watt, · 'The Papacy and Ireland in the Fifteenth Century', in R. B. Dobson (ed.), *The Church, Politics, and Patronage in the Fifteenth Century* (Gloucester, 1984). For attempts to control provisions to Irish benefices under York's administration see R. D. Edwards, 'The Kings of England and Papal Provisions to Irish Bishoprics, 1449–54', in J. A. Watts, J. B. Morrall, F. X. Martin (eds.), *Medieval Studies Presented to Aubrey Gwynn* (Dublin, 1961), 274–5.

[173] The new bishop was suffragan to Richard Beauchamp, bishop of Salisbury, with whom York enjoyed good relations.

[174] *Annals of the Four Masters*, ed. O'Donovan, iv. 963.

[175] Berry, *Statutes of Ireland*, i. 206–7.

[176] *Statutes at Large Passed in the Parliaments Held in Ireland* (Dublin, 1786), 10.

[177] Berry, *Statutes of Ireland*, p. 240–2. Simms, 'The King's Friend', pp. 221–2, points to the adoption by York of much that had been Ormond policy.

[178] Ibid. 175–9.

service as an alternative to a subsidy, for although the latter could be expected to yield about 700 marks per annum,[179] it was apt to be slow in payment, and York needed the money for troops for the forthcoming campaigning season.

Some time in the spring of 1450 York wrote to England in search of the monies due him, *inter alia*, as lieutenant. Evidently, he sent a fairly detailed statement, as on 17 May Henry told the English exchequer to pay him the 4,700 marks still due to him.[180] The exchequer, hard pressed for funds, was in no hurry to comply, and by 12 June York was writing in exasperation to his brother-in-law, the earl of Salisbury, to say that he was faced with a considerable military problem in Meath, that without funds the English would lose, and that he, York, would return to England rather than have it said that he had lost the province.[181] Alarmed by the tone of his lieutenant's letter, Henry sent Lancaster, king-at-arms,[182] but no money. York determined to return home.

This could not, however, be done immediately. His agreement with the O'Neills had brought no advantage, and O'Neill still occupied the vital area of the Fews between Ulster and the Pale.[183] In Meath, York was on the defensive against the Mageoghegans. Originally, he had intended to drive this family from Meath, and had made elaborate arrangements in the Drogheda Parliament to do so, but York had to be satisfied with a return to the status quo ante at Mullingar in June.[184] Departure also meant the appointment of a deputy, a delicate matter given the rivalry of Ormond and Desmond, and suitable shipping had to be commandeered, all of which took

---

[179] Richardson and Sayles, *The Irish Parliament*, p. 237.

[180] *PPC* vi. p. 92–3. There had been a variety of earlier warrants, on 30 July 1447, 7 Nov. 1448, 10 Feb. 1449, and 4 Dec. 1449 (E404/63/160; E404/65/59, 104; Stevenson, *Letters and Papers*, i. 487; E28/79/61). The second and the fourth achieved something, to wit 2,000 marks and £1,200 respectively (E403/774; E403/777). York's claim for a further 4,700 marks was therefore correct.

[181] *Calendar of Carew MSS: Book of Howth*, ed. Brewer and Bullen, p. 477.

[182] E404/66/184.

[183] Curtis, 'Duke of York as Viceroy', p. 170; 'Bonnaght of Ulster', pp. 89–100. York spent early August at Dundalk, presumably in consultation with the archbishop of Armagh (*Rotulorum Patentium et Clausorum Hiberniae Calendarium*, ed. E. Tresham, Irish Record Commission, (Dublin, 1828), 265). Immediately after York's departure, the Lord Deputy returned to Drogheda (R. Lascelles, *Liber Munerum Publicorum Hibernia*, 2 vols. in 3 (1824), i/2, 205).

[184] *Annals of the Four Masters*, ed. O'Donovan, iv. 967. n. 1. Lander, *Conflict and Stability*, p. 74, exaggerates, when he claims that York's administration was 'dangerously near to collapse'.

time. Not until late August was he able to set sail. He left Trim on 26 August,[185] was in Dublin on the twenty-eighth,[186] and set sail then or very soon after.

NOTE A

The duke of York presented his articles in the form of a bill against the bishop of Chichester on a Tuesday, Moleyns replying in person before the privy council in the presence of the archbishop of Canterbury. Which Tuesday is impossible to say. Although Pugh ('Richard Plantagenet as King's Lieutenant', p. 124) dates them to autumn 1445, they are certainly to be dated after 8 Dec. 1445, when the treasurer of Normandy returned to Rouen ('one of yeier thesurars of normandye was here'), and the phrase in York's submission, 'it lyked your highnese by aucthorytye of the same parliament', implies that Parliament is ended ('this same parliament', or similar, would have been adopted had Parliament been in session), and the articles, therefore, belong to a period after 9 April 1446. A minor consideration is that York was at Shrewsbury some time after the end of Parliament and before 11 May (Salop CRO Box viii. n. 377 m. 5d). The reference to Moleyns's last expedition to Normandy is to his embassy there in August–September 1445. As he was due to go again to Normandy shortly after 20 July 1446, it is very likely that the articles are to be dated between 9 April and 20 July 1446. Certainly, they cannot be later than Michaelmas 1446, as they refer to York's obligation to pay wages 'unto mihelmas last', which can only mean Michaelmas 1445 when his lieutenancy expired.

---

[185] *Rot. Pat. et Claus. Hib.*, p. 266.
[186] Ibid. 265. Medieval practice was against a deputy assuming responsibilities in the presence of his superior, so it is clear that York believed his departure imminent.

4

POPULARITY AND PROBLEMS

On 7 September Duke Richard arrived in Denbigh.[1] It had been a journey not without incident. Originally intending to land at Beaumaris, he had met with stiff resistance from local officials. They were acting not on their own intiative, as they made clear, but on orders which had their origins in the king's household, even from the king's chamber.[2] Against this opposition it is doubtful whether York managed a landing, and had he done so he would have had to negotiate Conway Castle, held against him by Bartholomew Bolde. More probably he sailed on thirty miles east to the Clwyd estuary where, as lord of Denbigh, he could feel more secure.

There can be no doubt that the local men were indeed acting under orders, and that similar orders had been sent to ports and towns across north Wales and the marches. Henry VI evidently had a deep-seated fear that Duke Richard intended to return to England and claim the throne. The reasons for this fear are not too hard to find.

When Adam Moleyns had been murdered in February 1450, an esquire, formerly in York's service in Normandy, Cuthbert Colville, had been party to the deed.[3] By March, the disturbances already present in the Home Counties[4] and East Anglia[5] had spread into London. A riot there, against Suffolk's release, was allegedly started by 'a poure olde man', a wine-drawer called Frammesly. Tried on 24 March, he duly suffered the penalties of treason, the council for some reason electing that his quarters should be sent to Winchester and Coventry, where there had been recent trouble, and to Stamford

---

[1] WAM 12166.

[2] R. A. Griffiths, 'Richard Duke of York and the Royal Household in Wales 1449–50', *Welsh History Review*, 8 (1976–7), 14–25, gives details of the events and of the officials responsible. Griffiths believes that York did effect a landing.

[3] KB9/109 m. 25; E101/53/33. Three weeks later Colville moved from Portsmouth towards Winchester, raising a revolt at South Waltham, and trouble continued for some weeks in Portsmouth itself (E28/80/15; C. L. Kingsford, 'An Historical Collection of the Fifteenth Century', *EHR* 29 (1914), 515).

[4] KB9/263/64; *Bale's Chronicle*, p. 128; E28/80/7, 16.

[5] Rymer, *Foedera*, xi. 262.

and Newbury.[6] There is no record of trouble in either town, but it cannot be a coincidence that both were towns of the duke of York.

While London rioted against Suffolk's release, a plot was being hatched in Suffolk by Thomas Johnson, yeoman of Driffield (Yorks., E. R.), and John Langley, of Barton on Humber (Lincs.). Assembling 10,000 men (or so it was alleged) at Ipswich on 3 March, they proclaimed that the earl of Douglas should lead an army of 40,000 men to overthrow the king and set up the duke of York, then in Ireland, and that the duke himself was likewise assembling a great force.[7] The plan now reads like the product of overheated imagination or too much ale, but the government could scarcely ignore such stories.

By April 1450 it began to look as though the government could not control its own capital, and Parliament was instructed to reassemble at Leicester at the end of the month. Again, rumours about York's intentions flared up. On the way to Leicester, Henry was waylaid at Stony Stratford by a shipman called Harries who claimed that 'the Duke of Yorke then in Ireland shuld in lyke manner fight with traytours at Leicester parliament and so thrashe them downe as he had thrashed the clods of erthe in that towne'.[8] For his impetuosity Harries paid the supreme penalty of the law.[9] Others were to tax the king in a similar way. The king himself later complained of 'oon Wastnesse which had suche wordes unto us'.[10]

Agitation continued throughout May and into June. No one supposed York to have had any hand in Suffolk's murder, but the immediate consequence of that event was a fear in Kent of severe punishment, fear which ignited a shire already resentful. By late June it was under the leadership of Jack Cade, who called himself Mortimer 'forto have the more favour of the people'.[11] Cade's

---

[6] Kingsford, 'An Historical Collection', p. 514; *CPR* 1446–52, 320; *PPC* vi. 107–9.

[7] KB9/265/21, 22. James I of Scotland had married Joan Beaufort, regent until her death (1445) for her son James II. In this she incurred the enmity of the earl of Douglas, who remained more or less constantly the focus thereafter for all discontent in Scotland (A. Dunlop, *The Life and Times of James Kennedy Bishop of St Andrews* (1950), 76 ff.).

[8] *English Historical Literature*, p. 371.

[9] *CPR* 1446–52, p. 383; E159/228 *Brevia Directa* Hilary Term m. 1ᵛ (writ of allowance to the sheriff for his execution).

[10] R. A. Griffiths, 'Duke Richard of York's Intentions in 1450 and the Origins of the Wars of the Roses', *Journal of Medieval History*, 1 (1975), 204. Wastness cannot be identified.

[11] Davies, *English Chronicle*, p. 64.

programme, which appealed to many soldiers, was explicitly in favour of York,[12] and included elements of propaganda sympathetic to him. So impressed was authority by Cade's Mortimer claim, that as late as October official records still referred to him as Mortimer, and only acknowledged the alias later in the year.[13] In fact, throughout the critical summer months the government thought of him as a claimant to the Mortimer political interest, and might well fear, as Stow was to allege a century later, that York, seeking the Crown, had stirred up the commons of Kent.[14].

While Cade marched the commons of Kent against the capital, provincial riots claimed the lives of William Aiscough, bishop of Salisbury,[15] and Robert Russell,[16] and there were determined assaults on the bishops of Coventry, Norwich, and Bath and Wells, and on the abbots of Gloucester and Hyde.[17] The king had good cause to suspect a broadly-based conspiracy against his councillors. Trouble continued despite Cade's death, and some of it again pointed, albeit haphazardly, to York.

His erstwhile manor of Hadleigh, lost in the recent act of resumption, remained lawless until early August.[18] His former tally-broker, Thomas Brown, was robbed on 9 July,[19] and in mid-August

[12] 'Item they enforme the kynge that the Comyns wolde ffurst destroye the Kynges ffreends and aftur hym selfe and thenne brynge in the duke of yorke to be Kynge, so that by there ffalse menes and lesynges they may make hym to hate and dystroye his verrey ffreendus and to cherysch his ffalse traytours that callen hem selfe his ffrendus' (Articles of the Commons of Kent: Oxford Magdalen College MS Misc. 306, printed in Hist. MSS. Comm. *Eighth Report*, App. 1 sect. 2, pp. 266–7; cf. *Fabyan's Chronicle*, p. 622).

[13] E403/783.   [14] Stow, *Annales*, p. 388.

[15] KB9/271/53; KB27/768 *Rex* m. 159ᵛ; see also J. N. Hare, 'The Wiltshire Risings of 1450: Political and Economic Discontent in Mid-Fifteenth-Century England', *Southern History*, 4 (1982), 13–31. Further assaults, on 28 Aug. at Erdington, were initiated by York's tenants from Allerholt and Gussage Bohun (KB9/264/60; KB27/768 *Rex* m. 103ᵛ; KB27/770 *Rex* mms. 136ᵛ, 147ᵛ, 160ʳ, and 176ʳ).

[16] KB9/109 m. 9. Russell was an intimate councillor of Adam Moleyns (KBB27/763 *Rex* m. 85ᵛ).

[17] Wright, *Political Poems*, ii. 225–9; Hist. Mss. Comm. *Report on the Manuscripts of the Dean and Chapter of Wells*, 2 vols. (1907–14), ii. 77; KB27/771 *Rex* m. 111ʳ. For the involvement of a Newbury butcher in the attack on the abbot of Hyde see KB27/771 *Rex* m. 108ᵛ. Gascoigne alleged that the Newbury conspirators widened their range of victims to include the clergy of Hampshire, and the rape of an 11-year-old girl. (T. Gascoigne *Loci et Libro Veritatum*, ed. J. E. T. Rogers (Oxford, 1881), 42 and 138–9.)

[18] Hadleigh had revolted the previous year at the election of the town's officers (SC6/1113/10), and it saw an attempt to raise support for Cade on 8 July. There were minor disturbances there as late as 6 Sept. (KB9/271/67; KB27/770 *Rex* m. 154ʳ).

[19] KB27/761 *Rex* m. 53ʳ.

a gentleman by the name of William Brenchenham was asserting that York intended to return from Ireland and claim the throne.[20] There was every reason why Henry should have feared York's return.

The duke had his reasons for alarm also, and he made them clear in two bills[21] submitted to the king, very probably in September. The first was a simple statement to the effect that while in Ireland 'I have bin informed that diverse language, hath bene sayde of me to your moste excellente estate whiche shoulde sounde to my dishonour and reproch, and charge of my person'.[22] The bill goes on briefly to declare his whole-hearted loyalty to Henry, and to invite him to summon his detractors so that the falseness of their accusations can be demonstrated. In tone, it is a cautious bill, convinced of an injustice, anxious that Henry should be in no doubt as to the author's loyalty. It is undated, but it might be suggested that such a document could well be the result of the meeting which York had with John Talbot, Viscount Lisle and Lord Wells in Shrewsbury on 12 September.[23]

The second bill is at once more aggressive and more explicit. It alleges that while in Ireland 'certayn commyssions ware made and directed unto divers persones which for the execucion of the same sette in certayn placis and the iniuries enpaneld and charged, the which jures certeyn persones laboured instantly forto have endited me of treson'.[24] It further complains of the hostile reception awaiting him at Beaumaris, and the military preparations set on foot with the alleged intention of imprisoning him in Conway, executing Sir William Oldhall, and imprisoning Mulso and Devereux.[25] It is a bill cast in very direct terms, suggesting a growing awareness of the political power with which popular sentiment was willing to entrust him. It is probably to be dated to the last fortnight in September.

[20] 'Ricardus dux Ebor' extra terram Hiberne (*sic*) infra quindenam tunc proxime sequente veniret in angliam et coronam dicti domini Regis de eodem Rege auferret et illud super caput eiusdem Ducis infra breve poni faciet' (KB9/85/1 m. 15).

[21] See note A p. 104.

[22] Griffiths, 'Duke Richard of York's Intentions', p. 203. The desire that he be declared true liegeman may support the contention that he had been banished to Ireland.

[23] Lisle 'mittitur ad impediendum', *Annales*, p. 769; £16 costs reimbursed to Lisle with a further £10 reward (E404/67/232, 28; cf. Minister's Accounts for the Borough of Shrewsbury, Salop CRO Box viii. no. 377 fo. 8ʳ).

[24] Griffiths, 'Duke Richard of York's Intentions', p. 203.

[25] Devereux was with him at Shrewsbury on 12 Sept. (Salop CRO Box viii. no. 377 fo. 8ʳ).

The claims about the circumstances of his landing and the general mobilization of north Wales can be shown to be well founded. His claims of legal processes against him, although lacking corroborative evidence, cannot, therefore, be dismissed out of hand. The king's reply to the bill denies that there were indictments, but is silent about the alleged commissions.[26] There were, in fact, several oyer-and-terminer commissions at work in the summer months, and the possibility cannot be excluded that some sort of allegations against York were put to a jury. In particular, York's reference to the intention of the king's officers summarily to execute Sir William Oldhall raises suspicions.

A set of indictments has survived, presented in the aftermath of the Dartford débâcle of 1452, in which Oldhall is indicted of a wide range of offences. One relates specifically to 1450, that on 6 March at Bury St Edmunds he, in the company of Sir William Ashton (who heads the indictment), John Framlingham esq., and others, plotted the death of the king, to which end various bills were composed claiming that the king by the counsel of the duke of Suffolk, the bishops of Salisbury and Chichester, Lord Say, and other lords about the king, had sold the kingdoms of England and France.[27] A further indictment, of Framlingham alone, adds that the king of France was to rule and, to prevent this, he wished that the duke of York should take the throne. Ashton was further charged with inciting the people of Bury, on 12 April, to support Cade.[28]

It is tempting to see in these indictments the vital explanatory link connecting York with Cade, but this is to ignore the context in which they were made. In February 1452 York accused Somerset of treason in his conduct of the war in France, implying that this was the reason for domestic disorder. Mindful of the course of Suffolk's trial (allegations about France followed by allegations about England), and conscious of the implication that at Dartford he had been in danger of being blamed for Cade's revolt, Somerset, after Dartford, turned the tables. He was not to blame for the rising of 1450. It was Oldhall and, by unspoken implication, York.[29]

---

[26] Griffiths, 'Duke Richard of York's Intentions', p. 204.

[27] Such accusations were independently in circulation in 1450 (*Six Town Chronicles*, p. 106; KB9/118/1 m. 30). There were tensions in Bury relating to the tenure of the former honour of the earldom of March (M. D. Lobel, *The Borough of Bury St Edmunds* (Oxford, 1935), 159–64).   [28] KB9/271/117.

[29] 'et consilium eidem duci [York] per alias litteras suas dederunt ad deponendum praefatum Regem Anglie de regno' (KB9/271/117).

All this is not to deny that Duke Richard was firmly of the opinion that attempts had been made to labour a jury 'forto have endited me of treson'. That such profound mutual mistrust should have developed between the king and the heir apparent in the summer months of 1450 was a grave disturbance to English political stability. York's initiative in Ireland had been ignored and ill-supported at home, and he returned convinced that a section, at least, of influential councillors sought his downfall. The political situation was further destabilized by independent factors; the loss of Normandy, the return of disgruntled soldiers, the break with the Hanse, and the swell of grievance of the shire communities. The final circumstance was of Henry's own making. The duke of Somerset was welcomed into the royal entourage on his return to England in early August, and the royal household, adrift and somewhat fragmented since the death of Suffolk, followed the royal lead, hesitantly at first, but by the end of the year with conviction.

The Beaufort–household alliance was an unfortunate, if understandable, development. Somerset was vulnerable to criticism over the loss of Normandy; the household were the recurrent targets of popular criticism. In turning to Somerset and to his own household the king was spurning the greatest magnate in the land, the heir apparent to the throne, a lord on whom the Anglo–Norman interest might well focus its loyalty, a peer of the blood in whom the domestic critics might put their trust. There had been other occasions when York seemed to Somerset a dangerous rival. Edmund Beaufort had his own, strong reasons for dissuading Henry from overmuch reliance on the Mortimer heir.

York set out for London in mid-September. By the time he arrived in the city he had some 3,000 men in his retinue.[30] He was joined by 'Western men' before he reached St Albans,[31] which suggests that he had made some effort to organize an adequate retinue, but otherwise the impression is that many joined him of their own accord. As he rode south, and the strength of popular hostility to the government became increasingly evident, so York's confidence grew. The abbot of Gloucester and Lord Dudley, terrified of popular vengeance, had already surrendered themselves

[30] *Bale's Chronicle*, p. 137, gives 3,000 men; *Annales*, p. 769, gives 4,000; *Benet's Chronicle*, p. 202, gives 5,000.
[31] Davis (ed.), *Paston Letters*, ii. p. 47.

into York's safe keeping at Ludlow.[32] He left them behind, lodged in the castle, and then moved east across the central midlands to Stony Stratford, and thence via St Albans to London.[33]

En route he made arrangements to meet the speaker of the 1449–50 Parliament, William Tresham.[34] This was not the summoning of a feudal retainer to swell the host. The reasons were more complex, and Tresham showed signs of unease about the proposed encounter. Preparing to ride in the early hours of the morning, he donned his collar of the king's livery, an honourable dignity, a public indication of loyalty, perhaps also a declaration to Duke Richard of royal protection, but he was to lose both livery and life before the encounter took place. York continued south.[35]

At St Albans he was joined by a Norman councillor, Sir Thomas Hoo, who had a ready welcome from his erstwhile colleagues in Rouen, but a violent one from the west country men.[36] Arriving in London, Duke Richard paraded his power through the city streets and on to the palace of Westminster where he humbly presented himself to his sovereign. The king, reportedly, received him graciously. York then took up lodgings in the bishop of Salisbury's house in the city.[37]

---

[32] *Benet's Chronicle*, p. 202. Dudley had marcher interests as keeper of Henry Gray's lands (*CFR* 1445–52, p. 149), which may account for his presence in the Ludlow area. *Benet's Chronicle* elsewhere (p. 199) records that he was captured in the west country in June 1450. Bouler's movements are uncertain as it was probably Beauchamp, elect of Salisbury, who, as bishop of Hereford, witnessed a warrant on 25 August (*PPC* vi. 101). Neither peer fully escaped York until the final days of the last session of the 1450–1 Parliament.

[33] For details see Griffiths, 'Richard Duke of York and the Royal Household in Wales', pp. 14–15.

[34] *Rot. Parl.* v. 211. J. S. Roskell, 'William Tresham of Sywell, Speaker for the Commons under Henry VI', *Northamptonshire Past and Present*, 2 (1954–9), 189–203, repr. in Roskell, *Parliament and Politics*, ii. 137–53.

[35] The journey across country has left no trace in surviving records, and must be presumed, Tresham's murder apart, to have been incident-free. The only recorded act of violence which might be related was an attack on a servant of Thomas Hopton esq. at Brome (Salop) on 11 Sept. (KB27/763 *Rex* m. 92ʳ). Thomas was the father of York's servant, Walter. The duke's arrival in London precipitated a riot at Newgate, where the warder, Gargrave, fled, subsequently to be arrested by York (*Bale's Chronicle*, p. 135; *English Historical Literature*, pp. 365, 297; Stow, *Annales*, p. 392.).

[36] Davis (ed.), *Paston Letters*, ii. 47.

[37] *Benet's Chronicle*, pp. 202–3. Richard Beauchamp did not receive his temporalities until 1 Oct., but the use of his house was probably by agreement rather than coercion, as York was to provide him with an escort to Parliament in November (Hampshire CRO MS 23M58/57b), and in 1453 duchy estate business was to be transacted in the house (BL Egerton Roll 8364).

Some time between 27 September and 6 October York put his
third bill up to the king. It was, in character, quite different to his
two previous bills. In those he had complained of personal affronts;
now he espoused the issues 'meche after the Comouns desyre'. Copies
of this bill were made freely available; indeed, by some contemporaries it was regarded almost as a manifesto, to be circulated as
widely as possible. Certainly it was drafted with an adroit eye to its
propaganda potential. York posed as the champion of 'reform'. To
add to Henry's unease, the tone of his proposals seemed to be almost
entirely derived from Cade and his Kentishmen, and, had Henry
allowed his request for full powers of execution, he would have given
York complete authority in the country, as William Wayte was quick
to grasp.[38]

Henry declined to do so. When he made his reply is uncertain,
but, given the circumstances, it is unlikely to have been long
delayed, and Henry himself expressed the hope of a decisive
settlement 'in schort tyme'. His formula for evading York's demands
was to put all to the chancellor and other lords of the council, with a
promise of a greater conciliar element in government decision-
making, a 'sad and so substancial counsaile', 'yow to be oon'.[39]

What York made of this promise is unknown. He left London on
9 October,[40] slightly later than was expected. His intention to go to
Walsingham was already well known, and he was expected there on
the eleventh. In all probability he rode thence to Norwich,[41] and so
to Bury St Edmunds, where he spent 15 and 16 October[42] in the
company of the duke of Norfolk. He was in Fotheringhay on
17 October, staying for at least four days. From Fotheringhay he
journeyed to Ludlow, arriving on 5 November, stayed eight days
and set off for Parliament.[43]

His reasons for travelling to Fotheringhay via Norwich can only
be tentatively established.[44] While in the Welsh march he was to

---

[38] Davis (ed.), *Paston Letters*, ii. 47–8. The text of the bill is given in Griffiths,
'Duke Richard of York's Intentions', p. 204.   [39] Loc. cit.
[40] *Benet's Chronicle*, p. 203.   [41] Davis (ed.), *Paston Letters*, ii. 53.
[42] Ibid. p. 54.   [43] Hampshire CRO MS 23M58/57b; cf. *Annales*, p. 769.
[44] His move into East Anglia was presaged by a new commission of the peace for
Norfolk and Suffolk (9 Oct.). Tuddenham, Daniel, and Heydon were dropped. York
continued as a JP in both shires. (*CPR* 1446–52, pp. 592, 595). There had been
considerable disorder in Sept., in Essex, in Suffolk, courtesy of the Framlingham
family, and in Norwich (KB27/759 *Rex* m. 96ʳ; 769 *Rex* m. 153ʳ; 770 *Rex* m. 161ʳ;
KB9/26/1 mm. 12, 15; KB9/118/1 m. 8; *CPR* 1446–52, p. 431; *English Historical
Literature*, p. 366).

recruit support for his return to London and Parliament. It may be reasonably supposed that he was similarly recruiting on his East Anglian estates. There was also the opportunity to weaken household influence in the area, a possibility which excited much optimistic comment and which York, to a modest extent, exploited. His main purpose, however, was to meet with the duke of Norfolk, and for York the outcome was entirely satisfactory. The two dukes— there were only four dukes of age at this time—agreed on nominees for the forthcoming shire elections, a public declaration of a ducal alliance in the Upper House.

Although his motives do not emerge until Parliament was in session, the royal household was, from the outset, afraid.[45] While York was in London the king dissembled a good countenance, but once York had left for East Anglia the king was summoning 'his men that be in the chekroll to awayte on hym atte parlement in their best aray'.[46] Meanwhile, Somerset rode into Kent to crush a further rising, returning by 27 October.[47] In London, the royal council cleared the way for a fresh expedition to Gascony,[48] and, as a gesture of good will, sent a schedule of resumed lands to the exchequer.[49]

The election of Nicholas Wyfold as Lord Mayor on 29 October was as welcome to the king as it was unwelcome to the soldiery, who sought to overturn the result by force.[50] The vigorous propaganda campaign waged throughout October[51] by supporters and critics of York came to a dangerous climax the following day; first the displays of the duke's arms being torn down, then the royal arms which replaced them being torn down in their turn. Only the continual policing of the streets by the mayor and an armed company prevented a further deterioration in order.[52]

---

[45] 'all the Kynges howsold was an is aferd ryght sore' (Davis (ed.), *Paston Letters*, ii. 47).

[46] Ibid. p. 50.

[47] Payment of £40 to Somerset for taking one John Smith, who called himself captain of Kent, and 20 marks per day, as he was going into Kent to restore order (*PPC* vi. 101; E404/67/38). This is a clear riposte to York's bill seeking appropriate powers. Somerset attended a council meeting on 27 Oct. (C81/1546/55).

[48] Vale, *English Gascony*, p. 136, states correctly that Rivers was formally appointed on 18 Oct., but the decision was taken on the fourteenth (C81/762/9277).

[49] B. P. Wolffe, 'Acts of Resumption in the Lancastrian Parliaments', *EHR* 73 (1958), 601.

[50] *Bale's Chronicle*, p. 136.

[51] *Gregory's Chronicle*, p. 195, reports that bills were posted everywhere 'sum at the Kyngis owne chambyr doore'.

[52] *Bale's Chronicle*, p. 136.

Parliament assembled on 6 November for the declared purpose of providing for the defence of the realm and of Gascony, the safeguarding of the seas, and the restoration of public order. Invited to present a speaker on the morrow, the Commons delayed over the weekend to Monday 9th, when they presented the duke of York's chamberlain, Sir William Oldhall.[53] In the mean time, the king appointed triers of English and Gascon petitions.[54] York was appointed to neither.

In electing Oldhall, the Commons were demonstrating their conviction that change was required and that York was the man to achieve it. The election was, therefore, a step of great significance for York, confirming him in his intention to oust the household men from government. For so long as money was necessary for Gascony, York, supported by Parliament, could exert appreciable pressure on Henry. This programme would, however, require considerable managerial skills, for even the most generous estimate can show only fourteen members closely aligned to York, with eleven others having some affiliations.[55] Admittedly, the number of household men returned was low,[56] despite royal attempts to manipulate the southern boroughs, and there were useful interest groups to which York might appeal. Fourteen veterans of the French wars sat in this Parliament, mostly as knights of the shire, and Thomas Par, a Scottish campaigner, sat for Westmorland. In addition, six other MPs were closely related to well-known soldiers.[57] The mercantile

[53] Bale (ibid. p. 137) claims that the Commons presented a petition on Sunday 8 November, that the duke of Gloucester be proclaimed a true knight. 18 November may be suggested as more probable.

[54] *Rot. Parl.* v. 210. Somerset was a trier of Gascon petitions.

[55] For details see Note B, p. 105.

[56] Three knights of the shire and fourteen borough representatives according to one estimate (J. S. Roskell, *The Commons in the Parliament of 1422* (Manchester, 1954), 136), although this is certainly too modest. To take only the shire MPs; John Norys and Edward Langford (Berks.), Thomas Wyle (Devon), Robert Stonham (Hunts.), and Thomas Stanley (Lancs.) were household men (cf. Wolffe, *Henry VI*, p. 217).

[57] William Herteshorn (Berks.), son-in-law of John Popham; Henry Bruyn (Portsmouth), son-in-law of Henry Retford; John Gresley (Staffs.), son of John Gresley (ob. 1449); Thomas Uvedale (Sussex), son-in-law of Henry Norbury; John Erle (Ludgershall), son-in-law of William Ludlow; John Melton kt. (Yorks.), father of John Melton esq. On 13 Apr. 1451 Norbury was given licence to export 1000 marks in bullion to pay his ransom (C76/133 m. 11). On 24 July 1451 substantial assistance was offered for Redford's ransom (*PPC* vi. 109–10). Such considerations must have affected the disposition of their MP sons-in-law in the crucial third session. Melton had already been given help in March 1449 (PSO1/17/891).

interest was strong, as might be expected, thirty-six members being
engaged in trade, but it cannot be supposed that they would behave
as a homogeneous group on specific issues, although an appeal for a
wiser commercial and foreign policy would have been generally
acceptable. York, then, could look to the shires for sympathy and
might have the respect of other groups, but Parliament's cooperation
could not be presumed. It would have to be managed. Oldhall, an
old soldier without experience as a member of Parliament, was not
necessarily, from York's point of view, the best person to occupy the
speaker's chair.

Having elected a speaker, Parliament awaited the duke's arrival.
York left Ludlow on 13 November.[58] No doubt he had already
recruited a following, but confidently expected that this would grow
substantially *en route*, as his agents had already set about drumming
up support. Later allegations presented these efforts as conspiracies
against the king. Thus, John Wykes and twenty others allegedly
assembled at Ripon on 10 November to plot the death of the king,
and in support of the duke of York.[59] On 11 November John Brown
and fifty-six others congregated at Stamford,[60] and Richard Salty
and others did so at Grantham.[61] The Mulso brothers, with twenty-
six colleagues, did the same at Fotheringhay.[62] York's Thaxted
tenants allegedly congregated at Chelmsford for a similar purpose
the following day.[63] On 13 November there was a riot at Walsingham
directed against the collectors of the fifteenth, in which they were
allegedly forced to write a bill in favour of the duke of York, binding
themselves to the will of the duke.[64] Clearly, Duke Richard was
determined to arrive in London in force, his ally the duke of Norfolk
being engaged in similar efforts in East Anglia. The duke of York,
his retinue about him, entered London on 23 November in most
provocative fashion, his sword born upright before him,[65] a gesture
whose profound symbolism cannot have escaped the London

---

[58] Hampshire CRO MS 23M58/57b.

[59] KB9/7/1 m. 10.

[60] KB9/65A m. 36.   [61] KB9/65A m. 12.

[62] KB9/94/1 m. 25. See also m. 2 for an earlier disturbance on 3 Nov., and also
KB9/278/51.

[63] KB9/26/1 m. 28.

[64] KB9/85/1 m. 16. Griffiths, 'Duke Richard of York's Intentions', p. 200, believes
these disturbances to be purely local demonstrations of support for the duke, but it is
difficult to see what would be gained by these activities in localities already well
disposed.

[65] *Bale's Chronicle*, p. 137.

crowds. The duke of Norfolk, again with a great retinue, arrived the following day.[66]

York had three problems on his hands. The first was practical. His sizeable retinue had to be maintained, as disorder would cost him much support, and this meant food and cash. The latter he borrowed, the former he brought in on the hoof, 999 sheep and 80 beef cattle. Stabling and pasturing were found at Camberwell and Dartford.[67] These arrangements worked well, and there is no record of York's men looting supplies.[68]

His second problem was discharged soldiers. Unruly and unpredictable, they had grievances of their own to press, and government attempts to appease them had, to date, had little effect.[69] Within the city walls their behaviour could be just about controlled, but it was less easy to be confident of preserving order in and around Westminster.[70] How far they would take orders from York was uncertain.

Finally, York needed to define his own political priorities. His main political rival was undoubtedly Edmund Beaufort, who had succeeded in replacing him in France and might now displace him in England. There was no reason to suppose, however, that this political rivalry would constitute a persistent threat to York's own safety. Recent experience suggested that it was the royal household which posed the personal threat, and that erstwhile followers of the duke of Suffolk were the most likely to seek to do him personal harm. Those of his councillors who had been in Normandy did not see the problem in quite the same way. They saw Beaufort as the enemy, the man who had surrendered Anjou and Maine but had pocketed the compensation, the man who had then gone on to lose Normandy. To these men, household politics were of little consequence, and they found no difficulty in the next few weeks in

[66] *Annales*, p. 770; Davis (ed.), *Paston Letters*, ii. 55.

[67] Hampshire CRO MS 23M58/57b.

[68] Some of York's followers may have exploited other avenues of advantage, e.g. 25 Nov., pardon to Richard Ellingham gent. for not answering a plea of debt (*CPR* 1446–52, p. 394).

[69] Payments to impoverished soldiers were made throughout Oct., and in one instance the government paid the funeral costs of a penurious soldier who died in Fleet St. (E404/67/23, 32, 55).

[70] William Bette of Manstoke (Essex) allegedly plotted the death of the king at Brentwood on 28 Nov. John Bagh of Holt, a soldier, and others, forcibly entered the house of John Trussel at Kensington and stole £20 (KB9/26/1 m. 14; KB27/770 *Rex* m. 161ᵛ).

restoring relations with Hoo, Scales, and Ogard, former soldiers who had, since 1445, drifted away from York towards the royal household.[71]

Nothing is known of the seven days after York's arrival, but on 30 November the scene erupted: 'the monday the last day of novembr was a marvelous and dredful sturmyng and noys of the comones and of lordes men at Westminster crieng and seieng to the lordes dooth justice upon the fals traitours or lett us be avenged'.[72] Benet explains that their anger was aroused by the king's refusal to proceed against Somerset and his allies for the loss of Normandy, and that this anger was given vent in a symbolic triple shout,[73] calling to mind the obligations sworn by the king at his coronation, a direct challenge to Henry VI as king. The impression given by both Bale and Benet is that this was a mass incursion by lawless soldiers and their captains, angered by the failure of the lords to move decisively against their enemies. Benet says they complained 'super omnes duces, comites et barones', which implies not so much a massed outcry against Somerset and the household, orchestrated for York's political advantage, as a vociferous, violent mob demanding justice to satisfy its own desire for vengeance.

Violence flared again the following day, 1 December, when the 'lordes men' took it on themselves, in a well-orchestrated raid, to try to seize and kill the duke of Somerset, then in Blackfriars. The earl of Devon saved Beaufort, smuggling him by boat out of Blackfriars to the Tower while the mob sacked the Dominican house.[74] According to one authority, Devon acted on York's orders,[75] and this may well have been so, for York could not afford to be associated with attempts at the summary execution of a peer of the realm, and of the blood. The plundering of a house of religion was more than sufficient embarrassment. When the soldiery turned their attention the next day to the houses of Hoo and Tuddenham, York intervened directly, riding through the city with a great force, taking one of the looters and dispatching him to the king, who sent him on to the earl

---

[71] Davis (ed.), *Paston Letters*, ii. 48; *CFR* 1445–53, p. 183; KB27/760 *Rex* mm. 74^r–76^v (Chancery suit on behalf of the duchess of Suffolk initiated by the earl of Salisbury, Oldhall, and Ogard relating to the estates of Sir John Clifton).

[72] *Bale's Chronicle*, p. 137.

[73] *Benet's Chronicle*, p. 203.

[74] Loc. cit.; *Bale's Chronicle*, p. 137; *Six Town Chronicles*, p. 106. Arrangements were made on this day to pay £3,000 for the wages of Calais (E404/67/97).

[75] *Benet's Chronicle*, p. 203.

of Salisbury for execution.[76] The next day the king and all his lords with their retinues rode through the city, and some degree of order was restored. On Saturday 5 December a commission of oyer and terminer assembled at the Guildhall to try other looters. It may also have committed Somerset to the Tower.[77]

It is not the violence of these few days which is surprising, but the fact that the violence was so long in coming. Hopes that Parliament might provide a settlement, especially on the arrival of the duke of York, no doubt explain the willingness to defer direct action until Parliament had assembled. *Benet's Chronicle* gives the impression that it was the failure of Parliament in the days following York's arrival which triggered off the violence. The soldiers were angry that nothing had been done about Somerset or anyone else whom they believed responsible for the loss of Normandy.[78] In this context, it would help if a Commons petition, requesting the removal of twenty-nine named persons from the king's presence forever, could be accurately dated. There is reason to believe that it belongs to this first session, and its demands for expulsion rather than death, for misdeeds in England rather than in Normandy, seem to imply a date sometime after 3 December.[79]

The petition itself is revealing, even if the list of names is derived entirely from earlier complaints. Somerset has pride of place, followed by Alice duchess of Suffolk.[80] Of the remaining twenty-seven, twenty had been indicted by the commons of Kent in August and Stephen Slegge in September.[81] The inclusion of Gay, Stacy,

[76] *Gregory's Chronicle*, p. 196, notices the attack on Tuddenham and Hoo, but dates it to 3 Dec. This authority's chronology makes better sense if it is advanced by a day, so that Gregory agrees with other sources in having the king ride through the city on 3 Dec. There is independent evidence to date the attack on Tuddenham's house to 2 Dec. (KB9/270A/42; KB27/769 *Rex* m. 164ʳ).

[77] *Bale's Chronicle*, p. 138.   [78] *Benet's Chronicle*, p. 203.

[79] *Rot. Parl.* v. 216–17. S. B. Chrimes and A. L. Brown, *Select Documents of English Constitutional History 1307–1485* (1961), 292, suggest either Dec. 1450 or Jan. 1451. J. S. Roskell, 'Thomas Thorpe, Speaker in the Parliament of 1453–4', *Nottingham Medieval Studies*, 5 (1963), 89, accepts Jan. 1451. In favour of the first session it may be urged that the operative date for the bill was 1 Dec., not, as one might expect for the second session, 1 Jan. There were only seven days available for business in Jan. Other evidence points to an improvement in the fortunes over the Christmas recess of some of those named, and the drift of Lord Scales away from his earlier accommodation with York is also noticeable over Christmas (Davis (ed.), *Paston Letters*, ii. 460).

[80] An attempt had already been made to charge her with treason (*Annales*, p. 770).

[81] *English Historical Literature*, pp. 364–5. Those indicted in Aug. but not included in the Commons bill were Bishop Lyhert of Norwich, Lord Rivers, Sir John

Halley, Babthorpe, and Le Vulre, although novel, followed the same pattern. John Newport had already been the subject of a Commons petition in the previous Parliament,[82] and Sir Robert Wingfield was a notorious opponent of the duke of Norfolk.[83]

Politically, this was a clumsy composite. Wingfield was obviously a sop to the Mowbray interest. The person who also need not have been on the list was Somerset. Without him, it was an indictment of domestic misgovernance. By including him, it confused Norman issues with domestic ones, and forced together two political interests not obviously aligned. York's own declared cause since October was the misgovernance of England, and he would have been wise to have stayed with it. Somerset's fate was largely of interest to ex-soldiers and the case against him was more contentious, more obviously the product of vested interest, than the case against William de la Pole's men. Arguably, the events of early December had already cemented a political alliance between Somerset and the Suffolk faction in the household. If so, whoever was responsible for the violence did York no service. If the petition predates these events, York must stand adjudged for pushing the two interest groups together.

Even as they were restoring order in the city, the Lords turned their attention to the maintenance of order in the shires, essentially the appointment of sheriffs.[84] Two shrievalties posed insuperable problems, and no sheriff was appointed. Of the remainder most went to known royal servants. John Barre (Hereford) and Thomas Herbert (Salop) had strong connections with Duke Richard; Thomas Wake (Northants.) was a servant of Viscount Bourchier.[85] In the one instance where the shire's interest is partially known, Norfolk and Suffolk, the opponents of Tuddenham and Heydon

---

Fortescue, John Hall esq., Robert Manfield esq., Thomas Thorpe, and the lawyers, Palmer, Vampage, and Greswold. Fastolf, a target of Cade, is not on the list (Davis (ed.), *Paston Letters*, ii. 313).

[82] *Rot. Parl.* v. 204. Newport had been in Normandy *c.* 15 Nov. to 6 Dec. 1449, victualling Honfleur and Harfleur, for which he was generously rewarded (E404/66/77, 95, 122). Malpractice on this expedition rather than misgovernance in the Isle of Wight may have been in the Commons' thoughts.

[83] In May 1450 he saw brief service under Somerset, and may therefore have been doubly suspect (C81/1265/10).

[84] *CFR* 1445–54, p. 186. The month's delay was the consequence of waiting for York's arrival (Davis (ed.), *Paston Letters*, ii. 56). Escheators were appointed on 7 Dec. (*CFR* 1445–54, p. 87). They were of a socially higher standing than usual, being mostly esquires.

[85] Wedgwood, *Biographies*, p. 913.

failed to secure one of their party, but the list was, otherwise, a favourable one for the household.[86]

On 5 December the king, the lords, and all their retainers rode again through the city to overawe the malcontents. If there was any particular issue which had triggered off a bout of unrest, it is not now known, but the fact that on this same day John Brown was appointed Beauchamp chamberlain of the receipt may be significant. He was forcibly removed from the office by the servants of the earl of Warwick two days later. To this, the duchess of Somerset promptly objected, and the row appears to have simmered for the remainder of the session and through the Christmas recess.[87] The remaining eleven days of the session were peaceful, giving the Commons time to discuss their most important initiative, resumption.

The first resumption bill which had commanded widespread public support had been approved by Parliament at Leicester in May, but it had been the subject of 186 exemptions, sufficient to wreck its political, if not its fiscal, purpose.[88] At much the same time as the Leicester Parliament had been considering resumption, the Irish Parliament, at York's prompting, were considering an Irish act along similar lines.[89] It was an adroit move on York's part, of little significance to the administration of Ireland, but immensely impressive to the English Commons. The earls of Ormond and Shrewsbury were exempted from its provisions, but York, with

---

[86] Davis (ed.), *Paston Letters*, ii. 51, 523–4. This may have been a victory for royal influence, but it should be noted that the subsidy of the 1450 Parliament, yet to be levied, was by assessment of the sheriffs. Reluctance to serve may have shaped the list as much as patronage.

[87] E159/227 *Brevia Directa* Hilary Term m. 33^r. Warwick's action may have been on the strength of a writ in his favour dated 7 Dec. (ibid. m. 6^v). On 24 Jan. 1451 the king delayed settlement of the dispute, appointing the treasurer and Lord Cromwell as joint holders (ibid. m. 33^r). The problem at issue was not just the tenure of the Beauchamp chamberlainship, but the succession to the whole inheritance of the lands of the duchy of Warwick, on which see R. L. Storey, *The End of the House of Lancaster* (1966), 231–41. Storey dismisses the claims of Duke Henry's sisters in the half blood, but the possibility of inheritance in the half blood could not be entirely discounted by contemporaries (cf. T. F. T. Plucknett, *A Concise History of the Common Law* (1940), 647). The challenge to Warwick's tenure implicit in the issue of the Beauchamp Chamberlainship lasted until 1453, and put Warwick firmly among the opponents of Somerset. Cecily, the dowager duchess, had married John Lord Tiptoft, but died in the course of the Christmas recess (23 Dec. 1450). Throughout the second and third sessions of Parliament custody of her estates was undecided (*CFR* 1445–52, p. 184). No write of *diem clausit* was moved either.

[88] *Rot. Parl.* v. 183–6. cf. Wolffe, 'Acts of Resumption', pp. 599–601.

[89] Berry, *Statutes of Ireland*, pp. 181–5. There are no textual similarities between the English and Irish acts.

remarkable shrewdness, allowed it to have full effect against all grants which he had made as lieutenant. The act was intended as much for English as for Irish consumption.

Parliament was prorogued on 18 December, rather than dissolved, because it at last began to show some signs of cooperation with the king. Supply was urgently needed if an adequate force was to be sent to Gascony. No money was voted in the first session, but the Commons had thawed to the extent of agreeing to expedite the collection of the subsidy of the previous Parliament.[90]

On 14 December York and his brother-in-law, Bourchier, were nominated to head a commission of oyer and terminer in Kent and Sussex to investigate all major crime, including treason.[91] This was a cunning ploy by Henry's advisers. York was clearly anxious to distance himself from public disorder, and might prove willing to reap a 'harvest of heddes' in Kent to sustain that image, but if he were to do so it might cost him much popular support. The commission never sat.[92] York left London on 19 December for Stratford-le-Bow, where he spent Christmas, returning to London by New Year's Day.[93]

Parliament reassembled on 20 January, but it is difficult to see how much of significance could have been done before late February, as the king, together with the dukes of Exeter and Somerset, the earl of Shrewsbury, and Lords Roos, Cromwell, and Lisle, rode into Kent on 28 January with some 3,000 men.[94]

---

[90] *CCR* 1447–54, p. 252. The shires continued to procrastinate (ibid. pp. 207, 223).

[91] *CPR* 1446–52, p. 435.

[92] No records survive, no chronicler mentions it, no payments to the judges for service in Kent in this period are to be found. A writ of *venire facias* for the commission of 1 Aug. 1450 was issued for as late as 17 Dec. (R. Virgoe, 'Some Ancient Indictments in the King's Bench Referring to Kent, 1450–52', in *Kent Records: Documents Illustrative of Mediaeval Kentish Society* ed. F. R. H. Du Boulay, Kent Record Society, 18 (1964), 216–17), and the record of the commission of 27 Jan. 1451 makes no mention of it, although it does mention that of 1 Aug. 1450. A new bench was appointed for Kent on 24 Dec. 1450, eliminating local men and replacing them with household officials (*CPR* 1446–52, p. 590).

[93] Hampshire CRO MS 23M58/57b: *English Historical Literature*, p. 372; *CPR* 1467–77, p. 62. He was still in London on 10 Jan. (SC6/1113/11).

[94] *Benet's Chronicle*, p. 204. Five other peers were certainly absent at this time: the earl of Oxford and Viscount Bourchier were sitting on a oyer-and-terminer commission at Colchester (C81/263/9343), the earl of Wiltshire was similarly employed in Dorchester (KB27/770 *Rex* m. 132), and Lord FitzWarin at Exeter (*CPR* 1446–52, p. 434). The earl of Northumberland was on private business in Beverlay on 15 Feb. (G. Poulson, *Beverlac*, 2 vols. (1829), i. 220).

Something very grave seems to lie behind the events of 20–8 January, the first week of the new session. The last days of the previous session had seen a rudimentary if strained, co-operation amongst the nobility themselves, including York, and between the king and nobility. This points to the existence of the 'sad and so substancial counsaile' promised by the king,[95] although its composition and deliberations are unknown. It is unlikely that an acute problem had arisen before 20 January, for, if it had, Parliament would have been prorogued; but the situation in the first week of the session clearly came to be viewed with such alarm that the king determined to absent himself from his capital with a number of leading peers, despite Parliament's being in session.

The reason for Henry's alarm was one Stephen Christmas esq., who had been engaged on 22 January in rousing the Kentishmen with the claim that the king intended to lay waste the county with the levies of Cheshire and Lancashire.[96] This much is revealed by his indictment. More emerges from *Gregory's Chronicle* which says that the king executed men 'for hyr talkyng a gayne the kyng, havynge more favyr unto the Duke of Yorke thenne unto the kynge'.[97] Henry, and probably Kent too, was well aware that Stephen Christmas had spent the year 1449–50 in the household of the duke of York in Ireland.[98] Fears that the duke was using the men of Kent to pressurize the royal household, with the undertones of Cade and his Mortimer claims, were more than sufficient reason to leave Parliament and ride forthwith into Kent with the two dukes of the Lancastrian blood.

Convinced that York lay behind this, the king broke with the conciliar formula of government, and instructed the exchequer to proceed in its usual processes and no longer require warrants bearing conciliar approval.[99] The broader-based council was rejected, York was not to be incorporated into government, his supporters were to be disciplined, and he was to be isolated and neutralized.

This reversion to customary procedures was convenient to other parties, as is shown by the warrant of 30 January to the exchequer, ordering further delays in their proceedings against a much-favoured

---

[95] Griffiths, 'Duke Richard of York's Intentions', p. 205.

[96] KB9/267/93. Christmas was not brought into court, sitting at Rochester, until 17 Feb. Fears of royal punishment of Kent for Suffolk's murder had been a major factor in Cade's revolt.

[97] *Gregory's Chronicle*, p. 196.

[98] *CPR* 1446–52, p. 264.   [99] *PPC* vi. 104.

household servant, Viscount Beaumont, for his tenure of the Bardolf estates.[100] Chedworth's elevation to the see of Lincoln[101] was probably decided in this week, against the claims of William Gray, a connection of York's and a friend of Kemp of London,[102] who was thought to be sympathetic to the Kentishmen's cause.[103] Chedworth, provost of King's College, was appointed, Gray was prosecuted under praemunire.[104] On 14 February Reginald Boulers, seemingly no longer in Ludlow Castle, was consecrated to Hereford by John Lowe of Rochester, acting alone, and in considerable secrecy.[105]

There is no evidence of any parliamentary business being transacted in the king's absence, although some sort of council must have remained in London, because executive documents for the period 28 January to 26 February survive, including some concerning York. On 11 February he was confirmed as lieutenant of Ireland.[106] Two days later, Nicholas Giles was given licence to surrender £1,200 in tallies given him by the duke, and to ship wool customs-free in lieu.[107] On 16 February a very favourable commission of the peace was issued, on conciliar authority, for Herefordshire, with York heading the list, and including John Barre, John Skidmore, Thomas FitzHarry, Robert Clinton, and John Wigmore.[108]

The king's reply to the resumption bill and arrangements for the Rivers expedition to Gascony appear to have occupied what remained of the session. York's only gain was confirmation of the office of Justice of the Forests south of the Trent.[109] With

---

[100] E159/227 *Brevia Directa* Hilary Term m. 4^r. This, the second delay, was ordered to the quinzaine of Easter, the first having been ordered on 30 Nov. (ibid. m. 25^v).

[101] His property, as provost of Kings, had been attacked in Sept. 1450 (KB9/133 m. 33).

[102] *Official Correspondence of Thomas Bekynton*, ed. G. Williams, 2 vols. Rolls Series (1872), ii. 157.

[103] Davis (ed.), *Paston Letters*, ii. 60.   [104] KB27/760 *Rex* mm. 30, 81^r.

[105] Emden, *Oxford*, p. 228. Boulers was not cleared of charges until May, and he did not fully escape York's influence until 6 June, when he replaced John Milewater (appointed on 16 Feb. 1451) with Sir John Talbot as constable of Bishop's Castle (*Registrum Reginaldi Boulers episcopi Herefordensis*, ed. A. T. Bannister, Canterbury and York Society, 25 (1919), 3, 6).

[106] *CPR* 1452–61, p. 465. The confirmation was intended to reaffirm the exemption of this appointment from the 1450 act of resumption, and to free York's hands for the (exceptional) summoning of an Irish Parliament (*Second Report of the Royal Commission on the Historical Manuscripts of Ireland*, App: Pl. III).

[107] E404/67/113.   [108] *CPR* 1446–52, p. 590.

[109] Ibid. p. 413. The office had been resumed in 1450. He failed to recover either the lordship of the Isle of Wight or Carisbrooke Castle. The Crown retained the

resumption agreed, York had only foreign policy as a stick with which to beat the government, but this could only be a useful weapon if wielded in conjunction with the Staplers, and York lacked a means of forging an alliance with them. The appointment of Stourton and Sudeley as treasurers of the household had, if anything, tied the Staplers more closely to the household, and, with rumours of a possible attack on Calais at the start of the 1451 campaigning season,[110] the immediate worries of the Staplers dictated their allegiance to the Crown, even if they would have had it otherwise.

Attempts to restore commercial links with Burgundy may have resulted from his influence,[111] and, if so, York's standing in the mercantile community can only have been enhanced, but the duke had little opportunity, except through Parliament, to consolidate such influence. As the session wore on, his grasp on events weakened steadily, and it was lost altogether by the end of the recess.

Gradually the household recovered its authority. Cromwell, hostile to Suffolk, but not noticeably allied to York, picked up the stewardship of the duchy of Lancaster.[112] The earldom of Pembroke, which in April looked as though it might fall to York,[113] slid inexorably away, to land in the lap of the queen in July.[114] New commissions of the peace for Kent (5 April), Gloucester (12 April), and Wiltshire (18 April)[115] saw in Gloucestershire a slight gain for York, as Thomas Young was added to the bench, but the Kent list was changed solely to add his opponent, Thomas Brown, and the Wiltshire list to restore the Hungerford interest. The earl of

---

former and granted the latter to John Baker esq. on 9 April 1451 (E404/68/83; *CPR* 1446–52, p. 445). He retained Baynards Castle, lost it by resumption in 1455, and recovered use of it by a lease in March 1456 (*CFR* 1452–61, p. 159).

[110] Davis (ed.), *Paston Letters*, ii. 37, 42.

[111] 3 Apr. despatch of Edmund Melette to arrange for embassies to Burgundy and Utrecht (E404/67/127). 1 Feb. commission to Richard Hanson (stapler) and others to investigate attacks on the Bay Fleet at Winchelsea (*CPR* 1446–52, p. 439). 16 Mar. order not to molest the Hanse (*CPR* 1447–54, p. 267). 29 May arrangements to repay Staple loan paid to Burgundy in restitution for damage done to Bay Fleet (E28/81/23; E404/67/167).

[112] Somerville, *Duchy of Lancaster*, p. 421.

[113] The commission appointed on 17 Apr. to inquire into its true value consisted entirely of colleagues of York in 1441: Sir Walter Devereux, Sir Hugh Mortimer, Sir John Skidmore, Thomas FitzHarry, Thomas Parker, and John Barre, the sheriff (*CPR* 1446–52, p. 445). The possibility was still alive in May when a royal judge had to be sent in haste to hold the sessions (E404/67/161).

[114] *CCR* 1447–54, p. 223.   [115] *CPR* 1446–52, pp. 588–9, 597.

Wiltshire obtained royal assistance for the ransom of his brother;[116]
Lord Dudley recovered, on very favourable terms, the custody of
the Grey inheritance.[117] This restoration of household influence may
well have prompted new disturbances in Kent during the Easter
recess.[118] Certainly, in East Anglia a Tuddenham resurgence was
feared in March, and by early May the influence of the household on
the sheriff was well known.[119]

Parliament reassembled on 5 May because the king needed
money. He was most likely to get it if a firm intention to relieve
Gascony could be demonstrated, but it could not. Rivers's expedition,
in the offing since the previous autumn, looked set to do more
damage to the Devonians than to the French,[120] and, unfortunately
for the government, the troops would not sail without payment—
and without departure the Commons were uneasy about voting the
money.[121]

The problem was complicated further by a Commons petition
which contrived to connect supply with the recognition of the duke
of York's title as heir to the throne. In fact, it was one of York's own
councillors, Thomas Young, who promoted the petition, and the
initiative clearly came from the duke. No contemporary source
advances a reason for his action, although there is general agreement
that Parliament was dissolved promptly on its submission.[122]

---

[116] An official hostage at the fall of Rouen, royal assistance for his ransom was not
unreasonable, and his feoffees raised part of the money (*Bale's Chronicle*, p. 126;
C76/133 m. 10).

[117] Dudley was granted involvement in any subsequent arrangement should his
proffer of £130 p.a. be exceeded (C266/61/12).

[118] Virgoe, 'Ancient Indictments Referring to Kent', pp. 244–6.

[119] Davis (ed.), *Paston Letters*, i. 238–9, ii. 68, 71, 73. Fastolf's fortunes,
improving steadily from autumn 1450 to Feb. 1451, thereafter took a turn for the
worse (P. S. Lewis, 'Sir John Fastolf's Lawsuit over Tichwell, 1448–1455', *Historical
Journal*, 1 (1958), 16.

[120] The musters were delayed from 2 Apr. to May, and were still due on 23 June
(*CPR 1446–52*, 444, 476, 478). The sheriff had later to be given an allowance for the
trouble caused in the shire (E159/230 *Brevia Directa* Hilary Term m. 23').

[121] Money was set aside from the customs of London and Southampton (E13/145A
m. 53 *Placita Coram Baronibus*; E28/81/55).

[122] 'and [the Commons] rightfully to electe hym [York] as heire apparent of
England, nought to procede in any other matters till that were granted by the lordes,
whereto the kyng and the lordes wold not consent' (Nicholas, *Chronicle of London*,
p. 137). Parliament was dissolved on 3 June, when both houses were still in session
(E404/70/2/52; *CCR 1447–54*, p. 354). Young went to the Tower, an overt sign of
Henry's displeasure, accompanied, according to the dean of St Martin-le-Grand, by
other councillors, officers, and domestics of the duke (A. J. Kempe, *Historical*

There is every reason to suppose that when Young raised the succession issue he was confident of the Commons' opinion, and confident in the expectation that a public statement of York's status would guarantee the duke's pre-eminence after the dissolution of Parliament. There were only two other families to take into account, the Hollands and the Beauforts.[123] As grandson of Henry IV's sister Elizabeth,[124] Henry Holland was closest in blood to Henry VI, and might, therefore, be regarded as heir presumptive, were it not for the parliamentary declarations of 1404 and 1406 explicitly settling the Lancastrian throne on Prince Henry and the heirs male of his body, in default of which to his brothers and their heirs male successively.[125] Parliament might, presumably, choose to set aside such provisions, as regards the throne of England, but Henry V's claim to the throne of France was, by implication in the Treaty of Troyes, one of succession to Charles VI, and, therefore, to be determined thereafter by Salic law. The Holland claim would require abandonment of a claim of the throne of France. In 1451 it was unlikely to be pressed.

The Beaufort claim was simpler and more sensitive. Legitimated by Richard II, they had been specifically excluded from the royal succession by letters patent of 1407, supposedly confirming Richard II's legitimation, but, in fact, interpolating a crucial clause excluding them from the succession.[126] Letters patent could, of course, be revoked, and an act of parliament would certainly carry as much if not more weight. The senior Beaufort was a girl, Margaret, but the problems of the French succession, together with the obvious Lancastrian predisposition to a settlement on heirs male, would probably, in 1451, have turned minds to Edmund Beaufort duke of Somerset. The option open to Henry VI was, therefore, to reply to Young's petition with a parliamentary declaration in favour of Somerset as heir presumptive.

Another option was to accept the petition. This would have been to confirm Duke Richard's status as heir presumptive by right of descent from Edmund, fifth son of Edward III; and the duke, in

Notices of the Collegiate Church or Royal Free Chapel and Sanctuary of St Martin-le-Grand (1825), 140).

[123] For an alternative opinion of the dynastic issue and its implications see R. A. Griffiths, 'The Sense of Dynasty in the Reign of Henry VI', in Ross (ed.), *Patronage, Pedigree, and Power*, pp. 13–36.

[124] *Complete Peerage*, v. 195–212.   [125] *Rot. Parl.* iii. 525, 574–6.

[126] Griffiths, 'Sense of Dynasty', p. 33 n. 18, and authorities there cited.

accepting such recognition, could arguably have been represented as having abandoned any claim as heir to Lionel, second son of Edward III by Philippa, later countess of March. This latter claim would have its difficulties for York in 1451, as he would have to consider himself as heir to the English throne via Philippa, and heir to the French throne via Duke Edmund, thus leaving a possible loophole for the Beauforts.

The petition was rejected for several reasons. This was not an opportune moment to settle the succession issue. Only one family would have been satisfied with the outcome, and Henry did not want more critics. Accepting York on the grounds of descent from Edmund of Langley might well be open to subsequent popular misunderstanding, and encourage the country at large to reflect on the claim through Lionel of Clarence. Popular support for the duke of York was already alarming, without further prompting through misconceptions of a constitutional settlement. Most important, neither Henry nor his household wanted York as first councillor for the foreseeable future. Young's petition must be considered unfortunate, in that it forced the king into a public declaration of his attitude to York. Excluded as first councillor, it is unlikely that he would have been willing to sit at the council-table thereafter in the company of the duke of Somerset. Duke Richard, through Thomas Young, had sought to confront Henry and had lost. His consequent exclusion from the council-table brought a decade of instability to Lancastrian England.

The duke of York had lost the battle in Parliament. In the countryside the violence also subsided. Attempts to stir up the Kentishmen in March, and again in April, failed.[127] Trouble rumbled on in Sussex, but the sentiments expressed were lollard and quasi-leveller, of no interest to York.[128] East Anglia, quiet in the spring,[129] grew restive as the household men were restored to influence and favour. This resulted in large-scale disturbances in Norwich on 16 July.[130] Hostility to the household evidently persisted in the provinces, as did the support for the grievances of

---

[127] Virgoe, 'Ancient Indictments Referring to Kent' p. 244. The indictment of Nicholas Waterman of Cobham alleges that, *inter alia*, he claimed Cade to have been a Mortimer and, therefore, the rightful king (ibid. 245).

[128] KB27/760 *Rex* m. 70; KB27/769 *Rex* m. 167; *CPR* 1446–52, p. 478.

[129] Sir John Wenlock and Drew Barantyne esq. attacked property of the duchess of Suffolk (KB27/764 *Rex* m. 64ᵛ).

[130] KB9/85/1 m. 6. The principal target was Thomas Hoo.

Cade's Kentishmen. Sir William Oldhall, and possibly Duke Richard, were not to overlook this.

Regrettably, the events of the summer of 1451 can only be most sketchily reconstructed. The starting-point must be the allegations made in 1452 that, on 20 July 1451 in the Great Hall at Westminster, Oldhall plotted to seize the king on 16 September following.[131] Two points need clarification; why Oldhall should manifest his (criminal) intentions before the justices of the King's Bench, and whether such a plot was indeed set in motion.

Two items in the patent rolls may be of significance for the first problem. On 18 July a commission had been appointed to arrest the vicar of Standon and four other, named persons of the village.[132] Oldhall, who held the manor from the duke of York at the time,[133] may have been lodging a protest against this commission before the Bench. Alternatively, or possibly additionally, on 20 July a commission was appointed, to hear an appeal by Thomas Gower esq. against a sentence of the duke of Somerset, as Constable, in a dispute over ransoms; a sentence which had gone against Gower.[134]

These are curious entries, but inconclusive.[135] The alleged 16 September plot does, however, have a certain plausibility. On 18 September there were riots at Ilminster and Yeovil, allegedly fomented by Lord Cobham, Sir Hugh Courtney, and others, to rouse the people to support the duke of York and his 'false and traitorous purposes' (unspecified).[136] As there had been intermittent trouble in the west country all year, this is indecisive, but on 20 September, or so it was alleged in 1452, Edward Clere esq. of Stokesly (Norfolk) received, at King's Lynn, treasonable letters from the duke of York, intended for the town and for notable persons of the shire.[137] The letters requested that the recipients be favourable to the duke of York in certain undertakings, again unspecified.

[131] KB27/777 *Rex* m. 106ᵛ.

[132] *CPR* 1446–52, p. 478. The trial of Stephen Christmas had resumed at Dartford on 13 July (KB9/267/93).

[133] *CPR* 1431–6, p. 531; SC6/870/4.   [134] *CPR* 1446–52, p. 466.

[135] There is no evidence to link York or Oldhall with the propaganda verses in circulation at that time emanating from William Tailboys, although the authorities may have been concerned about such a possibility, as York's name is explicitly included (R. Virgoe, 'William Tailboys and Lord Cromwell: Crime and Politics in Lancastrian England', *BJRL* 55 (1973), 480–1).

[136] KB9/2/90; KB27/771 *Rex* m. 96ᵛ; KB27/774 *Rex* m. 172ᵛ.

[137] KB/85/1 m. 10.

In the last week of September the king was in the Midlands, the heart of the duchy of Lancaster, and summoned there the duke of Buckingham, and the earls of Shrewsbury and Salisbury.[138] York's whereabouts at this time are unknown. He had been at Southwark on 7 September,[139] and by late September had some 2,000 men about him.[140] No further evidence exists about the state of English politics at this time, but the fall of Bordeaux had given York's parliamentary criticisms a new edge in July, and it is not impossible that he was engaged in a fresh political initiative. That he had 2,000 men at his command in September merits reflection.

The duke chose to take his retinue to the west country. *Benet's Chronicle*, the fullest account of events, says that dissension broke out on 17 September between the earl of Devon, with Lords Moleyns and Cobham on the one hand, and the earl of Wiltshire and Lord Bonville on the other. The duke of York intervened, and prevented further disorder and damage. The king, according to *Benet's Chronicle*, was angry at the widespread breach of the peace, and summoned all involved to court, proceeding to lodge Wiltshire and Bonville in Berkhamstead Castle, Moleyns and Cobham in Wallingford. His summons was, however, ignored by York and the earl of Devon.[141]

Another source gives a somewhat different slant, claiming that York intervened, supported by Lord Moleyns and Sir William Herbert, and stopped the siege of Taunton Castle; Bonville, besieged in the castle, surrendering himself to York.[142] This account is of help, as it permits York's intervention to be dated to 1 October. Why he intervened is less clear. The west country men had been fiercely hostile to the court interest in 1450, and York apparently sought their support in the shadowy plot of September 1451, support in part, at least, given him thanks to the Courtney family. Unable, for whatever reason, to advance his cause in September, York marched west to help his Courtney allies. In so doing, he administered a useful snub to the duke of Somerset, restoring order

[138] E404/68/96, 97, 99. Letters of some sort were also sent at this time to Lord Dudley and Sir Thomas Stanley (n. 176).

[139] Hampshire CRO Wrottesley MSS. 5M53 m. 92.

[140] *Benet's Chronicle*, p. 205.

[141] *Benet's Chronicle*, p. 205. For the background to this dispute, and details of the disturbances occasioned, see Storey, *End of the House of Lancaster*, p. 89.

[142] *Annales*, p. 779.

to the county from which the duke drew his title.[143] *Bale's Chronicle*, in a confused way, seems to be hinting at a further motive. It has the duke, on 12 October, committing Lord Berkeley and the earl of Wiltshire to ward.[144]

As it stands, this is highly unlikely. James Berkeley had no quarrel with the earl of Wiltshire.[145] His difficulties lay with the three daughters of Richard Beauchamp earl of Warwick by his first marriage, and principally with the eldest, Margaret countess of Shrewsbury. Her son, Viscount Lisle, had forced Berkeley to surrender Berkeley Castle on 6 September.[146] If York did intervene, it was more probably to help Berkeley, if only because the second of the Beauchamp daughters was wife to Edmund duke of Somerset.[147]

Whatever the details of York's activities, there can be no doubt that the king was very angry with him. East Anglian events may have goaded Henry further. According to later indictments, Sir William Oldhall, on 3 November at Hunsdon, plotted the death of the king.[148] How, when, and by what agency this was to be achieved is unstated, and the allegation might well be dismissed, were it not for the fact that on 23 November Oldhall took sanctuary in St Martins. According to the dean, Oldhall entered sanctuary before daybreak, fearing heavy imprisonment, possibly execution, because of accusations by Walter Burgh, an esquire of the king's household, that Oldhall had organized the robbery of Somerset's goods at Blackfriars the previous year. He also stood bound in sums of money to certain persons, and had been commanded by the king not to leave London. In fear, he fled to St Martins. Somerset tried to winkle him out, but the dean opposed this successfully.[149] On 2 December fresh

---

[143] Cf. letter of the duke of Norfolk 'we lete yow wete that nexst the Kynge our soverayn Lord, be his good grade and lycence, we woll have the princypall rewle and governance throwh all this schir, of whishe we ber our name' (Gairdner (ed.), *Paston Letters*, ii. 259).

[144] *Bale's Chronicle*, p. 139.

[145] There had been trouble between them in 1448–9 (KB27/770 *Rex* m. 134[r]; G. Wrottesley, *Early Chancery Proceedings* William Salt Archaeological Society Collections, NS, 7 (1904), 250–1).

[146] J. Smyth, *Lives of the Berkeleys*, ed. J. Maclean, 2 vols. (Gloucester, 1883), ii. 65–71.

[147] On 8 Oct. Berkeley settled part of his inheritance, including the castle, on himself for life, with reversion to the Beauchamp sisters, and made a gift of land in Slimbridge (Glos.), together with £1000 and the use of the castle for two years, to the earl of Shrewsbury (KB27/763 *Rex* m. 41).

[148] KB9/40/1 m. 5 & 6; KB9/278/52.

[149] Kempe, *Historical Notices of St Martin-le-Grand*, pp. 140–1.

attempts were made to arrest the vicar of Standon and his colleagues.[150] What all this amounts to, and whether York had any part in it,[151] cannot now be established, although it is clear that Oldhall retained York's confidence, as on 20 December he was appointed an arbitrator in the duke of York's dispute with Thomas Brown.[152] What is certainly the case is that by Christmas York, then at Ludlow,[153] was decidedly uneasy.[154]

NOTE A

The bills survive in a contemporary transcript in the archives of Beverley, and partially in Stow's *Annales* (pp. 666–8). The text of the Beverley transcript is printed in Griffiths, 'Duke Richard of York's intentions', pp. 203–6, and collated with Stow. Griffiths proposes that York submitted two bills, receiving a reply from the king to each bill. It is here suggested that there were in fact four bills, of which three now survive. The first bill is to be found only in Stow and starts 'Please it your highnesse' and ends 'in example of all other'. This bill was unknown to the Beverley clerk. He transcribed a separate bill having its own formal opening, 'plese it unto your excellence' and, subsequently, itemized in its particulars. The repetition of a formal opening is superfluous if this is, indeed, the continuation of the one bill, as Stow unfortunately prints it. The formality might just be explicable if it were continued in each element of the bill, but it is not. In style, the first bill, known only to Stow, is very generalized, relating to unspecified allegations against York. The second, known to both Stow and Beverley, is specific, and compromises York's allegations against other named persons. It is, however, probable that this bill had been preceded by a bill, now lost, which is alluded to by York, 'as I have wretyn to your excellence here be fore'. Griffiths is correct in his belief that there is a distinct bill, which he presents as the second bill. More widely known than its predecessors, it is certainly to be distinguished from the earlier bills and, from its content, does not appear to be the missing bill. There were, therefore, four bills, the first

---

[150] *CPR* 1446–52, p. 535.

[151] Theobald King was paid for riding from Fotheringhay to Melbury 'with letters of the lord' (i.e. York) on 4 Nov. 1451 (SC6/1113/11), but this cannot be taken as firm evidence that York was himself at Fotheringhay. Why York ordered, from William Milbourne 'payntour' of London, various items is also a puzzle (C1/22/176).

[152] *CCR* 1447–54, p. 326.

[153] SC6/1113/11 (31 Dec.). He exchanged New-Year's gifts with the queen (Myers, 'Jewels of Queen Margaret', p. 124).

[154] He made his only payment of the fee farm of Montgomery and Chirbury on 11 Dec., in cash. Presumably he was anxious to avoid exchequer process (E401/823).

known only to Stow, the second alluded to by York, and possibly by Henry in his reply to the third bill ('we have seen the billis late taken to us'—but Stow reads 'bill' for 'billis'), but which is now lost. The third is to be found in both Beverley and Stow. It is to this bill, starting 'Cosyn we have seen the billis', that Henry's first reply is addressed. There is, then, a fourth bill, starting 'Please it your hygnes tendirly to considere', to which Henry gives a separate response, 'Item, as touchyng your last bille'.

NOTE B

The fourteen are John Fillol (tenant of York at Gussage Bohun) and William Browning (Dorset), Sir John Barre (Glos.), Thomas Young (Bristol), Sir Walter Devereux (Hereford), Sir William Oldhall (Herts.), Thomas Mulso (Northants.), Sir William Burley (Salop), Sir Henry Bruyn (Portsmouth), Sir Roger Chamberlain and Sir Edmund Mulso (Suffolk), John Russell (Wilts.), Sir John Saville (Yorks.), and Thomas Palmer (Rutland).

The eleven possibles are: William Tyrell (Essex (whose brother-in-law Robert Darcy was also returned for the shire. Darcy's father often acted for the duke, and his brother-in-law was Henry Bruyn); Robert Poynings (Sussex) (whose allegiance to Cade would logically suggest support for York; when on 9 December 1450 he found sureties before the lords they included Walter Devereux and Edmund Mulso (*CCR* 1447–54, p. 238)); Thomas Barton (Lyme Regis) (who may have been York's receiver for Wigmore (SC11/818; the identification in Wedgwood, *Biographies*, p. 46 is precarious.)); Robert Browning (Wareham) (who was probably a relative of William Browning. York controlled the borough); William Canning (Bristol) (a close relative of Thomas Young); William Scot (Huntingdon) (who is unlikely to have been 'of Smeeth' (Kent) as Wedgwood suggests (*Biographies*, p. 752), and is more probably from nearby Chalney, and accompanied York in 1440 (E101/53/33)); Henry Gray, one of the candidates proposed by York for Norfolk (who may have been in the duke of Norfolk's interest (Davis (ed.), *Paston Letters*, ii. 55)); Robert Harcourt (who had, or very shortly acquired, Yorkist connections (Wrottesley, 'Plea Rolls', iii. 197)); John Lawley (Wootton Basset) (who was a relative of William Browning (Wedgwood, *Biographies*, pp. 125, 529)); Thomas Bonyn and John Weobley (who were elected in defiance of the aldermannic oligarchy in Hereford, and may well have been sympathetic to the duke; Weobley was to be associated with him in 1452 (Storey, *End of the House of Lancaster*, pp. 228–30)). (The Thomas Mallory who sat for Wareham has been identified with the author of the *Morte D'Arthur*, but this can only be tentative and makes little political sense (but cf. P. J. C. Field, 'Sir Thomas Mallory MP' *BIHR* 47 (1974), 30).)

This modest impact by a great nobleman on elections at a time of strong personal appeal supports the general opinion that although influence could be exerted it was only one of the factors determining an election result (cf. Roskell, *Commons in the Parliament of 1422*, p. 27).

5

DARTFORD

Some time over the Christmas season York received word that the king was publicly advertising his displeasure, and on 9 January he signed and sealed a declaration protesting his loyalty to his king.[1] Conscious, perhaps, that such protestations required a more public commitment, he invited the bishop of Hereford and the earl of Shrewsbury to Ludlow, there to tender him an oath on the sacrament and report his sincerity to the king. They were, further, to report his willingness to repeat the oath before nominees of the king, should he so desire it. The only thing York did not offer to do was to go to Henry and declare his loyalty in person. Duke Richard was a worried man. The whole tone of the letter is deferential in the extreme, yet, less than a month later, he was defiantly demanding the removal of the duke of Somerset, insisting that without this there would be no ease or tranquillity in the land. The change is so abrupt as to merit attention.

There is no evidence to suppose that in January he strayed very far from Ludlow.[2] The king was more active. On 17 January there assembled a council at Westminster 'for greet matiers concernying our worship, the wele of us and of this our land'.[3] Calais was certainly one of the 'greet matiers' discussed, and arrangements were made to impound Venetian and Genoese carracks for service, and arrange for appropriate payment.[4] By 26 January it was public knowledge that the king intended to cross to Calais, it being further

---

[1] Stow, *Annales*, p. 393, repr. in Gairdner (ed.), *Paston Letters*, i. 96. On 2 Jan. Shrewsbury town had received a letter from the king, the contents of which are unknown (Salop CRO box viii. n. 380 m. 1ʳ).

[2] The only known action of Duke Richard early in Jan. 1452 was to give one Richard Doughton an annuity of £2 p.a. (SC6/850/28). The distribution of liveries by Walter Devereux in and around Weobley on 4 Jan. does not seem to have anything to do with York, but was related to Devereux's quarrels in Hereford (KB9/34/1 m. 5; Storey, *End of the House of Lancaster*, p. 229).

[3] E28/82/9.

[4] G. L. Harriss, 'The Struggle for Calais: An Aspect of the Rivalry Between Lancaster and York', *EHR* 75 (1960), 31; E28/82/3; E159/229 *Brevia Directa* Michaelmas Term m. 34ᵛ.

declared that in the circumstances it was not possible to summon Parliament.[5]

The other 'greet matier' must have been the duke of York. On 28 January, and quite uncharacteristically, the king had William Oldhall forcibly taken from sanctuary. The dean protested, Henry's conscience stirred, and Oldhall was restored on the thirtieth. It is clear from the dean's record of these events that the instigator was the duke of Somerset.[6]

Whether in consequence of answers given by Oldhall, or in alarm at York's letter, or simply because York showed no sign of attending the council, Master Thomas Kent, the council secretary, was sent to the duke on 1 February.[7] It is unlikely that he met Duke Richard much before 7 February, by which time the duke's attitude had changed profoundly. In a letter to the city of Shrewsbury of 3 February,[8] York stressed the danger to Calais not just from the French but, it was implied, from its captain, the duke of Somerset, who had, he claimed, already lost Normandy and Gascony. He further asserted that his intention in 1450 had been, and by implication still was, to restore good government to the realm, again to find the faithless hand of the duke of Somerset against him. The third allegation explains York's change of heart: 'the said Duke of Somerset . . . laboreth continually about the King's highness for my undoing, and to corrupt my blood, and to disinherit me and my heirs, and such persons as be about me'.[9]

The pressure on his chamberlain alarmed the duke, for whom the failure of Young's parliamentary claim may have come to look increasingly disquieting as the months passed. Believing it to be a matter of his own survival, and, he claimed, the nation's, he proposed to march on the king and have the duke of Somerset

[5] *CPR* 1446–52, pp. 512–3, 537.

[6] The dean believed the abduction to be the consequence of an attack on Walter Burgh on 18 Jan. Burgh accused Oldhall of complicity in this attack. The dean ascribes Oldhall's restoration both to his own labours and to those of certain bishops (Kempe, *Historical Notices of St Martin-le-Grand*, pp. 141–2).

[7] Order to pay him 12 marks (1 Feb.) 'nowe going by the commandement of the lordes of oure counsaille unto oure cousin the Duc of York with certaine lettres and message' (E404/68/79). On 28 Jan. new justices of the peace were appointed for the West Riding (*CPR* 1446–52, p. 598). On 15 Feb. John Pilkington gent. of Sowerby, a property of the duke of York, was ordered to be discharged of all treason charges (KB27/773 *Rex* m. 67ʳ). In late Feb. Thomas Pilkington was brought before the council under pain of £1,000 (E28/82/26).

[8] Gairdner (ed.), *Paston Letters*, i. 97.

[9] Cf. *Six Town Chronicles*, p. 107.

removed. This was, he declared, in no wise to be seen as an act against the king's majesty. In a codicil he stressed that the whole enterprise was to be orderly. A letter similar in content was circulated to most of the towns of southern England, and by 17 February several had forwarded copies to the king.[10] He bade them ignore it and obey only royal proclamations.

But by this time the political situation had deteriorated further. York, as he had written to the city of Shrewsbury, was proposing to move in all haste. On 8 February Thomas Mulso was planning an operation from Fotheringhay, and his brother, Sir Edmund, and the Shrewsbury burgess and local squire, Fulk Eyton, were doing the same at Ludlow two days later.[11] The intention was to assemble supporters on or about Ash Wednesday at various centres, and thence to join up with York, hopefully already well on the way to London. Thomas Kent may well have gathered something of what was intended, as a commission of oyer and terminer for the south-western shires was issued the day after he returned to London,[12] and for Kent and East Anglia on the seventeenth.[13]

Despite the winter season, the duke was successful in rousing his tenantry. Assemblies are first reported on 20 February at Moulton and Hitchin,[14] and in the south west at Ottery and Cullompton.[15] It was Camber's turn the next day,[16] followed by Fotheringhay, Rowell, and Nassington on the twenty-second,[17] Huntingdon,

[10] *PPC* vi. 90–2; Storey, *End of the House of Lancaster*, pp. 98, 249; Griffiths, *Reign of Henry VI*, p. 710 n. 136. The recipients included the Kent towns of Canterbury, Maidstone, and Sandwich, and commissions to suppress rebellion in Kent were issued the same day. York evidently hoped for support from the Cinque Ports, which would have isolated the Calais garrison. Bristol, Winchester, Colchester, Oxford, and Sudbury have nothing in common, which implies that York circularized his letter throughout the southern towns at least. In Aug. 1452 Thomas Bright, a Canterbury fuller, was accused of having raised a rebellion on 21 Aug. at Hertlesham, claiming to possess letters sealed by the duke of York or the earl of Devon, though he could neither read nor understand them. That Bright claimed the possession of such letters shows a general familiarity still surviving in Kent with the possibility of receiving communications from the duke or the earl (KB27/778 *Rex* m. 116ʳ).

[11] KB9/94/1 m. 4; *CPR* 1452–61, p. 31; KB9/103/1 mm. 2, 16. Mulso was paid £28. 17s. 0d. by York's officials on 10 Feb. (SC6/1113/11). Storey, *End of the House of Lancaster*, p. 98, sees this, and all subsequent risings, as local demonstrations of support for the duke of York, but other indictments are clear that the purpose was to gather forces to join York *en route* (KB9/65A mm. 20, 21; KB9/270A/77; KB27/769 *Rex* m. 146ᵛ; C81/1371/31; *CPR* 1452–61, p. 24; cf. Griffiths, *Reign of Henry VI*, p. 695).

[12] *CPR* 1446–52, p. 537.   [13] Ibid. p. 577.   [14] KB9/118/1 m. 33.
[15] KB9/269/42; KB27/767 *Rex* m. 92ʳ.   [16] KB9/7/1.
[17] *CPR* 1452–61, p. 31; KB9/94/1 mm. 3, 4, 21. This was Ash Wednesday.

Grantham, and Thaxted,[18] and, in Devon, Camerside on the twenty-third,[19] and Stamford on the following day.[20]

This was an encouraging response, but other parts of the plan were proving more difficult. By 22 February he was in the vicinity of Northampton,[21] and had sent an herald on ahead to warn London of his approach.[22] Uneasy, the city sought advice from the king. Henry had already left London for Barnet on 16 February,[23] and by the time he reached Dunstable on the eighteenth he had sixteen lords with him, including the dukes of Exeter, Buckingham, and Norfolk, though not, interestingly, Somerset, together with a retinue in royal livery.[24] On 22 February he commissioned the bishop of Winchester, Viscount Bourchier, and Lord Stourton to negotiate with York.[25] They did so, trying to establish his motives for insurrection, but York denied that this was what he was doing, saying that his target was 'traitors'.

For the king this was an unacceptable answer, and he wrote firmly in reply to the city of London, commanding them to resist York.[26] London obeyed, and this proved the turning-point for York. He moved to Kingston on 26 February, lingered for three days, then marched on to Blackheath. Fresh attempts were made to negotiate while he was at Kingston, largely because the king had no wish to see the duke in Kent, but the bishops of Winchester and Ely failed to deflect him.[27] Henry, meanwhile, had been summoning men from far and wide. Thomas Yerde, as sheriff of Surrey and Sussex, brought men direct to Blackheath.[28] Robert Strelley, sheriff of Nottinghamshire and Derbyshire, was ordered to raise a force in

[18] KB9/42/1 mm. 16, 17; KB9/65A mm. 20, 21; KB9/26/1 mm. 24, 30. The Thaxted men assembled at Chelmsford.

[19] KB9/15/1 mm. 20, 37.

[20] C81/1371/31; *CPR 1452–61*, p. 24.

[21] *Benet's Chronicle*, p. 206, describes how the king, then at Northampton, sent a delegation to the duke which reported back the following day.

[22] Loc. cit.; *English Historical Literature*, p. 297.

[23] Griffiths, *Reign of Henry VI*, p. 695. Giles, *Chronicon Angliae*, p. 43, says that when Henry left London he had already summoned York to a council meeting in Coventry (cf. *Bale's Chronicle*, p. 139).

[24] *English Historical Literature*, p. 373. Somerset is noted as leaving London on 16 Feb. in the king's company (*Bale's Chronicle*, p. 139). Griffiths (op. cit. p. 695) is of the opinion that he did in fact stay with the king.

[25] *Benet's Chronicle*, p. 206.

[26] Loc. cit.; *English Historical Literature*, p. 297.   [27] Ibid.

[28] E404/69/143. Yerde was credited with a 'notable number' and received a £50 reward. Exchequer process against the important Surrey squire, John Pennycoke, a known opponent of York, was respited on 31 Jan. (PSO1/19/964).

Derby and hand it over to the duke of Buckingham. Strelley then raised a force in Nottingham, and brought it in person to London, where he stayed for four days.[29] John Troutbeck, the Cheshire esquire, was rewarded for his support at Blackheath,[30] and, as Robert Horne's career subsequently prospered, it is likely that he too, as sheriff of Kent, played his part.[31] The account of Strelley's contribution has one interesting feature, that he was in London for four days. Much the most likely period is 29 February to 3 March,[32] and this would imply that when York was at Kingston on 28 February he may have enjoyed sufficient numerical superiority to be tempted into Kent, only to find the king substantially reinforced.

The king had other forces than the shire levies. The duke of Buckingham and Lord Bonville were commissioned to raise forces in the South West,[33] and Buckingham, together with the earls of Shrewsbury and Salisbury, had been in constant attendance with retinues from 16 February.[34] Viscount Bourchier joined the king then, or shortly after,[35] and Stourton was also in his company, possibly with Finderne's professionals.[36] Warwick came in soon after,[37] and, of course, Somerset had every incentive to raise men. Retinues of the ecclesiastical peers, though modest, would have helped to swell the host.[38] This rapid acquisition of strength allowed the king to move into Kent only twenty-four hours after York, thereby forestalling any possibility of York employing a few days whipping up sympathy.[39] York had to hold the field with the forces available, but they were insufficient to force the issue.

[29] E159/230 *Brevia Directa* Michaelmas term m. 16ᵛ.

[30] *DKR* ii. 720. [31] *CPR* 1446–52, p. 577.

[32] The king, who was in Southwark on 28 Feb., moved to London from the Midlands, and paused there to add to his forces (*English Historical Literature*, p. 298; Giles, *Chronicon Angliae*, p. 43.

[33] *CPR* 1446–52, p. 537.

[34] E404/68/96, 97, 99. On 21 Feb. the king, writing for a loan to the south west, spoke of the force being assembled under Shrewsbury, which would land when and where thought advisable (E28/82/20). Such elements of this force as existed could also be employed.

[35] *Benet's Chronicle*, p. 206. [36] E404/68/80.

[37] *CPR* 1446–52, p. 523. One of his councillors, Walter Blount esq., was described as 'of London' on 12 Feb. (G. Wrottesley, *Extracts from the Plea Rolls of the Reigns of Henry V and Henry VI*, William Salt Archaeological Society (1896), 197).

[38] Convocation was in session at St Pauls from 7 Feb. to 3 Mar. The king may also have enjoyed a propaganda advantage from this.

[39] Henry was at Southwark on 29 Feb., and moved the following day to Welling. Sir William Pecche of Lullingstone brought men in to York, on 1 Mar., to the 'field of Sandhill' (KB27/784 *Rex* m. 99ʳ).

The chronicle sources divide sharply over events at Dartford, both on the timing of negotiatons and, more importantly, on their outcome. There were certainly negotiations on either 1 or 2 March, possibly both, Winchester and Ely again acting, together with Warwick, Salisbury, Bourchier, and Sudeley. *Benet's Chronicle* says that the practical outcome of these negotiations was that York, Devon, and Cobham presented articles against the duke of Somerset, kneeling before the king to do so, and that the king and lords then returned to London.[40] Three other sources agree with this, and a fourth, the *Chronicon Angliae*, is substantially in agreement, but says that York sought the king's mercy.[41]

A different, but mutually consistent, story emerges from five other chronicles: 'there was agreid that the duke of Somyrset shuld be hadde unto warde to answere soche articlys as the duke of yorke shuld lay unto his charge, upon which promyse made the duke of york brak up his ffeelde'.[42] The duke of York then came in to the king, only to find the duke of Somerset a free individual. If this was so, then the king was in gross breach of his word. The charge is, however, so grave and so flagrant as to excite doubts. It is inherently unlikely that the negotiators would have been party to such gross deception. It is no less unlikely that the king had need of it. He had the superior force which, unlike York's, could be readily augmented. He had only to fly his banner to call York's bluff. The professionals of Calais were not so very far away. He had a duty to hear York's complaints, and did so. Imprisoning Somerset would have given the impression of prejudging the issue.

The articles which York presented against Edmund Beaufort were probably compiled over the Christmas period at Ludlow, though they may well go back in substance to November 1450.[43] The intention was, as the preamble stated, to show that the political

---

[40] *Benet's Chronicle*, p. 207.

[41] *Six Town Chronicles*, p. 107; Davies, *English Chronicle*, p. 70; *English Historical Literature*, p. 373; Giles, *Chronicon Angliae*, p. 43.

[42] *Great Chronicle*, p. 186; (MS Vitellius A XVI, in *Chronicles of London*, p. 163, is an identical text for this year.) See also the very similar accounts in *Short English Chronicle*, p. 69, and Nicholas, *Chronicle of London*, p. 138. *Fabyan's Chronicle*, p. 627, has the same story, but at greater length.

[43] Gairdner (ed.), *Paston letters*, i. 103–8. the articles were formally presented on 2 Mar. (Griffiths, *Reign of Henry VI*, p. 697). London was formally advised of the agreement on 4 Mar. (C. M. Barron, 'London and the Crown, 1451–61', in J. R. L. Highfield and R. Jeffs (eds.), *The Crown and Local Communities in England and France in the Fifteenth Century* (Gloucester, 1981), 106 n. 40).

unrest in England was the result of the king's failure to punish those who had lost France. It was a difficult case to promote, and the articles submitted do not establish the causal connection fully or convincingly. Nor, as a recent study of Beaufort's government in Normandy from 1448 to 1450 has established,[44] does the surviving evidence always point unambiguously to sustained misgovernance.

The first charge, the dismissal of officers and the imprisonment of public servants, did have some substance to it, although the reasons prompting Somerset thus to act are unknown. The fortification of Mortain and St James de Beauvron, which York asserted was the main reason for the failure of the Anglo-French truce, did, indeed, take place, but, as Somerset had not been given sufficient powers to negotiate the future of the fortresses with Charles VII, it would be difficult to prove criminal intent. The more telling point was made in the earlier part of this second article: that Somerset knew of, and consented to, the sack of Fougères.[45]

The accusation that he reduced the strength of garrisons and failed to pay wages is plausible, but it might prove difficult to place all the blame on Somerset. There was, in 1448–50, a chronic shortage of ready cash, not of his making, as was well known. Financial shortages, no doubt, could also be advanced to explain his inability to provide reinforcements and supplies to other garrisons, the substance of York's next article. The strongest point comes towards the end of this article and in the next, that he put up inadequate resistance at Rouen, and surrendered other fortresses not then besieged. In fact, he had been give little option by Charles VII, but the duke of York did not trouble to mention this. The degree of military resistance possible in the circumstances was very debatable.

From an alleged willingness to sell Normandy, York went on to assert Somerset's intention to sell Calais. This somewhat gratuitous logic was at odds with circumstances in Calais, where the garrison had been very recently expanded to near wartime strength to meet the existing emergency, with Somerset only precariously funded.[46] Nor was the credibility of the charge improved by hints that Somerset intended secretly to surrender Calais, as dowry for a putative marriage of his daughter to the count of Charolais.

The suspicion is that the most important article was really the last,

[44] Jones, 'The Beaufort Family', pp. 21–5, 224, 229, 266–7, 272–4, 279.
[45] Keen and Daniel, 'The Sack of Fougères', p. 380.
[46] Harriss, 'Struggle for Calais', p. 31.

that Somerset had kept the 72,000 francs, given him to pass on as compensation to those who lost rights and property on the surrender of Anjou and Maine, that is to say, *inter alia*, Oldhall and Fastolf.[47] This suspicion is reinforced by the sole, almost throw-away, reference to the loss of Gascony in the indictment,[48] and the obvious feebleness of the supposed link between the loss of Normandy and English domestic troubles.[49] Trying to make Somerset responsible for Cade was a ploy which might well rebound. York saw Somerset as his political rival. His Norman councillors, led by Oldhall,[50] had persuaded him that the allegations of treasonable conduct were the best way of removing Somerset from power. They were wrong. The king and the lords were not impressed. The appeal to the commons, the most dangerous political action, forfeited their sympathy. York had to salvage himself from an ill-conceived enterprise.

The events of the next fortnight, a public declaration of loyalty at St Pauls and the adoption of arbitrators for the dispute between the two dukes, were probably agreed in general terms at Dartford.[51] So, too, must have been the offer of a general pardon, as York and his allies could not possibly have persuaded their followers to disperse without some guarantees of their future safety. That the formal declaration was made a month later 'in honour of the Passion' was simply a face-saving formula for the king.

For the duke of York there was little chance of saving face. To be obliged to take an oath of loyalty was itself humiliating,[52] and the terms of the oath were no less embarrassing. 'I am and ought to be humble subject and liegeman'; a statement of obligation the details of which the oath remorselessly set out: not to attempt anything

[47] Fastolf had complained about compensation on the day of the surrender (Wolffe, *Henry VI*, pp. 195, 198).

[48] York had contributed nothing towards loans for its relief (E28/83/49, 56; E207/16/5/K71).

[49] Suffolk's death removed the individual whom most felt responsible for misgovernance. In 1450 the plea was to bring back the dukes, not just Duke Richard. Somerset might yet prove to be a competent domestic minister.

[50] For a similar assessment of Oldhall's influence over York see C. Rawcliffe, 'Baronial Councils in the Later Middle Ages', in Ross (ed.), *Patronage Pedigree and Power*, p. 98.

[51] The first arbitration agreement, confirmed by the king on 4 Mar., bound the parties in 20,000 marks (Rymer, *Foedera*, xi. 362).

[52] The text of the oath is given in Giles, *Chronicon Angliae*, p. 43, in Stow, *Annales*, pp. 395–8, and in the rolls of the 1459 Parliament (*Rot. Parl.* v. 346), whence, possibly, Stow's confusion in having York take the oath at Coventry.

against the Crown, to inform the king of any such attempt, to come 'in humble and obeysant wise' when summoned.

The oath preserved the fiction that the events of 1452 were not a rebellion, and the arbitration with Somerset continued the charade. Nine arbiters, at least five of whom were to give judgement, were to receive claims in writing the following day, Tuesday, and to perform any award by Thursday. Failing an award, which, given the brief period allowed them, was a near certainty, the king was to give judgement before Michaelmas. The arbitration panel was imbalanced in favour of Somerset. Viscount Bourchier and his brother of Ely might perhaps be favourable to York, but the chancellor, the bishop of Hereford, the duke of Buckingham, and Viscount Beaumont were court men.[53]

While York was bracing himself for his humiliation at St Pauls, his supporters were still plotting. The Crown case against the principals —Oldhall, John Sharp 'of London gentleman', Robert Ardern esq. and John Maltman, yeoman, both of The Lodge (Warwicks.)—was that on 6 March at Baynards Castle they planned a rebellion in the Welsh marches, Kent, and elsewhere, claiming that the Crown of England is inheritable, and that Parliament could remove the king and elect another to rule because the king was not able;[54] that on 12 April at Westminster they plotted the death of the king;[55] and that on 20 April near Ludlow Sharp assembled forces in the house of the earl of Shrewsbury, marched on Ludlow, and there killed Richard Fazakerley, a valet of the king.[56] Presented as a sequence these events are deceptive, probably intentionally so.

The allegations of 6 March are the most interesting, as they show clearly the propaganda being disseminated in London on York's behalf, propaganda which does not shirk from implying York's title to the throne—and hence, perhaps, the need to have a public repudiation of such an implication in the St Paul's oath. The last charge, Fazakerley's murder, looks more like score settling and was

---

[53] *CCR* 1447–54, pp. 327, 334. The first panel, formed on or before 4 Mar., consisting of Canterbury, Ely, Buckingham, Wiltshire, Worcester, Viscount Beaumont, and Lords Cromwell and Stourton, was, if anything, more hostile (Rymer, *Foedera*, xi. 362). The terms of arbitration in the two bonds differ slightly. York's charges were to be 'not affecting the estate of the king and realm', Somerset's to be charges 'which concern not principally the estates of the king and realm'.

[54] KB9/103/1 m. 15; KB27/773 *Rex* m. 75ʳ.

[55] KB27/768 *Rex* mm. 98ʳ·ᵛ, 103ʳ; KB27/777 *Rex* m. 102ᵛ.

[56] KB9/270/34; KB27/768 *Rex* m. 98ᵛ.

seen as such by contemporaries,[57] but the plotting of 12 April does not ring true. For Oldhall, the falsification is demonstrable. On 22 March William Elton esq. and Thomas Harpur, yeoman of the Crown, were paid for daily attendance on Oldhall,[58] and on 16 April another yeoman, Richard Mikowe, was paid for the same.[59] Oldhall, closely watched in St Martins, was not at liberty to plot. The plot lay in the allegation itself, which post-dated the general pardon for offences before 7 April. Admittedly, some areas were restive in March and April, but it is not possible to demonstrate the existence of a co-ordinated plot, neither did one exist.[60] York left for Ludlow around 24 March,[61] and when requested to release Sharp in April, in accordance with his oath, did so.

Trouble continued in the shires for the rest of the year. A pedlar, John Wilkins of Stratford-upon-Avon, managed to stir up a sizeable revolt in Kent from 6–8 May, too late to help York, but interesting in its demands for the articles of the commons of Kent, and for the removal of the king's councillors, and, in one indictment, the allegation that the earl of March was coming with a great number of Welshmen, that Lord Cobham would sent them money, and that Cobham's brother would be their captain.[62] John Sharp, the conspirator of 12 April, was included in another indictment along the same lines. There was a treasonable assembly 'to aid other rebels' at Silam (Suffolk) on 6 July, though to what purpose is unknown.[63] There was further trouble in Kent at the end of the year,[64] and the sheriff of Yorkshire for 1451–2 had allowance for taking traitors in Warwickshire and Lincolnshire.[65] An approver alleged a plot at Cromer on 1 November 1452 to encompass the deaths of Somerset, Dudley, the bishop of Hereford, the abbot of St Albans, and Thomas Daniel, but he could identify only four conspirators.[66]

---

[57] *English Historical Literature*, p. 368.

[58] E404/68/100.   [59] E404/68/115.

[60] A commission of oyer and terminer was sent into Wiltshire on 6 Mar. (*CPR 1446–52*, p. 539).

[61] *Benet's Chronicle*, p. 207; Stow, *Annales*, p. 396, says he was released on the arrival of a Gascon embassy and went to Ludlow.

[62] KB27/770 *Rex* m. 154; KB27/774 *Rex* m. 180; Virgoe, 'Ancient Indictments Referring to Kent', pp. 257–9.

[63] KB9/118/1 m. 17; cf. *CPR 1452–61*, p. 55.   [64] Ibid. 58.

[65] E159/229 *Brevia Directa* Hilary Term m. 16ʳ.

[66] KB27/770 *Rex* m. 175ᵛ. There were a scattering of incidents on York's estates, none significant. William Browning's house was robbed in July 1452 (ibid. m. 9ʳ); two of Oldhall's Standon tenants made the mistake of advertising their Lollard beliefs (KB9/40/1 m. 4); there were thefts at Grantham (KB27/764 *Rex* m. 86ᵛ; *Rex* m. 81ʳ),

Despite these instances of discontent, it is clear that the house of Lancaster (Beaufort and all) had received the loyal support of the English nobility at Dartford, in a display of strength which could be readily appreciated by contemporaries. After Dartford, York was exposed and defenceless, and his systematic ruin might be steadily encompassed by his embittered, influential enemies. Indeed, he had been fortunate to escape charges of treason, an indulgence which was not to be extended to his associates.

It might be supposed that Duke Richard's supporters could seek safety in a general pardon, and most were to find it, eventually. But the mechanism of the pardons could be exploited to considerable advantage by Somerset, and he and his supporters were not slow to spot their opportunity. The general pardon had first to be sued, and then the pardon presented in court after indictment.[67] It was, therefore, possible to hold show trials to demonstrate the majesty of the king, the political pre-eminence of the duke of Somerset, and the political feebleness of the duke of York, powerless to save those on whom he depended—their salvation, instead, to rest on the benign mercy of the king. As a propaganda weapon it had immense potential, and was employed to the full; public confessions of guilt being staged even when no trial was taking place.[68] However, as one chronicler commented adversely on the sight of petitioners naked and bound, kneeling in the frost and snow, it may be that the plan ultimately rebounded on its perpetrators.[69] Whether it was obvious to the accused that theirs was a show trial is uncertain. John Wynnawey was sentenced on 20 October but not pardoned until 11 November.[70] Perhaps he was aware of the king's intention to Wakefield (KB9/149/1 m. 100; KB9/227/5, and Swanscombe, where villagers stole £80 due from St Martins, Canterbury, for a clerical tenth (E159/230 *Brevia Directa* Hilary Term m. 18ʳ; *CPR* 1452–61, p. 62); at Cowerne Parva there was an incident of rape (KB9/269/2)—a conventional catalogue of crime.

[67] Roger Ree appears to have been charged, bailed, sued for pardon, found sureties, and then come back into court to present his pardon (KB9/94/2 m. 36 for bail, C237/43/41 for general pardon). His bail was put up by different names from those who found surety.

[68] 'At oure last being at Leomynstre in oure Shire of hereford oure said besechers in the lowliest wise kneling in thaire shirts praied us of pardon' (C81/767/9744). No trial was staged at Leominster.

[69] *Six Town Chronicles*, p. 107; Storey, *End of the House of Lancaster*, p. 102, disputes the veracity of this, on the grounds that the events described took place in the summer. It more probably refers to trials in Hitchin and elsewhere in Jan. and Feb. 1453 (KB9/40/1; KB9/26/2). Somerset also owned property in Hitchin.

[70] *CPR* 1452–61, p. 23. The order of the king under the signet was dated 29 Oct. (C81/1371/30).

pardon him at the time of the sentence, but any delay in informing him would certainly merit the judgement of cruelty.[71] It seems to have been generally accepted that pardons could be refused without adequate sureties,[72] and this also afforded opportunities for delay. John Maltmann, one of the conspirators of 6 March, was only able to find surety in November 1455.[73] Some of the more influential victims were able to evade the whole process. Sir Walter Devereux, William Mulso esq., and Thomas Willoughby had signet letters ordering a halt to all processes against them.[74] Sir Edmund Mulso, Henry Griffith esq., and John Milewater simply found large bonds as security for good behaviour,[75] but for most there was public humiliation, the derision of neighbours, and not a little fear.

Pardons also give some indication of the scope of the support given to York. It cannot be supposed that all general pardons granted have been recorded,[76] nor that all persons involved in the events at Dartford sued for one. None the less, some points of interest emerge. There were 396 pardons issued for persons originating from York's areas of influence. Of these, Stamford, with 139,[77] and Hitchin, with sixty-three, provide much the largest contingents. Only one person each from the estates in Gloucestershire, Wiltshire, Somerset, and Hertfordshire (apart from Hitchin) sought a pardon, and only two from Buckinghamshire. Ludlow produced five, and, indeed, pardons for Shropshire men totalled only forty-eight. York certainly had much larger forces than this in the field, so it must be

---

[71] John Framlingham obtained a pardon on 6 Apr. 1453, found security in Chancery on 18 May, which was notified to the justices, and was dismissed in Oct. (KB27/770 *Rex* m. 130). If this procedure obtained for such as Wynnawey then he would have been aware of the artificial nature of the proceedings against him from the outset, but it does not follow that spectators were similarly aware.

[72] Gairdner (ed.), *Paston Letters*, i. 242.

[73] KB27/773 *Rex* m. 75ʳ. Sir Edmund Mulso was held in the Marshalsea until sureties had been found (KB27/769 *Rex* m. 146ᵛ). If this was standard practice, Maltmann was, in effect, imprisoned for three years.

[74] KB9/34/2 m. 33; KB9/94/2 mm. 37, 51.

[75] *CCR* 1447–54, pp. 400, 442.

[76] Storey, *End of the House of Lancaster*, p. 216, gives a total of 2,430 pardons for the 1452 grant, based on exchequer evidence. The Pardon Roll (C67/40) records 2,485, and it is unlikely that their lists are identical. William Willoughby esq. of Boston found surety before the sheriff and coroner of Lincolnshire (C237/43/276), and the vicar of Erdington arranged security before the sheriff and JPs in Oxfordshire (ibid, n. 60). In neither instance is a *dedimus potestatem* recorded.

[77] The largest group of Stamford men mentioned on a single charge sheet is forty (*CPR* 1452–61, p. 24).

supposed that prosecutions were selective, concentrating on the ringleaders with perhaps a flavour of local score-settling.

None felt the pressure of Beaufort hostility more than Sir William Oldhall, the duke of Somerset rightly regarding the articles against himself as largely a product of Oldhall self-interest. In May 1452 he was brought before the King's Bench.[78] He found surety on 27 June, having obtained a general pardon three days earlier,[79] but no attempt was made to inform the King's Bench of his surety in Chancery, and so he remained under legal duress, and probably remained in sanctuary.[80] He was indicted at Peterborough on 4 November 1452, before the earl of Wiltshire, and at Hitchin on 19 March 1453.[81] Despite his pardon, he was outlawed at the beginning of April 1453,[82] and his property, already much depleted,[83] was available for disposal. Some of it had already been granted away on 13 December 1452, and on 25 March 1453 most of his remaining lands went to the new earl of Pembroke, and his house at Hunsdon to the man who held him his bitterest enemy, the duke of Somerset.[84] In June 1453 Somerset set about Oldhall's attainder, as a supporter of Cade and a counsellor of those who took the field at Dartford.

Duke Richard was physically safer than his chamberlain, but his potential position was no less precarious.[85] He was restricted to his own estates,[86] a restriction to which he adhered. On 2 June 1452 he was at Ludlow,[87] at Bewdley on 28 July,[88] whence he moved on to Fotheringhay by 11 August,[89] probably to avoid the commission of oyer and terminer then in session, in the presence of the king, at Ludlow.[90] By this time, the arbitrators of 13 March having failed to produce a settlement, the king was supposed to have assumed responsibility for an award. A council-meeting was duly held at Coventry in September, but the king simply passed the problem on

[78] KB27/768 *Rex* m. 103ʳ.

[79] *CCR* 1447–54, p. 363; C76/40 m. 30.

[80] KB27/777 *Rex* m. 106ʳ; *CPR* 1446–52, p. 569.

[81] KB9/278/51, 52. He spent Christmas under guard, but on 20 Jan. was at the priory of Pulteney (E404/69/10; LR 14/153).

[82] KB27/771 *Rex* m. 102ʳ.

[83] He had lost his sheep to the escheator of Norfolk on 20 Dec., although friends, led by Edmund Clere esq., tried to recover them (E207/16/5/K13). His mill at Standon was also seriously damaged (SC6/870/5).

[84] *CPR* 1452–61, pp. 34, 103, 111.

[85] He received a general pardon on 3 June (BL Campbell ch. VI 10).

[86] *Croyland Chronicle*, p. 528.   [87] BL Egerton Roll 8364.

[88] SC6/1113/11.   [89] BL Egerton Roll 8364.

[90] Storey, *End of the House of Lancaster*, p. 102.

to a new, and unknown, panel of arbitrators in York's absence.[91] His next known whereabouts was Fotheringhay on 18 December, where Fastolf gave him a loan against a pledge of jewellery.[92] Summoned to the Reading Parliament,[93] it is unlikely that he attended or was encouraged to attend. Certainly, he was absent at Fotheringhay during the second session.[94]

Thomas Ferrers showed sufficient confidence in his lord to have him as a feoffee in November 1452,[95] and William Ashwell, a Northamptonshire yeoman (and blithely ignorant of politics), joined York and the duchess of Somerset in his modest enfeoffment.[96] Such efforts as were made to defend York's property rights were made on his behalf by his councillors, rather than in his name.[97] Thus, Sir Walter Devereux recovered properties mortgaged by the duke in 1449 to the bishop of St Davids,[98] and contested, successfully, the inheritance of the Cornewaille lands in which York had an immediate interest as mesne lord.[99] Devereux was also successful in contesting his rights to four parts of the Dymmock inheritance of Sir Richard Oldcastle.[100]

These were the only successes. The losses outweighed them. Much the most important was the Isle of Wight. Where others found

[91] *Annales*, pp. 770–1. He was at Ramsey (Wilts.) on 6 Sept. (Hist. MSS. Comm. *Various Collections*, i. 342).

[92] Gairdner (ed.), *Paston Letters*, i. 249. The final audits for the south western lands were held at Melbury in Oct. (SC6/1113/11), and for the northern estates at Fotheringhay the following month (SC6/1115/6), and it is possible that York attended these. His son, Richard, was born at Fotheringhay on 2 Oct. and, given the child's name, he may well have been present (*Annales*, p. 771).

[93] *Report on the Dignity of a Peer*, p. 932. He had played no part in the Great Council which met intermittently between 25 Nov. and 25 Dec. 1452 (E404/70/2/52).

[94] He was there on 27 May and 1 June (SC6/850/28; BL Egerton Roll 8364). A servant of his, Thomas Dogge esq., of Wareham (Dorset), was attacked near Baynards Castle on 6 Feb. 1453 (KB9/270A/72), but there is no means of knowing if his master was then in London.

[95] *CCR 1454–61*, p. 324.

[96] York also acted in a property exchange on behalf of John Lynn esq., but this was probably initiated by Lord Cromwell (*CPR 1452–61*, pp. 82, 92).

[97] Given York's vulnerability at this time, it is surprising that there are only two recorded instances of incursions on his property, by Somerset's men at Ware (SC6/1113/11), and by John Ingowe at Rayleigh (KB27/774 *Rex* m. 85).

[98] *CPR 1452–61*, p. 71. Devereux's fidelity had been confirmed at a particularly low moment in Apr. 1452 by the grant of the stewardships of Radnor and Usk (Longleat: Devereux Papers, box 1, n. 6, Oxford: Magdalen College: MacFarlane transcript).

[99] For the return of the inquisition *post mortem* and subsequent case see KB27/774 *Rex* m. 167[r,v]; C44/30/22; *CFR 1452–61*, pp. 30, 32–3.

[100] KB27/771 *Rex* m. 95[r,v]; *CPR 1452–61*, p. 49; *CCR 1447–54*, pp. 384–6.

it possible to negotiate leases for resumed lands, York did not. On 6 September 1452 the lordship of the island was granted to the duke of Somerset.[101] The decision to grant earldoms to the king's uterine brothers cost York the lordships of Builth and Hadleigh, and his London residence of Baynards Castle,[102] all lost originally by resumption. His office of Justice of the Forests south of the Trent he lost to Somerset in July 1453, in a grant mischievously acknowledging Somerset's good service 'on both sides of the sea'.[103]

In the second session of the Reading Parliament, on 12 May, York was deprived of the lieutenancy of Ireland, and it was given, on slightly better terms, to the earl of Wiltshire, now also earl of Ormond.[104] The new lieutenant promptly selected the archbishop of Armagh as his deputy.[105] It is generally supposed that York had maintained links with the province since his departure, although the evidence seems very inconclusive,[106] and in April 1452 it was the English council who had replied to messages from the Lord Deputy,[107] who, anyway, was the real power in Ireland. On Ormond's death there was renewed fighting,[108] which may also have provided a pretext for a change of lieutenant. Shipping for the new lieutenant's passage was ordered on 1 July 1453, but he never sailed.[109]

By July 1453, Somerset's position appeared unassailable. Parliament had proved co-operative, Talbot's Gascon expedition showed every sign of recovering a significant portion of the duchy, to the general satisfaction of public opinion. The Burgundians were soliciting

[101] *CPR* 1452–61, p. 18.   [102] Ibid. 79.   [103] Ibid. 88.

[104] Ibid. 102. For the terms of the indenture see E404/69/168. He was successfully assigned 4,000 marks on 8 July (E403/793; E401/831), having had livery of the earldom of Ormond on 8 May (*CPR* 1452–61, p. 75).

[105] Ibid. 82. The archbishop of Armagh had been studiously uncooperative with York in 1449–50, and his position had been strengthened by the papal suspension of Michael Tregurry of Dublin on 15 Mar. 1453 (*Calendar of Papal Letters x. 1447–55*, p. 251) and Tregurry's subsequent capture by pirates (W. Harris, *The Whole Works of Sir James Ware Concerning Ireland*, 2 vols. (Dublin, 1764), i. 340). A new treasurer of Ireland was appointed on 7 Sept., Sir Henry Bruyn (Lascelles, *Liber Munerum*, i/2, 210).

[106] E. B. Fitzmaurice and A. G. Little, *Materials for the History of the Franciscan Province of Ireland*, British Society of Franciscan Studies, 9 (Manchester, 1920), 203–7, but this seems to rest entirely on *CPR* 1446–52, p. 467. The king, in 1451, had presented directly to the parish church of Trim, already assigned by York to Edmund Oldhall (*Calendar of Papal Letters x. 1447–55*, pp. 229, 233).

[107] E28/82/29.

[108] *Annals of the Four Masters*, ed. O'Donovan, iv. 980 n. u.

[109] *CPR* 1452–61, p. 120.

English support, which further improved the already encouraging
position in Calais, and the murder of the earl of Douglas in Scotland
in February 1452 had sufficiently disturbed Scottish politics for the
northern border to be secure for the time being. The queen's
pregnancy, certain by Easter,[110] gave the prospect of dynastic
security which was essential to longer-term confidence in the
government of Henry VI.

In other circumstances Chastillon might well have swept all this
aside, a convincing demonstration of all York's indictments of
Beaufort incompetence and treasonable mendacity. It was, indeed,
bad news, and it triggered off unrest in the city of London,[111] but no
one thought to shout for the restoration of the duke of York.
Somerset had done his work well. York was too isolated to pose a
threat, even in the aftermath of so grave a military defeat.

It is very doubtful whether Somerset even paused to congratulate
himself on this achievement, for a far more serious problem faced
him. The king, who was proposing on 27 July to go soon on a
campaign of law enforcement in the provinces,[112] had fallen
mentally ill some days later. Without firm evidence as to the nature
of the king's illness, it cannot be said with any confidence whether
his lapse into insanity was persistent, or whether for some days the
unfortunate monarch had periods of lucidity. In either case, the
immediate, and not unreasonable, reaction in the early days of
August must have been to wait and see. The king's condition was,
therefore, carefully concealed, initially to avoid needless public
alarm, but, with the news of Chastillon circulating, it became a
matter of the utmost importance that as much time as possible
should elapse before the king's condition became public knowledge.
The duke of Somerset's political future depended on the king's
recovery.

Despite the need for secrecy, it would have been prudent for him
to have attempted, albeit covertly, to draw other peers into the
regime in the summer months. No such attempt was made.
Conciliar warrants for nine days of July survive,[113] showing
Somerset absent only on 18 July, and the chancellor only on the

[110] The queen spent a night in Apr. in Hitchin with the duchess of York
(BL Egerton Roll 8364; Davis (ed.), *Paston Letters*, ii. 248).
[111] *Benet's Chronicle*, p. 209, says the news arrived in early Aug.
[112] Wolffe, *Henry VI*, p. 270.
[113] E28/83/23, 24, 26, 28, 29, 31, 33, 34, 37; nos. 24 and 34 are printed in *PPC* vi.
143.

following day. The treasurer was absent twice (13 and 18 July), but, surprisingly, the privy seal was present only three times. Others attending were the bishop of Winchester and Thomas Thorpe, on five occasions, Lord Dudley and the Prior of St Johns, on three, and the dean of St Severins, twice, with the earl of Warwick attending on 10 July, and the earl of Salisbury on 18 July.[114] Councils were rarely well attended in the summer months, but this list of councillors was, in the circumstances, too narrow, and Somerset allowed this unsatisfactory position to deteriorate further in August.

Of the ten warrants surviving for that month, the treasurer appears on all, the dean of St Severins and Thorpe on eight, Dudley on 1 August, but not thereafter, and the prior of St Johns twice, both on 10 August.[115] No one else appears, and the change is as striking as it is intriguing. In effect, the exchequer was struggling to maintain some degree of support for the Gascon expedition,[116] the rest of the administration retreated.[117]

Clearly, this state of affairs could not be indefinitely protracted, but there was every reason to delay if possible until the queen was delivered, and her physical condition was, no doubt, of as much concern to Somerset as the king's mental state.[118] On the other hand, delay only emphasized the extent of the king's sickness, for the longer he was ill the less significant any signs of recovery would be. The king would have not only to recover, but to stay sane for a reasonable period, in order to give real conviction to the possibility of resumed personal rule.[119] The queen gave birth to a son on

[114] On 21 July the queen received a major charter of privileges giving her a remarkable administrative autonomy on her estates. The charter was witnessed by the chancellor, treasurer, privy seal, the archbishop of York, the bishops of London and Worcester, the dukes of Exeter and Somerset, the earl of Wiltshire, Lords Cromwell and Dudley, 'and others' (*CPR* 1452–61, pp. 114–16). After this meeting, business was largely concerned with the relief of Gascony and the problems of the north.

[115] E28/83/48, 49, 52–4, 56–9 (numbers 49 and 52 carry no year, but are almost certainly of this sequence); *PPC* vi. 152.

[116] Success was very limited. Lord Camoys was never paid (M. G. A. Vale, 'The Last Years of English Gascony, 1451–1453' *TRHS* 5th ser. 19 (1969), 135 n. 7).

[117] Messengers passed between the council and the court, at Clarendon (E403/795 m. 2).

[118] The queen had acquired a 'Council House' in Westminster in July (*CFR* 1452–61, p. 35). Somerset's appointment as constable of Windsor Castle was due to lapse at Michaelmas 1453 (PSO1/17/880).

[119] The presentation of the infant prince of Wales to the king by the duke of Buckingham shows that the verdict of physicians on the king's sanity was of no constitutional significance. In an age of only rudimentary psychology their verdict

13 October, and at the christening Somerset stood as godfather. But it was impossible to delay much longer. The decision to summon a Great Council was made, though when, and by whom, is unknown. Initially, it was intended to exclude York, but on 23 October a group of peers, Somerset and the chancellor being absent, decided to send for him through the agency of Sir Thomas Tyrell. Tyrell was instructed to say that the council was summoned 'to sette rest and union betwixt the lords of this lande'. The political fuse was fired with the next sentence, 'And for asmuch as there hath bee and yit as it is supposed is variance betwixt hym [York] and sum othre of the lords'.[120] The duke of York was to be allowed to press his charges against Somerset.

would count for little unless the peers of the realm were also individually convinced. For evidence that Henry's condition varied see Wolffe, *Henry VI*, pp. 271–3.

[120] *PPC* vi. 163.

6

THE FIRST PROTECTORATE

The summons to Duke Richard of York ran counter to a strong political tide. Power had rested with the duke of Somerset since 1451, and after Dartford he had virtually monopolized it. That power was now to be challenged, as the king's councillors were fully aware. Legitimacy, practical politics, the duke of York's inexorable arrival at the forthcoming session of Parliament, all demanded a solution, and these considerations, rather than personal favour, determined the council's invitation. Of the four laymen who signed the warrant, Worcester, the prior of St Johns, Sudeley, and Dudley, the last two had profited appreciably in the Somerset years, Prior Botiller's attitude is unknown, and Worcester, perhaps indifferent to Somerset, is best regarded as a willing servant of the king. Of the five bishops, three were king's men, Wainflete, Chedworth, and Lowe, and one was a former Suffolk protégé, now the queen's confessor, Walter Lyhert. The fifth, Richard Beauchamp of Salisbury, may have had some sympathy with York, but it is impossible to see how such a group could agree to summon York other than on grounds of legitimate right.

As the instruction to Tyrell shows, they were very well aware that their decision, whatever its basis might be in constitutional propriety, had profound implications for the duke of Somerset. Their hope was that the council could come to some agreement with both York and Somerset, in order to allow the kingdom to be governed. It is difficult to determine whether this was a sensible programme in the circumstances, albeit, in the event, sadly over-optimistic.

Where Tyrell found the duke of York is uncertain; Fotheringhay most probably.[1] He arrived in London on 12 November[2] with a

---

[1] York was at Stamford on 30 July, possibly to hamper an impending commission into recent treasons there (BL Egerton Roll 8364; *CPR* 1452–61, p. 124). A messenger, John Barbour, was paid on 5 Dec. for taking privy-seal letters to the duke at Fotheringhay, and it is likely that Tyrell found him there (E403/795).

[2] *Benet's Chronicle*, p. 210. There was a council meeting on 31 Oct., but no further

modest entourage, as requested. With him came the duke of
Norfolk, who immediately appealed Somerset of treason.[3] Some
such development had probably been anticipated, but originating
from York, and so giving grounds for hope of a possible accommodation between him and Somerset. Norfolk's intervention made
this much more difficult to organize, and gave York the political
advantage of the public support of another great lord. York
sustained the pressure by demanding, in effect, the liberty of
Oldhall, convicted of treason by the Reading Parliament.[4] Had the
council conceded this, it would, by implication, have allowed the
possible integrity of Oldhall's actions, and the doubtful legality of
those of Somerset, the subject of the 1452 charges.

By 30 November there were at least forty-six peers in London,
and, at a Great Council meeting, they jointly agreed to suppress
lawlessness and not to sustain each other in any lawless act. To this
each swore in turn.[5] In so doing, they accepted the authority of the
king's council henceforth to command attendance, and agreed to
co-operate in the execution of conciliar warrants.

The next problem was to settle the scope of conciliar authority
and, from York's point of view, to secure for himself a significant
role in such a body. Discussion to this end took place on 5 December
and, probably informally, before. The council which foregathered in
the star chamber on that day was, for the most part, similar to the one
which had agreed on 21 November to the restoration of York's
councillors. Missing were the bishops of Carlisle and St Davids, the
earls of Shrewsbury and Wiltshire, and the lords Sudeley and
Berners, with, as a newcomer, Lord Scales. Absence had, therefore,
pushed the balance away from the Beaufort interest, though not
necessarily towards York.

The agreement, subscribed to by only fourteen of those present,
was that the council would act, but only in substantial and necessary
matters essential to the 'pollytyque rule and gouerance of this his
[i.e. the king's] land and to the observaunce and kepynge of his lawes
as the nessecytye asketh and requyerethe'.[6] No attempt was made to

---

details are known (C81/1546/70). York probably occupied the bishop of Salisbury's
house (BL Egerton Roll 8364).

[3] *Benet's Chronicle*, p. 210.

[4] *CPR* 1452–61, p. 143; C49/53/13.

[5] R. A. Griffiths', 'The King's Council and the First Protectorate of the Duke of
York', *EHR* 99 (1984), 77–8.

[6] Ibid. pp. 78–9.

redefine council membership, so the effect of this decision was to entrust only the powers necessary to prevent a complete breakdown to a body whose composition had been for the most part determined in the days of York's eclipse.

For York this was unhelpful. Thus far, he had managed to remove Somerset, and to be involved in a decision-making process which recognized his importance in the circumstances of the king's illness, but was reluctant to give substantial expression to that recognition. Delay could only give others, including Somerset, a chance to enter the fray. What York may well have overlooked was the possibility that the household might yet become a serious threat in its own right. Certainly, he seems to have taken no steps to contain its influence, and it is his signature which stands at the head of the secular peers on a warrant of 6 December making hasty provision for the household's immediate needs.[7]

On the day York had arrived in London, Parliament had been prorogued at Reading, to meet again at Westminster on 14 February. Any further decisions on the form of government during Henry's illness would certainly be deferred until then, an unnecessarily extended delay. Some, no doubt, hoped for Henry's recovery more speedily than others.

It having been agreed that the council should do little more than keep the wheels of government turning, that was what happened. Between 23 November and 14 February forty-eight items passed under the great seal, of which twelve were passed in the first week in December, and another twelve in the ten days before Parliament reassembled, the last two weeks in December and the first three in January seeing only nine patents enrolled.[8] Such decisions as were being taken were modest, and, seemingly, at the initiative of the chancellor.

An active council can once more be identified on 6 February, when fourteen councillors warranted a decision, or rather a non-decision (the point is not without significance) concerning the lieutenancy of Ireland. By 9 February the number had risen by four to eighteen, the newcomers being the bishop of Hereford, the dukes

[7] *PPC* vi. 164. This was followed by a thorough scrutiny of the state of the exchequer (E401/795).

[8] *CPR* 1452–61, p. 141 ff. The totals exclude pardons for non-appearance, as these were issued automatically on receipt of the chief justice's certificate and, therefore, bear no relation to conciliar business. Patents issued by bill of the treasurer or chief butler are excluded for the same reason.

of York and Norfolk, the earl of Worcester, Viscount Beaumont, and the lords Stourton and Dudley. The earls of Warwick and Salisbury, present on the sixth, were not listed on the ninth, presumably because the patent was in their favour.[9] The absence of Lord Greystoke, also present on the sixth, is inexplicable. Two warrants of 13 February survive, carrying nineteen and twenty-seven names respectively. Of the nineteen, the bishops of Durham, Norwich, and Salisbury are new, along with the earls of Oxford and Shrewsbury, Lords Berners, Fauconberg, Greystoke, and FitzHugh, with the two archbishops, Beaumont, the prior of St Johns, Cromwell, and Dudley being the absentees.[10] Not surprisingly, it is the more important warrant of 13 February which carries the larger number of signatures, twenty-six in all.[11] Peers present on earlier warrants but not signatories to this warrant were the dukes of York and Norfolk, the prior of St Johns, and Lords Cromwell and Fauconberg.

Clearly, the peers were assembling for the parliamentary session scheduled to start on the fourteenth, but, despite the fact that Henry had now been ill for some six months, they showed themselves on the eve of parliament still very reluctant to provide a stable basis for the government of the realm. The queen's intervention troubled them most. John Stodeley reported, on 19 January, that she had submitted a bill of five articles, in effect demanding the powers of a regent, together with sufficient livelihood for the king, the Prince Edward, and herself.[12] The remainder of Stodeley's letter shows something of what was intended—the creation of a household government having the role of military protector of the king and prince, with sufficient income to sustain its authority and a royal power to be exercized on its behalf by the queen.

York could not have anticipated this. Margaret of Anjou had hitherto been a politically neutral figure, if anything sympathetic to

---

[9] C81/1546/73, 74. The dukes would appear to have been in London by 6 Feb. (*Benet's Chronicle*, p. 211), though enquiries were being made on 13 Feb., by the duchess of Suffolk, about Norfolk's preparations for going to London (BL Egerton Roll 8779; *CCR* 1447–54, p. 476).

[10] C81/1546/75. This warrant related to the replacement of the treasury keys lost by the earl of Warwick. His claim to the Beauchamp chamberlainship may lie behind this order.

[11] C81/1546/76. The two archbishops, London, Winchester, Ely, Norwich, Hereford, Salisbury, Lincoln, and Durham, the earls of Salisbury, Warwick, Devon, Worcester, Oxford, and Shrewsbury, Viscount Beaumont and Lords Greystock, Grey of Ruthvin, FitzHugh, Dudley, Clinton, Fitzwarin, Stourton, Scrope, and Berners.

[12] Gairdner (ed.), *Paston Letters*, ii. 297.

York, and she had had little opportunity, and probably little inclination, to intervene in the political crisis of the autumn months, having given birth on 13 October. Her motives for intervening in January can only be matter for speculation, but concern for Somerset does not seem to have been one of them. Rather, she seems to have been persuaded that the duke of York was a threat to the inheritance of her child. This made English politics yet more fraught. Thus far, events could be satisfactorily described by contemporaries in terms of the competition of two dukes for influence over the king. Margaret of Anjou's intervention implied that the dynasty itself was under threat. As Stodeley reports, the atmosphere was already very tense a full month before parliament was due to reassemble.

If anyone was in control of events it was Cardinal Kemp. He had contrived the absence of the privy seal, M. Thomas Lisieux, from all council meetings since Christmas,[13] thereby denying the executive powers of the privy seal to the council, and ensuring that warranty over the great seal was the only guarantee of legitimacy immediately available to the council. Kemp's powers of procrastination were, therefore, considerable, and, in the hopes, perhaps, of the king's early recovery, he used them.

It was Kemp who moved the major item of business of 13 February 'to whom the kinges power sholde be committed for the holding of the[14] at this tyme'.[15] As Parliament was due to assemble the following day, the question had clearly been deferred to the last possible moment,[16] and the terms of the question were intended to allow only the holding of Parliament, the powers of prorogation and dissolution being retained by the king's council. But the warrant itself, as it now survives, shows that Kemp's ploy to retain conciliar control over Parliament had failed, at least initially, for the councillors present gave 'the kinges power' to the duke of York and added the codicil: 'and to proceede ende and dissolve the

---

[13] That Lisieux was not out of favour with the council is shown by their consideration for him on 2 Jan., and his absence from the surviving lists might well be ascribed to their limited number, were it not for the major business discussed on 9 and 13 Feb. Moreover, the bill of 9 Feb. was noted as having been received by the chancellor the following day, so it is clear that Lisieux was discharging his responsibilities efficiently and promptly (*CPR 1452–61*, p. 152; C81/1546/74).

[14] MS damaged.

[15] C81/1546/76.

[16] Four days had been allowed in 1422 (J. S. Roskell, 'The Office and Dignity of Protector of England with Special Reference to its Origins', *EHR* 68 (1953), 197.

'said parlement and to do all thyng that shalbe necessairie thereto or to any of the premysses'.[17] York was thereby given complete discretion, only to lose it thanks to Kemp's manipulations, for, when the commission duly appeared over the great seal dissolution of Parliament was expressly reserved to the council.[18]

Despite Kemp's obstruction, York had made a significant gain. Whether the queen's bill for a regency was discussed at this time is unknown. It may well have been thought proper to present it to Parliament.[19] But this first vote on the constitutional deadlock had been in York's favour. This was important to York not just in its own right but because, although the novelty of the queen's proposition could be relied upon to discourage the more conservative peers, the Lower House had the highest proportion of household members in it of the reign.[20] This had shown itself in the Commons' willingness to support Somerset's initiatives in the Reading session, and, from York's point of view, most discouragingly, they had elected a known Beaufort associate, Thomas Thorpe, as their speaker. Recognizing the difficulties with which this would present him, York had been pressing a lawsuit against Thorpe even before Parliament had reassembled.[21]

At some time unstated, in the king's thirty-first year, Thorpe had detained property of the duke's at the London house of the bishop of Durham, allegedly to the value of £2,000.[22] York had brought an action in the previous Michaelmas Term,[23] and had obtained

[17] C81/1546/76.

[18] Rymer, *Foedera*, xi. 344. The text is almost a verbatim transcript, *mutatis mutandis*, of the commission given to Gloucester on 6 Nov. 1422 (*Rot. Parl.* iv. 169). The clause restricting York's authority is identical to the 1422 text. Only Cromwell survived of the 1422 council, and he was absent on 13 Feb.

[19] The queen arrived in London on 20 Feb. (Barron, 'London and the Crown', pp. 94 and 107 n. 42).

[20] J. S. Roskell, *The Commons and their Speakers in English Parliaments 1376–1523* (Manchester, 1965), 248; Wolffe, *Henry VI*, p. 217. Sections of the community were critical of the queen (KB9/273) m. 8), and her failure to bring a dowry still rankled (*Calendar of State Papers, Milan* ed. A. B. Hinds, (1912), i. 18–19).

[21] Roskell, *The Commons and their Speakers*, p. 250; 'Thomas Thorpe, Speaker in the Parliament of 1453–4', *Nottingham Medieval Studies*, 5 (1963), 93–5.

[22] The similarity of these charges and those levied against Oldhall for having stolen Somerset's property at Blackfriars in 1450 excites suspicions of a quid pro quo.

[23] Roskell, 'Thomas Thorpe', believes that the court action took place soon after 19 Jan., but, on balance, this seems less probable, as it would have brought the trial into a new law-term, a point not mentioned in York's very careful bill to the Lords on the matter, but one of sufficient administrative importance to merit mention (*Rot. Parl.* v. 239). Thorpe's articles against the duke, noted by Stodeley on 19 Jan., might, therefore, have been the substance of a petition to the House of Commons.

judgement against Thorpe, who was duly committed to the Fleet. It was of wider political importance to York that he should stay there, but this was a matter of some constitutional delicacy, and Thorpe was reportedly devising articles against the duke in January.[24]

When Parliament assembled, on 14 February, the Commons agreed among themselves to send a delegation to the Lords to know the cause of the continued detention of the speaker. In reply, York's council presented a petition on the following day to the Lords, arguing that the case had been brought and settled during a Parliamentary vacation and did not, therefore, infringe on the liberties of Parliament. The judges to whom the Lords turned concurred, Fortescue (*CJ*) propounding the judgment that there was no general *supercedeas* which would automatically override the legal capacity of a lower court, and that for parliamentary privilege to be effective in a lower court a writ of *supercedeas* had to be specifically moved.[25] Thorpe stayed in the Fleet. The Commons proceeded to elect as their new speaker Sir Thomas Charlton, a household servant, distantly related to the Nevilles,[26] possibly more closely related to York.[27] The connection should not, however, be overstressed, as there were several other members with much closer ties to Neville or York. Charlton's election disposed of a political enemy, but gave York no clear lever in the Commons.

It was important, too, that Somerset should stay in the Tower. He had been arrested on 23 November, but the progress of the case against him is now impossible to reconstruct. The sole surviving document is a bill put up by the duke of Norfolk to the Lords, demanding that they speed things up.[28] He wanted two distinct and separate trials, by French law for alleged treasons in France, and by English law for English misdeeds. It was his belief that Somerset stood condemned as a traitor should any one charge be established, and the way in which these charges are alluded to gives the impression that they were substantially those presented at Dartford. The main thrust of Norfolk's demand was, however, the separate trial for English and French crimes.

How this could have been done is difficult now to determine, and may have been no less so then. Was Norfolk angling for York to be

---

[24] Gairdner (ed.), *Paston Letters*, ii. 296. [25] *Rot. Parl.* v. 239–40.

[26] Roskell, *The Commons and their Speakers*, p. 255.

[27] If, that is, he was related to the Charlton who fought at Verneuil 'qui maritavit Amasiam ducis Ebor' (William Worcester, *Itineraries* , ed. J. Harvey Oxford, 1969), 4).

[28] Gairdner (ed.), *Paston Letters*, ii. 290–2.

given authority in France? One possible consequence was that Cardinal Kemp could be kept away from any 'French' trial, which would presumably be conducted by those with French peerages. That this may not be mere supposition is suggested by an entry in one chronicle, that Kemp had done his best to prevent Somerset's imprisonment, and that he subsequently became the target of the active hostility of the duke of Norfolk.[29] Tentatively, this might be dated to mid-January.[30] Wisely, the council did not release Somerset for the new parliamentary session, but they also took no further action against him. Frustrated, Norfolk seems to have started to press for Kemp's dismissal.[31]

With Somerset in the Tower and a new speaker in the Commons, York could now set about further consolidation of his position, which for the present depended entirely on Parliament continuing in session. There is no record of business for thirteen days, until on 28 February it was agreed to fine absent lords.[32] This act may indicate a feeling amongst the lords that they would soon have to take some difficult decisions, responsiblity for which they would prefer to share as broadly as possible. If this be allowed, then it would follow that, as yet, there had been no decision over the queen's bill for a regency.

The first indications of political movement surface on 9 March when Lord Cromwell introduced a bill against the duke of Exeter.[33] As the duke was a known ally of the Percy family, any settlement of this quarrel would at once establish York's authority in relation to Henry Holland, and determine the interest of the Neville earls. The punitive elements of the bill were to be debated on 11 or 12 March, but the matter was not settled until 20 March when judgment was given in Cromwell's favour.

[29] Giles, *Chronicon Angliae*, p. 44.

[30] Stodeley's news-letter, very probably intended for the duke of Norfolk, shows Kemp in need of a retinue for self-protection, and considerable tensions between duke and archbishop (Gairdner (ed.), *Paston Letters*, ii. 295–9).

[31] William Worcester, *Itineraries*, ed. Harvey, p. 153.   [32] *Rot. Parl.* v. 248.

[33] For the petition and its context see R. A. Griffiths, 'Local Rivalries and National Politics: The Percies, the Nevilles, and the Duke of Exeter, 1452–55', *Speculum*, 43 (1968), 608. There may have been a gesture of support for Cromwell in the commission of 23 Feb. to try Robert Collinson (*CPR* 1452–61, p. 171). The mechanics whereby York engineered this success are uncertained. Business seems to have been intiated in the council and only then passed on to the Upper House. How the two are to be reliably distinguished is unclear. A council meeting is recorded on 2 Mar. (C81/1546/77), five peers endorsed a warrant on 13., twenty-eight on the fifteenth (*PPC* vi. 166–7).

Between 9 and 20 March, therefore, York made significant political progress. This was further signalled in the events of 14 and 15 march. On 14 March the earl of Devon was formally indicted of high treason before the duke of Buckingham, acting as Steward, though by whose authority is unclear. Devon was acquitted, probably on the same day. York, who had been implicated in the indictments made against Devon, seized the opportunity to make a public declaration of allegiance, and to have all the peers then present recite simultaneously an agreed formula, accepting his status as 'true and feithfull Liegeman to the Kyng oure Soverain Lord'.[34]

On 15 March the infant Edward was created Prince of Wales.[35] York, a signatory to the council warrant initiating the act, may have viewed this development with mixed feelings. It demonstrated a willingness of the lords to settle matters of substantial constitutional importance, in this instance one which was an essential preliminary to any interim settlement of government before the prince should come of age. The drawback was, for York, that, whatever form the final settlement might take, authority over the principality of Wales would rest with the council of the prince.

While the Lords moved tentatively towards a constitutional settlement, the Commons debated a request of the chancellor, presented on 13 March, for a grant of £40,000. After six days of discussion the Commons declined to make any further vote of taxation, pointing out that they had already been notably generous, and that they were still awaiting the one thing closest to their hearts since the start of the first session, a sad and substantial council.[36]

The refusal of taxation was an uncomfortable development for York, for it was not outwith the bounds of possibility that Parliament would now be dissolved, and affairs conducted by a royal council after the manner of the minority of Richard II. Surviving records show no clear direction of parliamentary business after the Commons reply. It was the death of Cardinal Kemp which galvanized English politics. In any settlement of government there had to be a chancellor, and undue delay was unthinkable. This could also be to York's advantage, and privately he cannot have grieved over-much at the death of a skilled bureaucrat and prince of the

[34] *Rot. Parl.* v. 250; *Benet's Chronicle*, p. 211.
[35] *CPR 1452–61*, p. 171; *Calendar of Charter Rolls 1427–1516*, p. 127.
[36] *Rot. Parl.* v. 240.

Church, whose authority had been so effectively wielded in restraint of his ambitions.

Kemp died on 22 March. The following day the Lords sent a substantial deputation to the king. Above all else, the Lords wanted a sign of recovery, and their instructions to the deputation were to determine definitively whether the king's sickness endured. It did. Despite three pressing attempts to induce Henry to give some sort of sign, the king gave none. This they reported to the Lords on 25 March. There was no alternative. A chancellor would have to be appointed by the Lords.[37]

It is not now possible to explain satisfactorily why, on 27 March, the Lords elected Duke Richard of York Protector of the Realm and Chief Councillor.[38] It may be sufficient to say that Kemp was no longer there to stop it.[39] On the day after his election as protector, he submitted articles for the discharge of his new office.[40] He desired an act of Parliament declaring his election, which was accepted, the precedent of 1422 being explicitly cited. The Lords agreed to support him, giving him all due, lawful, and reasonable assistance in matters of the public good. This left the Lords the final arbiters of what was for the 'wele of the Kyng and of his said land'. To a request for a definition of York's authority as chief councillor of the king the reply again turned to the limitations imposed in 1422, allowing only a personal title, and a duty to attend to the defence of the realm against enemies or rebels. On the matter of remuneration, the council proposed to consult further with the duke, an interesting reply, as there was already a precedent for this in 1422. The fifth and final question was clumsy, desiring that the king's councillors, when chosen, would accept like responsibilities. If allowed, this would have restricted the scope of the council, and might have left open a possible interpretation that the council had defined its powers at York's request. The question was, understandably, evaded.

On 2 April Richard Neville, earl of Salisbury, succeeded Cardinal Kemp as chancellor. As a secular peer, he was an unlikely candidate, despite his Beaufort lineage, and his selection in such sensitive political circumstances was little short of sensational. The Neville interest was not necessarily inclined to York, despite the fact that

[37] *Rot. Parl.* v. 240–2; Griffiths, *Reign of Henry VI*, pp. 724–5.
[38] *Rot. Parl.* v. 242.
[39] *Benet's Chronicle*, p. 211: 'capitalis amicus . . . ducis Somersetie'.
[40] *Rot. Parl.* v. 242.

York was married to Salisbury's sister. The earl's political interest was set in the broad context of the confiscation of the Percy estates by Henry IV and, more recently, the internal squabbles in the Neville family consequent on Earl Ralph's second marriage to Joan Beaufort. Neither could Edmund Beaufort be viewed with detachment by Salisbury, as Beaufort was pursuing the Beauchamp inheritance to which Salisbury's eldest son enjoyed the substantial claim.

Both disputes had been pursued violently in recent months, and both had wide geographic remit. South Wales had seen violent skirmishing between Somerset and Warwick, and the northern shires were close to a civil war in a Percy–Neville dispute which had implications for the stability of the east Midlands, thanks to the duke of Exeter's interest.[41] Already, Parliament, at York's prompting, had exonerated Courtney. The rapid promotion of the Neville interest extended the prospects of partisan justice from the south west into Wales, the east Midlands, and into the north. It is difficult to believe that it was in the best interests of the nation that the earl of Salisbury should hold the great seal.[42]

The following day, 3 April, the duke of York took on himself the office of protector, by act of Parliament, for so long as it pleased the king, saving that, when Prince Edward should reach years of discretion, he might, should he so choose, assume the dignity and title himself. The proviso in favour of Prince Edward was, as it were, constitutional common sense. The decision that York should hold office during pleasure gave the royal council the ultimate power to dismiss him.

On the same day as York was admitted to office, most of the lords who were to be of the king's council assembled in the star chamber.[43] It was intended to be a balanced group, both in dignity and political interest—two dukes, Norfolk and Buckingham, the archbishop of York and five other bishops,[44] five earls,[45] the five most senior barons,[46] with Sir Thomas Stanley, John Say esq., and the Dean of

---

[41] Wolffe, *Henry VI*, pp. 268–9; Griffiths, 'Local Rivalries and National Politics', p. 606.   [42] Griffiths, *Reign of Henry VI*, p. 727.

[43] Griffiths, 'The King's Council and the First Protectorate', pp. 79–81.

[44] Winchester, Worcester, Norwich, Lincoln, and Chester. Worcester declined to serve.

[45] Salisbury, Warwick, Oxford, Shrewsbury, and Worcester.

[46] Viscounts Bourchier and Beaumont, the prior of St Johns, Cromwell, and Scales.

St Severins. It may reasonably be supposed that it was the intention that the new archbishop of Canterbury would be a member, once in possession of his see.[47] It is also very probable that three other barons, Sudeley, Dudley, and Stourton were intended to be members, but were unable to attend.[48]

Sir Thomas Stanley's ingenuous observation to this first meeting, that he thought himself merely a conciliar errand-boy, need not be taken too seriously. At a practical level, the advice of the junior members would be valuable. Stanley's suspicion that real power was to be found amongst the secular lords was, however, reasonable. Of the barons, Beaumont and Scales were Margaret of Anjou's servants,[49] and Bourchier, although York's brother-in-law, is not generally recognized as especially biased towards the duke.[50] The prior of St Johns was content to serve any administration. Cromwell, pleading, with some cause, sickness and old age, was reluctant to be included, but was pressed to serve. A firm opponent of Holland and Percy, his interests might intermittently coincide with those of York. The other barons were servants long trusted by the king himself.

There was more evident sympathy for York among the earls. The two Nevilles stood to benefit singularly from the protectorate. By the same token, the earl of Shrewsbury did not. Worcester had little direct interest to press, and, had he not been the treasurer , might well have been passed over in favour of the senior earl, Pembroke. Oxford could be expected to keep a wary eye on the household, and also on the duke of Norfolk.

The episcopal bench was less sympathetic. Only Carpenter of Worcester could be regarded as neutral, and he declined to serve. The others were hostile; Wainflete, Boulers, and Booth especially so. The duke of Norfolk had thus far been a vociferous supporter of his uncle of York. In other circumstances, the duke of Exeter might have been appointed in his stead. Buckingham, steady and loyal, and

---

[47] But cf. Griffiths, 'The King's Council and the First Protectorate', p. 77, who believes him to be a further addition.

[48] The first writ instructing this council to attend after the dissolution of Parliament includes these three (*PPC* vi. 174–5).

[49] Myers, 'Household of Margaret of Anjou', p. 96; 'Jewels of Margaret of Anjou', p. 125.

[50] The most sustained study of the Bourchiers accepts that York and Bourchier were initially sympathetic, but that in the 1450s the viscount's particular regard was for Humphrey duke of Buckingham (Woodger, 'Henry Earl of Essex', pp. 48, 60).

close to the Bourchiers, provided the serious prospect of good governance.

The lords of the council were already aware that Thomas Bourchier of Ely was to be the next primate, as the decision to promote him had been taken in the Lords, with Commons approval, on 30 March.[51] On the day York was made protector, the priory at Christ Church set in motion the procedure for electing a new archbishop.[52] On 6 April the temporalities were entrusted to a predominantly Bourchier group, and on the ninth, licence to elect was granted by the Lords.[53] This passed smoothly. There was a fight, however, over the bishopric he vacated, Ely. The Nevilles pressed the claims of George Neville, but it went to William Gray.

The Upper House next turned its attention to finance, more particularly to defence and the king's household. The refusal of the Commons to vote a substantial subsidy in February was mollified on 3 April, when they allowed the appropriation of tonnage and poundage for three years for the keeping of the seas, and the government was further licenced, on 16 April, to negotiate a loan against the security of this appropriation.[54] An act for the assignment of revenues to the household was passed on 17 April. Customs revenues aside, the act focused on the principality of Wales and the duchy of Cornwall, assigning £1,200 from these sources.[55] In effect, this restored the household income of the king, queen, and prince, approximately, to the level at which it stood before Edward was confirmed in the principality. The revenues of the earldom of Chester and duchy of Lancaster were not mentioned.[56]

Such was the logic of York's charges against Somerset, that he was obliged to assume the lieutenancy of Calais. Not that he was unwilling, but it was likely to prove difficult. As Dr Harriss has shown, Somerset's standing with the Calais garrison was very good, and York would have to offer considerable inducements if they were to admit him.[57] The key was the Calais Staple, but York had found it difficult during the session to establish a firm relation with the wool

---

[51] *PPC* vi. 168. [52] Ibid. 170.

[53] *CPR* 1452–61, p. 154; Rymer, *Foedera*, xi. 347.

[54] *Rot. Parl.* v. 244–5. On 21 Apr. commissioners were instructed to negotiate a loan against this security for the defence of Calais (*CPR* 1452–61, p. 148).

[55] *Rot. Parl.* v. 246.

[56] On 31 May the feoffees of the duchy of Lancaster were instructed to pay £1,000 into the household (E28/84/36).

[57] Harriss, 'Struggle for Calais', pp. 33–5.

interest, which was engaged in an internecine feud over the Partition Ordinance of 1429.[58] His decision to negotiate directly with the mayor of the Staple, Robert White, settled the partition issue temporarily, and York had, by the dissolution of Parliament, emerged with sufficient secure credit from the Staplers to start negotiations with the soldiers themselves.

Arbitrary seizure of their wool by the garrison in May forced the Staplers into more substantial co-operation with the protector, but, as such co-operation could only take the form of loans secured against the wool customs, aid from the Staple was likely to reflect the Staple's judgement of the political stability of the protectorate. It would be foolish to lend a large sum repayable over an extended term when the life of the protectorate could, with Henry's recovery, be short. York tried diligently to secure control of Calais throughout May and June, and he had a loyal aide in Viscount Bourchier, who, by hard cash and hard bargaining, brought York reasonable prospects of securing admission, such that on 17 July he was able to indent as captain.[59]

The other problem, Ireland, was rather easier. Already, on 6 February, the council had been persuaded to suspend assignments for its defence until the lieutenancy had been clarified, this despite the earl of Wiltshire's presence in the chamber.[60] The appointment of Rowland FitzEustace, Wiltshire's critic, as treasurer of Ireland, on 9 February,[61] suggests some confidence on York's part, but, judging from the terms of the final agreement of 15 April,[62] the council did

---

[58] *Rot. Parl.* v. 256. For the background see Thielemans, *Bourgogne et Angleterre*, p. 171; T. H. Lloyd, *The English Wool Trade in the Middle Ages* (Cambridge, 1977), 274; J. H. Munro, *Wool, Cloth, and Gold* (Toronto, 1972), 147.

[59] Harriss, 'Struggle for Calais', pp. 35–7. Much indirect effort was also expended to this end, e.g. the appointment of a new, more sympathetic, commission to inquire *post mortem* into the lands of Elizabeth Lady Strange, whose son John was son-in-law to Lord Rivers (*CPR* 1452–61, p. 169; M. Hicks 'The Changing Role of the Wydevilles in Yorkist Politics to 1483', in Ross (ed.), *Patronage, Pedigree, and Power*, p. 63), and the support given by York to Robert White over the issue of London tithes (*Calendar of Papal Letters x. 1447–65*, pp. 165–6; Sharpe, *Letter Book K*, p. 361).

[60] C81/1546/73; E28/84-1; *PPC* vi. 172. The earl of Wiltshire had been described as lieutenant only a fortnight earlier, in a letter of complaint from the FitzEustaces. The letter is dated 23 Jan. The chronology is a little tight, but it may be this letter which precipitated the conciliar debate (BL Cotton Charter IV n. 35).

[61] Lascelles, *Liber Munerum*, i./2, 210.

[62] *PPC* vi. 173. For a very brief discussion of these events see H. Wood, 'Two Chief Governors of Ireland at the Same Time', *Journal of the Royal Society of Antiquaries of Ireland*, 58 (1928), 270–1.

not settle the matter, but left it to the claimants to sort out themselves. York won.[63]

Parliament was dissolved some time between 17 and 21 April, and it was intended that the continual council should first meet on 6 May.[64] When invited to assume the responsibility of council membership, the nominees had been for the most part cautious. They were publicly uneasy about their health, about the commitment to persistent attendance, and about their rights to freedom of access, speech, and departure.[65] Beaumont was unenthusiastic on 3 April, and is not recorded as attending any council meeting before 1 July. Boulers of Coventry and Lichfield was merely cautious on 3 April, but he, too, made no subsequent appearance, failing even to attend the proposed Great Council in June. The two dukes bemoaned their ill-health, which evidently overcame Norfolk at the end of May, but Buckingham managed an erratic attendance throughout the period to early July. Cromwell, who may well have been sick, did not attend, nor did Sudeley. Scales, who declaimed on 3 April that 'he would not contyneally attend', did not do so at all. The earls of Shrewsbury and Warwick did not appear, perhaps through mutual antipathy, perhaps because of naval responsibilities. Oxford managed the second recorded meeting, but no other. The backbone of decison-making was the episcopal bench, Wainflete in particular, together with the chancellor and the treasurer. The other regular attenders were the prior of St Johns, Bourchier, Stourton, and Dudley.[66]

Wherever possible, it was to members of the continual council that the more substantial executive responsibilities were entrusted. Thus, four of the five earls responsible for the keeping of the seas were council members, Scales was ordered to quell the rioting directed against the king's new college in Cambridge,[67] and the Calais negotiations were entrusted to Bourchier. Immediately after Parliament, it was the archbishop of York who travelled north to

---

[63] In July 1457 he was paid as lieutenant, by force of his patent of 1448, a new patent coming into force in Dec. 1457; so it is unlikely that in 1454 a fresh patent was issued (E101/71/4/937; E403/810 m. 10). The next known appointment to an Irish post was on 23 May 1454 (Lascelles, *Liber Munerum*, i./2, 218). It is very possible that Wiltshire went over to Ireland in the summer of 1454 (BL MS Titus B xi. fo. 213ʳ).

[64] *PPC* vi. 174.

[65] Griffiths, 'The King's Council and the First Protectorate', pp. 80–1.

[66] Details of attendance are taken from the warrants in file E28/84 and *PPC* vi. 178 ff. [67] E28/84/54.

patch up a temporary truce,[68] and it seems likely that the original intention was to use this as the foundation for a more stable settlement, to be arranged by the council. Events, in fact, overtook this plan, although a last desparate attempt was made, on 11 May, to get Exeter to come south.[69] The council probably knew that this had failed by 16 May, and recourse was then had to the much less satisfactory expedient of sending the protector north. There may not have been much discussion about this, as the chronology smacks of haste,[70] and it seems likely that York travelled north only lightly escorted.[71]

York did not return to London until about 8 July,[72] and in his absence the council sustained the business of government without recorded reference to him, Salisbury's presence in the council giving it the necessary executive authority. Little, however, was done that was of consequence. In the period from the close of Parliament to York's departure north, only sixteen items of business passed under the great seal, and, in his absence, business under the seal increased only slightly, to a total of forty-one items, half of these falling in two separate weeks 12–18 May (eleven items) and 26 May–1 June (thirteen items). There was very little business done between 19 and 26 May (three items) and 16 and 22 June (one item). Of the total of forty-one items, thirty-two were of an administrative nature, mostly commissions. The remainder were either presentations to benefices, or exemplifications. The council, in York's absence, seems to have been anxious to avoid contentious grants.

Scrutiny of the exchequer rolls in the period shows a similar, though slightly less controlled, caution. The household officers were assigned just over £1200, of which only £43. 6s. 8d. went into the king's chamber, and household debts of the order of £700 were also discharged, by assignment. Defence was the other major item, with the keepers of the seas receiving £2,333. 6s. 8d.,[73] and Salisbury,

---

[68] *PPC* vi. 178.

[69] Ibid. p. 180 (E28/84/11).

[70] He was in London on 11 May (E28/84/12) and on 13 May (BL Cotton Vespasian MS F XVIII n. 99), and in York eight days later, though *Benet's Chronicle*, p. 211, says he left London about 19 May (cf. Griffiths, 'Local Rivalries and National Politics', p. 612).

[71] He was looking, unsuccessfully, to Sir Walter Devereux and Sir William Herbert for help in May (BL Cotton Vespasian MS F XVIII n. 99).

[72] Davis (ed.), *Paston Letters*, ii. 95.

[73] On 28 May it was ordered that they be assigned 2,000 marks as a gift, but it is not clear if this was ever done (E404/70/1/68).

as warden of the West March, £500.[74] In payments to private individuals York was treated much the most handsomely. On 7 May he was assigned £333. 6s. 8d. in annuities, while still in London, ten days later £146. 13s. 4d., for the same cause, a further 100 marks of annuity in cash on 20 May, and a reassignment of a £12 tally on 1 June.[75] No other individual received anywhere near this total (£558. 13s. 4d.), except by way of loan repayments. None the less, the figure was not extraordinarily high, still less excessive.[76]

While York was in the north it was agreed that a Great Council would be held on 25 June at Westminster, to discuss Calais and the pacification of the realm,[77] and writs of summons were issued, on conciliar authority, to the bishops and the secular peers of the realm; sixty-six in all. The response was imperfect. The bishops of Rochester, Chester, and St Davids, the earl of Shrewsbury, and Viscount Beaumont certainly failed to turn up, as did at least eleven others.[78] The best recorded attendance was twenty-four, on 18 July.[79] York himself was late, not returning from Yorkshire until 8 July.

York had done well in the north, though not without difficulty. He had entered York unopposed on 19 May,[80] but thereafter had lost the initiative. Surviving an assassination plot, he had retreated, gathered a force together, and had reoccupied York before 15 June, when he could hold a commission of oyer and terminer in York Castle.[81] Sessions continued through until 24 June, York setting off for London early in July. At his departure, the stability of the north was by no means guaranteed, but it was now more likely to be secured by political action in London than by the pursuit of lesser malefactors in the shires, and York was sensible to return.

The northern problem was really two problems—Neville hostility to Percy; and the duke of Exeter. The former problem, familiar to governments throughout the middle ages, was how to control irresponsible peers in remote regions, in this case Thomas Percy,

[74] Calais also figures frequently on the rolls, but, as it has peculiar problems at this time, it will be considered separately.

[75] E403/798.

[76] It was necessary on 11 July to halt a variety of exchequer processes which were being conducted against him (E28/85/25).

[77] *PPC* vi. 184–7.

[78] Ibid. 216; E28/85/1, 8.   [79] *PPC* vi. 207.

[80] For the substance of this paragraph see Griffiths, 'Local Rivalries and National Politics', pp. 612 ff.

[81] Writs of *venire facias* had been issued as early as 2 June (KB9/148/2).

Lord Egremond.[82] To this problem the fifteenth century lacked a permanent solution, but, providing the trouble could be contained, it need not become acute. Managing the problem really meant detaching the leading peers from involvement, and, in a particular manner, York achieved this by removing the Percies.

It was the duke of Exeter's behaviour which was the more serious threat, not just to the north but to the political stability of the realm. His immediate quarrel was with Lord Cromwell, and had been for some time. The Percies became prospective allies when Cromwell's niece and co-heiress Maud Stanhope married Sir Thomas Neville. This served to widen the Percy–Neville rift, and shift the focus from Cumbria to Wressle, the Yorkshire manor of Lord Cromwell, formerly of the earls of Northumberland.

In widening the geographic area of the dispute Exeter had done no service to central government, but his gravest action was to transform his territorial claims into a political programme. This does not appear until 21 May, when the protector was already in the city of York, and Exeter at Spofforth, where he allegedly negotiated with the Percies to assume the governance of the king and to claim the duchy of Lancaster.[83] Messages, presumably of similar intent, were then sent into Lancashire and Cheshire.[84]

Exeter was not simply providing the Percies with a pretext for their behaviour. His was a direct challenge to York, as protector, and it was not entirely an unreasonable one. Furthermore, he was consistent in his subsequent behaviour. Summoned on 3 June to the projected Great Council,[85] he responded to the summons, and was in London within a matter of days; a secret not too well kept.[86] But political sentiment on the council was against him, and he retreated into the, very proximate, sanctuary of Westminster Abbey.

It is difficult to dismiss Exeter's move to London as naïve or over-optimistic, for he may not have been entirely friendless there, and it is possible that his behaviour in the north, in particular in relation to

[82] York's attitude to the Percies can be best exemplified by his lease, on 3 July, of the town of Doncaster from Sir John Salvain for six years (*CPR* 1452–61, p. 584). Doncaster was originally Percy property, and the family was actively seeking its recovery (J. M. W. Bean, *The Estates of the Percy Family, 1416–1537* (Oxford, 1958) 79. Some Doncaster men supported Exeter in May (KB27/775 *Rex* m. 90ᵛ), and Percy men had attacked Salvain in March (Griffiths, 'Local Rivalries and National Politics', p. 610).

[83] KB9/149/1 m. 27; KB9/278/12; KB9/282/28; KB27/778 *Rex* m. 113ᵛ.

[84] Cf. Griffiths, 'Local Rivalries and National Politics', p. 613.

[85] *PPC* vi. 189–90.   [86] Davis (ed.), *Paston Letters*, ii. 92.

the duchy of Lancaster, was not without prompting from the capital. On 30 May the council intervened to authorize the privy seal alone to warrant the chancellor of the duchy of Lancaster, and not the Eagle signet as before.[87] On 9 June William Worcester reported Exeter's presence in London and followed this with the observation: 'And the Pryvee Sele ys examyned how and yn whate maner and by whate authorité prevye selys passed forth in that behalf, whych ys full jnnocent and ryght clere yn that mater, as it ys well knowen'.[88] With this cryptic utterance the evidence ceases, but the suspicion that Exeter's claims to responsibility in the exercise of duchy affairs were taken seriously in some quarters cannot be lightly dismissed.

York returned to London on 8 July.[89] He returned to face serious difficulties in sustaining the momentum which had brought him to office. He had now to defend himself from two directions, from the dukes of Exeter and Somerset, and from the possibility of his own insecurity spilling out into the provinces and rekindling violence—a political failure which would be held against him.

Exeter he solved by the peremptory expedient of abducting him from sanctuary, holding him briefly, then sending him, under guard, to the Lancastrian castle of Pontefract;[90] not, perhaps, the most obvious gaol, but it had, at least, the merit of distance from London. Only the monks protested. Ironically, it was the already incarcerated duke of Somerset who proved the bigger problem.

It cannot be coincidence that on the day after indenting for the captaincy of Calais York was obliged to make a declaration concerning the imprisonment of the previous incumbent. Somerset's fate was one of the explicit reasons for the summoning of the Great

---

[87] The privy seal was itself normally moved by conciliar warrant, though on at least one occasion the chancellor selected from a choice of draft warrants the final form to be sent out over the privy seal (*PPC* vi. 193). On four occasions York ordered privy seals to be made out by the authority of his own signet, though all four examples relate to presentations to benefices (PSO1/19/998–1001). The treasurer of the household also warranted bills to go to the privy seal (E28/84/14). On at least one occasion the great seal was used to move the duchy seal (*PPC* vi. 217). Lisieux himself was still rarely in attendance, and this may have caused inconvenience. Thus, a document of 6 July did not reach the chancellor until 11 July (C81/1546/83). Eagle signet was intended for the king's personal use in duchy affairs. who had been employing it in 1454 is unknown (Somerville, *Duchy of Lancaster*, p. 212; *PPC* vi. 188).

[88] Davis (ed.), *Paston Letters*, ii. 92–3.

[89] Griffiths, 'Local Rivalries and National Politics', p. 620.

[90] *Great Chronicle*, p. 186; *Benet's Chronicle*, p. 212; Davis (ed.), *Paston Letters*, i. 154. His guards, Sir Thomas Rempston and Sir Brian Stapleton, had been servants of his father in the 1440s (Marshall, 'English War Captains', p. 43).

Council, and this may well explain the attendance of only twenty-four peers.[91] On this low attendance York adroitly pinned his hopes; a large council had committed Somerset to ward; there ought, therefore, to be a large council to release him, which manifestly there was not. The argument was accepted, though York, when indenting the previous day for Calais, had obviously taken into account the possibility of failure.

This interim settlement of Somerset's fate could not, however, conceal the need for a more satisfactory resolution of his case. Trial could scarcely be delayed much longer, and on 28 July a date was fixed; 28 October.[92] Clearly this trial would be a show of political strength which York might well lose. Loans would be difficult to raise, insecurity would become evident, and the more financially precarious and insecure York became the more unconvincing his political position would appear.

He did what he could to consolidate his position during the last days of July. Excluding the payments for Calais,[93] assignments in his favour by 17 July (the last day of business) totalled £290. 13s. 4d.; £159 was paid him in cash, and he was paid a total of £252. 4s. 6d. by the customs of Hull and London in annuities.[94] Moreover, on 23 July he acquired authority to deliver the king's livery to eighty, unnamed, gentlemen, in a council meeting dominated by his supporters.[95] This force was almost certainly intended as a bodyguard to accompany him north.[96] He set off shortly after,[97] arriving in York by 3 August.[98] The duke of Exeter, rather than the Percies, was his target, and fresh indictments against the duke were heard on the third. So far as the Percy–Neville problem was concerned, he seems to have sought an accommodation with the earl of Northumberland, preferring to halt all proceedings and the

---

[91] *PPC* vi. 206. [92] Ibid. pp. 215–7, 218–9.

[93] On 24 July £1,000 in cash and £1,700 in assignments, including £200 against the Canterbury tenth (Stevenson, *Letters and Papers*, ii. 501–2).

[94] E403/798; Bean, 'Financial Position', tab. ii. On 19 July he secured the farms of the mines of Devon and Cornwall for ten years, his mainpernors being Thomas Colt, Salisbury's agent, and Thomas Witham, who had been appointed chancellor of the exchequer eleven days previously (*CPR* 1452–61, p. 158; E404/70/2/31). A loan of 100 marks on 24 May was repaid on the Bedfordshire tenth five days later (E401/839).

[95] *PPC* vi. 209. The bishops of London and Ely and the secular peers present certainly supported him in July.

[96] On 17 July Salisbury was retaining men in his capacity as warden of the march (C76/136 m. 5).

[97] He was in London on 24 July (C81/1546/83).

[98] KB9/149/1 m. 27; Griffiths, 'Local Rivalries and National Politics', p. 621.

execution of all judgments against him,[99] and to buy the acquiescence of the Nevilles to this.

Lord Fauconberg he permitted to evade the consequences of foreclosure in his surety for Edmund Arblaster in July.[100] Salisbury and Warwick were permitted to seal a joint indenture as wardens of the East March, for twenty years, at the improved rate of £1,250 in peace time, double in war.[101] He also secured for the earl of Warwick two manors in Norfolk,[102] and for Salisbury the fee farm of Carlisle, in the centre of Percy territory.[103]

York's whereabouts for the next six weeks can only be surmised; Sandal seems the most likely,[104] with the Nevilles either at Middleham or Sheriff Hutton.[105] The first firm date for his whereabouts is 19 September, when he presided over the oyer and terminer sessions at Derby.[106] He again disappears from view until 7 November, when he is found in attendance at a council meeting at Westminster.[107]

The paucity of sources for the last months of 1454 is most frustrating, especially as it seems to reflect the accidents of survival rather than any lack of government activity. It is true that analysis of the patent, close, and fine rolls shows very little administrative activity in September,[108] but thereafter business flows at a steady, if

---

[99] E28/85/62.   [100] *PPC* vi. 208.

[101] R. L. Storey, 'The Wardens of the Marches of England Towards Scotland, 1377–1489', *EHR* 72 (1957), 605.

[102] The gift was not above suspicion, as the manors, Bouilles and Walcotes, had had a tortuous history over the previous twenty years. The other interested party was Richard Doket, whose connections were with Tuddenham (*CCR* 1454–61, p. 77).

[103] *CFR* 1452–61, p. 98.

[104] The letter of York to John Paston dated 19 Aug. from Sandal seems most likely to belong to this year (Davis (ed.), *Paston Letters*, ii. 99).

[105] Warwick was at Middleham on 23 Aug. (Davis (ed.), *Paston Letters*, ii. 100). Several patents of this period are dated at Middleham (2 Sept.; *CPR* 1452–61, p. 196) or at Sheriff Hutton (e.g. 22 Sept.; ibid. 219). From this it would follow that Salisbury was at Pontefract, where Exeter was held, on 29 Sept. (ibid.). Apparently, the chancellor's sole authority was sufficient warrant for these patents, although one licence, dated 23 Sept. at Sheriff Hutton, was warranted 'by King and Council', presumably a convenient formula (Rymer, *Foedera*, xi. 358). Entries on the French Roll are dated at Malling (C76/136 m. 12 *passim*).

[106] KB9/12/1 m. 3[r]. The sessions had been postponed from July (E28/83/39).

[107] C81/1546/102.

[108] Seven letters patent (three dated Sunday 29), no letters close, one fine roll entry, the appointment of a new sheriff of Bristol (*CFR* 1452–61, p. 115). There was an outbreak of pestilence in the city and environs in late August–September, and the protector and chancellor, although expected, stayed away (Davis (ed.), *Paston Letters*, i. 156; R. S. Gottfried, *Epidemic Disease in Fifteenth-Century England* (1978), p. 105).

modest, rate until mid-December, when it again dries up. It is not clear who was taking the decisions in October, as only one writ carrying conciliar attestation survives, for 15 October.[109] The chancellor, treasurer, archbishop of Canterbury, and the dean of St Severins were noted as present. As they were all members of the continual council it must be supposed that it was this body which sustained the government machine. It had been intended to hold a Great Council on 21 October, and to keep it in session for at least a week. Fifty-four peers had been summoned.[110] The continual council, however, met even while the, delayed, Great Council was in session. Thirteen members attested a warrant on 7 November,[111] of whom nine were to be present at a further meeting six days later.[112] On 15 November there were eleven councillors, ten on 23 and 24 November, and single figures on warrants for 27 November and thereafter.[113]

The Great Council itself had been summoned for 21 October, but it is unlikely to have started punctually. Twenty-nine peers are noted as present on 13 November,[114] and the total number attending does not seem much to have exceeded this. One notable absentee on the thirteenth was the duke of Norfolk, and he may well have absented himself entirely.[115] This may be the explanation of the failure of the Great Council to settle the fate of the duke of Somerset, the original purpose of its summons, though his name certainly cropped up during the course of business.[116] The council's one known decision, the reform of the household, an idea close to the political interests of the duke of York, was carried through in an essentially impartial fashion.[117] A similarly studious neutrality may have kept Somerset in the Tower.

York would have had more difficulties with the ordinary council,

---

[109] C81/1546/100.

[110] *PPC* vi. 216–19. Some pruning of those summoned may well have taken place. On 25 Oct. the earl of Wiltshire was ordered to take the fealty of the new abbot of Cerne (*CPR* 1452–61, p. 197).

[111] C81/1546/102.   [112] C81/1546/86.

[113] C81/1546/86–9, 91–5.   [114] *PPC* vi. 233.

[115] On 3 Nov. he was reported to be daily expecting a summons from the king (Gairdner (ed.), *Paston Letters*, iii. 7). This is puzzling, as he already had one, dating from July. Either the duke was being ingenuous or was being deliberately kept away. The former is the more likely.

[116] On 4 Nov. he was fully discharged from all responsibilities at Calais (C81/1546/85; Rymer, *Foedera*, xi. 359).

[117] *PPC* vi. 220–33.

where the bishops tended to be the most regular attenders but, with the Somerset issue shelved, possibly indefinitely, the household being drawn into some semblance of control, and Calais now within his grasp, York's authority was too great to be checked, though it might be hampered.

The protector remained in and around London until the end of December,[118] and took advantage of his growing power to consolidate his hold over Ireland, where FitzEustace's death in October had left the province without a deputy. A ratification of his lieutenancy was secured in November,[119] but he appears to have had little trouble influencing events there earlier in the month, securing the post of deputy chancellor for Sir William Welles and appointing a new keeper of the Irish hanaper.[120]

He continued to receive money from the exchequer, £830. 7s. 4d. in all, including £287. 0s. 8d. in cash,[121] but he had no payment for any of his current responsibilities as protector or as lieutenant of Ireland.[122] He did best with annuity entitlements, drawing £2,650. 11s. 10d. in the financial year 1454–5.[123] This was a considerable improvement on recent years, but he was still in receipt of much less than he was due, and, although it can be said that he exploited his authority, he did not do so in any outrageous sense. This must have been to his political credit in the eyes of most.

Similar sums at this time were paid at the exchequer to Henry Percy, Lord Poynings (£837. 1s. 6d.) and the earl of Salisbury (£841. 0s. 5d.), reflecting the policy of accommodation adopted in the summer. Both parties made other gains in this period, the Percies at last making tentative steps towards the recovery of their Northumberland estates, hitherto held by the duke of Bedford or the Crown,[124] and Salisbury making an outright gain of Hawarden Castle, and also heading, with some success, a list of feoffees

---

[118] He attests many warrants throughout the period (C81/1546/91–3, 95, 97). See also BL Egerton Charter 2895.

[119] C81/1546/90 (enrolled the following day, *CPR* 1452–61, p. 22). For this he paid half a mark. It was a ratification rather than a new appointment (but cf. Powicke and Fryde, *Handbook of British Chronology*, p. 154).

[120] Berry, *Statutes of Ireland*, pp. 327, 456–9. On 10 Dec. he presented the absentee bishop of Kildare, Geoffrey Hereford OP, to his living of St Mary's, Pembridge (*Reg. Stanbury*, ed. Bannister, p. 192).

[121] E403/800. This includes a repayment of £100 loaned on 5 Dec. (E401/843).

[122] Despite a specific warrant to that effect (E404/20/2/99).

[123] Bean, 'Financial Position', tab. ii.

[124] Bean, *Estates of the Percy Family*, p. 75; *CFR* 1452–61, p. 113.

disputing the inheritance of Ogard's property on behalf of Joan Clifton.[125]

For the first time since he became protector York found a little time to help his retainers and servants.[126] Oldhall obtained a writ of error,[127] and an adjournment *sine die* of his trial. Nicholas Christmas obtained a writ of *exigend*,[128] Walter Devereux a licence for a modest enfeoffment,[129] and Edmund Blount managed to gain seisin of an equally modest group of properties,[130] though this last was not simply an act of grace and favour, as the dispute over the property had brought the Blount–Vernon quarrel as far south as Gloucestershire.

This modest largess one would expect to see complemented by an assault on the household, but, though the household ordinance is the one certain act of the Great Council, it is not at all clear from its provisions why it was enacted. In allowing a total of 393 persons, it extended the size of the king's household by twenty-three from the 1445 ordinance,[131] which does not seem to imply a search for economy.[132] Nor does it appear to have made any drastic change in the basic personnel from the era of Somerset's pre-eminence.[133] It may not even have been intended as a reform, just as a confirmation of tenure for existing incumbents. Only in the preliminaries, establishing two earls, a viscount, and two barons, rather than a duke alone, may it have been intended to hurt Somerset, though in so doing it reinforced the Lancastrian sympathies in the senior echelons. A caveat has also to be recorded, in that its provisions may well never have been effected.

[125] *Calendar of Deeds and Documents: iii.: Hawarden Deeds*, ed. F. Green (1931), 4.

[126] He had managed to gain the wardenship of Thomas Fastolf for his old councillor Sir John Fastolf in June, but this had provoked sporadic violence in Norfolk for most of the summer, and it took the intervention of the Bourchiers to ease the problem somewhat in Oct. (Davis (ed.), *Paston Letters*, ii. 93; *Catalogue of Ancient Deeds*, v. 182, A11669).

[127] KB27/777 *Rex* m. 102[r]. Oldhall did not recover his forfeited lands (*CPR 1452–61*, p. 198).

[128] KB27/774 *Rex* m. 87[v].

[129] *CPR 1452–61*, p. 215.   [130] *CFR 1452–61*, p. 118.

[131] A. R. Myers, *The Household of Edward IV* (Manchester, 1959), 63–75.

[132] Real numbers in the household were consistently a great deal higher (Wolffe, *Henry VI*, p. 283).

[133] Right of access to the king was in effect given to his half-brothers, Beaumont, Cromwell, Beauchamp, and St Amand, Sir Edmund Hungerford, Sir Philip Wentworth, four esquires and four gentlemen ushers. Only Cromwell looks remotely sympathetic to York.

Surprisingly, given his vulnerability to a change in the king's health, York had done little in the nine months of his protectorate thus far to reward his own retinue substantially, or to disturb the pro-Beaufort faction, or to infiltrate the household with his sympathizers. His powers as protector were, as Parliament intended, severely limited by a council of wider political interests. This presumes, however, that York had these as urgent political aims, which may be an unsafe assumption. His urgent need, in 1453, had been to survive, and, thanks to Henry's illness, he had done so. By December 1454 the longer-term prospects were beginning to open up. In the north, the battle at Stamford Bridge, in early November, had resulted not only in a Neville victory but in the capture of Egremond, easily the most persistent Percy trouble-maker.[134] Pursuit of a pacification policy was now that much easier and the settlement of Ampthill on Lord Grey also looked promising.

The more serious worry was the general upsurge of violence, a reflection of the political uncertainties of the earlier months of the year. In June there had been serious riots, and other violence, in the Bonville interest.[135] In south Wales the trouble had started somewhat earlier, in May, because of an insufficiently robust initiative by central government to exercise some control over the area, especially over Gruffydd ap Nicholas. The attempt failed, possibly because of divided councils at Westminster, and by August the area had slipped from central authority.[136]

In East Anglia, Thomas Daniel, with Norfolk's tacit support,[137] had embarked on a campaign of such bitterness against Henry Wodehouse that the latter was forced, in September, to destroy much of his inheritance.[138] An outbreak which York might privately have condoned was a riot at Baring, on the Isle of Wight, directed against the duke of Somerset's bailiff.[139] In Kent, the Poynings–

---

[134] Griffiths, 'Local Rivalries and National Politics', pp. 620–4.

[135] KB9/274/36; KB27/774 *Rex* m. 159ᵛ; KB27/776 *Rex* m. 100ʳ; KLB27/777 *Rex* m. 101ᵛ; Storey, *End of the House of Lancaster*, p. 165. Courtney's behaviour perhaps reflects an erroneous confidence, as an erstwhile ally of York, in the protector's willingness to close an eye to his transgressions.

[136] R. A. Griffiths, 'Gruffydd ap Nicholas and the Fall of the House of Lancaster', *Welsh History Review*, 2 (1965), 218–21. For problems in Flint see *DKR* 37/ii. 19.

[137] Daniel, described on 8 Jan. as 'of Framlingham' (KB27/775 *Rex* m. 59ʳ).

[138] William Worcester, *Itineraries*, ed. Harvey, p. 253.

[139] KB27/779 *Rex* m. 127. Trouble persisted there into the new year (KB9/280/18, 20).

Percy dispute seemed for the time being to have run its course,[140] but that did not bring order to the county, and by December commissions to inquire into violations of the law were being issued.[141]

Order in the shire was in the first instance the duty of the sheriff, and it was, therefore, of great importance to York to secure favourable nominations to the shrievalties when the new terms fell due in November, but, with two exceptions,[142] he failed. The appointments made on 4 November were, therefore, in all probability the work of the Great Council then in session. What emerged from their deliberations was a list of studious blandness,[143] county esquires, for the most part, with no prominent role hitherto in shire politics. One York annuitant was appointed, Sir John Barre (Herefords.), and Richard Quatremains, a man of uncertain Yorkist sympathies at this time, took Oxfordshire–Berkshire. John Stanhope was presumably appointed to Nottinghamshire–Derbyshire in the Neville or Bourchier interest, and John Huddleston (Cumberland) and Nicholas Husee (Surrey–Sussex) were soon to find their way into the Neville camp. Another in the Neville interest, though he also had connections with York, was Sir John Saville (Yorks.).[144] John Wingfield (Norfolk–Suffolk) was a Mowbray man,[145] with a record of service to York in France.[146] The selection for the most part of lesser men, however, suggests a search for a compromise-list, a worthy cause for York to support in public, but difficult, in that local disputes at the time needed a firmer hand than many of the sheriffs could hope to employ. York's reputation could only suffer from such breakdowns.

Another difficulty was London, where there was serious rioting against the Lombards, probably in the autumn,[147] though there is no

---

[140] R. M. Jeffs, 'The Poynings–Percy Dispute: An Example of the Interplay of Open Strife and Legal Action in the Fifteenth Century', *BIHR* 24 (1961), 156. Whether Poynings was, as Jeffs supposes, in prison is less certain (cf. Davis (ed.), *Paston Letters*, ii. 95 and KB27/774 *Rex* m. 135ʳ).   [141] *CPR* 1452–61, p. 224.

[142] Bedfordshire–Buckinghamshire where Edmund Rede was appointed retrospectively on 5 Nov. to collect what he could for the previous year, the new sheriff Thomas Singleton being appointed on the twenty-fourth; Warwickshire–Leicestershire where Thomas Berkeley, a Buckingham supporter, was appointed on 28 Nov. (Rawcliffe, *The Staffords*, p. 209).

[143] *CFR* 1454–61, p. 101.   [144] See App. III.

[145] *Descriptive Catalogue of Ancient Deeds*, iii. 379, C3535.

[146] BL Add. Ch. 8031; E101/53/33.

[147] *Gregory's Chronicle*, p. 199. For another cause of tension see *Calendar of Papal Letters x. 1447–55*, p. 166.

record of government intervention, and York, popular in London, may well have hoped that he would not be called on. Relations with the Calais Staple were not at their warmest,[148] the actions of the fleet had met with criticism,[149] and he had annoyed the east-coast merchants by his prohibition of the Icelandic trade.[150] This was not the time to irritate the merchant community further, especially as relations with Burgundy were strained.

The concern of the protector over Anglo-Burgundian amity had been shown very early in his protectorate, when one of his own council, Sir Edmund Mulso, was sent with Louis Gallet, the French secretary, to the duke of Burgundy, to negotiate the return English goods, seized in retaliation for Bonville's piracy.[151] Mulso failed because his master had failed to restrain Bonville.[152] More acts of piracy in the summer brought the arrest of English shipping in Middleburgh.[153] There may, too, have been some unease among merchants about the foreign-policy intentions of Philip the Good. His declaration of intent to go crusading was well known, but probably not treated too seriously[154] until two months later, in April, when he attended an Imperial Diet at Regensburg.[155] This move towards better Imperial–Burgundian relations was disquieting to the merchant community, as it might presage an improvement in Hanseatic–Burgundian relations at a time when England's strained attitude towards Lübeck was hindering renewal of closer ties with the Hanse as a whole.[156]

By Christmas 1454 the duke of York's position was politically secure, though not above criticism. Ireland was his; Calais was almost his. The north was quieter, though other areas now required similarly firm treatment. There was need for a more coherent foreign policy and for a broader, more creative outlook within the council, but these were not insuperable difficulties, and the duke and his

---

[148] For attempts in this period to repay outstanding Staple loans see *CPR* 1452–61, pp. 210–1, 226.

[149] Gairdner (ed.), *Paston Letters*, i. p.303.

[150] *CPR* 1452–61, p. 172.   [151] E404/70/1/83.

[152] Davis (ed.), *Paston Letters*, ii. p.93.

[153] Thielemans, *Bourgogne et Angleterre*, p. 161.

[154] The English council had been evasive on this issue in July (Rymer, *Foedera*, xi. 355).

[155] R. Vaughan, *Philip the Good* (1970), 297–9.

[156] M. M. Postan, 'The Economic and Political Relations of the Hanse from 1400 to 1475', in E. Power and M. M. Postan (eds.), *Studies in English Trade in the Fifteenth Century* (1933), 131.

supporters could reasonably hope that, given time, such short-comings would be remedied.

The time was not given. York attended a council meeting on 30 December[157] at Westminster, and the king's health was probably the principal item of business, for, by the New Year, Henry was regarded as recovered.[158] York could only await events, but something of what followed, a Great Council and Somerset's release, must have been expected. The protectorate was no longer necessary, and York surrendered his office early in the New Year.[159]

The Great Council which assembled on or before 5 February was reasonably well attended, twenty-seven peers accepting the case for Somerset's release.[160] Of the great peers present, only York is likely to have been hostile, the archbishop of York having been consistently pro-Beaufort, and the archbishop of Canterbury and the duke of Buckingham being now enthusiastic for his release, whatever their earlier attitudes.[161] Of the seven bishops, only two might have opposed, supported by the Neville earls and the earl of Devon. Worcester was uncommitted, and the two viscounts almost certainly favoured release. The attitude of the lords Cromwell and Greystoke must be uncertain,[162] but Roos, Sudeley, Bonville, and Stourton are unlikely to have opposed, and Fitzwarin probably followed the Bourchier line, taking Say with him.

The mood of the council was certainly against York, but it is probable that even with a more balanced group he would have lost. The failure to present charges may have disturbed the ecclesiastical peers in particular. Their sense of constitutional propriety had brought York out of the wilderness in 1453. Clause thirty-nine of Magna Carta must have weighed on them. The practical difficulty

---

[157] C81/1544/97.

[158] *Benet's Chronicle* dates his recovery to 31 Dec. (p. 212; cf. MS Gough London 10, in *Six Town Chronicles*, p. 158). Rawlinson B 355 (ibid. 108) puts it after Christmas. It is likely that the king showed sustained signs of improvement after Christmas, which by the year's end were deemed sufficiently permanent to permit his restoration to authority. However, the bishop of Winchester and the prior of St Johns were relieved to find him still in good health on 7 Jan. (Davis (ed.), *Paston Letters*, ii. p. 108; cf. *Bale's Chronicle*, p. 141).

[159] He is not styled protector on 5 Feb. Unofficially, Somerset had been released from the Tower on 26 Jan., and it may be safely supposed that he had lost office before then.

[160] Rymer, *Foedera*, xi. 361; CCR 1454–61, p. 9. Seventeen peers, including York, but not Somerset, witnessed a petition on 5 Feb. (C81/1546/98).

[161] *Benet's Chronicle*, p. 212.

[162] Cromwell was still prosecuting his suit against Exeter (KB27/775 m. 48[r]).

was the absence of the duke of Norfolk, who would have done something to balance the scales of prestige in York's favour, and whose presence was essential if charges were to be pressed. Norfolk's absence was bad for York, although the case itself did not fail by default, Somerset being only bailed,[163] but for York this was tantamount to acquittal. Only Henry's renewed insanity could give him any hope of recovering lost ground.

What happened over the next month is unknown,[164] but it is unlikely to have afforded York aught for his comfort, for on 4 March, at Greenwich,[165] Somerset was able to secure a declaration of his innocence in all criminal charges against him, leaving all other matters to arbitration.[166] Dismissed from the captaincy of Calais on the same day,[167] York was joined in relegation by the earl of Salisbury three days later.

---

[163] He was bailed until the morrow of All Souls. With the possibility of a relapse in Henry's health, Somerset cannot have wished to see so lengthy a deferral.

[164] A warrant of 5 Feb. carries seventeen names, including those of Wiltshire and Scales (C81/1546/98). This is the only warrant of the period. On 21 Feb. the duchess of Somerset had a warrant for payment of £100, which implies Somerset influence (C81/768/9893), but a six-man commission of 22 Feb. into the alleged misdeeds of John Cassy, a man of Yorkist connections as steward of Newent for Fotheringhay College, included Sir John Barre, Walter Devereux esq., and Giles Brugge, so it is possible that York, through Salisbury, still exerted some influence, though Warwick may also have had an interest in the case (*CPR 1452–61*, p. 223; KB9/287/35; C. Carpenter, 'Sir Thomas Malory and Fifteenth-Century Local Politics', *BIHR* 53 (1980), 38 n. 61).

[165] Windsor was in Neville hands.

[166] C81/1546 99; Rymer, *Foedera*, xi. 361.

[167] Ibid. 363.

7

THE SECOND PROTECTORATE

At no time described as a Great Council, the Greenwich meeting was, none the less, well attended. Thirty-three peers assented to the proceedings, an appreciably higher number than that found in the protectorate Great Councils, though, again, the duke of Norfolk was absent. The king clearly intended his declaration of Somerset's innocence to be final, the last word on an issue which had been exploited for five years to weaken the Beaufort regime. The terms of arbitration between Somerset and York, agreed on the same day, implied that the remaining matters were of a civil rather than a criminal nature, thus persisting with the idea first adopted after Dartford, although now with less hostile arbitrators, only three of the eight, Wiltshire, Beaumont, and Stourton, being seemingly biased.[1] What the populace at large thought is unknown, but, in the context of politics in 1455, was not likely to have been immediately significant. If he was to prosper, the duke of York needed a new political weapon to attack Beaufort, one which, preferably would rouse popular sentiment. There was none immediately to hand, making his political position uncomfortably exposed. Somerset was as well aware as York that he was dependent on the king's good health for his continuing political well-being. Somerset needed, therefore, to act as quickly as possible. It had taken only eighteen months after Dartford to reduce York to a political shadow, but that might be too long. The process needed to be more energetically pressed, and Somerset started immediately.

Exchequer payments all but dried up.[2] There were difficulties in the law courts.[3] York's recent farm of the king's mines was ignored.[4] Little things all, but for York, in isolation in Sandal Castle,[5] they could only be seen as the thin end of the wedge. The political

[1] *CCR* 1454–61, p. 49.
[2] One tally, for £60, was cleared on 6 May, nominally to York, in fact to Thomas Barker, with £25. 18s. 3d. remitted (E403/801 m. 2).
[3] KB27/776 *Rex* m. 31ᵛ. Deferral of York's case against John Ingowe.
[4] *CPR* 1452–61, p. 217.
[5] BL Egerton Charter 7189.

isolation of 1453 was too recent and dangerous an experience to be forgotten, especially as Salisbury and Devon were receiving similar treatment.[6] By contrast, the archbishop of Canterbury had a £200 gift,[7] and the Percies moved a little nearer to the £6,400 owed them by the exchequer.[8] The only enemy of York's still in difficulty was the duke of Exeter.[9] This rapid shift of favour was bound to disturb, and it did. Tensions rose. Soon after Easter, York and Somerset quarrelled publicly.[10]

The king's behaviour between Christmas and Easter had been imprudent. He was correct in discharging York, and the continued detention of Somerset was legally unacceptable, but it would have been a simple matter to have given authority to a third party, Buckingham or the Bourchiers seeming an obvious choice. The speed with which Somerset was restored to power was bound to alarm York, and the Nevilles also, and it was evident, to any who chose to reflect on events, that Somerset would have to seek York's elimination from politics as quickly as possible. Somerset needed now, while the king was sane, and by immutable royal authority, to settle the form government should take in the event of a relapse. Only by this means could Somerset feel secure. The summons to a very particular group of councillors to meet on 15–18 April[11] must be judged in this context. The next step, the summons of a Great Council to Leicester, was essential to give authority and dissemination to any proposed settlement. Once declared, it would be irrevocable, and York would be finished. Duke Richard had to prevent the Great Council from taking place.

The duke of York retired north and, together with his Neville allies, no less alarmed than he, set about raising forces. A deputation comprising the bishop of Coventry, the earl of Worcester, and the prior of St Johns was sent, but the sole source for this embassy goes on to say that York simply detained them.[12] Whether because of their failure to return, or on the basis of some other military

---

[6] See *CPR* 1452–61, pp. 217, 288.

[7] E404/70/2/59.   [8] E404/70/2/77.

[9] Even he was allowed to leave Pontefract (Rymer, *Foedera*, xi. 365), and Cromwell's case against him was deferred to the autumn (KB27/777 *Rex* m. 95ʳ).

[10] *Benet's Chronicle*, pp. 213–14.

[11] C. J. Armstrong, 'Politics and the Battle of St Albans, 1455', *BIHR* 33 (1960), 12. The argument of Mr Armstrong, that the council was summoned to discuss the future safety of the king, is not inconsistent with this thesis.

[12] Op. cit., 16. All details of events before and at St Albans are taken from this article without further acknowledgement.

intelligence, Somerset woke up to the scale of York's military preparations, and on 18 May sent out summonses far and wide. Armstrong makes a strong case for believing that Somerset ordered military forces to join him at St Albans. There is, however, an alternative viewpoint, that on 18 May Somerset sent for aid to come to the king 'whersoever we be',[13] and that, although he expected trouble, he expected it within the vicinity of Leicester rather than as far south as St Albans.

It would be a help if York's movements could be reconstructed, but they cannot. It is known that he was at Royston on 20 May. If he had been further north at, say, Fotheringhay, some days earlier, it might reasonably have been supposed that his intention was to turn west to Leicester.[14] Somerset would not cherish armed retinues at Leicester, but they could probably have been contained. Only when York moved further south with the obvious intention of preventing the king from gaining Leicester could the full scope of his intention have been suspected. Even then, those around the king might reasonably suppose that he would shrink from a direct assault on the royal party. By the evening of 21 May the king was at Watford, by which time York and the Nevilles were somewhere to the west of Ware. The king left Watford the next morning, intending to dine at St Albans, probably hoping to make Dunstable by early evening, to be advised *en route* that York was moving towards him. Only at this stage does it appear to have occurred to a section of the court that York might indeed attack the royal party.

The king decided to relieve Somerset as Constable, appointing Buckingham in his stead, and, following his new Constable's advice, moved on to St Albans and sought to negotiate. For Somerset this was a most unwelcome development, as negotiations could only concern his own fate. Buckingham's initial confidence in negotiation proved correct, and the royal party were able to enter St Albans unmolested, despite the town's potential for defence. This did not trouble the Yorkist lords unduly. It would be sufficient to delay the king in St Albans and prevent the Leicester council.

The dukes of York and Buckingham entered into serious negotiations immediately. Both dukes were hampered by other issues. Somerset was deliberately provocative, sending Lesparre

[13] Letter to the city of Coventry, quoted op. cit., 17.
[14] *Benet's Chronicle*, p. 213, says that York was riding towards London. *Brut*, ii. 521, in a confused entry, seems to imply that York's movements were unexpected.

pursuivant to York, and following him with Bonville's herald. For his part, York was restrained, confining his request to the points at issue between himself and Somerset, but he was again hampered by the ambiguous behaviour of the duke of Norfolk. But York's insistence on the charges against Somerset put Buckingham in an impossible position, for, however full his powers might be, they could not include the power to concede what the king had already denied. Anyhow, Somerset would scarcely have co-operated. Buckingham appears to have sensed the impasse before York, and to have stalled for time, aided by the king. Delay could only augment the royal army. If anything was now to be achieved by York it would have to be done quickly. Warwick grasped the point and opened the fighting while the last embers of negotiation still flickered.

Once the fighting had started there was no going back. The king's banner was displayed, making York and his supporters traitors, and defeat would mean death and forfeiture. On the positive side, there were ransoms and plundering and the settling of old scores. Both sides had plenty of stomach for a fight; that the Yorkists won seems to have been the result of some neat tactics by Warwick, and lack of preparation by the household men.

St Albans was not the first battle of a civil war. York was fighting to be rid of Somerset. Arguably he had to, as Somerset might also argue. English politics had swung increasingly uncontrollably from the one interest group to the other, since the first seeds of jealousy were sown in 1440 at York's appointment to the French lieutenancy. Somerset was not a great duke. Without Henry he could have been brushed aside by York, but Henry, in an age when policies were identified with people, was insufficiently ruthless to sacrifice him. Somerset's regime was too closely associated with failure, but ministers who loyally discharged Henry's policies were loyally supported in return, a commendable but politically naïve attitude. Henry should have abandoned Somerset discreetly after Dartford and sought support from the Staffords. Instead, he stood by Somerset and allowed him to plan York's destruction. That was why Henry was waylaid at St Albans.

The throne was not imperilled at St Albans. Henry himself was wounded, as must have been appreciated at the time, and he retired into a tanner's house. He could readily have been killed behind its doors and no witness survive. The royal standard had been abandoned, Henry and the kingdom were in York's hands—and were safe. York did his best, too, and in the king's name, to stop indiscriminate plundering once the battle was won.

Discipline was apparently restored fairly quickly, as there are no accounts of outrages in the St Albans area in the following days,[15] but order had to be breathed into the king's government, and respectability into the duke's actions, as quickly as possible. Parliament was clearly the most useful single step to achieving this, and writs were sent out on 26 May,[16] as early as was practical.

Meanwhile, every effort was made to diffuse an atmosphere of normality. The king was escorted to London 'in greet honour', lodged in bishop Kemp's house,[17] not the Tower, and the Whitsun festivities conducted with determined jollity. Few can have been deceived. The tension was evident at St Pauls on Whitsunday itself, when the king insisted that York, not the archbishop, place the crown on his head; and after Trinity Sunday the king dissociated himself from affairs, and moved to Windsor, and thence to Hertford. York remained a little longer, then withdrew to Ware 'to tymme the Parlement be gynne'.[18]

There were some matters which could not be delayed until Parliament, in particular the disposal of Somerset's offices, several of which, not the least being Calais, were of increased importance in the aftermath of St Albans. Windsor Castle, where the king was most likely to reside, was committed to the custody of Fauconberg and Sir John Bourchier on 2 June.[19] Calais went to Warwick almost immediately after St Albans and the Treasury to Viscount Bourchier.[20] The biggest block of grants was in Wales, where Somerset was replaced by Warwick in Monmouth and Three Castles,[21] and by Edward Bourchier at Kidwelly.[22] The dependence on Neville and Bourchier is striking, and York in these early days looked like heading a narrow factional government. The grant of Calais to Warwick looks especially significant, as York had spent much of the previous year trying to get it for himself. The impression is strong

---

[15] Only two cases of any sort involving violence are to be found, at Bylawe on 1 June and at Long Whatton on 12 June (KB27/773 *Rex* m 25ᵛ; KB27/783 *Rex* m. 23ᵛ).   [16] *Benet's Chronicle*, p. 214.

[17] *Six Town Chronicles*, p. 142; Gairdner (ed.) *Paston Letters*, iii. 29.

[18] Ibid. 32. York, Salisbury, and Warwick all spent the next weeks in the Hertford area, presumably to forestall any inclination by the king to raise forces.

[19] *CPR 1452–61*, p. 243.

[20] Patent dated 29 May (ibid. 242), but to 30 May by exchequer warrant (E404/70/2/80); Davis (ed.), *Paston Letters*, ii. 116.

[21] Somerville, *Duchy of Lancaster*, p. 648.   [22] Ibid. 640.

that York was being forced to concede more to Neville interests than was either publicly politic or privately his intention. The York–Neville alliance was a recent phenomenon, no doubt in need of strengthening, but the Nevilles looked now to be the stronger party.

As ever, York avoided the temptations of self-reward. He took the largely honorific post of Constable and the functional post of constable of Carmarthen,[23] but otherwise nothing. In personal rewards he gained, to his political credit, very little from St Albans.

The plums fell to the Nevilles and the Bourchiers, and the Nevilles, in particular, continued to do very well throughout the summer and autumn. Salisbury was given the confiscated goods of Lord Camoys,[24] and on 20 August the justices of oyer and terminer handed down gratifying fines totalling 9,080 marks on the Percies.[25] These were, of course, punitive fines which would not accrue to the Nevilles, but they would serve to keep the Percy family in line. More immediate financial rewards came from the exchequer, £583. 18s. 11d. being assigned to Salisbury over the period, at a time of acute stringency.[26] There were even attempts to pay the Nevilles as wardens of the march,[27] though Fauconberg received very little, just a licence to trade, to repay his ransom.[28]

The Nevilles gained because they could exert pressure and, by and large, surprisingly little was done to offset this pressure by a wider distribution of rewards. The earl of Oxford, the Shrewsburys, and Lord Stanley received licences to trade with France, and Stourton's prisoners were permitted to arrange their ransoms.[29] As concessions they cost nothing, and in general terms the English peerage did not profit from the first battle of St Albans. The Nevilles and Bourchiers scooped the pool.

There were precious few rewards for the gentry either. Even families such as the Ogles, who deserved well of York, were ignored. There are six rewards which might just relate to service at St Albans: to Oldhall,[30] Sir Henry Retford,[31] Sir Thomas Lumley,[32] John Denstone esq.,[33] Henry Unton,[34] and Robert Burton,[35] not a lengthy list even if the surmise is true. Commissions of gaol delivery

---

[23] *CPR* 1452–61, p. 245.   [24] *PPC* vi. 251.
[25] KB27/778 *Rex* m. 108ʳ.   [26] E403/801.   [27] E404/70/3/73.
[28] C76/132 m. 2; C76/138 m. 34. At St Albans he had fought for the king.
[29] C76/138 mm. 31, 33; C76/137 mm. 9, 12.
[30] Allowed to plead his general pardon on 20 June (KB27/777 *Rex* m. 106ʳ).
[31] *CPR* 1452–61, p. 242.   [32] *PPC* vi. 259.   [33] E28/86/17.
[34] *CPR* 1452–61, p. 242.   [35] E28/86/5.

may also have released prisoners sympathetic to York, Neville, or Bourchier, though in the circumstances their presence at St Albans would have been most improbable.[36] York did very little for his own supporters, though he did his best to ensure a smooth succession for William Hastings to his father's property,[37] and he granted £10 from his Bisley estates to Giles Brugge on 27 May.[38] The confirmation of the stewardship of Chirk to Otwell Worsley,[39] and the lease of Margaret Lady Darcy's lands to William Claxton, show the Nevilles seeking to reward at least some of their supporters.[40]

The explanation for the scarcity of rewards after St Albans lies in the likelihood of an act of resumption in the forthcoming Parliament, when a list of exemptions in favour of York's supporters at St Albans would create a very bad impression, as well as weakening the force of the act. If this is so, York, as so often in the past, was in an unfortunate position, mindful of the need to reward loyalty, unable to do so for fear of jeopardizing his current political programme. Certainly, resumption was worthwhile, even at the price of disappointing his supporters, as it was a fair assumption that it would be popular with the Commons and, more important, would provide an opportunity to weaken the household, the last Beaufort stronghold. With an amenable household, and broad support amongst Lords and Commons, York need not fear the dangerous political isolation of 1451 and 1452–3, which had come so near to ruining him. Much, clearly, depended on Parliament.

Writs of summons were issued on 26 May, except in Lancashire where they were delayed until 30 June.[41] York was summoned simply by the style of duke.[42] Although John Jenny was to express to John Paston doubts about the wisdom of seeking election,[43] it is not clear that his opinions were widely shared. The duke of Norfolk

---

[36] For commissions see *CPR* 1452–61, pp. 255, 257, 258. Of those mentioned, only Thomas Cornewaile and his associates can be politically labelled, as an anti-Stafford group (KB27/767 *Rex* m. 65ʳ).

[37] C44/31/7, 8. [38] SC6/850/28.

[39] *CFR* 1452–61, p. 249. For the Neville connection see BL Egerton Ch. 8542. Chirk may already have been in the hands of Joan Neville, countess of Arundel (*CPR* 1461–7, p. 228).

[40] *CFR* 1452–61, pp. 120, 125, 129, 134. One mainpernor, Robert Kelsey, was a servant of Robert Neville, bishop of Durham, and the Claxtons were also in his service (*DKR* 37/ii, 218, 199).

[41] *CCR* 1454–61, p. 25; J. S. Roskell, *The Knights of the Shire for the County Palatine of Lancaster, 1377–1460* Chetham Society, NS, 96 (1937) App. B.

[42] *Report on the Dignity of a Peer*, ii. 936.

[43] Davis (ed.), *Paston Letters*, ii. 120.

certainly exerted his customary pressure on the shire,[44] and the one election for which record survives, Kent, shows no lack of contenders.[45]

Returns for 204 out of 288 MPs survive for the Parliament. Of these, 128 had not sat either in 1450–1 or the 1453–4 Parliaments, forty-seven had sat in 1450–1, and thirty in 1453–4. Given the bias of the 1450–1 Parliament, these figures suggest a Lower House marginally disposed towards York, although MPs of demonstrably Yorkist sentiment number only eight,[46] with Neville and Mowbray similarly represented. Representation of the household was indifferent, with only twenty-six members, mostly for borough seats,[47] and, although the exchequer had an interest of similar strength, this may have been of as much use to the Bourchiers as to the court. It seems safe to say that York had little to fear from a house of such composition.

The return of a favourable Lower House was obviously of advantage to York, but in early July he was more immediately concerned with the attendance of peers. Some, such as Exeter, he could well do without, and he was, no doubt, grateful for the problems of the northern border as a reason for the earl of Northumberland's absence, but, in general, York needed a large attendance to avoid any impression of repugnance among the peers, consequent on St Albans.[48] Probably to his surprise, certainly to his gratification, he got it.

A variety of factors explained the lords attendance. Civil war, with Cade a recent memory, was in no one's interest. York had clearly shown that Henry was to be given all reverence as king, and all

[44] Ibid. 117.

[45] E13/146 m. 11 *Coram Baronibus* Michaelmas Term. It seems to have been a purely Kent affair, with Richard Culpepper being struck from the writ at a second election, in favour of Gervase Clifton. The current Culpepper genealogy is unsatisfactory (J. Comber, *Sussex Genealogies* (1931)), but there is nothing known about the three Richard Culpeppers then living to suggest any anti-Yorkist tendencies which might explain his failure.

[46] William Browning (Dorset), Giles Brugge (Gloucs.), Thomas Young (Bristol), Walter Devereux (Herefs.), John Clay (Herts.), Leonard Hastings and Thomas Palmer (Leics.), and Thomas Harrington (Yorks.). In addition, William Canning (Bristol) and John Young (London) were closely related to Thomas Young, as was Alexander Browning (Wareham) to William Browning (Nichols, *Collectanea Topographica et Genealogica*, vi. 357). The other MP for Wareham, a town which York controlled, was Richard Chalcote, who received a licence to trade on 24 July (C76/136 m. 1).

[47] Wolffe, *Henry VI*, p. 217.   [48] E28/86/21.

property owners stood to gain from the restoration of recognized royal authority. From patronage some might well stand to gain more than others, and vested interest must have played its part. There may, too, have been a genuine hope that with Somerset dead a more positive accommodation between the king and the duke of York might form the basis for more stable government. Certainly, the items of business presented to the Upper House were the important issues which a new regime ought to have submitted for consideration.

It is regrettable that so little is known of the business procedure of the Upper House in the late middle ages, as the decision to set most of the business of Parliament before committees of peers looks novel, at least in so far as it merited entry on the Parliament roll. The entry is valuable, as it is also records the items of business intended for discussion, although it does not indicate whether other items were excluded.

Eight subjects were proposed, and five of these, the household, Calais and the northern Marches, safe-keeping of the seas, bullion shortages,[49] and peace-keeping in Wales, were put into committee. Except in his capacity as a Welsh Marcher lord, which automatically included him in the Wales committee, York was on none of these, although he was a trier of both English and Gascon petitions.[50] It may be significant that Viscount Bourchier (the treasurer) and his brother (the chancellor) were also excluded from committees, presumably because their offices were deemed to give them more general responsibilities. In this light, York's exclusion may also imply a transcendent position in government,[51] although too much should not be made of this. The committees themselves give, in their composition, every impression of a studious concern for the balance of interests.

The three items not put into committee were much the most sensitive, the setting of 'a parfite love and rest amonge the Lordes of this lande', the establishment of 'an ordinaire paiement' for the Calais garrison, and 'to advertise and ordeyne howe and when the XIIIM. Archers graunted in the last Parlement shall be emploied'.

The lords made no progress in settling their various quarrels. For

---

[49] York's farm of the west country mines may have reflected an interest in this problem.

[50] *Rot. Parl.* v. 278.

[51] On 9 July, at Parliament's opening, he obtained a patent confirming his salary entitlement when protector. This may have been intended as a heavy hint (E13/146 m. 56 *Coram Baronibus* Trinity Term).

those who had been at St Albans there was an urgent need for a full, authoritative, and final exoneration, such that they would be actionable in neither the criminal nor the civil courts. The act which resulted was most ingeniously structured around the declarations of loyalty made before the battle itself. In casting Somerset as the traitor and the king as misinformed, St Albans became a loyal action, and by repeating, and enrolling, the letters written before the battle, York was, in effect, making a profuse declaration of loyalty to the house of Lancaster. Whatever the truth of his loyalties at St Albans, at Parliament he was the loyal subject of the rightful king, and this loyalty he publicly affirmed by an act of personal homage before Henry, and was followed in this by every other peer present.

Somerset was not made to carry the blame alone. Lord Clifford, Sir Ralph Percy, Thomas Thorpe, Thomas Tresham, and William Joseph were initially identified as the culprits. It is difficult to see how Clifford and Percy could have played a similar role to the other three, who were household men. In the stiff fighting at the barricades they may well have inflicted casualties on the followers of York or Neville, but it was no part of this act's intent to put those who fought for the king in the wrong. They were dropped. For reasons unknown, so too was Tresham. Thorpe and Joseph remained to bear the allegations of deliberately misguiding their king. Interestingly, the word 'treason' appears nowhere in the act.

The thoroughness of these actions (and this very thoroughness must give some indication of public scepticism) brought some immediate assurance of York's loyalty, but it did nothing to dispose of the other legacy of St Albans, the internecine rivalry of the great families. It was beyond the powers of the Upper House to heal their divisions. Only the king had the transcendent authority to do that. Later he was to try, and fail; for the moment his personal authority was in abeyance.

Whatever the committee for Calais[52] achieved, the crucial problem, excluded significantly from its remit, that of immediate payment, was not resolved. 'Ordinarie paiement', the committee's problem, had to come from the wool customs; the merchants had therefore to co-operate; they would not co-operate without the

---

[52] The three Nevilles, the bishop of Ely, and the prior of St Johns were sympathetic. Buckingham needed to safeguard his own Calais settlement, Booth of Chester, Boulers of Hereford, and Stourton must be counted hostile (*Rot. Parl.* v. 279).

restoration of, or reimbursement for, their lost wool; that could come only by extraordinary means and those means—discussed by whom?—could not be found.[53] The one thing that made the problem slightly less urgent was that Somerset was dead.

Why the 13,000 archers were mentioned is impossible to say.[54] Foreign policy in 1455 is largely obscure, but the most hopeful prospects and useful employment for such a force were in Scotland, where the earl of Douglas had rebelled, and, by August, was in receipt of rewards from the English exchequer.[55] York may himself have toyed with a French expedition, but the king's policy, recently restated,[56] was peace, and this view was likely at least for the time being to prevail, especially as York had no formal constitutional status. The possibility of the use of the archers for the restoration of control over Calais may be safely dismissed. In fact, nothing at all was done about the Reading archers.

The committees had varying degrees of success, but the results of their deliberations are not of immediate consequence. Presumably, they reported to the whole of the Upper House, who in turn passed business down to the Commons. What the Commons did independently is uncertain. They elected Sir John Wenlock as speaker,[57] but thereafter assumed a passive role in the determination of major items, as supply was not requested.

This is not to say that the attitude of the Commons was overlooked. The act for the restoration of Duke Humphrey's good name was probably initiated by York's supporters, but seems to have been generally popular.[58] Attempts to sort out the late duke's debts were, no doubt, similarly well received.[59] A lot of popular

[53] A warrant of 3 June ordered assignment of 7,000 marks to the Staplers, with a codicil ordering assignment of a further 3,000 marks added after the dating clause. A discussion a few days after 3 June could have been attended only by York, the Nevilles, and Devon, and such ecclesiastical peers as were in London (E404/70/1/73). The problem seems to have been deferred to August.

[54] *Rot. Parl.* v. 279.   [55] Stevenson, *Letters and Papers*, ii/2, 502.

[56] *Calendar of State Papers, Milan*, ed. Hinds, p. 16.

[57] His connection with the Bourchiers has been stressed (Roskell, *The Commons and Their Speakers*, p. 261), but he had fought for the king at St Albans and was the queen's chamberlain. If he had a change of heart, as Armstrong has suggested ('Politics and the Battle of St Albans', p. 56), it is open to question how well this was known.

[58] *Rot. Parl.* v. 335. *Six Town Chronicles*, p. 146, and *Reg. Whethamstede*, i. 181 note the act.

[59] There may be a link between the need to restore the duke's good name and the intention to repay his debts. Any threat of posthumous attainder might have been making the settlement of his estate difficult.

resentments seem to have been solved in a series of short acts, and the wider problems of bullion shortage[60] and household insolvency were tackled with Commons approval.

Both the Commons and the duke of York had an interest in Thomas Young's case, if for differing reasons. As a petition,[61] it spoke only of the rights of free speech and carefully avoided mentioning what had been said in 1451. Yet this must have been fairly general knowledge. The lords of the council who discussed the petition certainly knew it, so did some of the Commons. Surreptitiously, therefore, York was engaged in a propaganda exercise emphasizing his claim to conciliar pre-eminence by encouraging Young's petition. Either the Commons consolidated their privileges, and so condoned Young's utterance, or they rejected the petition because of what was left unsaid, and thereby condoned an unfortunate precedent. The Commons chose to try and tighten their grip on free speech but they may not have been averse to York's conciliar pre-eminence, especially given the realities of July 1455.

The ambiguity of the petition's circumstances was not lost on the council, who contrived to avoid a formal confirmation by the king of a putative Commons right, by having the king refer the petition to the council, so that it could be regarded, and treated, as any other petition for an act of grace by the king. Thomas Young was acting in all of this as a loyal servant of the house of York, not as the vanguard of the fight for liberty of speech in the Commons. He won the battle of propaganda for York, the battle for the liberties of the Commons was really little more than a skirmish, the Crown conceding nothing.[62]

The proceedings closed on 31 July with the declaration of a general pardon for all offences before 8 July. It was to be taken up by rather fewer persons than its 1450 or 1452 predecessors.[63] The earliest recipients include Lord Egremond and his brother Richard, on the second day of issue, 6 August, the duke of Exeter on

---

[60] A new controller of the Mint, Thomas Montgomery, was appointed on the last day of the session (*CPR 1452–61*, p. 246).

[61] The original is SC8/28/1387; cf. *Rot. Parl.* v. 337.

[62] For other interpretations see B. Wilkinson, *The Constitutional History of England in the Fifteenth Century* (1964), 287–8; J. E. Neale, 'The Commons Privilege of Free Speech in Parliament', in R. W. Seton-Watson (ed.), *Tudor Studies* (1924), 265.

[63] The pardon roll has 2,021 entries (C67/41). Storey, *End of the House of Lancaster*, p. 216, notes 2,057 entries on the exchequer roll.

18 August, the bishop of London, the earl of Arundel, and Lord Fauconberg. Many of the recipients were armigerous, and most of them had played a part in one or other major disturbance in recent times. As most of these disturbances were essentially local vendettas, the pardons were likely to intensify, rather than pacify, local antagonism; a possibility which must have occurred to the council. The attractions were, probably, a simplification of the flow of judicial business and the hope that bygones might now be bygones, with the further hope that a strenuous law-enforcement programme would contain renewed violence.

Pardons cost the government nothing, which was, perhaps, as well, as loans were keeping the exchequer afloat, Parliament had voted nothing, and the wool trade was in disarray. The uncertainty seems to have disturbed the workings of the exchequer itself, as the entries on the rolls are not always straightforward. The picture which emerges is that, loan repayments aside, the earl of Salisbury with £583. 18s. 11d. assigned, and the duke of York, assigned £326. 13s. 4d., together with £20 in cash, were much the largest beneficiaries in a very lean period.[64] There were no payments to the household until the Michaelmas Term—£80 on 13 October—and payments thereafter were very modest until 16 December, when £1,844. 16s. 7d. was assigned to various departments of the household. In this term, York and the Nevilles received practically nothing.

In an attempt to cut through the financial problem, the council resorted to the drastic expedient employed by Lumley in 1447–9—changing the customs officers. York had first employed the expedient in April 1454, at the start of his protectorate. On 4 April 1454 eight ports had lost at least one customer, Boston, Lynn, and Ipswich losing both. London had lost one of its collectors of alien subsidies the same day, another, twelve days later, and its searcher on 15 April. Bristol, Southampton, and Yarmouth had also lost a customer in that month.[65] Thereafter, there had been only the very occasional change, the Bristol searchers being, however, singled out for sustained attention.[66]

Somerset's recovery of authority had brought a block of changes in March 1455, nine posts losing at least one customer, but this was

---

[64] E403/801; E403/806.   [65] *CFR* 1452–61, pp. 57–60.

[66] This was not a politically motivated campaign. There were allegations that major customs frauds were being perpetrated at Bristol (KB27/775 *Rex* m. 114ʳ).

modest when compared to York's changes in June, when ten customers, ten searchers, and two collectors of tunnage and poundage were dismissed.[67] The changes in customs officers were presumably intended to invalidate tallies, the changes in searchers to prevent smuggling, which, given the uncertain conditions prevalent at Calais, must have been a sore temptation.

With Parliament in session, and the king often present, a superficial normality developed, but it is clear that real normality was elusive. The king and his council deliberated on various issues in the first days of August.[68] The council then broke up in an atmosphere of considerable political uncertainty. Its next recorded meeting was on 27 October, but it is likely that it met earlier in the month.[69]

Over this period the king kept his sanity, but his bodily health gave cause for concern. Kymer had attended him in June,[70] and three surgeons attended him in July.[71] Their actions seem to have been efficacious, as there is no record of subsequent illness, and he was able to move between Westminster, Windsor, and Waltham,[72] and in late August to Hertford.[73]

What part he took in government is unknown, but some decisions, such as the licence to elect a new bishop of Exeter on 8 October,[74] could not have been taken without his knowledge. Neville's selection, a month later,[75] simply shows Henry's awareness of political realities; whoever rules must do so with York's approval. Anyone tempted to side with the king against the York–Neville coalition could easily suffer Somerset's fate. For the moment, the great lords had accepted York, and until Henry actively repudiated him his position was unassailable by lesser men. What is puzzling is York's failure to rule more vigorously after Parliament's adjournment at the end of the first session; unless, that is, he found the Bourchiers

---

[67] *CFR* 1452–61, pp. 105–11.

[68] Principally on Calais (C81/1546/103–6; C76/137 m. 8). The king's sign manual is to be found on several warrants of this period (e.g. *PPC* vi. pp. 255, 257–8, 259–60).

[69] C81/1546/107.   [70] Rymer, *Foedera*, xi. 366.

[71] E404/70/2/89.   [72] E28/86/25; E404/70/3/2, 12.

[73] Fears for his health were expressed in Oct. 1455 (Davis (ed.), *Paston Letters*, ii. 127), and in Nov. 1457 an approver included in his report 'he [the king] slepeth to myche therto he was hurte at Seynt Albones' (KB9/287/53). Useless as direct evidence about Henry's physical well-being, these observations do show something of the concern in popular circles.

[74] *CPR* 1452–61, p. 282.   [75] Rymer, *Foedera*, xi. 367.

reluctant to comply. Certainly, he left London, not to return before 31 October.[76]

With no one at the helm the state drifted. Again, trouble flared up in Derbyshire, and this despite Buckingham's best attempts at arbitration in September.[77] The same month saw riots in London.[78] But the greatest outburst of violence was in Devon, where the Courtneys rampaged for most of October against Lord Bonville and his affinity,[79] murdering Nicholas Radford in the process—a murder which aroused widespread repugnance and predisposed many to a protectorate.[80] These events may well have swayed the Bourchiers, as Sir William Bourchier was one of the early targets.[81] Parliament was due to reassemble on 12 November, with a Great Council scheduled for 6 November, presumably to ratify the appointment of sheriffs, possibly also to fix an agenda.[82] On 10 November this council was invited to appoint the duke of York as the king's lieutenant in Parliament, and the thirty-eight peers present assented. Within a week York was once again protector.

It has been persuasively urged that the protectorate was not necessitated by any mental relapse of the king, but that it was the product of unscrupulous opportunism on the part of a faction close to the duke of York.[83] Certainly, Henry was nowhere reported as sick. As his original illness is unknown, it is, unfortunately, impossible to know whether the fear voiced in the Commons, that the demands of law enforcement might precipitate a relapse, was the voice of genuine concern or of constitutional propriety. Granted, however, that the king was not ill, need the motives of York and his supporters necessarily have been so reprehensible? If the king was indeed fit and well, then the decision to nominate York as lieutenant

[76] C81/1546/108. Fifteen other peers were present.

[77] For earlier attempts to calm Derbyshire see *PPC* vi. 250–1. For Buckingham see I. H. Jeayes, *Descriptive Catalogue of the Charters and Muniments of the Gresley Family* (1895), 96–7.

[78] *Benet's Chronicle*, p. 215; KB27/782 *Rex* m. 1656ᵛ, m. 169ʳ.

[79] Storey, *End of the House of Lancaster*, pp. 165 ff; KB9/16 m. 63.

[80] G. Radford, 'Nicholas Radford, 1385?–1455', *Report of the Transactions of the Devonshire Association for the Advancement of Science, Literature, and Art*, 63 (1931), 278. The news reached London on 21 Oct., and was being broadcast within a week (Davis (ed.), *Paston Letters*, ii. 126.

[81] KB9/16 m. 88; KB27/780 *Rex* m. 40ʳ; cf. *CPR* 1452–61, p. 305.

[82] This Great Council nominated George Neville to Exeter when twenty-one peers were present (Rymer, *Foedera*, xi. 367).

[83] J. R. Lander, 'Henry VI and the Duke of York's Second Protectorate, 1455–6', *BJRL* 43 (1960–1), 46–69.

in Parliament is decidedly odd. There is nothing in the composition of the Great Council which approved this step to suggest any particular predilection for York,[84] and the composition of the Upper House did not significantly alter over the following month.[85]

The Lords could have resisted Commons pressure. It was articulated, not by the speaker, Wenlock, but by William Burley, which, for the obstructively-minded, would have offered opportunities of delay.[86] The pressure was not exerted directly until 15 November, when the Commons refused to discharge any further business until a protector was appointed.[87] This might not, in fact, have amounted to much of a threat. Parliaments can always be dissolved, especially by kings in full possession of their faculties. What is striking is that the Commons' wishes were, in fact, met four days later,[88] by a very restricted proposal which satisfied York also.

The proposal advanced for discussion on 17 November, was that York be protector, as he had been in 1454. At his own request, a council was to be nominated 'to whoos advis, conseill and assent, I wull obey and applie myself', as had been the case the previous year. A committee was appointed to establish the limits of York's powers, comprising four spiritual peers, York, Rochester, Norwich, and Ely, and four temporal peers, Buckingham, Warwick, Bourchier, and Stourton; a sympathetic group, but by no means subservient. They allowed York rather more generous financial provision, otherwise keeping his powers to those of 1454. There was one change of significance, the definition of the circumstances in which York might be dismissed. In 1454 it had been at the king's pleasure. This time it was to be by the king, with the assent of the lords spiritual and temporal in Parliament. This clause suggests that as the king was not ill his recovery could not be regarded as the *terminus ad quem* for York's authority. The need was, instead, to allow the lords to determine when the circumstances had arisen which would terminate the need for York's services. In typical medieval fashion they gave one definition of these, the majority of the prince of Wales, but the lords in Parliament were not anticipating so long a period. York was to be given the king's power, but restricted,[89] and for a

---

[84] *PPC* vi. 261.   [85] Ibid. 267.

[86] Lander, 'The Duke of York's Second Protectorate', p. 84, points out the careful discussion of York's terms of service in the Lords.

[87] *Rot. Parl.* v. 285.   [88] Ibid. 288, 322.

[89] Ibid. 286–7. It is noteworthy that on 19 Nov. his sign manual stood highest on the council warrants, but thereafter was kept below that of the archbishop

very limited intention, as the Commons had requested—the restoration of order in Devon.[90]

There are thirty-eight names on the warrant creating York Lieutenant in Parliament on 10 November, and on the warrant of 11 December licensing him to adjourn Parliament there are thirty-three, so there had obviously been a fairly constant attendance in the Lords.[91] This impression is confirmed by the thirty signatures to a warrant of 4 December.[92] Ordinary council meetings had about ten members, though this rose to seventeen on 12 December,[93] for no very evident reason, and was the same the following day, when the more significant topic of Calais was discussed.[94] At ordinary councils the protector, with the chancellor, Winchester, Norwich, and Ely of the prelates, and Salisbury, Warwick, and Fauconberg of the lay lords, were the best attenders, which can only have been to York's advantage. His last recorded attendance of the year was on 16 December,[95] but, unfortunately, this is also the last surviving warrant of the series, and it is, therefore, impossible to discover who thereafter ran the council.

Business appears to have been conducted without fear or favour, and without much reference to the Commons. In fact, it is difficult to determine what, if anything, the Lower House did, which may in turn have adversely affected attendance in the next and final session. In the Upper House resumption and its consequences had to be thought through. Foreign policy may also have been a concern.

The evidence for this comes from a series of depositions made between August 1456 and February 1457 to commissioners appointed by Charles VII to inquire into alleged treasons committed by the duke of Alençon.[96] Each witness spins a different tale, but they can be fairly readily woven together to provide a story which started in June 1455 when Huntingdon Herald went to visit Alençon, reporting *inter alia* the death of Somerset at York's hands. Alençon

---

of Canterbury, an order which was sustained until 12 Dec., after when no apparent order of signature can be discerned (E28/87/3, 8, 9, 10, 12, 15, 17).

[90] Before Christmas, when he was committed to Devon, York was reassigned £338. 15s. 4d. After Christmas this fell to only £46. 13s. 4d. (E403/806; the issue roll gives a pre-Christmas total of only £281. 13s. 4d., E401/848).

[91] *PPC* vi. 261–2, 274–6.   [92] Ibid. 265–6.

[93] E28/87/16.   [94] *PPC* vi. 276–9.

[95] E28/87/23. He was not, however, a signatory to a warrant of the same day in favour of the duchess of Somerset (*PPC* vi. 282).

[96] Bib. Nat. MS Fr. 18441.

sent a sounding-mission to Calais which was joined by the herald in July. Late in August Alençon's emmissaries arrived in London, where they were told to await an assembly of the Lords three weeks before Christmas. On 23 November Alençon's contact in Calais, Sir Richard Harrington, notified the duke of York of Alençon's plans, and six days later York himself saw the emissaries. He was suspicious of one, Thomas Gille, but respected the other, Edmund Gallet, as he was the son of Louis Gallet, one of the king's French secretaries. Sporadic talks took place, Gille returning to Calais on Christmas Eve, and to his master on 6 January.[97]

The duke of York's interest is clearly attested, and the more plausible because several witnesses recall his general scepticism, and all connected with the negotiations recount a close examination by York and his colleagues.[98] Those consulted by York in November– December are given as the chancellor and the treasurer, Buckingham, Salisbury, Warwick, and Wenlock, with Wenlock being the principal interrogator, except on the projected marriage of York's son to Alençon's daughter, where Mulso asked most of the questions. Wenlock and Clay also quizzed Gille about the attitudes of the king of Aragon and the count of Armagnac.[99] It is doubtful whether York gave serious thought to a possible invasion of France,[100] but both he and fellow councillors may have been exercized as to just what Huntingdon Herald, pursuivant of the duke of Exeter, might have been up to the previous summer, and with what possible consequences.

The problem to which York had most strenuously to address himself was the west country, a problem for which he had full powers, as was Parliament's intention: 'Obey hym and kepe his commaundements as ye wolde and owed to obey us yf we were there in oure owne persone';[101] an impressive command, and it struck fear into Bonville, who ran to the king; but the king sent him to York.[102] The earl of Devon, the real culprit in the Radford affair, was still

[97] Fo. 41ᵛ, 62ᵛ, 46ᵛ, 64ʳ.   [98] Fo. 47ʳ, 63ʳ, 110ᵛ.

[99] Fo. 52ʳ. The marriage proposal was again discussed in Jan. (fo. 105ʳ). The king of Denmark was hoping to draw Aragon into an anti-English coalition at this time (E. M. Carus-Wilson, 'The Iceland Trade', in Power and Postan (eds.), *Studies in English Trade in the Fifteenth Century*, p. 179).

[100] Policy in March 1455, after Somerset's release, had been to seek an extended truce with France (*Calendar of State Paper Milan*, ed. Hinds, p. 16).

[101] E28/87/22 (letter, 'by the King' to the mayor and commonalty of Exeter. It bears no other warranty).

[102] *Chronicles of London*, p. 166.

rampaging around Powderham on 19 December,[103] though York
evidently expected him at Shaftsbury[104] in obedience to his
summons. Eventually he was apprehended, seemingly without a
fight, and both he and Bonville were imprisoned; by order, however,
of the council, not the protector.[105] Order was restored in the west,
and Radford's heir felt secure enough to start proceedings against
Courtney.[106]

The duke of York had done well in the west country. This was
entirely commendable, and was very much after the Commons'
desire. Henry, in an imaginative moment, had a mind to retain his
obviously very useful talents as a law enforcer, but without such an
exalted constitutional status.[107] Whether he would have been able to
give substance to this idea must be debatable, but the king was given
no real chance, and for this a political misjudgement of Duke
Richard must take the blame.

His error was in his handling of resumption, the principal
problem of the second parliamentary session. York, who had
rewarded Wenlock over Christmas,[108] was well supported by the
Commons, if the evidence of *Benet's Chronicle* is to be accepted.
The opposition came from the Lords, unanimous, save one—again,
according to the same authority.[109] Why this should have been so is
not easy to establish, as it is not clear what stage in its meta-
morphosis the original petition for resumption had reached. The
evidence points to the petition having been first presented in July,[110]
but prosecuted more severely on or after 19 November. This is
evident from the fact that the original petition appends as its final

---

[103] KB27/780 *Rex* mm. 65[r], 76[r], 87.   [104] *Six Town Chronicles*, p. 109.

[105] If Devon was apprehended in late Dec., he spent an appreciable time with
York, as he was not handed over until York came to Parliament (*Chronicles of London*,
pp. 109–10, 166). York was in London by 24 Jan. (*PPC* vi. 285).

[106] KB27/779 *Rex* mm. 84 ff.

[107] Gairdner (ed.), *Paston Letters*, iii. 75.

[108] £20 p.a. 'for good service and counsel' (SC6/850/4). Wenlock was also able, on
8 Nov., to recover some of the fines incurred because of his Henley riots (KB27/779
Rex m. 28[r]).

[109] *Benet's Chronicle*, p. 216. Only one warrant survives for this session, dated
24 Jan., ten days into the session. Twenty-two peers signed (*PPC* vi. 285). York was
able on 2 Feb. to sustain his parliamentary campaign against Thomas Thorpe (SC8/
152/7596; *CCR* 1454–61, p. 108).

[110] Wolffe, 'Acts of Resumption', p. 610 and id., *Royal Demesne*, p. 138. Wolffe
bases his dating on the indecisive expression 'Michaelmas next'. Firmer evidence
comes from the structure of the petition where the first petition concludes before the
codicil exempting the prince of Wales and York as protector (*Rot. Parl.* v. 303;
cf. Griffiths, *Reign of Henry VI*, p. 769 n. 194).

clause an exemption in favour of Prince Edward and the duke of York as protectors, which was neither applicable nor relevant in July. This amended petition was then debated, and the process of examining exemptions was set in motion. The Commons, in an attempt to prevent additional exemptions, then introduced in the final session, on or around 14 February, a revised resumption-petition so drastic that it provoked the determined opposition of the Lords.[111] It was, therefore, around this second petition that the dissension flowed.

John Bokkyng's letter of 9 February[112] gives some indications of a possible chronology: a resumption petition presented in the first fortnight of the new session of Parliament with York's support;[113] the queen, 'a grete and stronge laboured woman', struggling to exempt herself from its provisions; only Warwick riding in support of York to Parliament in array sufficient to forestall hostile action by their peers. If this is so, then York was already very vulnerable to dismissal by the Upper House, as the terms of his patent provided. Benet's story of the lords 'crossing over' to bring Henry to Parliament, to repudiate resumption and receive York's resignation, seems increasingly plausible.[114] Certainly, on 25 February York resigned as protector, and left London before Parliament ended. He did not appear at the council-table again that year.

---

[111] *Rot. Parl.* v. 328; cf. *Benet's Chronicle*, p. 216.

[112] Gairdner (ed.), *Paston Letters*, iii. 74.

[113] York stood to gain personally from the measures, as he might hope once again to set hands on the Isle of Wight, lost in 1451, and Baynards Castle, specifically excluded from one of the provisos of the first petition (*Rot. Parl.* v. 309).

[114] Huntingdon Herald reported that Henry and Duke Richard quarrelled soon after 25 Feb., and that York then left London. Edmund Gallet reported a conversation with the king after this, in which Viscount Beaumont figured largely, together with Sudeley and Stanley (Bib. Nat. MS Fr. 18441 fo. 112^r).

8

LOVEDAY TO LUDLOW

Duke Richard spent the summer of 1456 at Sandal,[1] whence he was supposedly defending the northern border, but was, in fact, expending most of his energies composing flamboyant letters of defiance to the Scottish king.[2] Invasion scares in Cornwall (May), the Isle of Wight (June), and Kent (August)[3] may have given his aggressive posturing a ready acclamation in the southern shires.[4] In the North, his sympathies for the Nevilles left him with a more prejudiced audience.

The senior Nevilles had not accompanied him north. Salisbury remained in London, appearing occasionally on the council, and he was one of only three lords to present themselves on 7 June for a proposed Great Council[5] Warwick was preoccupied with Calais. The one lasting achievement of the final session of Parliament had been the act for the settlement of Calais, an act whose passage may well have been instrumental in keeping Warwick close to York in the difficult February days. In fact, the control of Calais was settled by the Staplers, who had taken matters into their own hands the previous December, and had then realized that the admission of Warwick was in their own interests. Nonetheless, an act of Parliament was necessary to secure the financial settlement, and Warwick had needed to ensure its passage before Parliament was dissolved. The manner of Warwick's subsequent take-over was smooth, if technically somewhat complicated, and by July he was well established, and able to resist the large French force which, rumour suggested, was in the vicinity.[6]

---

[1] DL29/8899/560; Davis (ed.), *Paston Letters*, ii. 141.

[2] *Correspondance of Bekynton*, ed. Williams, ii. 143; Rymer, *Foedera*, xi. 383; cf. Dunlop, *James Kennedy*, pp. 139–42. The threat from the Scots was sufficiently serious, however, for the justices to hold no sessions at York from 20 June to 27 Aug. and from then to mid-Oct. (Just. It. 1/1546 mm. 10ᵛ, 16ʳ).

[3] *CPR 1452–61*, pp. 309, 307, 311.

[4] *Benet's Chronicle*, p. 217, exaggerates both the threat and the response.

[5] Davis (ed.), *Paston Letters*, ii. 148.

[6] Harriss, 'Struggle for Calais', pp. 43–7.

Henry may not have wished to oppose Warwick. The signs are that he was trying hard to retain his loyalty, and also that of his father, enlarging on this tolerance of the Nevilles with modest rewards to the Bourchiers, as well as to old supporters.[7] Of these last, the duchess of Somerset did best, recovering the lands given to her husband and, since February, resumed—lands which included, once again, the Isle of Wight,[8] for which York had angled so often. But there was no concerted attempt to buy support, as there had been in 1452 after Dartford. Instead, as a measure at once practical and tactful to the Commons, most of the proceeds of resumption were vested in the prince of Wales. Largess was not distributed to the barons, and commoners did no better.[9]

If anyone did well it was York. His lease of the Cornish mines was confirmed in May,[10] and he was reassigned fourteen tallies, totalling £936. 16s. 0d., with another two worth £53. 6s. 8d. redeemed for cash.[11] Attempts were made to settle sums due to him as protector. During his second protectorate, £193. 17s. 8d. had been paid to him of the 2,000 marks due, and it was arranged, on 9 March 1456, that he be entitled to ship wool free of customs to the balance outstanding.[12] The king's motives may not have been entirely innocent, as this settlement would prevent York raising the idea of a protectorate under a financial guise, but as a financial settlement it seems to have benefited York, and by November he was trying to purchase Caister from Fastolf.[13]

Financially, he may have felt more secure, but by November 1456 York was politically very exposed. In early May the commons of Kent had again produced a 'Mortimer'—this time a tailor called John Percy of Erith, where York had property—and for a week there had been major disturbances in north Kent.[14] What the Kentishmen's

---

[7] *CPR* 1452–61, pp. 275, 286–7; C76/13 m. 6. Humphrey Bourchier and Thomas Neville were jointly created chamberlains of the exchequer on 3 March, but pressure may have been exerted on them, as they, in turn, chose Simon Grimsby as keeper of the counter tallies (E404/71/5/40). On the same day, Alice Lovell was licensed to enter her portion of the Cromwell lands (*CPR* 1452–61, p. 278). Somehow, Henry seems to have alienated Buckingham (Davis (ed.), *Paston Letters*, ii. 141–3).

[8] *CFR* 1452–61, p. 153; *CPR* 1452–61, pp. 277, 291.

[9] Thus, the Gurney estates went to the prince, except for Curry Mallett, which William Browning, one of York's councillors, was able to lease in March (*CFR* 1452–62, p. 158).

[10] Ibid. 150; *CPR* 1452–61, p. 291.   [11] E403/808.

[12] *CPR* 1452–61, p. 278.   [13] Davis (ed.), *Paston Letters*, ii. 149, 167.

[14] KB9/49 mm. 2, 4–6; KB9/288 mm. 58, 59; *PPC* vi 287–9; *CPR* 1452–61, p. 307.

rising owed to the violent anti-Lombard riots in London in late April[15] is impossible to say, but both revolts were alarming to the king, and his punitive action was sufficiently vigorous to leave both London and Kent resentful.[16]

No sooner had these troubles been solved than disturbances flared in the west Midlands. Two of York's men were at the root of the violence, Sir William Herbert and Sir Walter Devereux. The latter had started things in April by seizing the mayor of Hereford, then Herbert attacked the earl of Wiltshire's property at Orcop. These local quarrels escalated in June into an attempted raid on Kenilworth, with the alleged intention of killing the king.[17] The two then joined forces in August and attacked the earl of Richmond at Carmarthen Castle, an action intended, no doubt, for their own advantage, but, as the castle was still technically under York's jurisdiction, the action readily took on a broader and more disconcerting significance. On 25 October Herbert raided Glamorgan and Llandaff, in an insurrection organized from Abergavenny, but for what purpose is unknown, the indictment being very brief.[18] James II of Scotland was meanwhile, mischievously claiming that Duke Richard had sought his aid in an attempt on the throne.[19]

The government was itself going through a process of upheaval. The queen had already determined to establish herself, together with the prince and their respective households, in the west Midlands, and by September Henry had joined them. For the next four years England was to be governed from Coventry, but with the routine bureaucratic functions still discharged in Westminster. It was an ill-conceived notion which did much to enfeeble royal authority for the rest of the decade.[20]

In early September York was in London, at the bishop of Salisbury's house,[21] where he was treated to a particularly savage propaganda spectacle. The heads of five dogs were impaled outside his lodgings in Fleet Street, each carrying a scurrilous verse in its

[15] *Six Town Chronicles*, pp. 143–4.
[16] *Letter Book K*, ed. Sharpe p. 377; Davis (ed.), *Paston Letters*, ii. p. 148.
[17] KB9/35 mm. 40, 115, 32.
[18] KB9/35 mm. 25, 52.
[19] Stevenson, *Letters and Papers*, i. 324.
[20] Griffiths, *Reign of Henry VI*, p. 777 ff; Wolffe, *Henry VI*, p. 309. The patent of 28 Jan. 1457 establishing tutors for the prince of Wales states 'quorum tutela et regimine ipse et sua cunta habent disponi et administrationi (Rymer, *Foedera*, xi. 385).
[21] *Benet's Chronicle*, p. 217; *Six Town Chronicles*, p. 144.

jaws.[22] Their message was as direct as its presentation was brutal. The son of a traitor, York deserved to die, but, instead, he left others to pay the price for his offences:

> What planet compellyd me, or what signe
> To serue that man that all men hate?
> y wolde hys hede were here for myne
> ffor he hath caused all the debate[23]

If York's evasiveness angered the author 'the debate' at least was to provide an obliteration,—no doubt gratifying—of York's political hopes. There had been talk of a council to meet in London on 8 October,[24] but, in fact, it met at Coventry on the sixteenth.[25] York attended, having first visited Sandal.[26] As a council it was a disaster, and was, more than any other single event, responsible for the deterioration of English political life to the turmoil of 1459–63. The household, led now by the queen, staged a coup. Chancellor, treasurer, and privy seal were dismissed. York and the Nevilles were isolated.[27] For the duke of York this was scarcely a novel experience, and he was all too well aware of the likely consequences, but not even he, at his most pessimistic, could have anticipated the aftermath. On 5 November, Exeter, Somerset, and Shrewsbury attempted to ambush Warwick, who was journeying to London.[28] On 1 December it was York's turn to be attacked, this time at Coventry, by the young duke of Somerset.[29]

Meanwhile, the queen had moved swiftly in the autumn, negotiating adroitly with Gruffydd ap Nicholas, and using his undoubted, if maverick, influence to restore royal authority in south Wales, especially in the principality.[30] Other bureaucratic pressures

---

[22] Loc. cit.

[23] *Historical Poems of the XIVth and XVth centuries*, ed. R. H. Robbins (New York, 1959), 189–90.

[24] Davis (Ed.), *Paston Letters*, ii. 161. On 3 Sept. Henry had ordered that no one enter London except peaceably and with a modest retinue (*Letter Book K*, ed. Sharpe p. 377).

[25] *Benet's Chronicle*, p. 217; cf. E403/809.

[26] He was at Sandal on 30 Sept. (DL29/8899/560). He was reportedly in London on 11 Oct., as a witness to the surrender of the great seal (*CCR 1454–61*, p. 211).

[27] Davis (ed.), *Paston Letters*, ii. 164. Annoyance at Bourchier's loss of the great seal may have caused the council to be transferred to Coventry.

[28] *Six Town Chronicles*, p. 144; Griffiths, 'Local Rivalries and National Politics', p. 627.

[29] *Bale's Chronicle*, p. 159. The mayor saved him.

[30] Griffiths, 'Gruffydd ap Nicholas and the Fall of the House of Lancaster', p. 226.

could also be brought to bear on York, and in November he found himself on the losing side in a chancery action, as a feoffee for the late Sir Leonard Hastings.[31]

The attempt to pin-point responsibility for the Herbert–Devereux disturbances was made at a Great Council which opened at Coventry on 15 February 1457 and closed some time before 14 March.[32] No immediately contemporary account of this council survives, but there is, in the preamble to the 1459 act of attainder of the duke and his supporters, an account of an assembly which is probably this council.[33] According to the preamble, the chancellor made 'divers rehercels' to the duke of York, following which the duke of Buckingham, on behalf of all the lords temporal, stated that York could only lean on the king's grace. This he implicitly requested on York's behalf, by going on to demand that York should be punished, should there be any repetition. Unfortunately, the preamble does not say of what.

The purpose of the preamble was to persuade Parliament in 1459 that York's attainder could be justified, and it is, therefore, a hostile source, but it does look as though some sort of accord was struck at Coventry, for when the indictments of Herbert and Devereux were drawn up for the oyer and terminer commission sitting at Hereford from 2 to 7 April, it was a careful document making no direct allegations against York.[34] This makes it very difficult to know just what part he was supposed to have taken in the 1456 disturbances. The charges relating to trouble at Hereford and Orcop do not seem likely to have had much to do with him, but the charges against Herbert and Devereux, of attempted assault on the king at Kenilworth and the foray against Edmund Tudor, may carry echoes of the suspected complicity of York. There is a problem with the former charge, however. The king was nowhere near Kenilworth in June, [35] and it is possible to explain the latter charge, without reference to duke Richard, in terms of an opportunistic exploitation of the military stalemate between the earl of Richmond and Gruffydd ap Nicholas. Herbert, in particular, had hopes of

---

[31] C44/31/7, 8. The following Feb. he made his one and only payment of the £110 farm of the gold and silver mines of Devon (E401/854).

[32] *The Coventry Leet Book*, ed. M. D. Harris, Early English Text Society, pt. ii. (1908), 277.

[33] *Rot. Parl.* v. 347.

[34] KB9/35; KB27/784 *Rex* mm. 88ʳ, 100, 102ʳ.

[35] Wolffe, *Henry VI*, p. 370.

diminishing Gruffydd's influence.[36] Where York may have played a part was in the later, now obscure, disturbances of 25 October, only two weeks after the change of major office-holders.[37] It was probably an impossibility to assemble, at Coventry in 1457, sufficient proof to persuade York's peers of his guilt, especially as at least one of them, the powerful Marcher duke of Buckingham, had also been offended by the October purge. Discretion suggested that the matter be fudged, and in this presumption of innocence York was recompensed, on 21 April, for the loss to the earl of Pembroke of the castles of Carmarthen, Aberystwyth, and Carreg Cennen, although he was never to see any of the £40 per annum settled on him as compensation.[38] The renewal of his Irish lieutenancy on 6 March, not technically necessary for another six months, may also have been intended as a warning.[39]

For Herbert and Devereux the legal process rumbled on for some months. Herbert, the better connected, received a general pardon in June. Devereux was imprisoned.[40] For York, the king continued his presumption of innocence through the summer months, and modest gestures of reconciliation were attempted; a weekly market for Fotheringhay,[41] an assignment of £446 as lieutenant of Ireland,[42] a commission of array in Suffolk.[43] It is difficult to ascribe this generosity, albeit subdued, to the queen or her advisers. It was the king's work, a preliminary to an attempt to draw York back into conventional political activity.

This was a highly commendable intention, but it is difficult to see what Henry anticipated as the longer-term outcome of such a venture. The tone of English political life in 1457 is, admittedly, peculiarly elusive. One longer-term trend, the consolidation of household power in the midlands and the north west, is clear, but government intentions towards the Nevilles and, in a different manner, towards London and Calais, are vague; perhaps a genuine reflection of the king's hesitancy as to just how such problems were

[36] Griffiths, 'Gruffydd ap Nicholas', p. 224.
[37] Griffiths, op. cit., p. 225, sees all the events of 1456 as instigated by York.
[38] Rymer, *Foedera*, xi. 388; *CPR* 1452–61, p. 340.
[39] *CPR* 1452–61, p. 341. He did not indent for the post until 17 Apr. (E101/71/4/937).
[40] Griffiths, *Reign of Henry VI*, p. 780.
[41] *Calendar of Charter Rolls 1427–1516*, p. 128.
[42] 15 July, paid by the hands of Thomas Blount (E403/810).
[43] *CPR* 1452–61, p. 402, warranted by king and council.

to be tackled. Any settlement with York would have to take its place in such a context.

Henry himself seems to have believed it possible to produce a negotiated settlement between the various hostile families, and to have believed that in so doing the destructive tensions of English politics would be unwound. There was some sense in this. The difficulty is to see what policies Henry could offer to which a newly-united baronage could give effect under his leadership. Social and commercial policies were not widely regarded as government issues. Unlike their forbears, the English nobility had at this time no well-established taste for secular building, for collecting, or for patronage, which might have kept them at home, and Henry's court offered little by way of elegant distraction. The one policy which might have worked, war, was unacceptable to the king. When Henry determined on the reconciliation of his leading baronial families, he embarked on a worthwhile and laudable enterprise, but one which, in isolation, offered no prospect of long-term stability.

Henry first set about a reconciliation in a Great Council meeting at Westminster in November. The little that is known of this comes from a writ issued at the end of the month, in which the king summoned a further council to meet on 27 January 1458, with a view to concluding, and sufficiently providing for, the matters as yet unresolved.[44] Those matters cannot now be identified, but Henry had done well to bring this first council to pass at all. In order to provide sufficient security he had summoned levies from the shires in October, and had paraded them ostentatiously, in order to subdue the Londoners and restrain less-disciplined lordly retinues.[45] The exercise was certainly sufficient to reassure Duke Richard, who arrived in London some time before 10 November.[46] Not all of the council's actions will have pleased the duke, however—Thomas Thorpe's creation as keeper of the privy wardrobe in particular[47]—

---

[44] *PPC* vi. 290–3.

[45] Griffiths, *Reign of Henry VI*, p. 805. Griffiths believes these levies to have been summoned according to the terms of the Reading Act of 1453. This is uncertain. The later writ of 17 Dec. was issued on the basis of the act, and would, therefore, require four months' notice before practical results could be obtained. The king seems to have been in a frame of mind to attempt to pacify the lords during Lent, with the inducement of an army at Eastertide to be led on campaign, the king at the head of his people in defence of his realm. The duke of York was commissioned to raise archers in Northamptonshire, Essex, and Yorkshire (*CPR* 1452–61, pp. 406–10).

[46] SC6/1114/2. York had been at Shrewsbury in October (Salop CRO Box viii. n. 385 m. 3ʳ).   [47] *CPR* 1452–61, p. 392.

but there was a sensitivity in the decision of 5 November to make a twelve-year lease of the Isle of Wight to the duke of Somerset. Three weeks earlier it had been a grant during pleasure.[48] Likewise, the grant of a pension to the earl of Douglas was reassuring to the wardens of the Marches, and of interest to York as a recent campaigner on the northern border.[49] The new naval commission for the earl of Warwick gave him further autonomy in Calais.[50] For his part, Henry was able to draw the Courtneys back into the fold.[51] Such tentative achievements, and the very fact that the Great Council had not collapsed into open violence, gave Henry the confidence, evident in his writ, to try again.[52]

The duke of York arrived in London on 26 January, the day before the scheduled opening of the council, and took up residence in Baynards Castle.[53] The earl of Salisbury was already lodged in the Arbour. For Henry this was most promising. Somerset arrived on the last day of the month,[54] and Exeter, Egremond, and Clifford shortly after. Unfortunately, they then attempted to ambush York and Salisbury as they rode to Westminster.[55] They failed, but the practical problem remained of how to conduct serious sustained negotiations without losing all in a disastrous attempted vendetta. Henry withdrew to Chertsey, leaving the Lord Mayor to restore order.[56]

When Warwick arrived in London on 14 February, Henry returned to Westminster, and the wording of a writ sent that same day to the earl of Arundel, ordering him to attend forthwith, suggests that Henry had been awaiting the younger Neville earl before attempting anything very substantial.[57] Now he sought 'to sette apart suche variaunces as ben betwixt divers lordes of this oure reaume'. This he envisaged as the elimination of the personal

[48] Ibid. 390–1.
[49] Ibid. 418.
[50] Ibid. 413.
[51] *CPR* 1452–61, p. 393.
[52] The process against Pecock in Dec. may also have been envisaged by Henry as part of the pacification of Church and State.
[53] *Brut*, ii. 525; *Chronicles of London*, p. 168. The entry for this year in the *Great Chronicle* is identical. He brought 'hys oune housold onlye', according to William Worcester (Davis (ed.), *Paston Letters*, ii. 532), but 400 men according to the London chronicler.
[54] Gairdner (ed.), *Paston Letters*, iii. 125.
[55] *Six Town Chronicles*, p. 159.
[56] Barron, 'London and the Crown', p. 95.
[57] *PPC* vi. 293.

antagonisms generated by the battle of St Albans, together with other specific points of personal dissension between magnates.[58]

Of these latter, one may have been Ireland,[59] another was certainly the keeping of the seas. The earl of Warwick was confirmed in this post on 4 March, a decision which left the duke of Exeter with feathers still ruffled a week later.[60] These were, however, side-issues by comparison with St Albans. Any settlement of this problem was likely to be taxing, and Henry somewhat prejudiced his chances of a broadly-based accommodation of peerage sentiment by moving, on 20 February, to Berkhamstead.[61] This left intermediaries (who had presumably to work to a brief) to solve a problem which was more one of attitude than of financial compensation. It also had the unfortunate effect of making the king inaccessible to the duke of York, confined within the city, the retinues of the duke of Somerset and his supporters without. It might be urged that Henry, in staying at Berkhamstead to 14 March, wished to distance himself during discussions, in order to disseminate an attitude of impartiality. If so, he should not have allowed Somerset, Exeter, Clifford, and Egremond to come to him on 23 February.[62]

The arrival of the earl of Northumberland, on 26 February,[63] allowed further scope to negotiations about St Albans, and they proceeded usefully, an agreement to enter into recognizances to keep the peace until Michaelmas being a fairly immediate outcome.[64] This preliminary pacification achieved, more substantial matters could be pursued, and by 5 March it was possible for several of the parties to enter into mutual bonds with the two chief justices.[65] York was not involved in these arrangements, neither was Exeter, nor Somerset, and the bonds, for £100, were modest, which suggests modest issues. In fact, the main problem, vendetta, became more serious, with an attempt by Somerset and Northumberland to ambush Warwick on 9 March.[66] The earl had been riding towards

---

[58] Wethamstede places Henry's intentions firmly within the context of St Albans (*Reg. Whethamstede*, i. 296).

[59] 6 Mar., licence for the earl of Wiltshire to be absent from Ireland (*CPR 1452–61*, pp. 417, 419; *CCR 1454–61*, p. 276).

[60] *PPC* vi. 294.

[61] *Reg. Whethamstede*, i. 298; Wolffe, *Henry VI*, p. 371.

[62] Davis (ed.), *Paston Letters*, ii. 533.   [63] *Six Town Chronicles*, p. 160.

[64] Davis (ed.), *Paston Letters*, ii. 533.

[65] *CCR 1454–61*, p. 282 (cf. the bonds of £500 entered into by the chief justices on 6 Mar.).

[66] *Six Town Chronicles*, p. 160.

Westminster, and this second attempted assault seems to have persuaded Henry of the need to construct a new mechanism for negotiation. His persistence, despite the provocative actions of York's critics, is impressive. On 16 March he came to Westminster, and the following day led a public procession for peace.[67] In the afternoon he was joined by the queen.

He then set in motion negotiations to solve the main issue, instructing the archbishop of Canterbury to act as intermediary between the York–Neville group, meeting in the mornings at Blackfriars, and the others, meeting in the afternoons at the Whitefriars house on Fleet Street, Henry himself remaining at Westminster. By 23 March the essentials had been completed, and mutual bonds were agreed by the principal parties to accept the king's arbitration, York's being the largest at £10,000.[68] At the palace of Westminster the following day the terms of the settlement were promulgated.[69] Henry had achieved his Loveday.

Unfortunately, he had expanded much effort on the solution of one issue, St Albans, only to overlook another, in many respects more serious. The issue on which constructive, long-term political stability depended was the political relationship between Duke Richard, on the one hand, and the queen and the royal household on the other; an issue obvious to all since the coup of October 1456. Admittedly, it would have been difficult to incorporate the queen into any written public agreement, as she enjoyed no obvious political role within the constitution of the realm as then understood, but it should not have been impossible to propose a reallocation of office-holders, and to award York some distinctive role in government. By allowing England's political problems to be reduced to the level of family squabbles, Henry was overlooking issues of much deeper significance which had been troubling the body politic since 1450, if not earlier. But then, had Henry been able to see so clearly, many of the deeper problems would not have taken root.

In so far as the terms of arbitration have survived, they would

---

[67] Loc. cit. The king's movements are unclear (cf. Griffiths, *Reign of Henry VI*, p. 842 n. 208). MS Vitellius A XVI may be correct in saying he came to Westminster four days before mid-Lent, Sunday, 7 March, but this may be a transcription error for four days after mid-Lent. *Benet's Chronicle*, p. 221, as Griffiths notes, states that the king came to Westminster on 20 Mar., but Benet states that he came from the city.

[68] *CCR 1454–61*, p. 292.

[69] *Benet's Chronicle*, p. 221; *Six Town Chronicles*, p. 160; *CPR 1452–61*, p. 424.

appear to have had two elements: a cash recompense to the families who suffered by York or Neville hands at St Albans, and, secondly, a perpetual memorial in the form of a chantry, in the abbey church of St Albans, for the slain, to be financed from a landed endowment devised by York and the Nevilles.[70] As a settlement, this seems very one-sided, but scrutiny of such evidence as survives suggests that York had driven a very hard bargain. In theory, he was to pay out some 5000 marks in compensation, but, in fact, it was agreed from the outset that the payment would be in tallies, yet to be issued, for sums due to York as lieutenant of Ireland. These tallies, as yet notional, were then transformed, by agreement, into a licence to York to export wool to the customs value of 10,000 marks.[71] If the necessary time was available to effect such shipments, York stood to make 5000 marks of his salary from the deal; far more than he had hitherto been paid. In fact, York was to make no attempt to hand over the money, although he may have shipped some wool.

Potentially more costly was the promise to settle land to a yearly value of £45, as such land might have a purchase-value in the order of £900, but a two-year respite was allowed, providing that £45 was paid each year. York and the Nevilles paid up in 1459.[72] By 1460 events had overtaken the Loveday settlement, so their long-term intentions of honouring the agreement must remain speculative. However, had they refused to amortize the land, it is difficult to see how Henry could have coerced them, without precipitating that very conflict which the Loveday sought to avoid.[73]

What was obvious, then as now, was that the Loveday arrangements themselves give the lie to the importance of the arbitration. When York emerged from St Pauls, it was hand in hand with Queen Margaret, not with the duchess of Somerset. The 'reconciliation' was presented as political, not familial, but the only solid negotiation had been the discussion of compensations and obits, which was an evasion of the real issue. But, as that issue was the control of the king, it was, perforce, unlikely that Henry would have been aware of it. That he rejoiced with a genuine heart and voice one cannot doubt,

[70] Rymer, *Foedera*, xi. 434; *CPR 1452–61*, p. 424; *CCR 1454–61*, 369.
[71] *CPR 1452–61*, pp. 424, 546. For the licence see C76/140 m. 16. The wool could be exported by Sandwich or Southampton only.
[72] *CCR 1454–61*, p. 369.
[73] A breach of the terms of the settlement was to be punished by forfeiture of the bonds; the proceeds, interestingly, to be applied to the household (*Reg. Whethamstede*, i. 307).

but it is difficult to dispel the image of weary cynicism on the faces of the other participants.[74]

For a while the public pretence of reconciliation was sustained. By the end of the Trinity Term assignments had been made to York totalling £686. 13s. 4d. to cover pension arrears.[75] Such commissions of the peace as were issued included York, where appropriate, although he was not added to any bench on which he had not previously sat.[76] He was summoned, in August, to a council in October, but he may not have attended. When, on 30 October, a major reshuffle of offices took place, he was absent, and was not present at any recorded November meeting.[77] He was, however, summoned in February 1459 for a Great Council scheduled to meet on 2 April.[78]

Superficially, all was well, but the real thrust of politics no longer lay in the royal council but in the competition for influence in the shires. First in the midlands, then in the south east, the Crown contrived to secure the major strong points and the leading county families. New marriages bound leading court families together, and patronage variously rewarded, or bought, loyalty.[79] Against this there was little York could do. His one crumb of comfort was the king's ham-fisted involvement in London's affairs, which left very influential sections of the City community with little cause for gratitude. The attempt to murder Warwick in February 1459 showed the true nature of political feeling, Loveday or no Loveday.[80]

In late June 1459 a Great Council assembled at Coventry. The archbishop of Canterbury, the duke of York, the bishops of Ely and Exeter, the earls of Salisbury, Warwick, and Arundel, and Viscount Bourchier were absent, and, at the queen's prompting, they were, according to *Benet's Chronicle*, indicted of charges unspecified.[81] According to an allegation made later in the year at the Coventry

---

[74] There may have been attempts by the household to conceal from the king the limitations of his Loveday (*Gregory's Chronicle*, p. 203).

[75] E401/861; E403/814; E404/71/2/70, 73. The assignment of £110 against his own farm of the west country mines had only notional value. Of the real worth of the others one can only be sceptical.

[76] *CPR* 1452–61, pp. 660 ff.

[77] Stevenson, *Letters and Papers*, i. 361–9. He was absent from the Garter chapter on 22 Apr., as were the earl of Salisbury and Viscount Bourchier (Anstis, *Order of the Garter*, ii. 162).

[78] *PPC* vi. 298.

[79] Griffiths, *Reign of Henry VI*, p. 802.

[80] *Great Chronicle*, p. 190.

[81] *Benet's Chronicle*, 223.

Parliament, Sir William Oldhall and Thomas Vaughan esq. were engaged in a treasonable conspiracy at 'Garlickhythe' on 4 July.[82] It has been suggested, most plausibly, that their crime was to communicate the outcome of the Coventry council to the earl of Warwick at Calais.[83] By 1 August, again according to the Coventry Parliament, Alice countess of Salisbury was engaged in a treasonable conspiracy at Middleham.[84] There may be some truth in this, as the bailiff of Bawtry was, in mid-August, allegedly inciting his colleagues to treasonable acts.[85] The town of Shrewsbury received a letter from the duke of York at this time, the contents of which are unknown.[86]

Why the queen should have chosen to challenge the duke and his Neville associates publicly in June is difficult to say. The impression is that Henry had tried, since the Loveday, to construct an aristocratic council and to base it at Westminster. Murderous family rivalry thwarted this initiative. On the negative side, the growing independence of the earl of Warwick in Calais would certainly have to be challenged, and the queen grasped that this would have to be done away from London, and quickly.[87] There is nothing in the conduct of the duke of York to suggest that he was responsible, either directly or indirectly, for this decision. The queen was worried about Warwick.

Benet may have exaggerated the numbers of those charged in late June, but the behaviour of the Neville earls, and of York, shows that, irrespective of the others, they believed themselves to be in danger. Accordingly, they sought to gather together, in order to present a united case both actually and symbolically to the king. The intention was to gather in strength in the west midlands and then negotiate directly with Henry. Warwick had no difficulty in persuading London that his intentions were peaceful, and was admitted on 20 September[88] with a significant force, marching on towards his town of Warwick the following day. He was shadowed very effectively by the duke of Somerset, who forced him north of

---

[82] *Rot. Parl.* v. 349.   [83] Griffiths, *Reign of Henry VI*, p. 847 n. 274.
[84] *CPR 1452–61*, p. 518.   [85] KB27/800 *Rex* m. 11ʳ.
[86] Salop CRO Box viii. n. 387 m. 1ʳ.
[87] Griffiths, *Reign of Henry VI*, p. 809. There were rumours in the winter months that if Parliament could be summoned it would expel Warwick from Calais (Stevenson, *Lettes and Papers*, i. 368).
[88] *Gregory's Chronicle*, p. 204; *Short English Chronicle*, p. 72; *Benet's Chronicle*, p. 223, says he had 500 men.

the town, and so on to Ludlow. Salisbury was similarly shadowed by Lord Audley, who sought to prevent him crossing the river Weaver. The young Somerset was, presumably, uneasy at confronting the Calais veterans. Audley had no such reservations, and Bloreheath resulted.[89] It was understandable that there should have been violence. For the royal affinity, the simultaneous movement of armies from the north and the south east, together with York's troops massing at Ludlow, could only be understood as a co-ordinated, three-pronged attack on the king's midland stronghold. In this they misjudged their enemies' immedite intention, which was to lobby the king from strength, rather than attack.[90]

The three lords made no hostile move after Bloreheath, and the government was obliged to reflect on its next actions. For a fortnight nothing happened. Then, rightly concluding that the balance of advantage lay in making the next move political rather than military, the Crown, at Leominster on 9 October, made public its intentions; Henry's perhaps, the queen's certainly. Parliament was summoned to assemble at Coventry on 21 November. York, Warwick, and Salisbury were not summoned.[91] Evidently, they were to be either impeached or attainted.

Events now moved quickly. The bishop of Salisbury, sent by the king with an offer of pardon, met with a brisk response. Such offers were useless, came the reply. The Yorkist lords had a right of summons which was being flouted; a disingenuous reply, for all involved must have been aware of the implications of their non-summons, and, as Warwick correctly pointed out, their safety at previous councils gave little confidence in such guarantees. This reply ruled out any possibility of compromise. The lords at Ludlow would not consider a pardon, and, by implication, their guilt. The recent events which they so conveniently overlooked the Crown chose, naturally, to exploit, and so, having declared them rebels, a direct message was sent by the hands, significantly, of Garter, to York and the Nevilles, who were then at Worcester. In reply, the three peers, in Garter's presence, before the high altar of Worcester cathedral, took a solemn oath that they acted 'for the prosperity and

---

[89] Some local score settling lay behind the engagement (KB9/263/21, 22).

[90] For a differing interpretation of the military circumstances surrounding Bloreheath and Ludlow see A. Goodman, *The Wars of the Roses: Military Activity and English Society, 1452–97* (1981), 25–31.

[91] *Report on the Dignity of a Peer*, ii. 941.

augmentation of [the king's] high estate',[92] and jointly signed a letter
for the herald to take to the king. In this, they justified their
assumption of arms with a plea of self-defence against those lords
about the king; 'regii collaterales' in Whethamstede's happy phrase.[93]
Already, Warwick had cited the incompetence of these lords as
justification for the Yorkists' actions. Now, they added the very
astute observation, that those same lords were motivated primarily
by their desire for the lands, offices, and goods which would be
forefeit to the king.[94] At court, not surprisingly, such claims made
no impression, but they did have a wider audience. Whethamstede
reports three general vindications for the Yorkists' conduct in
circulation at the time, the removal of evil councillors, and the
removal of the household men, which two motives he balanced with
a third, the creation of Duke Richard as king.[95] The *Brief Latin
Chronicle* reflects a similar public uncertainty about the motives of
all concerned.[96]

The oath taken, the rebel lords moved from Worcester to Ludlow,
but via Tewkesbury, an odd route which can only imply an attempt
to move south, a move successfully contained by the royal army,
which then forced them to retreat across the Severn to Ludlow.[97]
This took place on 11–12 October, bringing the two armies to
Ludlow field, which York fortified in the hope, perhaps, that
fortification might induce an attitude of negotiation, as it had at
Dartford.[98]

Whethamstede no doubt enjoyed himself composing his descriptions
both of the hesitancy of the troops, and of the Yorkist lords rallying
their despondent followers with stirring speeches, but one suspects
that he was correct only about the despondency and about the
continual discussions in the rank and file.[99] The king's general
pardon had only a few days to run.[100] Trollope's defection, along
with the Calais garrison, was certainly the decisive event, but

[92] Stow, *Annales*, p. 405; Davies (ed.), *English Chronicle*, p. 81.
[93] *Reg. Whethamstede*, i. 337.
[94] The Beauchamp inheritance was also a factor.   [95] Loc. cit.
[96] *Brief Latin Chronicle*, in *Three Fifteenth-Century Chronicles*, ed. J. Gairdner,
Camden Society, NS, 28(1880), 168.
[97] *Benet's Chronicle*, p. 224.
[98] *Gregory's Chronicle*, p. 205.
[99] *Reg. Whethamstede*, i. 338. Goodman, *Wars of the Roses*, p. 29, accepts the
abbot's account, although on p. 124 he points to an element of creativity in the
descriptions.
[100] *Rot. Parl.* v. 348.

Reginald Grey esq. may well have defected earlier in the day,[101] and the 'oulde soudyers'[102] who slipped away may not have been just Trollope's men. One chronicler even speaks of possible treachery.[103] In such circumstances, running away was sound military sense. York abandoned Ludlow to its fate.[104] The court retired to Worcester, harrying all in its path for no very obvious reason.[105]

Surprisingly, no effort was made to pursue the lords, and for a while there seems to have been uncertainty as to whether the earl of March was still in the country. The chancellor was reported in October as worried that March would lay claim to an earldom designated, thanks to damage to the manuscript, as 'Ha . . .';[106] probably Aumale. The worry was not unreasonable, as any debate on this claim would have reopened two issues: why the Yorkist lords had not been summoned, with the implicit a priori assumption of guilt, and, secondly, by a distinct implication of that particular title, the right of the duke of York to the throne.

Just what the court should do after Ludlow was not at all clear. Some sort of case would have to be presented to Parliament, but there were difficulties. York had taken up arms against the king in person, the royal banner being displayed.[107] Salisbury could be indicted for Bloreheath, Warwick for misconduct at Calais. It had the makings of a good case, weakened, however, by the well-known fact that the three peers had persisted to the last in declarations of loyalty to the king, and had made accusations against household peers which enjoyed a considerable measure of popular sympathy. If these points could be countered, this was, undoubtedly, the best opportunity yet of ridding the queen's interest of one of its most persistent and dangerous critics and, through the distribution of forfeited lands, of giving a broader group of influential men a stake in the security of the Lancastrian dynasty.

Parliament would require some managing if this were to be achieved, but the venue, if unpopular in some quarters,[108] offered

---

[101] *CPR* 1452–61, p. 573.   [102] *Gregory's Chronicle*, p. 205.
[103] *Benet's Chronicle*, p. 224.
[104] *Calendar of Charter Rolls 1427–1516*, p. 155.
[105] *Gregory's Chronicle*, p. 207; *Benet's Chronicle*, p. 224. York's estates lay for the most part to the west of Ludlow.
[106] Davis (ed.), *Paston Letters*, ii. 185.
[107] *Benet's Chronicle*, p. 224; J. G. Bellamy, *The Law of Treason in the Later Middle Ages* (Cambridge, 1970), 201.
[108] Hist. MSS. Comm. *Seventh Report*, i. 431.

encouraging prospects, and elections might perhaps be massaged
into producing a sympathetic house. The very hostile *English
Chronicle* alleges that such election management did take place,[109]
but, if so, the results do not seem very impressive. More was
required than manipulated elections, even if such were possible, and
the king's advisers set about the creation of what they hoped would
be an impressive and compelling case in favour of their proposed
course of action, attainder. The *Somnium Vigilantis*, composed in
advance of the Coventry Parliament, shows the way the arguments
of York's enemies were being developed.[110]

The argument is presented in a highly stylized manner, having its
own rules of composition and presentation,[111] but, essentially, the
rebels were allowed six points of defence: that mercy was a necessary
attribute of a king; that the realm needed its nobility; that the cause
of reform was an honourable one; that there were no specific charges
levelled against them; that the defence of the realm required them;
and that, should circumstances change, mercy requested now might
later be coerced. So one-sided is the presentation of the case that this
defence was ignominiously routed, to the total satisfaction of the
author. An impartial critic might be less readily satisfied. The very
lengthy reply to the defence that reform is inadequate justification
betrays an unease that this issue was likely to receive close scrutiny.
The argument that York had no God-given right to judge was
reasonable, but the inability to prefer specific charges against him
was legally uncomfortable. Internal dissension could well cause
trouble with the enemies of the king's peace within and without the
realm.[112] Speed alone would contain such a problem. Unless some
stiffening of sinews could be achieved, Henry might yet pardon
them all, even if it might be 'cruelnes to have mercy apon themm'.

The reply to the second article betrayed the true nature of the
problem, 'the restorynge of thaim were none other but a wylfull
submyssioun and exposynge of the kynge to thare wylle'. Those
about the king had to see York and the Nevilles crushed. Henry had

---

[109] Davies, *English Chronicle*, p. 83.
[110] J. P. Gilson, 'A Defence of the Proscription of the Yorkists in 1459', *EHR* 26
(1911), 512–25.
[111] M. Kekewick, 'The Attainder of the Yorkists in 1459: Two Contemporary
Accounts', *BIHR* 55 (1982), 29.
[112] In 1458 York had shown some sensitivity to the dangers of internal dissension
in the face of external threat (Stow, *Annales*, p. 403). Similar rumours occupied the
Cinque Ports in 1460 (Hist. MSS. Comm. *Fifth Report*, p. 493).

to be held to this, and Parliament would have to be persuaded both of the justice of the case and of the constitutional desirability of the act of attainder by which it was to be achieved. The preamble to the act was, in consequence, a most carefully-worded indictment.[113]

From his youth, it was claimed, the duke of York had been 'cherished and favoured', but, despite the favours of high office in France and Ireland, he had gone on to stir up Cade, then directly to defy, and to seek to usurp, the royal power. He had broken his most solemn oath, had levied war against the king at St Albans, and, despite royal clemency, had gone on to stir up insurrections in Wales, at Bloreheath, and finally at Ludlow. A manifest traitor, on whom clemency was wasted, Parliament must perforce proceed to judgment.[114]

The two houses were persuaded, and the duke of York and twenty-three others, by an act of novel form based on the process of 1450 against the duke of Suffolk, were accordingly attainted.[115] The case against York was a good one, and was never satisfactorily refuted by his supporters, and it remains a plausible basis for interpreting his actions, even when all due allowance has been made for the partiality of the compilers. As the Mortimer claimant, his political attitudes were of more profound political consequence than even consideration of his great wealth would necessitate. He could never be just another government critic, and the attainder of 1459 enjoyed its plausibility precisely because Duke Richard had not sought to be just such another critic. He had sought to use his right by blood to determine the counsel which the king might receive. Failure in France and mismanagement at home had given him a large constituency to whom he might appeal, and at Dartford he had pressed his case. He failed then, and thereafter, because he could not persuade his peers. They accepted as a constitutional axiom that it was for the king to choose his councillors. The coercive attempts of Duke Richard, however well supported by the lineage of his blood, were an accroachment on the royal power. This was the case against York: that he had sought to coerce the king to accept his counsel and, increasingly, his alone. Theories of popular sovereignty might, perhaps, have given a more stable basis to York's claims, but such

---

[113] *Rot. Parl.* v. 347–9.
[114] Notoriety alone, since the reversal of the judgement on Roger Mortimer in 1354, was insufficient grounds for conviction (Bellamy, *Law of Treason*, p. 83).
[115] Op. cit. 187.

theories were scarcely regarded in England at this time, and certainly
would not have been exploited by the duke, had they been available.
The only manifestation of popular assent constitutionally admitted
was at the coronation of a new sovereign.

The Coventry Parliament, which assembled on 20 November,
moved slowly and cautiously towards attainder. Three days to elect a
speaker was average, but then it hesitated as to what to do next.
Around 30 November the king made his offer to pardon all who
submitted within eight days,[116] and this allowed the bill of attainder
to be pushed further forward. By 7 December York and other
leading figures were already attainted, but who to include and who to
exclude of the smaller fry had yet to be determined.[117] Four days
later, sixty-six peers took an oath of loyalty to the king, queen, the
prince of Wales, and the heirs of the prince, lawfully begotten.[118]

The act of attainder brought all York's property into the king's
hands, but it was a difficult to act to which to give immediate effect.
To some extent this must have been anticipated, as royal power in
Wales and the North had been weak for some years, and it was
unlikely that Crown servants would find much of a welcome. Such
steps as were taken, however, were honourable. No attempt was
made to dismember the estates, only small parcels of land being
handed out, and the possibility of a restoration of the ducal lands was
not made administratively impossible. A clause in the act explicitly
safeguarded any jointure lands of the wives of the attainted, although
in the case of Duchess Cecily no jointure settlement appears to have
been in effect. On 20 December Henry settled revenues of 1,000
marks per annum on a group of feoffees to her use, the leading
secular peer in the enfeoffment, the duke of Buckingham, being
entrusted with her custody.[119]

Surviving records give the impression that this was one of the few
actions of central government concerning York's estates which had
any practical effect. The immediate intention of the Crown was to
raise loans against the security of the confiscated estates, employing
the money to cover the costs of resistance to the duke and his

---

[116] The duchess of York came to Parliament on 6 December, presumably to seek a
pardon (*Gregory's Chronicle*, p. 206; Davis (ed.), *Paston Letters*, ii. 188).

[117] Loc. cit.   [118] *Rot. Parl.* v. 351.

[119] *Rot. Parl.* v. 350; *CPR* 1452–61, p. 542; *Gregory's Chronicle*, p. 206. For a
partisan account see Davies, *English Chronicle*, p. 83. A grant of the office of parker of
Miserden, an enfeoffed estate, was made to John Mody from Stamford on 2 Jan. 1460
by unknown authority (SC6/850/29).

adherents.[120] This, perhaps as much as sensitivity to criticism of estate dismemberment, required the smoothest possible transition of ownership, which in turn required the retention of both the administrative structure and the personnel of the former owners, whenever possible. Between 6 and 14 December this essential administrative framework was constructed.[121] In counties where York held very modest estates these were administered in conjunction with the forfeited estates of other supporters, but the division was for convenience' sake rather than out of malice.[122] The Crown was helped by the fact that the treasurer, the earl of Wiltshire, had at one time been a ducal councillor. Just how diligent York's other erstwhile councillors were in the service of their new master is uncertain, but there were difficulties in the winter months in the southern marches,[123] and it may be significant that the account roll for the lordship of Fotheringhay for this year is blank.[124]

As would be expected if the revenues were already pledged, grants of land from the ducal estates were initially very limited. Almost all grants related to south-western properties, mostly in favour of the earl of Wiltshire. There is evidence that he took immediate economic advantage of his new holdings.[125] The next stage in the exploitation of the forfeited lands came on 16 March, when a team of exchequer officials was given overall control of all their revenues for the next three years.[126] This arrangement opened the way to leasing, and Lord Dudley, the duchess of Somerset, and the earl of Pembroke took advantage of the opportunity.[127] The leases themselves were usually for twenty years and were for very modest parcels of property. The duchy was essentially preserved intact.

With due allowance for those minor bureaucratic confusions

---

[120] *CPR 1452–61*, pp. 597, 576. On 24 Feb. 1460 the exchequer was ordered to pay 3000 marks to the earl of Wiltshire to cover the costs incurred 'late in our progress and in especial upon the field against the rebels' (E404/71/4/30).

[121] *CPR 1452–61*, pp. 526, 530–1, 539. John Milewater, John Vincent, John Eyleriche, and, later, William Browning, all duchy servants, were re-employed by the Crown. Milewater entered into a bond for good behaviour for 200 marks (Palgrave, *Antient Kalendars*, p. 238).

[122] See, for example, ibid. 547 (Herts.), 561 (Lincs.). The latter carries the date 14 Oct. 1459, but the patent may well be of later origin, retrospectively dated.

[123] Griffiths, *Reign of Henry VI*, p. 851 n. 332.

[124] SC6/1115/7.

[125] For a grant of Petherton to the earl see *CPR 1452–61*, p. 542. For his enjoyment of the profits of Knole, Steeple, and Creech see SC6/1113/14.

[126] *CPR 1452–61*, p. 572.

[127] *CPR 1452–61*, pp. 261, 265, 267, 273; Rymer, *Foedera*, xi. 434.

which invariably punctuate the more complex administrative adven-
tures of medieval government, it must be said that the transition of
ownership of the ducal estates was, on paper, a success. In practice it
is less easy to be sure. On 13 March 1460 Denbigh and other castles
unspecified were reportedly in the hands of rebels,[128] and, although
Denbigh probably fell soon after, other castles were apparently still
holding out a month later.[129] Whether the Crown ever gained
complete control of the Welsh marches before the landing of the
Yorkist earls in Kent must be open to doubt. It was not for want of
trying. Letters patent always made explicit reference to castles, both
in the March and elsewhere, and the Crown regularly exempted
them from the control of erstwhile Yorkist estate officials.[130] In the
North, John Talbot esq. was granted Sandal, and Egremond
Conisbrough, though they may have had some difficulty in securing
possession. Fotheringhay went to the duke of Exeter, a useful base
for any venture against Ampthill, Sir Philip Wentworth took Clare,
and Viscount Beaumont, in all probability, held Stamford.[131]

Thus was the duchy disposed of, but, realistically, Henry's
advisers anticipated the duke's return. Commissions of array to resist
him were issued in December and again in late February.[132] This
was, essentially, a defensive policy, but the aggressive initiative of
sending Somerset to Calais, after some striking preliminary successes
had failed,[133] so there was little else Lancastrian supporters could do
except wait. This was a difficult policy to sustain, partly because
maintaining a continual watch was costly in money and goodwill,[134]
and partly because the habit of governing from the Midlands had left
the coastal periphery bereft of serious royal interest in recent years.
Scotland too, with the Nevilles out of the country, could not be
ignored, despite the four-year truce of 1459.

As for the Yorkist lords, there can be little doubt that the duke and
his second son, Rutland, left Ludlow in order to go to Ireland,[135]

---

[128] CPR 1452–61, pp. 574, 576, 578, 605.   [129] Ibid. 602.

[130] Cf. ibid. 534, 550, 574, 585–8. Surprisingly, Herbert retained control of Usk
(p. 549). Of those nominated to aid in the royal recovery of Wales only one, Sir John
Barre, remained loyal to Henry VI after Northampton. The rest were all acceptable to
the Yorkist lords in Nov. 1460 (cf. pp. 602, 632).

[131] CPR 1452–61, pp. 570, 534, 547, 536, 533.

[132] Ibid. 557–60, 605.

[133] Harriss, 'Struggle for Calais', p. 48.

[134] Sharpe, *Letter Book K*, pp. 402–3; Goodman, *Wars of the Roses*, p. 149.

[135] Once there, bills notifying that the duke 'ys at Devylyn strengthed wyth hys
erles and homagers' were circulated lest, like Thomas earl of Lancaster, he be indicted

but it is much less clear that Warwick, with the earl of March, left with the certain intention of going to Calais. The two sources for his movements, Waurin and the *Great Chronicle*,[136] agree that he ended up on the Isle of Jersey, but Waurin lands him there by accident, as the result of errors in navigation in the Bristol Channel compounded by the prevailing wind, the *Great Chronicle* putting him on board ship in South Devon courtesy of John Dinham esq. There is a strong possibility that both are correct, that Warwick did, in fact, board ship in Wales, was blown on to the North Devon coast, crossed the county to the English Channel, and took ship to Jersey. It follows that the earl of March accompanied Warwick as an insurance against the capture of his father's party, or against his boat foundering in the autumn weather of the Irish sea. Warwick was, in fact, heading for Ireland, expecting to join York there. That he eventually ended up in Calais, and in command, on 2 November, was very bad luck for Henry VI, and, given the behaviour of the Calais soldiers at Ludlow, entirely unpredictable.

Once in Calais, Warwick lost no time setting about its defence, to such effect that by March 1460 he felt able to leave Calais and set sail for Ireland, leaving behind the earl of March to avoid unnecessary risk to his life. However, the fact that his eldest son was, and was to remain, in Neville hands, must have been a persistent consideration in York's mind. It must also have been evident to York, as Warwick's twenty-six ships sailed into Waterford harbour,[137] that the earl was not only a very able commander but that whole companies of men and ships were defecting from the Lancastrian regime to serve the earl. Such defections had been singularly absent from York's career hitherto. The duke might have the blood of kings in his veins, but it was Warwick who knew the way to his potential subjects' hearts.

as having fled 'to the wode as an outlawe' (Davis (ed.), *Paston Letters*, ii. 540; Bellamy, *Law of Treason*, p. 50).

[136] Waurin, *Croniques*, v. 277; *Great Chronicle*, p. 191.

[137] *Calendar of Carew MSS: Book of Howth*, ed. Brewer and Bullen, p. 471. Waterford, a Talbot town, seized this opportunity to throw off the earl's authority, and was duly rewarded (*Calendar of Charter Rolls 1427–1516*, pp. 171–6). York was to take additional action against the Talbots, depriving the earl of his Irish chancellorship, which went to Rutland (Lascelles, *Liber Munerum*, i/2, 203), and forcing concessionary leases, for his private advantage, from Thomas Talbot, prior of the Hospitallers (Berry, *Statutes of Ireland*, pp. 752–5).

9

FAILURE

According to Waurin, the Waterford conference, which must soon have transferred to Dublin, decided to look for more support from the English nobility, and agreed that York, having assembled an army in Ireland, should land in the north, Warwick in the south. The sympathy of Kent was noted, with the obvious implication that Warwick should land there. Just how reliable a record this is must be open to some doubt. Waurin, for example, has the duchess of York and the young George and Richard present at Waterford, which is wrong. Waurin may well be speculating, but his central proposition, a co-ordinated landing, has a plausible sound to it.[1]

Some additional observations might be made. York was in a much safer position in Ireland than Warwick was in Calais, where his need to finance himself through piracy would sooner or later produce an international military response. The duke could afford to be in less of a hurry, which was, perhaps, as well, as he had to ensure sufficient security in Ireland to persuade men to follow him to England, and the agriculturally-based revenues of Ireland were much slower to exploit than dramatic seizures of merchantmen. The outcome of the Waterford–Dublin negotiations was an agreement for a co-ordinated invasion of England in the summer months, on or about the feast of St John the Baptist. Whether anything further was agreed is unknown.

This plan gave Warwick rather more time than he needed, York rather less. The duke had not been dilatory since his arrival in Ireland. Parliament had been summoned to Drogheda for 7 February, was adjourned to Dublin on 22 February, and, with a brief adjournment from 3 to 7 March, met there until 5 May.[2] York was to play a complex game in this Parliament, with some skill. The

---

[1] Waurin, *Croniques*, v. 286. Prior to 1459 this chronicle's entries are confused and unreliable. From that year onwards they are detailed, are substantially independent of London chronicle sources, and show a determination to preserve the reputation of the earl of Warwick which suggests a source close to the earl in the 1460s.

[2] Berry, *Statutes of Ireland*, p. 638.

essentials of the scheme were to exploit nationalist sentiment in order to exclude Henry VI's influence and give York *de facto* regal authority in Ireland, without conceding any *de jure* right to self-government for Ireland, which might ultimately weaken any future Yorkist regime in England.

In Ireland, the duke's authority rested on the letter patent of Henry VI of 6 March 1457, creating him lieutenant of Ireland for a second term from 8 December following, with the same financial provisions as previously.[3] In fact, the Crown had been marginally more conscientious in discharging its financial obligations than York had hitherto been in the discharge of his governmental functions. In July 1457 he was paid £446. 0s 11d.,[4] and on 28 March 1458, as part of the Loveday settlement, he had been licensed to ship wool free of customs to a total of 10,000 marks; a sum regarded as due to him as lieutenant of Ireland, presumably, at least partly, owing to him from his first term. York's sole contribution to the government of Ireland was to revoke Richard Tame's appointment as second engrosser of the Irish exchequer, made in September 1457, in favour of Thomas Kent, promoted the following November.[5] The earl of Kildare as deputy was the effective ruler.

Despite this neglect, or perhaps because of it, the Anglo-Irish welcomed York, although the decision to summon Parliament to Drogheda, in York's own county of Meath, rather than to Dublin, may reflect an initial wariness on his part. As for the Gaelic Irish, circumstance favoured York. Successive deaths among the O'Neills had put the two families of Tyrone and Clandeboy once again into violent confrontation, this time over the control of Omagh.[6] For a brief period in 1459 the quarrel was patched up, but the resolution of the internal feuds of the O'Donnells permitted the reconstruction of the customary Clandeboy–O'Donnell alliance, and the whole of Ulster was once again in confusion. In 1460 there was a brief lull, but there is no evidence that the Great O'Neill was likely to find much support in Ulster for a raid on the Anglo–Irish. The problems in 1460 lay to the west, where the O'Connors inflicted a heavy defeat on the Anglo-Irish some time before September 1460.[7] This was

---

[3] E101/71/4 n. 937; *CPR 1452–61*, p. 341.
[4] E403/810, by authority of a privy seal, citing, correctly, the patent of 1447.
[5] *CPR 1452–61*, p. 399.
[6] *Annals of the Four Masters*, ed. O'Donovan, iv. 1005.
[7] Loc. cit.; *Annals of Ulster 1379–1541*, ed. B. MacCarthy (Dublin, 1895), 201, 207.

essentially a threat to the earl of Kildare's power-base, and York could afford to leave the problem with the earl, but what appears to be a separate threat, from the O'Reilly's, had to be met in a pitched battle on 3 September. In a related operation York used Thomas Barrett (bishop of the somewhat notional see of Annadown, and hitherto suffragen of George Neville in Exeter) to stir up trouble on the O'Reilly's western flank, in a war against the archbishop of Tuam.[8] When York appointed William Sherwood as bishop of Meath in place of Edmund Oldhall, it was evidently intended that he should act as York's agent, containing any further O'Reilly threat. Just how the duke acquired the services of this highly qualified doctor of canon law is, regrettably, a mystery.[9]

Containing the military threats of the Gaelic Irish was important for York's own security and for domestic Irish opinion, but much more important was the need to establish a legitimacy for York's actions, as, without a consensus of opinion on his constitutional status, there was every possibility of civil war in the province. The Irish Parliament pushed its opportunities to the limit, and the king's lieutenant did little to restrain them. By the end of the first session, on 3 March, it had ratified his patent of appointment, a major constitutional concession by York, and agreed that the lieutenant, in the absence of the king, represented 'son trespluis noble persone et estate', thereby making attempts on the duke's life treasonable.[10] The influence of William Sherwood might well lie behind the claim that as a corporate entity Ireland could be bound only by the laws of its own Parliament, from which it followed that the exercise of appellate jurisdiction outside Ireland in Irish affairs was *ultra vires*.[11] But Parliament shied away from a declaration of independence, and York had nothing to gain in encouraging them in such a venture. An act ordering the arrest of four men carrying English privy-seal letters into Ireland to the king's Irish enemies, inciting them to take up arms against York, contented itself with a denial that the privy-seal letters were legitimate, and did not challenge the jurisdictional authority which the putative letters represented.[12] In

[8] *CPR* 1452–61, p. 655.

[9] Oldhall died in August 1459. For Sherwood's career see Emden, *Oxford*, iii. 1694.   [10] Berry, *Statutes of Ireland*, pp. 641–5.

[11] For a detailed study of the historical justification for such a claim see A. Cosgrave, 'Parliament and the Anglo–Irish Community: The Declaration of 1460', *Historical Studies*, 14 (Belfast, 1983), 25–43.

[12] Berry, *Statutes of Ireland*, pp. 740–5.

a similar case, concerning William Ovary of Kildare, it was declared that the introduction of English letters of privy seal into Ireland was contrary to the liberties of Ireland.[13] The sovereignty of Henry VI was thus preserved, but in a most tenuous manner.

In the time available, the duke did what he could to promote the province's interests. His most important single action was the creation of an autonomous Irish currency, which stopped the over-valuing of English coinage. This stemmed the outflow of silver.[14] Attempts to make trading conditions easier for Irish cloth-merchants probably related to this monetary change.[15]

There is general agreement that Irish sympathies for the house of York were first aroused during this Parliament, but the duke himself was in search of more than sympathy. He needed men and money. Parliament did what it could, voting him a mounted archer from every twenty liberate holders for so long as he was in Ireland, and making some attempt to raise the £360 subsidy voted in 1458.[16] This was helpful, in so far as it went, but York's particular need was for men to accompany him to England. He tried to raise some funds to cover their recruitment, by selling a royal charter over the great seal of Ireland to the English merchants in Dublin, licensing them to form a guild.[17] These, and other efforts unknown, must have had some success, as the Irish were believed in March 1461 to be a factor in Edward IV's military success.[18]

Those Englishmen who had accompanied York to Ireland could be relied upon to produce a nucleus of support. Twenty-one English exiles can be identified,[19] but one, John Higham, was murdered in April 1460.[20] Of the rest, most of the leading gentry-figures were of Neville rather than York affinity. For their part, the Anglo-Irish

---

[13] Ibid. 676–9.

[14] R. H. M. Dolley, 'Anglo-Irish Monetary Policies', in J. C. Beckett (ed.), *Historical Studies*, 7 (1969), 52–3. The new master of the Mint was Germain Lynch, a London goldsmith (Lascelles, *Liber Munerum*, i/3, 8; cf. *CPR 1461–7*, p. 40).

[15] Berry, *Statutes of Ireland*, pp. 784–7.   [16] Ibid. 644–9, 674–7.

[17] J. T. Gilbert, *Calendar of Ancient Records of Dublin*, i. (Dublin, 1889), 305. The Dublin record implies that this was done some time before 24 June.

[18] *Calendar of State Papers, Milan*, ed. Hinds, p. 59.

[19] Nicholas Strangeways, James Dockray, John Bolyngton, Thomas Colt, Sir John Wenlock, John Cornwalsh, John Gogh, Thomas Newbury, William Griffitz, John Bourchier, Sir James Pickering, Roger Eyton, Thomas Browe, John Roos, Thomas Tryme, James Newton, John Parker, John Cleaton, William Whelpdale, Nicholas Harpisfield, and Master Thomas St Just (Berry, *Statutes of Ireland*, pp. 724–9, 794–9).

[20] Ibid. 768. His son was rewarded by Edward IV (*CPR 1461–7*, p. 76).

seem to have volunteered to help York in some numbers. Some, such as the Barringtons, were traditionally hostile to the Butlers.[21] Others were closely interrelated, Robert Preston, Lord Gormanstown, Sir Rowland FitzEustace, and Sir Thomas Plunket;[22] and others again, such as the Bernewells, were probably responsible for the administration of York's Irish estates.[23] They were to prove over the next twelve months to be loyal servants of the house of York.[24]

Raising these men, and organizing their transport[25] and their private affairs, took time, and the .Anglo-Irish families were still obtaining licences from Parliament to leave Ireland as late as 21 July,[26] by which time the first news of the battle of Northampton must have been filtering through.[27] The Irish Parliament was dissolved on that date,[28] but York made no move to leave Ireland until 8 September, at the earliest. It is possible that he was waiting for the English Parliament to assemble, in which case he left a month too soon, and anyway had little to gain from the wait. Possibly he could not leave until the defeat of the O'Reillys but, if so, he must have placed great value on the security of Ireland.

The first session of the Irish Parliament had ended on 5 May, and Warwick, whose subsequent actions were to have important consequences for Duke Richard, left soon after.[29] He could not afford to linger, as the Channel Islands had fallen to the Lancastrians by early May[30] and a large fleet had put to sea under the duke of Exeter. He successfully evaded the duke, but, once in Calais, his opportunities

---

[21] *CPR* 1441–6, p. 404.

[22] Berry, *Statutes of Ireland*, p. 794; *CPR* 1461–7, pp. 117, 178; *Complete Peerage*, iv. 551, vii. 250, x. 598.　　　[23] Ibid. xii/2, 35.

[24] *Calendar of State Papers, Milan*, ed. Hinds, p. 59; cf. *CPR* 1461–7, pp. 117, 178, 186.

[25] The earl of Desmond may have been primarily responsible for raising shipping in Ireland (*Annals of the Four Masters*, ed. O'Donovan, iv. 1023). Lord Clinton was responsible for procuring shipping from England, but it is not impossible that his earliest actions were actually piratical, subsequently tidied up for the council of Edward IV (Scofield, *Edward IV*, i. 101).

[26] Berry, *Statutes of Ireland*, p. 792. The licences were 'to attend upon [York's] person, and to do him such service as agrees with their duty according to their abilities'.

[27] York maintained contacts with England, but the method is uncertain. The English government suspected merchants and fishermen. Bristol may have been particularly helpful (*CPR* 1452–61, p. 602; *CPR* 1461–77, p. 193). York was able to circulate propaganda news-sheets in England (Davis (ed.), *Paston Letters*, i. 505), possibly claiming that Henry was personally in favour of them (Rymer, *Foedera*, xi. 455).　　　[28] Berry, *Statutes of Ireland*, p. 638.

[29] *Annales*, p. 772.　　　[30] C76/142 mm. 9, 12, 13.

for communicating with York must have been few, if any, before Northampton, and he acted, necessarily, virtually independently of York. However, his actions prior to Northampton were to have serious implications for Duke Richard on his own return.

From Calais the lords issued a letter of grievance which was widely circulated.[31] It is obvious from the content that it had been drawn up in Dublin, one clause making explicit reference to York,[32] and the introduction asserted that the letter had been drawn up in the duke's name. It is, therefore, the best, indeed the only, source available for understanding opposition intentions in 1460, and for estimating the nature of the response which they met. In its surviving form, the letter may represent a version of a Dublin agreement subsequently amended by Warwick and his Calais companions, but whether this is the case, and, if so, in what particulars, cannot now be determined.

The letter sets out twelve heads of complaint. Following the pattern first established in Magna Carta, the Church is promoted as the first grievance; perhaps, as has been suggested, a genuine one, if somewhat vaguely expressed.[33] The remaining clauses were to be much more substantial, even specific. Clause two attacked purveyance, clause four returning to the theme, with the strong implication that there ought to be a resumption act. The promotion of purveyance so early in the list of grievances suggests that it was believed to be a serious and widespread problem, although there is no direct evidence in support of this contention since the days of Cade and the 1450–1 Parliament.[34] How the royal household had been supporting itself in the midlands is unclear, just as the extent of Somerset's requisitioning in Kent in the winter of 1460 is obscure. The mechanisms whereby the fleet was provisioned are no better known, but such was the financial position in 1460 that it is difficult to believe that either army or navy received much direct government aid.[35]

[31] Stow, *Annales*, pp. 407–8; Davies, *English Chronicle*, pp. 86–90. The texts are identical. Stow's hand features in the margin of the chronicle, according to its editor (cf. *Gregory's Chronicle*, p. 206).

[32] 'which letters the same Irish enemies sent unto me the said Duke of Yorke'.

[33] R. L. Storey, 'Episcopal King-Makers in the Fifteenth Century', in Dobson (ed.), *The Church, Politics, and Patronage*, p. 90.

[34] Southampton either had, or was soon to get, a taste of large-scale purveyance (Stow, *Annales*, p. 408).

[35] Before the Calais earls landed in Kent, they reportedly received many articles of grievance from the commons (*loc. cit.*; *Gregory's Chronicle*, p. 206). In order to get Exeter and Fulford to sea 2,500 marks was 'chevished' (E404/71/4/36).

On taxation, the lords were clear. In spite of high taxes, France had been lost. This was still a useful charge in 1460, despite the passage of a decade since Formigny, because it carried implications of peculation, of profiteers as yet unpunished. Much sharper was the criticism of the king's decision, modelled, it was alleged, on French practice, that every town should contribute on a permanent basis to a standing army.[36]

'Tallage', that useful pejorative of generations of critics, was scattered throughout the clauses. Its purpose may have been purely an embellishment of spite, but it may have had a specific referent, the practice, increasingly frequent since 1457, of distraining knights.[37] The *English Chronicle*, a very biased source, also alleges that the earl of Wiltshire had recently raised a loan by force.[38] Accusations of tallage had more than merely emotive value. Coercive finance had been a feature of Richard II's reign. Other echoes of that monarch's failure whisper through the charges.[39]

The laws, it was claimed, 'be partially and unrightfully guided'. Thus vague, it was a convenient charge to which a fair number might subscribe, and it did little to exemplify its general allegations for obvious reasons. Two charges it did develop, the murder of the duke of Gloucester, and the banishment, without trial, of great lords, that is, themselves. Again, there was the implicit reminder of the failures of Richard II.[40]

With their remaining allegations the Yorkist lords hinted at the likely finale. France had been lost in dubious circumstances. Recently, those around the king had written privy seals to the very enemies of their lord in Ireland, inciting them to open rebellion. In the full knowledge that Calais was in danger, those about the king had forbidden its provisioning and sustenance, as was well known.[41]

---

[36] 'Every tounshyp to fynde men for the kynges garde (Davies, *English Chronicle*, p. 87; cf. *Coventry Leet Book*, ed. Harris, p. 308).

[37] Rymer, *Foedera*, xi. 389; Griffiths, *Reign of Henry VI*, pp. 787, 836. n. 101.

[38] Davies, *English Chronicle*, p. 90; K. B. McFarlane, 'Loans to Lancastrian Kings, the Problem of Inducement', *Cambridge Historical Journal*, 9 (1947), 57. The demand for 36,000 ducats from Venetian merchants may also be relevant (*Calendar of State Papers, Venice*, ed. Rawdon Brown, i. 88).

[39] The queen 'made her sone called the Prince yeve a lyuery of Swannys to alle the gentilmenne of the countre' (Davies, *English Chronicle*, p. 79).

[40] Bellamy, *Law of Treason*, p. 198.

[41] Order dated 26 Sept. (Barron, 'London and the Crown', p. 95; cf. *Calendar of Plea and Memoranda Rolls: 1458–82*, ed. P. E. Jones (Cambridge, 1961), 11; *Annales*, p. 772).

Clearly, these lords intended that the whole realm of England should be handed over to its enemies. And so the time came to name names, the earl of Shrewsbury, the earl of Wiltshire, and Viscount Beaumont, 'oure mortalle and extreme enemyes'. It was their removal that was vital to the safeguarding of the realm, for it was they who procured at the Coventry Parliament the ruination of great nobles, untried and unheard, and then proceeded to rob and despoil them of goods and property to their own private profit, and, lest their infamy should still be in any way in doubt, it was alleged that they 'now procede to hangyng and drawyng of men by tyranny'. The truth of this was also well enough known. Newbury, in revolt against the earl of Wiltshire's taxmen,[42] was, in June 1460, visited by the earl himself, together with Scales and Hungerford, as justices of oyer and terminer.[43] Some they hanged. Seventy-five others they took to Wallingford, a castle of the prince of Wales.[44]

The letter was good propaganda; good, because so many of its charges were public knowledge. And it was not the only propaganda in circulation which had its origins in the Yorkist cause. The *English Chronicle*, in its résumé of the politics of 1459–60, seems to be drawing on a propaganda source in speaking of the wealth amassed by the queen and her affinity, and by Wiltshire, who 'peled the pore peple', and in accusing the queen of seeking to have Henry abdicate in favour of her allegedly illegitimate son.[45]

The same chronicle also includes a ballad composed, contrived even, by an unknown Canterbury clergyman. It is a difficult piece, which, as has been pointed out,[46] probably passed over the heads of most of its readers, but the refrain, which any of Canterbury's many clergymen would readily have identified, is of particular interest. The refrain itself, 'omne caput languidum, et omne cor merens', was borrowed from Isaiah,[47] and from a particularly pregnant context, in which the prophet of Israel is branding the nation as wholly sinful, as a betrayer of trust, without any soundness from its head

---

[42] Waurin, *Croniques*, v. 270. Newbury had been farmed by the earl of Pembroke since Easter (*CFR* 1452–61, p. 267).

[43] Davies, *English Chronicle*, p. 90; *CPR* 1452–61, p. 613.

[44] Ibid. 648. If Newbury was, indeed, what the Calais manifesto was referring to, and this seems very probable, then it is unlikely that the letter was issued much more than a week before the Calais lords landed, successfully, in Kent. This would support Stow's report that the letter in its final draft reflected grievances already heard in Kent.

[45] Davies, *English Chronicle*, pp. 79–80.

[46] Griffiths, *Reign of Henry VI*, pp. 861–2.   [47] Isaiah 1: 5 cf. vv. 4–9.

downwards, assaulted by strangers, the destruction visited of old on
Sodom and Gomorrah now imminent. But God has left a few
survivors faithful to the divine call. . . .

Whoever wrote this ballad was tackling the major issue: what was
to be done about Henry VI? The Calais manifesto was clear in its
insistence that Henry was the nation's true king, that the Yorkist
lords were his true subjects, and that no harm was intended to his
person. Indeed, only Shrewsbury, Wiltshire, and Beaumont were
explicitly cited as fit objects for punishment, despite the obvious
active hostility of the duke of Exeter and the earl of Pembroke. This
might seem to imply that the Yorkist lords would have been
contented if the three named lords were permanently removed, but,
short of their execution, it is not clear how this could be achieved.
Probed further, the document issued from Calais is significant in
what it does not say. Had an accommodation been acceptable,
subject to the removal of the three lords, then it would have been
possible to have signalled this in phraseology which reflected the
oath to the house of Lancaster taken at Coventry in November 1459.
But the prince of Wales is not mentioned. Neither is the queen.[48]
There is no hint of loyalty to the king's lineage, only to his most
noble person. The Calais manifesto was, in its essentials, the result
of long reflection, and it is clear that in June 1460 the Yorkist lords
were very uncertain what to do about the throne of England. That
they would have to fight to achieve their manifesto aims was evident.
That victory for them would also mean death for their opponents
had also been decided.[49] However, Pembroke was not on the list, nor
was Exeter.[50] The latter had control of the navy,[51] the former of
Wales. There was every sense in encouraging them to step to one
side, but would they, could they, do so if the person of the king was
in danger?

Sensible and obvious though this programme might seem in
Dublin, delicate even in its evasion of the problem of the monarch, it

---

[48] Treason legislation aside, any challenge to the queen would risk the allegation
that this would invite French intervention.

[49] This may explain Wiltshire's flight to Holland (Stow, *Annales*, p. 408).

[50] Both figure prominently in the poem 'The Ship of State' which identifies leading
government figures of the late 1450s (*Historical Poems*, ed. Robbins, pp. 191–3).

[51] Failure to secure Venetian ships, combined with Wiltshire's defection, was to
make the navy's role less significant (*Calendar of State Papers, Venice*, ed. Rawdon
Brown, p. 88). Part of the navy, under Gaston de Foix, may have changed sides
(cf. *CPR* 1452–61, p. 598).

had yet to be presented to a nation with its own views, and, whatever the subtlety of their reservations about Henry, time and time again, before Northampton, the Calais lords found themselves confirming Henry's legitimate authority. In Calais itself, they gave a written pledge of their loyalty to Henry VI to the papal legate, Coppini,[52] and were obliged to reassure the Kentishmen of their loyalty to Henry.[53] London's concern was largely with its own safety from the advancing, and predominantly Kentish, horde. As in 1459, so now, Warwick was able to reassure them, but as part of this reassurance a public oath at St Paul's was deemed an essential concession. Nothing, it was sworn, was to be done against the person of the king.[54] The earl of Warwick contrived to preface this oath with a detailed recitation of the points of misgovernance of the realm.[55] Privately, perhaps, the congregation was sympathetic, but publicly they would not renounce Henry.

On the eve of Northampton the public position of the Calais lords was clearly that of subjects loyal to Henry VI. However, it is notable that whenever negotiations were conducted Warwick did the talking, but always in the name of the earl of March.[56] Secretly, another plan may have been under consideration. Early in March Pius II, relying presumably on Coppini, could record a conversation between the legate and Warwick, in which the earl asserted that the duke of York ought to be on the throne.[57] The discussions at Dublin accepted the need publicly to suppress such intentions, but the secret counsels of the Calais lords may well not have abandoned them, and it must

---

[52] *Calendar of State Papers, Milan*, ed. Hinds, p. 23.

[53] *Reg. Whethamstede*, i. 371; Waurin, *Croniques*, v. 293. The original intention of the Sandwich landing may have been to secure the customs revenue for the garrison, prejudiced by a royal decision of 21 June (*CPR 1452–61*, p. 600).

[54] *Annales*, p. 773. It has been suggested that, in agreeing to admit the earls, London became Yorkist (Barron, 'London and the Crown' p. 96). This may be too strong. Scales held Southwark, but was at odds with the Common Council. The bishop of Ely failed to persuade him to accept the Calais lords, and he withdrew to the Tower (Waurin, *Croniques*, v. 294). Providing sufficient guarantees of good conduct could be found, London had strong financial reasons for co-operating with the Calais garrison. Scales's withdrawal had left them vulnerable. The oath at St Paul's was their insurance against subsequent recrimination, the earl of Salisbury their defence against Lord Scales.

[55] Stow, *Annales*, p. 408.

[56] Cf. negotiations with the Cinque Ports (Hist. Mss. Comm. *Fifth Report*, p. 492) and London (Waurin, *Croniques*, v. 294–5). March had precedence over Warwick as an earl, but he was still, in law, a minor.

[57] The text is cited in C. Head, 'Pius II and the Wars of the Roses', *Archivum Historiae Pontificiae*, 8 (1970), 149.

have weighed on their minds that if a change of dynasty was envisaged then the men were at hand to do it, a papal legate and the archbishop of Canterbury.[58]

From York's point of view the outcome of the battle of Northampton was satisfactory, but less than ideal. The deaths of Henry and the prince of Wales would have simplified matters enormously, but the prince and his mother had evaded capture, and as Henry was never known to take up the sword his death in combat could not reasonably have been expected. At St Albans he had taken shelter. At Northampton he was in his tent. March and Warwick must have hoped that he would flee, but if not then they expected to take him alive, and their actions on taking him—in making immediate obeisance to him—have the air of the premeditated.[59]

The casualty list was, nonetheless, impressive, with Buckingham, Shrewsbury, and Beaumont dead, and Wiltshire, Wainflete,[60] and Booth in flight. For all practical purposes the administrative system was at the disposal of the victors, and they rapidly set about consolidating their hold at all levels of central government. As in 1455, so in 1460, the Nevilles and the Bourchiers, with their adherents, took most of the plum positions, and the Nevilles managed a disproportionate share. York was given virtually nothing. Some may have seen this as suspicious.

Northampton eased the problems of regional government. Only Pembroke and Stanley[61] now had serious claim to influence in Wales and the Marches, and in the North Egremond's death had eased the Neville position. The principal regional problem was the South West, where the earl of Devon's hostility had to be assumed.[62]

It was a very narrowly-based government which assembled in London in late July. Seven bishops, the three Calais earls, Viscount Bourchier, and the lords Beauchamp, Grey of Ruthin, Fauconberg, and Scrope of Bolton witnessed the creation of George Neville as

---

[58] In 1463 the assistance of Archbishop Bourchier was officially recorded (*Calendar of Charter Rolls 1427–1516*, p. 192).

[59] As recently as 3 July Coppini had described the Calais lords to Henry VI as 'servitores vestrae Majestatis', but this had publicly to be demonstrated. (*Original Letters Illustrative of English History*, ed. H. Ellis, 3rd ser., 4 vols. (1846), i. 89).

[60] Wainflete surrendered the great seal three days before Northampton (*CCR 1454–61*, p. 459).

[61] Margaret of Anjou was wooing him on 24 June, but on 13 July he was ordered to take care of the recently released Nevilles (DKR 37/ii, 677, 499).

[62] The duke of Exeter's fleet was in the Dartmouth area (Waurin, *Croniques*, v. 289).

chancellor.[63] By 11 August only seven peers were with the king at Canterbury,[64] three of them Nevilles and two Bourchiers. With so little aristocratic endorsement, there was much sense in summoning Parliament, and writs were issued at the earliest practical moment; according to one source, as soon as the king was back in London on 16 July.[65] Richard duke of York was by that title summoned.

Decisions had now to be made. From York's point of view it was unfortunate that all major business could not be deferred until Parliament, or at least until he arrived, but it could not, and so the Nevilles and the Bourchiers made the decisions and profited from them.

In July there were two practical problems. The Tower had to be retaken—which it was, Scales being murdered soon after, which probably saved much trouble in East Anglia.[66] Calais was the other headache. The immediate threat came from the duke of Somerset in Guisnes. In one sense this was acceptable, as it kept Somerset out of England. The dispatch of just sufficient force to keep him in Guisnes therefore had its attractions, but Somerset was well aware that he would be of better use in England, and, anxious to disengage himself, was proposing to give Guisnes to the count of Charolais.[67] This unwelcome Burgundian dimension was further complicated by the presence of the dauphin at Duke Philip's court. Fortunately for Warwick, dauphin and duke read the situation alike. The promotion of Warwick was the promotion of civil war in Lancastrian England, which in recent years had come to look increasingly pro-Valois. Charolais was ordered to decline the offer. In mid-August Warwick sailed to Calais and negotiated the surrender of Guisnes.[68] The price he paid was high, an indication of the significance he attached to the security of Calais; and Somerset, together with the Guisnes garrison, was freely permitted to move to Dieppe, from where, in

---

[63] *CCR* 1454–61, p. 455.

[64] The archbishop, the chancellor, the bishop of London, March, Salisbury, Beauchamp, and Wenlock.

[65] *Short English Chronicle*, p. 74. The writs themselves are dated 20 July (*Report on the Dignity of a Peer*, iv. 945). The earl of March was also summoned.

[66] Griffiths, *Reign of Henry VI*, p. 863. On 9 July London lent 500 marks to allow the siege to be tightened, and thought it prudent to offer a further loan to the earls returning towards London with their soldiers (Barron, 'London and the Crown', p. 103).

[67] Waurin, *Croniques*, v. 291.

[68] *Annales*, p. 774.

October, he was reportedly poised to cross to Devon.[69] By this action, however, Warwick had brought immediate safety to both London and Calais, a point not lost in either city.

There was also the problem of Scotland. Just as Burgundy might see Warwick as a useful foil against Valois influence, so the French saw the restoration of Margaret of Anjou as their best hope of influence in Lancastrian England. Consequently, Margaret's flight to Scotland, after Northampton, breathed new life into a Scottish alliance which since 1445 had been an embarrassment to French policy in England. However, this neglect of Scotland had prompted James II's marriage to the Burgundian Mary of Gueldres in 1449. This alliance gave support to rumours in Calais that the lords were planning an invasion jointly with York in Ireland and James II in Scotland.[70] In a sense the rumours were correct, as James was indeed assembling an army to attack Roxburgh,[71] but it is difficult to see what the Nevilles could hope to gain from a Scottish invasion of the North. James II's behaviour looks opportunistic. It was an impulse which cost him his life on 3 August, and when a commission was issued on 12 August—significantly to the earl of Salisbury alone[72]— to resist the Scots, it was already unnecessary. Roxburgh had indeed fallen, and the Scots had gone on to slight Wark, but thereafter the assault had faltered.

The more serious possibility was that northern castles might well surrender to the Lancastrian prince of Wales at the head of a Scots army.[73] That this did not happen was due to the anti-French policies of Mary of Gueldres, which forced Margaret of Anjou to wait on Bishop Kennedy's return to Scotland. Scottish policy cannot, however, have been very clear in London, and York was in due course to go north, in December, to consolidate control of the region, in advance of an anticipated Scottish threat in the spring.

Domestic difficulties in August 1460 gave even more headaches than foreign ones. The biggest problem was to secure sufficient control in north Wales and the marches to permit York to return. Roger Pulleston held Denbigh against the duke, on the earl of

---

[69] Davis (ed.), *Paston Letters*, ii. 216; Stow, *Annales*, p. 409, says he crossed in September (cf. Griffiths, *Reign of Henry VI*, p. 869).

[70] The substance of this and the following paragraph derives from N. Macdougall, *James III: A Political Study* (Edinburgh, 1982), 41–8.

[71] In Dec. 1459 the earl of Douglas was rewarded for good service against the duke of York (Rymer, *Foedera*, xi. 437).

[72] *CPR* 1452–61, p. 589.   [73] Ibid. 649.

Pembroke's behalf, and Lord Powis held Montgomery.[74] Other castles were also holding out for the house of Lancaster. In addition, rumours abounded in every shire and hundred, there was widespread local mayhem and score-settling, and no obvious means of restoring order quickly.[75]

Such inducements to loyalty as could be found were employed to as useful effect as possible. Thus, Philip Courtney, one of the few supporters of the new regime in the south west, was rewarded with a licence to trade to defray his ransom,[76] and the rolls are filled with similar examples, usually costing little or nothing to the Crown, and all distributed in the hope of loyal service. Not that the regime had much idea of who its loyal servants were. In the case of commissions of the peace, only eight counties had their bench changed before Parliament assembled, and they frequently failed to exclude known supporters of the house of Lancaster.[77] Given the conditions, sessions of the peace may have been difficult to hold anyway. In the midlands Warwick acquired *carte blanche* to arrest whom he would.[78]

Patronage generously and judiciously employed might have bought the loyalty of vested interest, but there was precious little to give. Before Parliament, there were three leases made of land, none very large. The Crown was penniless. Most of Henry's jewels and ready cash had been stolen in July at Gayton (Northants.),[79] and the only immediate source of revenue was the customs, and so, not surprisingly, the customs officers in all major ports were replaced in early August.[80] New purveyors for the household, sensitive appointments in the light of the Calais manifesto, were made in the course of the same month.[81] In a further attempt to widen the opportunity of rewards, writs of *diem clausit* on the victims of Northampton were issued on 27 July,[82] but there would be an inevitable administrative delay before any wardships, or similar benefits which might accrue, could be identified and distributed.

---

[74] *PPC* vi. 303–5.

[75] Cf. *CPR* 1452–61, pp. 607, 612, 652; Hist. MSS. Comm. *Third Report*, p. 315.

[76] C76/143 m. 17.

[77] *CPR* 1452–61, pp. 660 ff.   [78] Ibid. 647.

[79] *DKR* 37/ii, 677. On 6 April they explicitly cited 'his great poverty' (C81/778/10829).

[80] *CFR* 1452–61, pp. 254 ff.   [81] *CPR* 1452–61, pp. 601 ff.

[82] *CFR* 1452–61, pp. 246–7. Excepting the earl of Shrewsbury, whose writ was delayed to 20 Aug., perhaps to give Lord Berkeley a chance to renegotiate his 1457 settlement (Smyth, *Lives of the Berkeleys*, ed. Maclean, i. 75).

Northampton had given the Calais earls the king, but not the kingdom. By September 1460 they were in control of London and Calais, and had shared the offices of government to the advantage of themselves, their Neville and Bourchier kinsmen, but mostly Neville, together with a handful of other supporters.[83] Their political influence waned as the miles from London grew. In the south-west, in Wales, and in the north they had little practical power. Without control of the person of the prince of Wales the longer-term outlook was very uncertain. Without money and some measure of public acceptance the short term seemed no less precarious. Parliament might offer some chance of persuading the gentry to co-operate, in the interests of establishing local order. It might just be possible to cajole the Commons into a tax, on the basis of the Franco-Scottish threat, though this would probably have to await developments, and was unlikely to be generally popular. Much depended on Parliament's conviction of the desirability and practicality of the Yorkist programme.

York landed near Chester, on or about 9 September.[84] According to Whethamstede, an uncertain source, he had been summoned by amicable letters from the king,[85] together, possibly, with the royal commission to hold the sessions in the marches, as Christopher Hanson reported.[86] Whichever version is preferred, it is clear that he did not come in response just to a parliamentary writ of summons. He was in Chester on 13 September, and, after a stay in Ludlow, Shrewsbury, and, probably, Hereford, was in Gloucester by 2 October, whence he moved on to Abingdon.[87] Although a circuitous route to London, there was some sense in a steady progress through the marches. His tenantry had to be reassured that he was back and intended to stay, a necessary reassurance after

---

[83] Attendance at a council on 23 Aug. comprised Canterbury, Exeter, the earls of March and Salisbury, Bourchier, the Prior of St Johns, Wenlock, Say, and the dean of St Severins (BL Cotton MS Vespasian F XIII n. 77; cf. *PPC* vi. 307).

[84] *Annales*, p. 774. His landing spot, Redbank, is at the north-west tip of the Wirral, and is usable only at high tide. It would appear that he dared not risk a landing at Chester itself, nor in the Clwyd estuary, where Denbigh was held against him. The *Annales* entry implies that he had few men with him (cf. *PPC* vi. 304–5).

[85] *Reg. Whethamstede*, i. 368.

[86] Davis (ed.), *Paston Letters*, ii. 216. The only recorded commission in which York is nominated is for Yorkshire for 24 Aug. (*CPR* 1452–61, p. 608).

[87] *CPR* 1461–7, p. 60; Waurin, *Croniques*, v. 312; *Annales*, p. 774; Marquis of Bath: Longleat MS 10494 (Magdalen College: McFarlane transcript); *Gregory's Chronicle*, p. 208).

Ludlow. Protection and rewards for the loyal, summary justice for defectors, all had to be meted out. And there was the problem of Jasper Tudor, now the base of Lancastrian hopes in Wales. It was necessary not only to contain him but, in so far as it was possible, to capitalize on the sharp polarity in Welsh affairs now that Buckingham was dead.

It also gave time for recruiting, and there is every indication that, from his first landing in the Wirral, York was anxious to increase his retinue. It is well known that by the time he reached Gloucester York was retaining without reference to Henry VI, or even to his regnal year. McFarlane, in demonstrating this point, suggested that York had, in fact, already renounced his allegiance at Chester, and there is much to commend this viewpoint. Not least is the fact that although we have only the indentures of 2 October (made in Gloucester) their text, reciting an obligation not only to York but to March, seems to match very closely the reported text of the Chester indentures in two particulars; the inclusion of March and, as McFarlane noted, the omission of the regnal year.[88]

It cannot, therefore, have been a well-kept secret that York had renounced his allegiance to Henry VI, and there is every indication that Warwick knew what was going on. By 17 September news of York's arrival in Chester had reached London, and on 23 September Duchess Cecily left Southwark with a view to meeting him at Hereford. The earl of March she left in London.[89] Warwick, who was in the midlands,[90] presumably heard the news somewhat earlier, and reportedly met York at Shrewsbury, where the two stayed for four days. Warwick then returned through the midlands to London.

[88] K. B. McFarlane, 'The Wars of the Roses', *Proceedings of the British Academy*, 50 (1964), 92–3 (repr. in id., *England in the Fifteenth Century*) and the authorities cited there. It is possible that York's arrival precipitated some sort of crisis in Chester's internal politics, as York recruited the mayor. Then, or soon after, the abbot of St Werburgh was imprisoned in Chester castle (*DKR* 37/ii, 779). By the end of the year, if not earlier, the Stanley and Savage families held the city for York (Bib. Nat. MS Fr. 20136 fo. 75'). Of the Lancastrians, 400 had reportedly defected to the Calais lords before Northampton (Waurin, *Croniques*, v. p. 296).

[89] Davis (ed.), *Paston Letters*, ii. 216. March did not leave London throughout the summer although his early presence in the west would have helped to consolidate the Yorkist hold on his father's estates (*Tropenell Cartulary*, ed. J. S. Davies, Wiltshire Archaeological and Natural History Society, 4 (1908), i. 73). The duke and duchess probably met some time before the duke arrived in Abingdon (*Gregory's Chronicle*, p. 208).

[90] Waurin, *Croniques*, v. 309. The author later says (p. 310) that the earl was at 'Lislefil' (?Lichfield).

York moved on to Ludlow, where an assembly of local gentry, in words very close to York's later petition to Parliament, invited him to assume the Crown. Waurin reports another, similar, meeting a day or so later. Waurin is, however, careful, throughout his narrative of events at this time, to give the impression that the preparations for York's attempt on the throne were done without the knowledge of Warwick, thereby exonerating the earl of breach of good faith in the oaths given at St Paul's and elsewhere.

It could just be, that in this latter contention Waurin is right, but there are two more plausible explanations: that York outlined his intentions to Warwick who disagreed and, having failed to dissuade the duke, left; or that Warwick encouraged York to be more public in his intentions, organizing popular assemblies from town to town 'inviting' him to take the throne. No further evidence exists to support either option, but in view of later events the latter explanation seems the more probable. Warwick, in late September, encouraged the duke to claim the throne, and the duke parted from him at Shrewsbury convinced that the earl went ahead to drum up support.[91]

If this is not so, then York's assumption of the full arms of England and his arrival into London, processing in the style and manner of a legitimate monarch, would seem to be an act of supreme stupidity. York genuinely expected popular applause. He did not get it and was forced to seek the throne by siege; a protracted business from which he emerged with his credibility sorely strained.

Reconstructing events in the 1460 Parliament is very difficult. The Parliament roll provides some dates.[92] These appear, on scrutiny, to be trustworthy. It is the linking sentences and the purported explanations which must be treated cautiously. The roll is correct about the preliminaries, the opening of Parliament on 7 October and the election of John Green as speaker on the tenth. It then recounts how, on 16 October, York presented a petition claiming the throne, which claim the Lords put successively to the justices and the serjeants, and then, on 22 October, debated it themselves, eventually to accept, on 25 October, that the duke's claim was valid but inopportune, thereby leading to the final settlement on 31 October. This calendar of events studiously omits

[91] There is a slight hint of this in Waurin, who says that Warwick arrived in London to announce the impending arrival of the duke (p. 312).
[92] *Rot. Parl.* v. 373–8.

all of what is politically significant. The problem is to know where to turn for a fuller account.

Much the most detailed published narrative comes from Waurin,[93] but it is biased, anxious always to show Warwick in the best possible light. In conjunction with other chronicle sources it does, however, give a political depth to events, which the official record fails to do. The narrative starts with Warwick's announcement of York's approach on 6 October. The following day the earl of March, the Neville earls, Fauconberg, and the archbishop of Canterbury organized a full assembly of both houses, and seated the king before the full Parliament in royal regalia. The archbishop of York then narrated the alleged misdeeds of government from a text seemingly dependent on the Calais manifesto.

Parliament then proceeded, amidst considerable confusion,[94] to elect Green, a Bourchier man,[95] as speaker, on the tenth, and, with Parliament thus properly constituted, York arrived the same day from Barnet, and took up residence in the king's chamber, placing the king under his own guard.[96] What happened next can best be described in the words of an unknown secretary writing to John Tiptoft, earl of Worcester, then in Venice:[97]

Most leinginc[98] And bountefulle good lorde youre moste comfortable lettres fro Venys of the last of August I resseivid heer the xiij day of octobre that is to say uppon Saynt Edwarde day whan ther was like to have ben atte Westmestre a mervelous werk for thewhiche great multitude of pepill drew thedir withoute any of the lordes to have seen who have shulde have goon on procession crownede. And my lorde to describe this werk hit passeth my power witte but I know for certein hit hathe caused many a slep to be broken thus hit began here fryday by for the feest a bove saides. The kyng whith lordes spirituelle and temperalle as the archbusshoppis of Cant' and York, busshop is of of Excetter Ely Linclon [*sic*] London Worcestre and

---

[93] Waurin, *Croniques*, v. 313.

[94] 'inchoatum erat' (*Brief Latin Chronicle*, ed. Gairdner p. 170).

[95] Roskell, *The Commons and their Speakers*, p. 267.

[96] 'more regio potius quam ducali' (*Reg. Whethamstede*, i. 377; Barron, 'London and the Crown' pp. 98, 108 n. 74). The king was lodged in the queen's household soon after. Another source says that York did not speak to the king for three weeks (*Benet's Chronicle*, p. 227). According to Pius II, Parliament's first action was to rescind all the legislation of 1459 (*Commentaries*, bk. iii. 270).

[97] Bib. Nat. MS. Fr. 20136 fo. 65. Fo. 66 is a seventeenth-century transcript. The whole is written in a neat secretary-hand, without subscription and direction. At some time, before the seventeenth century, the manuscript was folded. Tiptoft's attorneys in England were Robert Ingleton and Henry Chevele (C76/141 m. 19).

[98] Reading uncertain.

Chichestre, the Duke of Northefolk Erlys of Marche Warwik Salisbury with many abbats and Baronys sittyng in the parleament chambre except the kyng the commyens beyng in ther place acustumed in Westm' ther cam my lorde of york with viij hundred horse and men harneysed atte x of the clok, and entred the paleis with his swerde born uppe right by for him thorowe the halle and parleament chambre. And ther under the cloth of estate stondyng he gave them knowlich[e] that he purposed nat to ley daune his swerde but to challenge his right and so t[o]ke his loggyng in the qwenys chambre ha . . force and more and . . .[99] . . . nte whiche and toke uppon the rule of alle maner offices of that plac[e] and purposed no man shuld have denye[d] the croune fro his hed. How be hit alle the lordes above saide that he faunde they departed from thens and kept ther counsaille atte the blak Freris and sum tyme sent and som tyme wrotte to my lorde of York tille atte the last yt was agreed to take such direction as they wolde avise him.[100] Wherein my lorde of Warwik be had him soo that is fame is lik to be of great memory. And the kyng oure sourverain lorde to enjoye his owne and estate the gouvernaunce of the Realme with the protection and enheritaunce of the same to whom shalle be assigned atte this parleament in yet hit is not knowe. I shalle write as I may know to youre lordship.

Unfortunately, the letter is undated, but it is possible to eke out its information. Waurin recounts that the manner of the duke's arrival upset the Londoners; probably the merchant community, who must have viewed the growing turmoil with some alarm. They, in turn, protested to Warwick. The earl then sought the archbishop of Canterbury's mediation, but the archbishop refused. Thomas Neville was sent instead. This is to be dated 11 October, as Waurin recounts, and Tiptoft's correspondent agrees, that the lords met in conference at Blackfriars the following day.[101]

This meeting, evidently well attended, tried to persuade the earl of March to go to his father, to point out that the king's safety had been a matter of many previous assurances and, significantly, that the Londoners were very restless.[102] Deposition, they said, was out of the question. In the event, the bishops of Rochester and Ely, a

---

[99] MS damaged along the first fold of the letter, with minor damage along the second fold. There is space for about five words.

[100] Cf. *Reg. Whethamstede*, i. 376–7; *Chronicles of London*, p. 171.

[101] For the substance of this and the next three paragraphs see Waurin, *Croniques*, v. 315–18.

[102] The public indignation is noted in *Reg. Whethamstede*, i. 377–8. Pius II records the objections to York's claim as being the oaths to the king, his long reign, and his father's victories in France (*Commentaries*, trans. Gragg, bk, iii. 271).

baron,[103] and a citizen, Master Guy, went instead.[104] York replied to this embassy point by point, concluding that he proposed to seek coronation the following day, 13 October, St Edward's day.[105] On hearing this, the baronial council adjourned overnight. Reassembling early the next day, they again sent Thomas Neville to York, whom he found preparing for coronation. Whatever was then said is unknown, but Neville's mandate must have been both blunt and bluntly delivered. Despite the crowds assembling at the Abbey, York deferred his proposed coronation, and it was agreed that he accept the guidance of the baronial council.

Presumably it was, therefore, with their agreement that York submitted his claim to the throne to Parliament, on 16 October.[106] The Lords bought time by submitting the matter to the lawyers, and did not address themselves publicly to the issue until 22 October, when the chancellor recited that the king required that the lords discuss this matter, thus giving them the necessary freedom of speech on the issue. The outcome, reported on the twenty-fifth, was to accept York's claim, but to decline to give it effect. This seems to be the stage reported by Titptoft's correspondent; Henry to have the Crown for his lifetime, the rest uncertain.

By 31 October the Lords believed that they had produced a satisfactory settlement, giving the inheritance of the Crown to York and his heirs. York and March publicly subscribed to this in Parliament, but the duke then ran into difficulties with his own supporters. *Gregory's Chronicle*, recounting the agreement, goes on to say that, that same night, the king was removed against his will by unidentified persons to the house of the bishop of London.[107] The duke of York there visited him, again claiming to be king. It may be that in the light of the agreement York was hoping to persuade Henry to abdicate. If so, this was a monstrous political miscalculation, in the circumstances. That he was responding to pressures in his own camp seems much more likely. Certainly, two days later one of his men, Everard Digby esq. and a hundred or so others, were arrested, presumably with York's agreement, although

---

[103] Waurin says 'lord d'Oudeley (?Dudley).

[104] *Reg. Whethamstede*, i. 377–8.

[105] Since 1444 this had been an official holy day (*Gregory's Chronicle*, p. 185). It was also the date of the coronation of Henry IV.

[106] York omitted the regnal year in a letter over his signet dated 15 Oct. 1460 (SC6/870/4).

[107] *Gregory's Chronicle*, p. 208.

they had allegedly been rioting on his behalf.[108] Henry had processed, crowned, to St Paul's the previous day.

If this reconstruction of events is correct, it has important implications for any assessment of York's behaviour. It does look as though the duke and the earl of Warwick were working to an initially successful plan which then misfired.[109] The idea seems to have been for York to whip up support *en route* for London, while Warwick went on ahead to negotiate with the small baronial clique in London for the indictment of Henry VI, hoping thereby to declare him deposed, and so leaving the throne vacant for York to challenge it and take possession. The plan miscarried because Thomas Bourchier refused to co-operate. Once the timing misfired, there was every chance of a civil war fought out on the streets of the capital. This had at all costs to be avoided; Warwick prudently backed away from the plan,[110] and without Warwick York was as nothing. The eventual compromise, though obviously much indebted to the Treaty of Troyes, was, nonetheless, a very skilful piece of work, giving much needed stability to the status quo, even to the extent of giving York a long-term interest in the political stability of the kingdom.

It is just possible that the whole scheme was not dreamt up by Warwick and York at Shrewsbury in September, but had been in the air since July. On 7 July it was reported from Bruges that the Calais lords proposed to make a son of the duke of York king by passing over the king's son, about whom rumours of illegitimacy were circulating.[111] That some such idea was current might explain an otherwise pointless riot in Holborn by Walter Ingham gent., on 7 August, a riot in favour of the duke of York.[112]

Precisely why Warwick failed to carry Bourchier can only be guessed. As was pointed out in Parliament, several oaths had at

---

[108] KB9/941/87. On 1 Nov. York again made a grant without reference to the regnal year, but cited it in a grant dated 4 Nov. (*CPR 1461–7*, pp. 96, 14).

[109] Pius II, presumably following Coppini, says that the whole circumstances of York's claim was due to the boldness of Warwick (*Commentaries*, trans. Gragg, bk, iii. 271).

[110] By 21 Oct. York's claim was being discussed in Norfolk. The main fear there was that Warwick was proving too accommodating to the pre-Northampton regime (Davis (ed.), *Paston Letters*, i. 259).

[111] *Calendar of State Papers, Milan*, ed. Hinds, p. 27.

[112] KB9/941/88. But cf. the poem on the battle of Northampton, decidely Yorkist, and reflecting the official promulgation of York's loyalty, which ends, 'save the kyng and hys ryalte' (R. Brotanek, *Mittelenglische Dichtungen* (1940), 121; cf. Rymer, *Foedera*, xi. 460).

various times been taken by York and his colleagues. There was also
the fact that it was very difficult to establish any personal failing in
Henry.[113] The personal conduct of the Lord's Anointed was beyond
reproach. Edward II and Richard II had, all too obviously, been the
authors of their own actions. Henry VI was, all too obviously, not,
as, indeed, the Calais manifesto itself implied. The archbishop
refused to go along with the scheme, and a coronation without him
was unthinkable.

How far men's minds were swayed by the academic arguments for
and against York's claim in the days between 16 and 31 October
cannot be adequately determined.[114] The suspicion is, very little. As
might be expected, York's claim was strongest where Henry
Bolingbroke's claim had been at its weakest, hereditary succession.
But he was in difficulties over details. Why allow so long before
pressing the claim; why no demonstration of his lineage in his
customary coat of arms; what of York's own oaths and those of his
fellow peers? York dealt with the objections competently enough.
He wriggled a bit on the question of oaths,[115] denied Henry IV's
right by conquest, denied superiority of title by Parliament over title
by blood, but made his most appropriate observation when
commenting on the question of arms,[116] that he abstained from
bearing them 'for causes not unknown to all this Reaume'.[117]

Some of the objections to York's claim were unuttered, but, no
doubt, lingered in men's minds. What effect would Henry's
deposition have on his debts, some of which the Yorkist lords had
themselves negotiated in his name.[118] If Henry was not the rightful

[113] R. Lovatt, 'A Collector of Apocryphal Anecdotes: John Blacman Revisted', in
Pollard (ed.), *Property and Politics*, pp. 183–5.

[114] Parliament in 1461, nevertheless, was to reverse the act of attainder against his
father, the earl of Cambridge (*Rot. Parl.* v. 484).

[115] Coppini had probably already absolved York from his oath (*Reg. Whethamstede*,
i. p. 383; cf. Ellis, *Original Letters*, pp. 85–8).

[116] His arms were France ancient and England quarterly with a label of three points
argent, each charged with as many torteaux. *The Book of Saint Albans*, ed. W. Blades,
(1881, no pagination), following Nicholas Upton, claims that a label of three points is
appropriate to a second son.

[117] *Rot. Parl.* v. 377.

[118] Richard Lee, Lord Mayor with effect from 1 Nov., had been party to a loan to
the earl of Salisbury in the summer months. Despite Wedgwood's assertions, Lee
looks to have been more pro-Neville than pro-Lancastrian, which may help to explain
his election (Wedgwood, *Biographies*, pp. 530–1). During Parliament, Laurence
Barbarigo and Homo Bonegrete received licences to export wool free of £5,000 in
customs duty (*CCR 1454–61*, p. 469).

king then by what right did men hold grants of his gift?[119] Would this presage wholesale resumption? York had recently promoted an act of resumption through the Irish Parliament, and was known to be in favour of the idea in England.[120] Probably the most serious reservation was whether allowing the claim would, in fact, settle the dynastic issue. It was much more likely to precipitate a civil war, in which France would have good reason to intervene.

Duke Richard had a claim, and he had several hundred armed men to back it up, but by 16 October he had little more. York and Warwick had been in too much of a hurry. Unlike Henry of Bolingbroke, they had allowed hours rather than weeks for men to digest the new state of affairs; the claim and its implications. A conservative reaction was almost inevitable in such circumstances. As York was slightly older than Henry, and Henry might well have twenty years or more yet to live, it was unlikely that the settlement of 1460 would ever advantage York personally. Possibly his son might benefit, but much water could be expected to flow under the bridge before that happened, unless, that is, the young Lancastrian prince of Wales were to die.

When Bishop Neville opened Parliament, he chose as his text lines from the prophet Joel;[121] in the circumstances a shrewd choice. The prophet's call was for repentance, self-sacrifice, and unity of purpose in the face of an invading army, the invader from the north. The bishop had a useful theme, and it eventually yielded the most practical acts of the Parliament. York was given full authority to suppress trouble in England, with power to ask, as the king could, for support from all subjects.[122] This power was further extended to permit him to raise forces necessary to resist the Scots and

[119] No grants of significance were made between 8 and 16 Oct., when Stillington was granted a general pardon and £600, in repayment of a loan. Vaughan, for £1,000, was granted Sir Thomas Brown's lands on 18 Oct. (*CPR* 1452–61, p. 631).

[120] The politically sensitive decision to give control of the English lands of the duchy of Buckingham jointly to the dowager duchess and the archbishop of Canterbury (taken on 23 Oct.), and of the Welsh lands of the duchy to Warwick, together with the earl of Shrewsbury's lands (4 Nov.), was executed by means of a lease, not a grant of custody during minority (*CFR* 1452–61, pp. 284, 287). All grants of the duchy of Lancaster since 1450 were, in fact, resumed in this Parliament, and the grant of the principality of Wales to York was a grant of all lands held on 1 July 1442 (*Rot. Parl.* v. 384, 380).

[121] Joel 2: 15b–16a. Cf. vv. 15–20.

[122] The act of settlement had already formulated the constitutional novelty that encompassing the death of the duke, as the heir apparent, was treasonable (Bellamy, *Law of Treason*, p. 132).

French.[123] Financial provision for such eventualities, or, indeed, for anything at all, was much more precarious, as it was neither opportune nor practical to approach Parliament for a tax. Instead, York was assigned 10,000 marks, half for his own maintenance, 3,600 marks for the earl of March, and 1,000 marks for the earl of Rutland. To secure this sum he was granted the principality of Wales, the duchy of Cornwall, and the earldom of Chester.[124] This grant was a logical consequence of Prince Edward's disinheritance, and, had it been effective, it would have made York much the most powerful subject in the realm, as well as first councillor to the king. Any idea that Warwick, having captured the king, systematically thwarted York of the Crown in the 1460 Parliament in order that he might retain his own control of the State, has to account for this massive concession of potential power to York.

The decision to go north, implicit in Neville's sermon, was not an easy one to take in November. Some, at least, thought Queen Margaret to be in Wales with the earl of Pembroke, robbed of her cash, but confident of reinforcements.[125] They were wrong, as York and his advisers may have known, but even had she not been in the north there was an urgent need to intervene there as quickly as possible, partly to prevent vital castles being handed over to the Scots or the queen, or both, partly to restore order before the trouble could spill south. This was not just a problem of localized rioting. The earl of Northumberland was actively constructing an army in Yorkshire, ordering all men aged between sixteen and sixty to enlist to rescue the king.[126] The queen was believed to be trying to assemble forces in Hull.[127] In the West March, where Penrith was still in Lancastrian hands, the Yorkist council, in mid-November, could only order supporters to cope as best they could.[128]

[123] *Rot. Parl.* v, pp. 382–3.

[124] Ibid. 380–1. The figures are as given in the roll.

[125] *Gregory's Chronicle*, pp. 209–210. *Annales*, p. 773, notes that she took ship from Wales to Scotland. A letter received by the Common Council on 2 Dec. from the queen, the prince of Wales, and Jasper Tudor may have given rise to this impression (Barron, 'London and the Crown', p. 98).

[126] *Annales*, p. 774; Poulson, *Beverlac*, p. 231; C1/27/435. Beverley did not co-operate (Poulson, op. cit., p. 234). The earl also wrote to London (Barron, 'London and the Crown', pp. 98, 108 n. 76). Warwick was reportedly nearly captured by one of Northumberland's supporters in East Anglia (Waurin, *Croniques*, v. 309).

[127] *Gregory's Chronicle*, p. 210. The queen was in touch with London in early Dec. (Barron, op. cit., pp. 98, 108 n. 75).

[128] *CPR* 1452–61, pp. 651–2.

The purpose of the expedition to the north was to recover control of the castles of Pontefract and Wressle, and to establish reliable authority in York.[129] As a preliminary, this would require that York recover control of his lands in the West Riding. Clearly, a significant force would be necessary, and November was spent recruiting it.[130] There were problems, however, with both recruitment and finance. Kent and the Cinque Ports provided a sizeable force, which, in the event, was not to prove entirely reliable,[131] and York managed to obtain a little support from his Home-Counties estates, variously granting or confirming offices or annuities,[132] but there were other, no less pressing, demands on manpower. Calais had to be defended. It was necessary to send the earl of March to Shrewsbury to prevent Pembroke from joining up with the queen,[133] and there seems to have been no reliable person powerful enough to keep the west country men pinned down.[134]

Since Northampton, the regime had survived on loans, mostly modest, and for the most part from exchequer officials. Loans from twenty-two officials on 4 September amounted to £798. 14s. 1d., repaid by assignment in October.[135] Robert Stillington, the privy seal, raised 2000 marks from unknown sources, also in September.[136] John Say lent £2,076. 10s. 0d. on 8 October, and Henry Viscount Bourchier £2,538 on the same day.[137] In December an attempt to raise 1,000 marks in the city ran into difficulties.[138] There were probably other funds available, as the exchequer rolls for this term are only a partial guide to financial activity. They do not, for

[129] Duke Richard attempted to dissuade the Scottish regency government from further involvement with Queen Margaret (Bib. Nat. MS Fr. 20136 fo. 68).

[130] York took no recorded part in government throughout November, although he remained in London.

[131] Davies, *English Chronicle*, p. 108; Hist. MSS Comm. *Fifth Report*, p. 523. The sheriff, John Scot, had his farm waived on 8 Sept. (C81/779/10982).

[132] *CPR* 1461–7, pp. 14, 46, 57, 89. There are signs that York was short of money, and had debts to settle with London merchants (SC6/870/4).

[133] March was in the Gloucester area in late Dec., having passed, in all probability, through Oxford (*Short English Chronicle*, p. 72; Martin, *Archives of All Souls*, p. 159). He was reported as being in Shrewsbury from Christmas Day until the battle of Mortimers Cross (*Annales*, p. 775; *Gregory's Chronicle*, p. 211).

[134] Most reliance was placed on William Bourchier of Fitzwarin and, optimistically, on William Lord Bonville (*CPR* 1452–61, pp. 652, 654).

[135] E403/820.   [136] E404/71/5 n. 2.   [137] E403/820.

[138] Barron, 'London and the Crown', p. 103. Private individuals may have arranged loans in the city. John Wynne, goldsmith, arranged a loan of £1,403. 10s. 5d. His wife had been Duchess Cecily's companion on the voyage to Ireland in 1449 (*CCR* 1454–61, p. 473; E364/90).

example, record two payments of £100 ordered, on 28 September, in favour of the earl of March and the earl of Salisbury,[139] although it is likely that these warrants were obeyed. Tallies in York's name are recorded as honoured on 26 November (£50) and 5 December (78s. 4d.).[140] Despite these difficulties in the precise identification of available funds, it is unlikely that very large sums flowed into the administration's coffers.

York, Salisbury, and Rutland left London on 2 December,[141] Warwick staying behind. Who stayed with him is very uncertain. On 11 November nine peers had been recorded as present in the council.[142] It is unlikely that the number grew, a factor enhancing Warwick's authority.

At some point York set his own affairs in order. He had made a will, but when, and what its contents were, is unknown, as his executors refused to act.[143] He further enfeoffed on the archbishop of Canterbury, the earl of Warwick, and others his West-Riding and Northamptonshire estates, Rayleigh, and probably others.[144] The intention was that they should settle his debts and perform the other directions of his will. There were certainly debts,[145] possibly in the order of £6,000 or more,[146] but it would be unwise to regard this as the result of long-term financial distress. He had lost the revenues of his estates for over a year, and their administration was, doubtless, in some confusion. The pretensions of kingship had no doubt been costly, and the raising of a retinue to go north cannot have been cheap. If he died heavily in debt, and he probably did, this reflects recent misfortune rather than any long-term financial crisis. If anything, the scale of York's debts points to the willingness of creditors to lend in 1460.

---

[139] E404/71/5 n. 2, 3.   [140] E403/820.

[141] *Chronicles of London*, p. 193; *Benet's Chronicle*, p. 228, gives 5 Dec.

[142] Canterbury, Exeter, Ely, the earls of Warwick and Salisbury, Dudley, Stanley, Wenlock, and Stourton (*PPC* vi. 307).

[143] *Registrum Thome Bourgchier, Cantuariensis archiepiscopi, 1454–1486*, ed. F. R. H. Du Boulay Canterbury and York Society, 54, (1956), 200. The earl of Salisbury made his will in May 1459 (*Testamenta Eboracensia*, ed. J. Raine Surtees Society, pt. ii (1855) 207–9).

[144] *CPR* 1476–85, pp. 261, 269, 279, 341; *CCR* 1476–85, n. 920; *Excerpta Historica*, ed. Bentley, p. 370; *Calendar of Inquisitions Post Mortem: Henry VII*, i. 50, n. 124.

[145] Bean, 'Financial Position' p. 197.

[146] The arrangement of Edward IV in 1462 with Thomas Colt would, if it had been operative, have yielded about £1,000 p.a. and was obviously intended to run for some time (*CPR* 1461–7, p. 107).

The duke marched north through Nottingham, although by what route is uncertain. Fotheringhay, Stamford, and Grantham is just possible, but there is no evidence that anyone from these hitherto loyal areas joined him. If he went via Leicester he may well have hoped to gain William Hastings's support, but it does not seem to have been forthcoming. He ought to have marched in haste, and by the most direct route necessary, to prevent the earl of Devon making the city of York from the west country.[147] He did not. Admittedly, a rapid march would have cost York the reinforcements he urgently needed, but it is very unlikely that he was aware of the need. He had yet to see for himself the scale of the problem facing him, and he may have felt secure in the support of a useful number of north-country gentry, the recently recruited Fitzwilliams,[148] John Harrow of London and Richard Hanson of Hull,[149] Edward Bourchier and the old campaigner Sir Henry Retford, together with the northern knights Thomas Par, Thomas Harrington, and James Pickering.[150] This was a suffcient base for a routine law-and-order campaign, and York was able to add to its numbers at a lower social level. He picked up a modest recruit in the person of Richard Ford on 5 December,[151] the bailiff of Wakefield, William Burton, reportedly stayed loyal,[152] and York reputedly enjoyed popularity amongst the lower classes.[153] It cannot, however, be pretended that he commanded a large, well-armed and well-trained, retinue.[154]

When he arrived at Sandal on 21 December, the position was much more difficult than he could reasonably have anticipated. Northumberland, Clifford, Dacre, and Thomas Neville had been systematically destroying both York's and Salisbury's property in the area.[155] Somerset was garrisoning Pontefract, and the earl of Devon was in York with a sizeable force.[156] Somehow, Queen Margaret had

---

[147] His was certainly not the customary threefold march of an army advancing to battle (cf. Goodman, *Wars of the Roses*, p. 167. His point (p. 175) that Harrow led an infantry contingent may explain York's slow progress).

[148] *CPR 1461–7*, pp. 14, 46, 121, 479.

[149] *Great Chronicle*, p. 193; *Calendar of Plea and Memoranda Rolls 1458–82*, ed. Jones, p. 156. [150] *Annales*, p. 775.

[151] Appointed parker of Southfrith at £2 p.a. (WAM 12168).

[152] DL29/8899/560. [153] *Reg. Whethamstede*, i. 381.

[154] Only £4. 6s. 7d. was spent on his household in Sandal in Dec. (DL29/8899/560). Possibly Lords FitzHugh and Greystoke were intending to join him (*Annales*, p. 775). [155] DL29/8899/560.

[156] Recruited in Devon, Bath, Cirencester, Evesham, and Coventry (C. L. Kingsford, *Prejudice and Promise in Fifteenth-Century England* (1925), 177–9; *Annales*, p. 775).

persuaded the political community of the north to reject the declaration of the Parliamentary settlement, and, lacking control of the area, there was little York could do to counter this. Given these circumstances, prudence suggested that he gain as much sound military intelligence as possible, but he failed to do so.[157] An additional drawback was strong local dislike of Salisbury. The only encouraging feature was that Conisbrough castle was in the loyal hands of Edmund Fitzwilliam, who had taken the opportunity after Northampton of seizing Talbot's artillery from Sheffield and mounting it in the castle.[158]

In the circumstances, there was little else York could do but sit tight. His difficulty was lack of supplies, as the northerners had encamped around the town[159] and there had been no attempt to victual the castle in advance of his arrival. There may be some truth in one source's assertion, that York negotiated a truce with Somerset to last the twelve days of Christmas, and that the truce was deliberately broken,[160] but there can be little doubt that York met his end thanks to a sortie in strength.[161] This afforded the possibility of a pitched battle, and the northerners seized the chance.[162]

The young earl of Rutland died in combat at the hands of Lord Clifford on Wakefield Bridge. Trollope's men caught Salisbury in hiding that night, and he was executed at Pontefract the next day.[163] According to Whethamstede, York was taken alive, crowned with a paper crown and mocked by the soldiery, and was then beheaded.[164] No doubt, the parallel was intended to appeal to the new regime, but, in truth, York, who had appealed to violence to solve political problems so often in the past, died fighting those same political enemies. His head was severed from the corpse and displayed on the gates of York, a paper crown placed upon it in gruesome jest.

---

[157] Goodman, *Wars of the Roses*, p. 177.

[158] DL29/8899/560. York had also brought artillery with him (E404/71/5/38).

[159] *Reg. Whethamstede*, i. 381.   [160] *English Historical Literature*, p. 154.

[161] *Annales*, p. 775; *Reg. Whethamstede* i. p. 382. Even the confused account of de la Tour points to a large-scale sortie for supplies (*Calendar of State Papers, Milan*, ed. Hinds, p. 42).

[162] Some time was available to them to prepare their forces. The earl of Northumberland knighted two men before the battle was joined (C. H. Hunter Blair, 'Members of Parliament for Northumberland, 1399–1558', *Archaeologia Aeliana*, 4th ser., 12 (1935), pp. 99, 105).

[163] *Annales*, p. 775. According to this source, the bastard of Exeter executed him; according to his widow, John Sharp gent. of Pontefract was responsible.

[164] *Reg. Whethamstede*, i. 382. James Luttrell, a Devon squire, was later charged with the crime (*CPR* 1467–76, p. 522).

Seven days later the Londoners and the Burgundian artillery rescued the Yorkist cause from the catastrophe of Wakefield, and the young Duke Edward did much for his father's house at Mortimers Cross. At Towton, by force, he put himself in the right of kingship, and his father's severed head could, with dignity and decency, find its rest. Sixteen years were to elapse before his mortal remains were finally laid to rest in the chapel of Fotheringhay, amidst the splendours of the full arms of England and a golden crown held aloft by a reverential angel.[165] Had he worn the crown in his lifetime he would, no doubt, have ruled with justice and vigour, but devoted to the lost cause of English rule in France, as much a prey to self-interested counsel as was King Henry VI.

[165] BL Harleian MS. 48, fos. 78–91.

APPENDIX I

London: Public Record Office, Ancient Deeds, Series C (C146/6400)

This endenture made at ffoderingey the xxxti day of Januier the xxxvjto yere of the Regne of oure souverain lord kyng henry the sext betwix the right high and mighty prince my lord Richard Duc of york on the toon part and George Darell squier on the other part. Bereth witnesse that the saide George is belaste and witholden with my saide lord the duc for terme of his lyf promotting by the feith of his body and binding him by thees endentures forto doo true and feithful service unto my saide lord the duc. And with him forto (be)[1] agenst all erthly creatures of what estate preeminence or condition soo evere thay bee next the kyng our souverain lord and his yssu kyngs of England and of france. For the which witholding the saide George shal take of my saide lord the duc yerely the some of x li sterlings to bee taken of the yssues proufits and revenues of his manor and lordeship of Fasterne in Wiltshire by the handes of the receveurs fermers and other occupiers of the same for the tyme being Atte festes of the Annunciation of oure lady and mighelmasse by even portions. Unto the tyme that the saide George bee provided by my saide lord the duc unto an office or an other resonable reward of the valeu of xx mark by yere as by lettres patentes and lettres of warrant made theruppon unto the saide George undre the seel of my saide lord the duc hit may more clerely appere. In witnesse wherof to the toon part of thees endentures remaynyng towards the saide George my saide lord the duc hath doo set his signet the day place and yere aforesaide.

Signet seal, mutilated, on tongue; sign manual, 'R york', in left margin.

---

[1] Interlineated.

APPENDIX II

C OMMISSION OF THE DUKE OF Y ORK AS L IEUTENANT G ENERAL
OF F RANCE , 8 M AY 1436 (Paris: Bibliothèque Nationale Manuscrit
Francais 5330 fo. 137; a transcript in a fifteenth-century secretarial hand).

La commission et povoir donne par le Roy nostreseigneur amonsieur le duc
de york pour le gouvernement du Royaume defrance et Duchie de
normandie.

Henry par lagrace dedieu Roy de france et dengleterre Atous ceulx qui ces
presentts lettres verront salut. Comme pour les grans affaires qui nous
souvanenment de Jour en Jour, tant acause de nos royaumes de france et
dangleterre, comme dautres nos seigneuries soyons occupes en telle manere
que pour le present ne povons aller en personne puroveoir ala nescessite de
nostre dit royaume defrance duchie et pais de normandie. Combien que ce
sort entre les choses mondaines celle que plus nous touche acuer. Savoir
faisons que nous desirans nosdit royaume de france duchie et pais de
normandie et seugneuries de par dela tant en iustice, bonne pollice fait de
guerre de finance et aultrement, estre devenment et raisonnablement par
aulcun grant prince de nostre sang et (linguage)[1] lignage gouverne comme il
apperceut, Confans a plain es grave sens prudente loyaulte et vaillance de
nostre beaucousin Richart duc de york, qui nous est si prouchain desang
comme chermi[2] stait en sur ce grande et meuve deliberation tant avecques
nos beaulx oncles le duc degloucestre et le Cardinal dangleterre, comme
autres de nostre sang et lignage et gens de nostre grant conseil. Icelui nostre
beaucousin Richart duc de york anous per ladvis que dessus, fait cree
ordonne institue et establi, et par ces presentes faisons, creons, ordenons,
instituones et establissons nostre lieutenant general et gouveneur de nosdit
royaume de france duchie et pais de normandie et aultres nos domaines et
seigneures de par dela pour iceulx royaume et pais gouvernez pour nostre
nom et souver nostre scel en chief et en membres tant au regart de Justice et
pollice, comme de laguerre et finances collations, presentations et dispositions
de benefices et offices et autres choses quelconques conservans nosdit
royaume et pais. Excepte tant seullement les offices de connestable,
chancelleur, mareschal, tresoreurs et gouverneurs de finances que recevons
pour en disposes anostre voullente et plaisir. En donnant de nostre plaine
puissance strente auctorite royal et par ladvice que dessus a nostre dit
beaucousin le duc de york plain povoir, auctorite, commission et mandement

---

[1] Cancelled in MS.
[2] Reading uncertain.

especial par ces presentes de faire ce que dit est. Et oulter de donner, transporter, ceder, et declaisser atoutes personnes telles que bon lui semblera toutes manieres deterres et seigneuries nobles ou non nobles anous eschever ou aischeoir en iceulx royaume et pais par confiscation reversion ou aultrement en quelque maniere que cesort jusques ala valleur de mille salus dor de revenue par an, et au dessouver pour en joir aterme de vie ou pour eulx et les heires masles perpetuelment come de leur propre charge. Par my ce quils seront tenus de demourez sur icelles terres et seigneuries, et generalment de faire en tooutes aultres choses souver les nomes de lieutenant et gouverneur tant (sil)[3] seullement, tout ce que de bon gouverneur et lieutenant doit faire et que nous mesmes faire demuoe et pouvrions si presens yestions en nostre personne. Si donnons en mandement a tous les trois estats de nosdit royaume de france pais et duchie de Normandie tant gents deglise, secullaires, nobles, et aultres de quelque auctorite, dignite, premynence ou condition quils soient ou usent, et achacun par soy que avandit beaucousin le duc de york, et aset ordonnances, mandements et commandements obbeissent et entendent dilligauncent comme anostre lieutenant general et gouverneur de nosdit royaume et pais sans aucune opposition ou contredit. En testimony de ce nous avons fait mertre nostre scel aces presents. Donne en nostre pallays de Westm' le viije jour de may, lan de grace mliiij^{c}xxxvj Et de nostre regne le xiiij^e par le Roy en son grant conseil par lui tenu en son pallais de Westm' ouquel monsieur le duc de gloucestre, monsieur le Cardinal d'angleterre, les evesques de bathe, chancelleur dangleterre, de Norwyk, de Salisbury, de saint david et de Rocestre, le conte de suffolk, le sir de hongrefford, messre guillaume chambellain et autres plussieurs est. l Calot.

[3] Cancelled in MS.

APPENDIX III

SERVANTS AND ANNUITANTS OF DUKE RICHARD OF YORK

This list does not provide a full biography of the individuals named, but seeks only to identify their involvement with Duke Richard. In the reign of Edward IV individuals were rewarded for good service to the king and the king's father. Although in some instances there is a very strong likelihood that those rewarded did, indeed, serve Duke Richard, they are not listed here unless other evidence supports their inclusion. Minor estate officials such as local bailiffs are not listed.

ADE AP HOWELL. 1442/3 receiver of the gifts of Glasebury, Clifford, and Dynas (SC11/818).

THOMAS ALEYN. 1451/2 auditing clerk for the lordship of Fotheringhay, and in 1461 auditor for Duchess Cecily. Auditor in 1452/3 (SC6-764/10; SC6/1115/6; BL Egerton Roll 8784).

WILLIAM APPLEYARD. 8 Dec. 1439 granted £3 p.a. for life from Clare, and paid 20-mark annuity from customs for 1443/4. Probably not the bailiff of Thorne 1434/5 (WAM 12165; BL Egerton Roll 8703, 8782).

PHILIP ASHLEY, or ASTLEY. A lost brass at Standon described him as of the household of the duke (Cussens, *Hertfordshire*, i. 176).

JOHN AUSTYN. Before 1459 bailiff of Cranborne (*CPR* 1452–61, p. 590).

EMMA BAILLY. 1442/3 in receipt of £1 p.a. from Hughely (SC11/818).

JOHN BARKER. 1437 receiver of Bucks. and Oxon. (BL Egerton Roll 8781).

JOHN BARRE kt. 25 April 1433 granted £20 p.a. for life from Madwardine, paid 1442/3, confirmed 1460. In York's retinue 1436 and 1441 (*CPR* 1452–61, p. 548; C76/118 m. 12; E101/53/33; SC11/818).

WILLIAM BARROWE. 1442/3 in receipt of £2 p.a. from Cleobury Foreign (SC11/818).

THOMAS BARTON. Before 1442 receiver of Wigmore (SC11/818).

JOHN VISCOUNT BEAUMONT. He figures so frequently in York's property arrangements that he was almost certainly a councillor in the 1440s (*PPC* v. 136–8; BL Harleian Ch. 43 E 49.

M. ROBERT BEAUMONT, clerk. Very probably a councillor in 1436 and continued until 1441 BL Harleian Ch 53 H 17; *PPC* v. 136–8).

THOMAS BERNARD esq. 27 Oct. 1447 seneschal of Cambs. and Hunts. for life at 10 marks p.a.

ROBERT BOLD esq. 13 Sept. 1460 constable of Denbigh for life (*CPR* 1461–7, pp. 51, 60).

HENRY BOSSE. 1448/9 seneschal of Cranborne hundred, and bailiff of the same the following year (SC6/1113/9; BL Egerton Roll 8783).

JOHN BOTILLER. Before 1442 receiver of Shropshire (SC11/818).

EDWARD BOURCHIER esq. 27 Dec. 1456 granted 20 marks p.a. for life from Glos. (SC6/850/28).

HENRY VISCOUNT BOURCHIER. Councillor in 1449 and very probably from 1440 or earlier to 1460 (BL Egerton Roll 8783).

HUMPHREY BOURCHIER esq. 1459/60 seneschal of Stamford, fee £3. 6s. 8d. p.a. (SC6/1115/7).

ISABELLE LADY BOURCHIER. 25 April 1436 granted £100 p.a. for life from issues of Norfolk, Suffolk, and Essex, paid 1448/9 and £100 arrears from Clare (*CPR* 1461–7, p. 97; SC6/1113/10).

JOHN BOURCHIER. By 1459 steward of the honour of Clare and constable of Clare Castle (*CPR* 1452–61, p. 536).

JOHN BOYES. June 1454 a domestic servant (*Excerpta Historica*, ed. Bentley, p. 9).

WILLIAM BRADSHAWE esq. Jan. 1452 granted 100s. from Wakefield, and on 20 Nov. 1460 granted 20 marks from Soms. and Dors., confirmed 22 Nov. 1461 (*CPR* 1461–7, p. 57).

THOMAS BRADWEY esq. 19 May 1438 parker of Bardsley at a fee of £3. 0s. 8d. and a bonus of the same sum (paid 1447–9, 1451/2, 1457/8). 1 Jan. 1439 granted free housing in Bardsley, and at some stage he assumed the farm of the lordship (SC6/850/26–8; SC6/1115/6; *CPR* 1452–61, p. 548).

HENRY BROMFLETE, LORD VESCI. 1441/2 seneschal of Wakefield and Sowerby (DL29/8899/560), possibly a councillor in 1440s (BL Harleian Ch. 43 E 49).

WILLIAM BROWNING esq. Accompanied York to France in 1441. 27 May 1447 surveyor of Somerset and Dorset, and overseer of the receivership, and principal bailiff for life, at a fee of £5 p.a. for each office. As receiver in 1449/50 enjoyed a fee of £8 13s. 4d., and still receiver 1459/60. His effigy in Melbury Sampford church bears the collar of suns and roses (SC6/1113/11, 14; E101/53/33; BL Egerton Roll 8784).

GILES BRUGGE esq. 27 May 1455 granted £10 p.a. from Bisley. His step-father was John Browning, father of William Browning (q.v.) (SC6/850/28).

THOMAS BRUGGE. 12 Jan. 1456 granted 10 marks p.a. from Glos. for life (SC6/850/28).

WILLIAM BURLEY. 1442/3 lawyer retained in the lord's council at a fee of £13. 6s. 8d., seneschal and master forester of Denbigh (£40 p.a.), and seneschal of Montgomery (£20 p.a.). Still a councillor in June 1448 and very probably to death, 10 Aug. 1459 (SC11/818; SC6/1113/9).

MANDE COUNTESS OF CAMBRIDGE. 1437–9 in receipt of annuity of £100 p.a. (E213/385).

THOMAS CANDOVER DCL. Proctor in Rome (Emden, *Oxford*, iii. 2158).

ROGER CAPPES. 1436 lieutenant of Richard Dixton and William Prelatte at Bisley (SC6/850/28).

JOHN CARUS. 1442/3 paid £3. 6s. 8d. annuity from Llantrissam (SC11/818).

JOHN CASTEL. 1448/9 seneschal of Pimperne (SC6/1113/9).

ROGER CHAMBERLAIN, kt. 1451 seneschal of Swanscombe (KB9/265/109).

RICHARD CHAPELYN. 1451/2 'servant' (SC6/1113/11).

JOHN CHAUNDELL. 1448/9 clerk of the marshal (SC6/1113/10).

HENRY CHAUNDLER. 1453 'servant' (BL Egerton Roll 8784).

CLAREMENTINE (*sic*). 1448/9 paid £2 annuity from Clare.

JOHN CLAY. Treasurer of the household in Normandy in 1440s (BL Add. Chs. 12193, 12231).

WILLIAM CLETON. May 1454 'servant' (*Excerpta Historica*, ed. Bentley, p. 9).

JOHN LORD CLINTON. 27 Dec. 1456 granted 20 marks p.a. for life from Glos. In retinue of duke in 1441, with twenty lances and fifty-eight archers (SC6/850/28; E101/53/33; C76/123 m. 27).

WILLIAM COGGESHALE. 3 Sept. 1453 appointed parker of Hunsdon by Duke Richard, not William Oldhall, at a fee of £4. 11s. 4d. p.a. (SC6/1114/2).

JOHN COLSTON. 1448/9 paid £2 annuity from Clare (SC6/1113/10).

HENRY COOK. 1 Oct. 1446 yeoman of the kitchen with £5 p.a. from Usk, confirmed in 1461 (*CPR* 1461–7, p. 82).

JOHN COTES. 1437 receiver of Norfolk, Suffolk, and Essex. 21 Aug. 1443 parker of Fotheringhay at a fee of £2 p.a., paid 1451/2. Receiver of Thaxted. (BL Egerton Roll 8781, 8353; SC6/1115/6).

HUGH CRESSET. Before 1442 receiver of Montgomery and Shropshire. 1442/3 constable of Montgomery castle at a fee of £6. 16s. 0d. p.a. (SC11/818).

JOHN CROKER. 1437 receiver of Bucks. and Oxon. (BL Egerton Roll 8781).

RALPH LORD CROMWELL. Councillor Feb. 1445, and paid 100 marks annuity for 1443/4 (SC6/1115/6; BL Egerton Roll 8782).

ROGER CROSSE. 3 Sept. 1452 chaplain to the duke. 26 July 1456 archdeacon of Dublin with licence to be absent from Ireland (*Calendar of Papal Letters x. 1447–55*, p. 146; Berry, *Statutes of Ireland*, p. 460).

ROBERT DARCY. Lawyer, certainly a councillor by June 1448, at a fee of £20 p.a., paid since 1445, and probably a councillor in 1441. 1447/8 farmer of honour of Rayleigh for 100 marks p.a. (SC6/1113/9; WAM 12163, 12165; *PPC* v. 136–8; BL Egerton Roll 8782). Died 3 Sept. 1448.

GEORGE DARELL. 30 Jan. 1458 granted an annuity of £10 p.a. (C146/6400).

THOMAS DAVY. 1448/9 seneschal of Gussage Bohun (SC6/1113/9).

WALTER DEVEREUX, esq. 7 April 1452 seneschal of Radnor and Usk (Longleat: Devereux Papers Box 1 n. 6; McFarlane Transcripts).

WALTER DEVEREUX, kt. 1442/3 paid an annuity of £20 from lordship of

Pembridge. Before 1459 constable and porter of Wigmore castle. He accompanied York to France in 1441 (SC11/818; E101/53/33; *CPR* 1452–61, p. 586).

NICHOLAS DIXTON, clerk. Although there is no certain evidence, it is very likely that he was a councillor to York in 1441 (*PPC* v. 136–8).

RICHARD DIXTON. 1435/6 seneschal of Bisley. 1437 receiver-general. Attorney-general and feoffee for duke during first lieutenancy in France, and attorney-general again in 1442 and 1444 (SC6/850/26; C76/118 m. 4; C76/124 m. 12; C76/127 m. 4; BL Egerton Roll 8781; Harleian Ch. 53 H 17).

WILLIAM DONELL. 16 Sept. 1446 granted 5 marks p.a. for life from Winstone, paid 1457/8. 13 Jan. 1448 parker of Miserden at a fee of £3. 0s. 8d., paid 1447–9. Lost this office by 1457 (SC6/850/26–8).

JOHN DOREWARD the elder. 20 July 1447 granted 5 marks p.a. from Bardfield, and 1448/9 with Edmund Mulso joint seneschal of Rayleigh at a fee of £10 p.a. (WAM 12167; *CPR* 1461–7, p. 83).

ROBERT DOUGHTON. 13 Jan. 1451 granted £2 p.a. from Glos. for life, disallowed before Easter 1458 (SC6/850/28).

ROBERT DOVEDALE. Attorney of York in Ireland, date uncertain (SC1/44/ 45).

JOHN SUTTON, LORD DUDLEY. Surety for York in 1432, councillor by 1448/ 9 (*CCR*, 1429–35, pp. 190–2; SC6/1113/9).

Master THOMAS DUNKAN. 29 Sept. 1440 granted £26. 13s. 4d. p.a. for life from Glos., not paid 1457/8. Paid £10 from customs annuities of duke for 1442–5. Since 1423 rector of two portions of Bisley. Physician to the earl of March (SC6/850/28; BL Egerton Roll 8782; Emden, *Oxford*, p. 605).

JOHN ELTONHEAD. Before 1441 receiver of Denbigh (SC11/818; cf. KB27/ 783 *Rex* m. 16ʳ).

JOHN EYLERICHE. 1442/3 receiver of Shropshire at a fee of £5 p.a., and appointed receiver of Shropshire, Worcestershire, and the lordship of Bewdley after the Coventry Parliament (SC11/818; *CPR* 1452–61, p. 539).

JOHN FASTOLF, kt. June 1441, as councillor, granted a pension of £20 p.a. for life. May 1445 councillor, and paid as such, still councillor in June 1448 (SC6/1113/9; WAM 12165; BL Add. Ch. 14598; Egerton Roll 8781).

JOHN FEANTEVER. 1442/3 paid £2 5s. 6d. from Radnor (SC11/818).

NICHOLAS FENAY. 1432/3 receiver of Bucks. and Northants, 1451/2 receiver of Fotheringhay and auditing clerk (BL Egerton Roll 8774; SC6/1115/6).

THOMAS FITZMAURICE, EARL OF KILDARE. 1456/7 seneschal of the liberty of Meath (Berry, *Statutes of Ireland*, p. 462).

EDMUND FITZWILLIAM, esq. Before 4 Nov. 1460 appointed constable of Conisbrough castle (*CPR* 1461–7, pp. 14, 479).

JOHN FITZWILLIAM. 14 Nov. 1460 granted 10 marks p.a. for life from Yorks (*CPR* 1461–7, p. 121).

RICHARD FITZWILLIAM, esq. 14 Nov 1460 granted 10 marks p.a. for life from Yorks (*CPR* 1461–7, p. 46).

JOHN FLEGGE. 28 March 1440 parker of great park at Bardfield, and on 24 Jan. 1443 parker of the lesser park, drawing £3. 0s. 8d. and £3. 15s. 10d. respectively, paid 1447/8, 1450/1. 1 Oct. 1446 granted the manors of North Fambridge and Latchley Hall for himself and his wife, a grant not above suspicion. 15 Oct. 1446, with wife Agatha, had a grant of £2. 15s. 11d. p.a. from Latchley, paid 1460/1. 1448/9 bailiff of Deptord at a fee not less than £4. 11s. 3d. 1449/50 custodian of Stratfield Mortimer and of the great park there at fees of £3. 0s. 8d. and £6. 0s. 8d. respectively. Served with York in France and was captain of Bernay for the duke in 1444. (WAM 12165–8; SC6/1113/10; SC6/1115/1; *CPR* 1461–7, pp. 14, 45; *CPR* 1476–85, p. 179; E101/53/33; BL Add. Ch. 12236).

JOHN FOLKSWORTH. 1437 receiver of Northants. (BL Egerton Roll 8781).

RICHARD FORD. 5 Dec. 1460 seneschal and forester of Southfrith for life at a fee of £2 p.a. (WAM 12165).

JOHN GARGRAVE. 1429 attorney for York in King's Bench, and receiver-general in York's minority to 1429 (BL Egerton Roll 8759, 8774).

EUSTACE GERARD. 14 Sept. 1449 joint parker of Rayleigh at a fee of £3. 0s. 8d. (WAM 12167).

WILLIAM GLASIER. 1449/50 had allowance from Wotton Vetus of £6. 10s. 0d. for robes (SC6/1115/1).

REGINALD GREY, esq. Enjoyed 20 marks p.a. from Grantham and Stamford, but withdrew from York at Ludlow and had annuity confirmed by Henry VI on 25 Mar. 1460 (*CPR* 1452–61, p. 573).

THOMAS GREY, esq. Early 1450s 'servant' (SC1/51/92).

HENRY HAKLETON. 2 Oct. 1460 granted annuity of 10 marks p.a. from Herefords. (Longleat MS 10492).

JOHN HALL. 1442/3 paid an annuity of £3. 6s. 8d. from hundred of Barstaple (WAM 12167).

M. JAMES HAMELIN. Chaplain (*Calendar of Papal Letters ii 1431–47*, p. 237).

WALTER HARDY, or HARDING. 1448/9 seneschal of Cranborne Chase, having been appointed ranger of the same on 16 Feb. 1444, and confirmed in officer 1461, but fee of £6. 1s. 4d. in respect of the rangership was not paid in 1445. (SC6/1113/9; BL Egerton Rolls 8783, 8784; *CPR* 1452–61, p. 572; *CPR* 1461–7, p. 54).

RICHARD HARE. 1442/3 had a fee of £1. 6s. 8d. from Denbigh, possibly a lawyer (SC11/818).

JOHN HARPSFIELD. Aug. 1445 'servant', 1460 created chancellor of green wax, and chief remembrancer and clerk of the rolls of the duke's chancery at Trim (BL Add. Ch. 12267; Berry, *Statutes of Ireland*, p. 796).

JOHN HARPUR. 1458 auditor of Denbigh (*CPR* 1452–61, p. 570).

LEONARD HASTINGS, kt. 5 May 1435 granted £15 p.a. from Clarethall, and a further £15 p.a. from the same on 30 Sept. 1440. 1442/3 rider of Ludlow Chase at a fee of £5 p.a. Surrendered Clarethall grants on 1 Oct. 1448, in exchange for lands of duke at Cottingham at a rent of 15s. od. and seisin given on 4 Oct. At Agincourt with earl of March, in France in 1441 with Duke Richard (SC11/818; E101/53/33; BL Cotton Ch. v. n. 23; Hist. MSS. Comm. *Report on the Hastings Manuscripts*, i. p. 158).

JOHN HEMMINGBROUGH. A cook by profession, at one time in the service of Humphrey duke of Gloucester In York's service by 1451. Ranger of Cleobally in Rockingham forest at some time. Later chief cook to Edward IV (*CPR* 1446–52, p. 255; *CPR* 1461–7, pp. 48, 80).

HENRY AP GRIFFITH. 1442/3 master forester of Inan for life at a fee of £10 p.a. He also had £10 p.a. from Clifford. In York's retinue 1441 (SC11/818; E101/53/33).

JOHN HIGHAM. Servant, murdered in Ireland in 1460 (Berry, *Statutes of Ireland*, p. 786).

GEORGE HILTON. 2 Oct. 1460 granted an annuity of £5 p.a. from Wakefield (*CPR* 1461–7, p. 94).

THOMAS HOLCOTE. 2 Oct. 1460 granted annuity of 10 marks p.a. from Herefords. (Longleat MS 10491; McFarlane Transcript).

WALTER HOPTON. Prior to 1459 steward of Montgomery, Chirbury, Alcester, Tertref, Ceri, Cydewain, and Newton (*CPR* 1452–61, p. 552).

Hugh ap Meredith. 1442/3 paid an annuity of £1. 6s. 8d. from Montgomery (SC11/818).

EDWARD HULL, kt. 4 Apr. 1435 granted an annuity of £10 p.a. for life from Petherton, paid 1449/50. An attempt to pay him a fee of £5 as constable of Bridgewater Castle was cancelled in 1448/9, but paid 1451/2. In retinue of duke in 1436, constable of Bordeaux in 1440s (BL Egerton Roll 8783; SC6/1113/9, 11; C76/118 m. 14).

ROBERT HUNGERFORD, kt. Keeper of Cranborne Chase at a fee of £5 p.a., paid 1452, 1453 (BL Egerton Roll 8784).

JOHN HURLESTON. 1447/8 and still in 1450/1 receiver of Clare (WAM 12165, 12167).

JOHN AP JANKYN PIERS. 1442/3 paid an annuity of £3. 6s. 8d. from Llantrissam (SC11/818).

JOHN AP MEREDITH. 1442/3 lieutenant of the seneschal of Montgomery at a fee of £6. 13s. 4d. (SC11/818).

ROBERT KAY. 1452 paid £8 as life annuity from receipts of Kelby (SC6/1115/6).

JOHN KENDAL. 1451/2 cofferer of the household and probably in York's service to 1460 (SC6/1115/6; *CPR* 1476–85, p. 275).

WILLIAM KIRBY. 1447 'servant' BL Add. Ch. 12315.

JOHN KYRIELL. 1456–60 parker of Standon at a fee of £3. os. 5d. p.a. In 1460 he was owed £9 in wages (SC6/870/4).

JOHN LANE. 12 July 1445 appointed parker of Southfrith for life at a fee of £2 p.a., paid 1449–51 but lost by Dec. 1460. An archer of this name was with York in 1441 (WAM 12166, 12167; E101/53/33).

JOHN LANGLEY. 28 March 1434 granted £4 p.a. for life from Winstone, paid 1457/8. Accompanied York to Ireland in 1449 and 8 March 1449 granted £20 p.a. from Holmfirth in lieu of a like grant from Marshwood, confirmed 16 Jan. 1462 (SC6/850/28; KB9/252/2/53; E101/53/33; *CPR* 1452–61, p . 228; *CPR* 1461–7, p. 146).

HENRY LANGSHAWE. No date, appointed parker of Blakedon, confirmed Nov. 1461 (*CPR* 1461–7, p. 51).

JOHN LARDENER. 1453/4 'servant' (C1/24/20).

ROBERT LEGH. 4 Dec. 1454 appointed constable of Denbigh for life, confirmed 7 Aug. 1461 (*CPR* 1461–7, pp. 51, 60).

AGNES LENCHE. 1442/3 paid an annuity of £20 p.a. from Wigmore (SC11/818).

ROLAND LENTHALE, kt. 1442/3 paid an annuity of £26. 13s. 4d. from Wigmore, where he had previously enjoyed an annuity from the earl of March (SC11/818; *CPR* 1422–9, p. 380).

JOHN LEYLAND. 1448/9 seneschal of Fotheringhay (BL Egerton Roll 8437).

JOHN LLOYD. Before Dec. 1460 had annuity of 66s. 8d. from Denbigh (SC11/866).

HARRY LOVEDEYNE. 3 June 1454 groom of the kitchen (*Excerpta Historica*, ed. Bentley p. 9).

MAURICE LUDLOW. Enjoyed an annuity of 10 marks from Stanton Lacy (*Letters and Papers of the Reign of Henry VIII*, ed. J. S. Brewer, i. n. 1118).

THOMAS LUYT. Attorney in King's Bench in Hilary Term 1445. The following year he acted for Margaret of Anjou (KB27/774 *Rex* mm. 30ᵛ, 85ʳ).

ROGER LYGH (Clarenceux Herald). 1448/9 paid an annuity of £5 p.a. from Clare (SC6/1113/10).

JOHN MALPAS. 24 Aug. 1445 parker of Marshwood for life at a fee of £3. os. 8d. p.a., paid 1448–52. With Joan his wife, on 20 Jan. 1449, granted annuity of £5 p.a., paid 1449–52. Controller of the customs of Dublin and Drogheda. 1453 valet of wardrobe, formerly valet to Humphrey of Gloucester (SC6/1113/9, 11; BL Egerton Rolls 8783, 8784; E159/227 *Brevia Directa* Mich. Term m. 3ʳ; Berry, *Statutes of Ireland*, p. 187).

WILLIAM MAYELL. May 1454 servant (BL Cotton Vesp. F xiii. n. 99).

SIMON MILBOURNE. 2 Oct. 1460 granted annuity of 10 marks p.a. from Herefords. (Longleat MS 10495; McFarlane Transcripts).

THOMAS MILD. 1452 'Supervisor' in Essex (BL Egerton Roll 8353).

JOHN MILEWATER. 1442/3 receiver of Montgomery (fee £10 p.a.), and still acting in 1459/60, of Wigmore (£6. 13s. 4d. p.a.), of Radnor (£6. 13s. 4d. p.a.), of Maelienydd (£13. 6s. 8d. p.a.) and receiver-general of the earldom of March. 1446–60 constable of Clifford Castle, 1449/50 receiver-general, 1457/8 auditor of the lordship of Denbigh (SC11/818; BL Egerton Roll 8737; *CPR* 1452–61, pp. 547, 570).

JOHN MODY. 1457/8 parker of Miserden for life at a fee of £3. 0s. 8d. p.a., confirmed 1 Jan. 1460 (SC6/850/28, 29).

JOHN MONTGOMERY, kt. 10 Oct. 1438 seneschal of Thaxted, but lost office by 1448. 1437/8 seneschal of Clare (SC2/173/90 m. 1; SC6/1113/10; SC2/171/51 m. 9).

THOMAS MONYNGTON. Before Dec. 1460 had grant of annuity of £6. 13s. 4d. from Radnor (SC11/866).

ALICE MORTIMER. 1448/9 paid an annuity of £6. 13s. 4d. from Clare, and by grant of 20 Jan. 1449 paid an annuity of £6. 13s. 4d. from Somerford Keynes (SC6/1115/1; *CPR* 1452–61, p. 551; *CCR* 1454–61, p. 408).

JOHN MOYLE. Before Dec. 1460 had annuity of £10 from Denbigh (SC11/866).

WALTER MOYLE. No date, valet of the cellar, died before June 1461 (WAM 12168).

EDMUND MULSO, kt. 27 June 1446 seneschal and constable of Fotheringhay for life at fees of 5 marks and £10 p.a. respectively, and still paid 1451/2. 1448/9 joint seneschal of Rayleigh with £20 p.a. annuity from Clare. 21 Nov. 1447 rent-free grant of tenement in Gussage Bohun, and 1447/8 paid £4 p.a. for life from proceeds of the courts at Thaxted. He held Finmere and Barton for an unknown period, and in 1450/1 had compensatory grant for loss of lands in Erbury. He had briefly enjoyed the manor of Greys in 1443–4 (SC6/1115/6; SC6/1113/9, 10; WAM 12165, 12167; *CPR* 1461–7, p. 83). In retinue of duke in 1441, and household servant in Rouen and captain of Neufchatel to 1445. (E101/53/33; Bib. Nat. MS. Fr. 26074 n. 5305; Bib. Nat. Nouv. Acq. 2320 n. 265; *CCR* 1461–7, p. 115). 1449 accompanied York to Ireland and created seneschal of Meath, with power to appoint a deputy with authority to establish a town called Mulsoescourt in Fercullen. Granted tenements in Dublin (*CPR* 1446–52, p. 233; R. Butler, *Some Notices of the Castle of Trim* (Trim, 1840), 69; Berry, *Statutes of Ireland*, p. 214; *Rot. Pat. et Claus. Hib.* p. 265). In later life excused all royal service (C266/61/53).

WALTER MYMME. Oct. 1458 auditor of lordship of Denbigh (*CPR* 1452–61, p. 570).

JOHN NEVILLE, kt. After I St Albans he enjoyed jointly with Sir James Pickering all the offices and annuities formerly of Sir William Skipwith (q.v.).

JOHN NEWDIKE. 1437 receiver of Worcs. (BL Egerton Roll 8781).

THOMAS NEWNHAM. 1437 auditor (BL Egerton Roll 8774).

JOHN NEWPORT. 1443/4 'familiar' of the duke. 1448–?50 steward of the Isle of Wight, dismissed by York (E404/62/235; *Rot. Parl.* v. 204).

RICHARD NORMAN. Before 1441 receiver of Wigmore (SC11/818).

ROGER NORTON. 1449/50 paid £2 p.a. from Stratfield Mortimer (SC6/1115/1).

ANDREW OGARD, kt. May 1445 and in June 1448 described as councillor (WAM 12165; SC6/1113/9), and councillor in France Jan. 1443 (Bib. Nat. MS Fr. Nouv. Acq. 2320 n. 259). He did not employ York as a feoffee in 1448 (*DKR* 37/ii, 569). Died 13 Oct. 1454.

WILLIAM OLDHALL, kt. June 1447 councillor, chamberlain by 1448/9 to death, seneschal of honour of Clare at £15 p.a., and constable of Clare at £13. 6s. 8d. p.a., seneschal of Thaxted at £5 p.a. (BL Add. Ch. 496; SC6/1113/10). 1448/9 enjoyed half of all revenues of York's Gloucester- shire estates, and had grant of Wratting at death of Sir Thomas Hengrave (SC6/850/27; SC6/1114/2). SC6/1449/50 seneschal of Hitchin at £3 p.a. and 28 Oct. 1447 farmer of lands at Erbury for £4. 6s. 0d. p.a. (BL Egerton Roll 8364; WAM 12165). Councillor and chamberlain March 1449 (*CPR* 1446–52, p. 231). 1449 seneschal of Ulster at a fee of 100 marks (*Reg. Johannis Mey*, ed. Quigley and Roberts, p. 133; Oxford Bodley MS Eng. Hist. c 34 i).

JOHN ORAM. Clerk of the spicery 1432, 1437, clerk of the itinerant household 1453 (BL Egerton Rolls 8774, 8784, 8786).

JAMES ORMOND, EARL OF WILTSHIRE. 24 March 1446 seneschal of all lordhips in Dorset for life at a fee of £13. 6s. 8d., and of Marshwood for life at £2 p.a., both paid 1449/50 and 1451/2. 22 June 1446 granted for life the manors of Tarrant Gunville, Wareham, Steeple, and Creech, at an unspecified rent. 1459 he held the court at Marshwood and appointed the bailiffs for that year, and also William Kennyshame as receiver of Wiltshire (*pace* Rosenthal). 1459/60 annuity of £40 from Knole (BL Egerton Roll 8783; SC6/1113/11, 14).

THOMAS OTLEY. 1437 receiver in Kent (BL Egerton Roll 8781).

THOMAS PALMER. 1451/2 seneschal of Grantham at a fee of £4 p.a. (SC6/1115/6).

JOHN PARKER. 1424 parker of Netherwood for life at £3. 0s. 8d. p.a., confirmed Dec. 1459 (SC6/1113/1; *CPR* 1452–61, p. 528).

THOMAS PARKER. 1460 granted annuity of £15 from fee farm of Bromwich (SC6/1115/4).

WILLIAM PARKER. 1434 parker of Blakedon at £3. 0s. 8d. p.a. (SC6/1113/1).

JOHN PAYNE. 28 Nov. 1456 attorney in chancery for the feoffees of Sir Leonard Hastings, headed by York (C44/31/7).

NICHOLAS PEMBERTON, esq. 18 April 1452 granted £5 p.a. for life from Wakefield, confirmed 20 July 1461 (*CPR* 1461–7, p. 97; *CCR* 1461–7, p. 21).

JAMES PICKERING, kt. After I St Albans he enjoyed jointly with Sir John Neville all the offices and annuities formerly of Sir William Skipwith (q.v.).

JOHN PLASEDEN. 30 June 1437 'laudier' and 'palisser' of Conisbrough park (*CPR* 1461–7, p. 122, date corrected).

JOHN POPHAM, kt. 16 July 1440 granted 100 marks p.a. for life from Dorset in recompense for an annuity granted by the king from Builth, paid 1449– 53 (BL Egerton Rolls 8783, 8784; SC6/1113/11; *CCR* 1435–41, p. 150; *CPR* 1436–41, p. 134). With York in France in 1436 (E404/52/331).

WILLIAM PRELATTE. 1435/6 receiver of Bisley, 1448/9 receiver of arrears in Glos. and 1457/8 receiver of Glos., accounting until Easter (SC6/850/26, 27, 28).

STEPHEN PRESTON. 24 Aug. 1460 constable of Bridgewater and keeper of Petherton at a fee of £5 p.a., confirmed 1 Nov. 1460 (SC6/1113/16; *CPR* 1461–7, p. 96).

JOHN PROFOOT. 1447 receiver-general of Norman lands (BL Add. Ch. 8031).

ROGER PYRE. July 1461 late yeoman of the chamber (*CPR* 1461–7, p. 27).

RICHARD QUATREMAINS. 1448/9 lawyer, councillor. 1460/1 senior auditor in south west, probably by appointment of Duchess Cecily, who on 29 June 1461 made him supervisor of all her lands. His monumental brass in Thame (Oxon.) repeats his title of councillor (SC6/1113/10, 15; SC6/764/10).

EDWARD RANDOLF. 10 June 1440 parker of Blakedon at a fee of £2. 6s. 8d. p.a., paid 1451–3 (SC6/1113/11; BL Egerton Roll 8784).

ROGER REE. 18 April 1439 yeoman of chamber with corrody from Hamon Abbey. 1 Jan. 1440 valet of the chamber and parker of Rayleigh for life at £3. 0s. 8d. p.a., but on 14 Sept. 1449 joint parker at same fee. 12 Nov. 1446 grant for £5 p.a. for life from East Woodbury, and 1450/1 had £4. 13s. 4d. p.a. for life from hundred of Barstaple. 1 Jan. 1451 usher of the chamber, pardoned 'of Fotheringhay' 21 Jan. 1456, and served York to 1460 (WAM 12165, 12167; *CCR* 1435–41, p. 272; *CPR* 1461–7, p. 139; *CPR* 1467–76, pp. 62, 531; C67/41 m. 10).

SIMON REYHAM. 1448–50 cofferer of the household, losing office c.1451. 1451/2 receiver-general of earldom of March (BL Egerton Rolls 7360, 7364; SC6/1113/10, 11).

JOHN ROCKLEY. 1447/8 parker of Thunderley at £4. 13s. 6d. p.a.; paid only 45s. 6d. in this year, but in full 1449/50 (WAM 12165–6).

JOHN RUSSELL. ?1448/49 seneschal of Winstone and of all Wiltshire estates 1449/50. Held office at Fasterne to Dec. 1459 (*CPR* 1452–61, p. 574).

Dr THOMAS ST JUST. 1460 orator, chaplain, and almoner to duke (Berry, *Statutes of Ireland*, p. 794; Emden, *Cambridge*, p. 503).

JOHN SAVILLE, kt. 1427/8 seneschal of Sowerby, April 1458 seneschal of Wakefield, and probably master forester of Sowerby and constable of Sandal. Before 1461 farmer of the iron workings at Ossett, paying £14. 6s. 8d. p.a. (DL29/8899/560; KB9/289 m. 44; (*CPR* 1452–61, p. 532).

JOHN SAY. 4 Dec. 1453 seneschal of Hitchin, 1459/60 seneschal of Standon and Anstey (SC6/870/4).

THOMAS LORD SCALES. June 1448 councillor (SC6/1113/9). 1452/3 councillor of Margaret of Anjou (Myers, 'Household of Queen Margaret', p. 426). A councillor in Normandy in 1438 (C76/126 m. 5), but not in the 1440s.

THOMAS SCUDAMORE. 1442/3 receiver of Ewyas Lacy at a fee of £2 p.a. In retinue of Henry Lord Bourchier in 1441 (SC11/818; E101/53/33).

JOHN SEARLE (DE LA SELER). 4 Nov. 1460 parker of Bardfield at a fee of £3. 0s. 10d. p.a., paid 1461. He was described as 'of Bardfield, parker' in a general pardon of 14 Sept. 1452. Before 1459 enjoyed a fee from Fasterne (SC6/1114/2; C237/43/83; *CPR* 1461–7, pp. 14, 574).

RICHARD SHERBOURNE BA. Almoner (*Calendar of Papal Letters ii 1431–47*, p. 463).

JOHN EARL OF SHREWSBURY. 1442/3 paid £200 annuity, and in April 1447, from Ludlow, Builth, Clifford, and Wigmore (SC11/818).

JOHN SKELTON, esq. In 1445 paid £20 for arrears of 20-mark annuity (BL Egerton Roll 8782).

WILLIAM SKIPWITH, kt. 1 May 1454 grant of £20 p.a. for life from Hatfield, confirmed Aug. 1461. Before May 1455 he was seneschal of Hatfield and Conisbrough and chief parker there, and in receipt of £20 p.a. of York's annuity-entitlement at the Hull customs (*CPR* 1461–7, p. 53; *CPR* 1452–61, p. 552).

JOHN SMITH the younger. 1459/60 receiver of Herts., and at some time of the honour of Clare. July 1461 receiver of all lands of the duke of York and earl of March for good service to the duke (SC6/870/4; *CPR* 1467–76, p. 432; *CPR* 1461–7, p. 18).

JOHN SOUTHWORTH. 13 Sept. 1460 granted £10 p.a. for life from Denbigh (*CPR* 1461–7, p. 129).

RICHARD STALWORTH. Aug. 1452 'formerly valet' (BL Egerton Roll 8364).

JOHN STANLEY, esq. 1442/3 constable of Denbigh at a fee of £10 p.a. (SC11/818).

WILLIAM STANLEY OF HOPTON, esq. Before Oct. 1458 receiver of Denbigh (*CPR* 1452–61, p. 570).

JOHN STANLOW. 1448/9 councillor. Treasurer of Normandy for Richard Beauchamp, earl of Warwick, then for York (S6/1113/9; E404/53/324; BL Ad. Ch. 8435; Palgrave, *Antient Kalendars*, ii. 193). What connection he retained with York after 1450 is unknown, cf. Griffiths, *Reign of Henry VI*, p. 652 n. 26.

THOMAS STAYNDROPE. March 1453 collector of fines and amercements in Hadleigh (KB27/774 *Rex* m. 85ʳ).

JOHN STODEHAUGH. 28 Oct. 1448 seneschal of Southwold for life at a fee of 10 marks p.a., paid 1450/1. 1448/9 lieutenant of Sir John Montgomery in unknown capacity at a fee of £1. 10s. 0d. (WAM 12167; SC6/1113/10).

JOHN STOKKYS, esq. Parker of ?Bekkeley (Oxon.), confirmed 13 Mar. 1461 (*CPR* 1461–7, p. 8).

EDWARD STONE. 1432 receiver in Dorset (BL Egerton Roll 8774).

JOHN STORKE. Lawyer, councillor May 1447. Granted an annuity of £2 p.a., on 25 Dec. 1446, paid 1449/50 and 1451/2. 1453 auditor, 1459/60 held court at Marshwood (SC6/1113/9, 11, 14; BL Egerton Rolls 8783, 8784).

THOMAS STOTFIELD. 26 March 1434 yeoman of the chamber and parker of Bardfield for life, 1448/9 valet of the chamber, paid £5. 6s. 5d. p.a. from Clare (SC6/1113/10; *CPR* 1461–7, p. 15).

THOMAS STRINGER. 5 Nov. 1460 porter of the outer gate of Denbigh, and surveyor of the works, confirmed 1461 (*CPR* 1461–7, p. 89).

JOHN STURGEON. Bailiff of Hitchin at a fee of £5 p.a. He paid £2 p.a. for the tolls of Hitchin (SC6/870/4).

RALPH BUTLER, LORD SUDELEY. 24 May 1438 granted £26. 13s. 4d. p.a. for life from Lechlade, but cancelled in 1457/8 (SC6/850/28).

JOHN THYKKETHORP. 1450/1 groom of the chamber (C1/18/22).

WILLIAM TRESHAM. Lawyer, councillor 1448/9 (SC6/1113/9). Died 23 Sept. 1450.

JOHN TRUSSEL, kt. Receiver-general until death in 1437 (BL Egerton Roll 8781).

JOHN TYRELL, kt. A feoffee in 1436, and very probably a councillor (Reaney and Fitch, *Feet of Fines for Essex*, p. 23).

JOHN VAMPAGE. 1448/9 receiver of arrears in Dorset, probably the father who was a lawyer (SC6/1113/9).

ROGER VAUGHAN. 1442/3 receiver of Builth at fee of £3. 6s. 8d. (SC11/818).

JOHN VINCENT. 1432 and 1437 receiver in Yorks. 1457–9 receiver of Compton and Bardsley, and again in Michaelmas Term 1460, and 1457–61 receiver for Yorks. (BL Egerton Rolls 8774, 8781; DL29/8899/560; *CPR* 1452–61, p. 567).

JOHN WALDEN, alias GERARD. 1432 receiver in Essex, Norfolk, and Suffolk. 1444/5, 1448–53, 1455/6 receiver of Clare (WAM 12165–7; SC6/1113/12; BL Egerton Roll 8784; KB9/26/1 m. 25). 1448/9 clerk of the kitchen. He authorized payments, Feb. 1436, at Rouen to purveyors of poultry to the duke (SC6/1113/10; BL Egerton Ch. 7361).

JOHN WALL. 1460 chaplain (Berry, *Statutes of Ireland*, p. 796).

RICHARD WARNEFORD. 1437 and 1449/50 receiver in Wilts. (BL Egerton Roll 8781; SC6/1115/1).

JAMES WATER. Attorney in Ireland (SC1/44/45).

WILLIAM WELLES, kt. 26 Aug. 1450 seneschal of Meath (Butler, *Notices of Trim*, p. 69.

JOHN WENLOK, kt. 1 Jan. 1456 granted £20 p.a. from Hitchin, paid 1459 (SC6/870/4, 5).

REGINALD WEST, LORD DE LA WARE. Councillor June 1448 (SC6/1113/10). Died 27 Aug. 1450.

THOMAS WHITGREVE. Before 1442 receiver-general of Wales and Marches. By grant of June 1419 enjoyed lands in Worcs. to value of £10 p.a. for life. By 1435 in service of the Staffords (SC11/818; C139/18/40; Rawcliffe, *Staffords*, pp. 213, 225).

JOHN WIGMORE. June 1434 exchequer attorney, 14 Mar. 1438 attorney-general, 15 May 1438 attorney to collect annuities. 1442/3 paid an annuity of £20 p.a. from Arley. Attorney for York in absences in France and Ireland (E101/335/24; E159/214 m. 2^v Trinity Term 16 Henry VI.; SC11/818; C76/118 m. 4; C76/127 m. 4; E403/750, 781; *CPR* 1452–61, p. 392).

RICHARD WIGMORE, esq. Steward of the household and surety for York in 1432, 1451 receiver in Essex (*CCR* 1429–35, p. 190; BL Egerton Rolls 8353, 8779).

ROGER WIGMORE. Before 1442 receiver of Denbigh (SC11/818).

M. WILLIAM WILFLETE. 1453 commissioner of audit. 1455 confessor to duke. (BL Egerton Roll 8784).

WILLIAM AP JOHN. Before 1442/3 receiver of Ewyas Lacy at a fee of £2 p.a.

WILLIAM AP THOMAS, kt. Feb. 1444 councillor, and probably in 1441. 1442/ 3 chief steward of Maelienydd, Usk, and Caerleon, at a fee of £20 p.a. each (*PPC* v. 136–8; BL Egerton Ch. 7358).

THOMAS WILLOUGHBY. 1439/40 auditor in south west (SC6/1113/9), auditor of all lands of the earldom of March at a fee of £13. 6s. 4d., and a mark for robes, 1451–3 auditor of all lands in England at a fee of £21. 6s. 8d., with one mark for robes (SC6/1113/9, 11; BL Egerton Roll 8784). 1451/2 auditor of lordship of Fotheringhay (SC6/1115/6). 1453 treasurer of the household (BL Egerton Roll 8784; E403/798). Described as councillor in a papal indult in 1456. Descriptive categories in such letters tend to be loose, but this is probably correct (*Calendar of Papal Letters xi. 1455–64*, p. 227).

RICHARD WIMBUSH. 24 May 1436 attorney-general in York's absence in France (C76/118 m. 4).

JOHN WINNERSBURY, esq. Surety for York in 1432 (*CCR* 1429–35, p. 190–2).

WILLIAM WOLLASTON. 24 May 1436 agent for York at the exchequer, and a feoffee in York's retinue in 1441 (E403/724; Reaney and Fitch, *Feet of Fines for Essex*, p. 23; E101/53/33).

JOHN WOODEROVE. 1460/1 receiver of lordship of Sandal, possibly appointed by Duchess Cecily (DL29/8899/560).

JOHN WYKES. Before July 1449 seneschal of Ulster (*Reg. Johannis Mey*, p. 176).

THOMAS YOUNG. 26 Feb. 1447 seneschal of Easton in Gordano at a fee of 53*s*. 4*d*., paid 1448/9. He farmed Easton in Gordano at £16. 13*s*. 4*d*. p.a., and in 1459/60 owed £200 in arrears. 1449 attorney for duke in Ireland (SC6/1113/9, 14; *CPR* 1446–52, p. 245).

BIBLIOGRAPHY

MANUSCRIPT SOURCES

London, Public Record Office

Chancery
Early Chancery Proceedings (C1).
Miscellanea (C47).
Parliamentary and Council Proceedings (C49).
Patent Rolls, Supplementary (C67).
Treaty Rolls (C76).
Warrants for the Great Seal, Series 1 (C81).
Inquisitions *Post Mortem* (C138).
Inquisitions *Post Mortem* (C139).
Ancient Deeds, Series C (C146).
Mainpernors (C237).

Court of Common Pleas
Feet of Fines (CP25).

Duchy of Lancaster
Ministers' Accounts (DL29).
Miscellanea (DL29).

Exchequer
Exchequer of Pleas, Pleas Rolls (E13).
Treasury of Receipt, Council and Privy Seal Records (E28).
Treasury of Receipt, Ancient Deeds, Series A (E40).
King's Remembrancer, Accounts, Various (E101).
King's Remembrancer, Memoranda Rolls (E159).
King's Remembrancer, Sheriff's Accounts (E199).
King's Remembrancer, Bille (E207).
Pipe Office, Rolls of Foreign Accounts (E364).
Exchequer of Receipt, Receipt Rolls (E401).
Exchequer of Receipt, Issue Rolls (E403).
Exchequer of Receipt, Warrants for Issues (E404).

Justices Itinerant
Assize rolls (Just. It. 1).

Court of King's Bench
Crown Side, Ancient Indictments (KB9).
Coram Rege Rolls (KB27).

Privy Seal Office
Warrants for the Privy Seal, Series 1 (PSO1).

Special Collections
Ancient Correspondence (SC1).
Ministers' and Receivers' Accounts (SC6).
Ancient Petitions (SC8).
Rentals and Surveys (SC11).

London, British Library

Additional Charters.
Campbell Charters.
Cotton Charters.
Cotton Manuscripts, Vespasian E vii. F viii. Titus B xi.
Egerton Charters.
Egerton Rolls.
Harleian Charters.

London, Westminster Abbey Muniments

6643, 12165, 12166, 12167, 12168.

Hampshire County Record Office

23M58/57b (Household Account of Duke of York for 1450).
Wrottesley Manuscripts.

Hampshire, Winchester College, MS 19811

Oxford

Bodleian
MS Dugdale 2.
Lat. MS b119.

Magdalen College
MS Misc. 306.
McFarlane Transcripts.

Paris, Bibliothèque Nationale

Manuscrits Français.
Manuscrits Français, Nouvelles Acquisitions.

Salop Count Record Office

Box viii (Minister's Accounts for the Borough of Shrewsbury).

Primary Authorities

ANSTIS, J., *Register of the Most Noble Order of the Garter*, 2 vols. (1724).
Annals of the Four Masters, ed. J. O'Donovan (Dublin, 1851).
Annals of Ulster 1379–1541, ed. B. MacCarthy (Dublin, 1887–1901).
BASIN, T., *Histoire de Charles VII*, ed. C. Samaran (Paris, 1933–44).
BAYLEY, J., and CALEY, J. (eds.), *Calendarium Inquisitionum Post Mortem sive Excaetarium*, Record Commission (1806–28).
BENTLEY, S. (ed.), *Excerpta Historica* (1831).
BERRY, H. F. (ed.), *Statute Rolls of the Parliament of Ireland*, ii. *Reign of Henry VI* (Dublin, 1910).
The Book of Saint Albans, ed. W. Blades (1881).
BREWER, J. S. and BULLEN, W. (eds.), *Calendar of the Carew Manuscripts Preserved in the Library at Lambeth*, v. *Book of Howth* (1867–73).
BROTANEK, R., *Mittelenglische Dichtungen* (1940).
The Brut, or the Chronicles of England, ed. F. W. Brie Early English Text Society (1906–8).
Calendar of Ancient Records of Dublin, ed. J. T. Gilbert, (Dublin, 1889).
Calendar of Charter Rolls, 1427–1516 (1927).
Calendar of Close Rolls, 1409–1485 (1932–54).
Calendar of Deeds and Documents, iii. *Hawarden Deeds*, ed. F. Green, (1931).
Calendar of Entries in the Papal Registers Relating to Great Britain and Ireland: Papal Letters, 1431–1471 (1913–56).
Calendar of Fine Rolls, 1422–1485 (1935–61).
Calendar of Inquisitions Post Mortem: Henry VII (1898–1956).
Calendar of Letters and Papers, Foreign and Domestic: Henry VIII, 1515–1518 (1864).
Calendar of Letters and Papers, Foreign and Domestic, Henry VIII, I (1509–13), ed. J. S. Brewer (1920).
Calendar of Patent Rolls, 1391–1485 (1905–11).
Calendar of Plea and Memoranda Rolls of the City of London, 1458–82, ed. P. E. Jones, (Cambridge, 1961).
Calendar of State Papers, Milan, ed. A. B. Hinds, (1912).
Calendar of State Papers, Venice, ed. R. Brown (1864).

CHRIMES, S. B., and BROWN, A. L. (eds.), *Select Documents of English Constitutional History, 1307–1485* (1961).
A Chronicle of London 1189–1483, eds. N. H. Nicolas and E. Tyrell, (1827).
Chronicles of London, ed. C. L. Kingsford, (Oxford, 1905).
Collections of a London Citizen, ed. J. Gairdner, Camden Society, 2nd ser., 17 (1876).
The Commentaries of Pius II on the Memorable Events of his Times, trans F. A. Gragg, ed. Leona C. Gabel, Smith College Studies in History, 22, 25, 30, 35, 43 (1937–57).
COOPER, C. P., *Report on Rymer's Foedera: Appendix D: Archives of France* (1836).
The Coventry Leet Book, ed. M. D. Harris, Early English Text Society (1908).
Les Croniques de Normandie:1223–1453, ed. A. Hellot, (Rouen, 1881).
DAVIES J. S. (ed.), *The Tropenell Cartulary*, Wiltshire Archaeological and Natural History Society, 4 (1908).
Descriptive Catalogue of Ancient Deeds (1890–1915).
DUGDALE, W., *Monasticon Anglicanum*, ed. J. Caley, H. Ellis, and B. Bandinel (1817–30).
An English Chronicle, ed. J. S. Davies, Camden Society, 1st ser., 64 (1856).
FABYAN, R., *The New Chronicles of England and France*, ed. H. Ellis (1811).
FRY, E. A., and G. S., *Full Abstracts of the Feet of Fines Relating to the County of Dorset*, Dorset Records, 9 (1896).
GASCOIGNE, T., *Loci et Libro Veritatum*, ed. J. E. T. Rogers (Oxford, 1881).
GILBERT, J. T., *Facsimilies of the National Manuscripts of Ireland* (Southampton, 1874).
GILSON, J. P., 'A Defence of the Proscription of the Yorkists in 1459', *English Historical Review*, 26 (1911), 512–25.
Great Chronicle of London, ed. A. H. Thomas and I. D. Thornley (1938).
GREEN, E., Pedes Finium *for the County of Somerset: Fourth Series: Henry IV to Henry VI*, Somerset Record Society, 22 (1906).
HARRISS, G. L. and M. A. (eds.), 'John Benet's Chronicle for the years 1400 to 1462', in *Camden Miscellany*, 21 Camden Society, 4th ser., 9 (1972), 151–233.
Historical Manuscripts Commission: Second Report, (1871); *Third Report*; (1872), *Fifth Report*, (1876); *Seventh Report*, (1879); *Eighth Report*, (1881); *Report on the Manuscripts of the Dean and Chapter of Wells*, (1907–14).
Historical Poems of the XIVth and XVth Centuries, ed. R. H. Robbins (New York, 1959).

Incerti Scriptoris Chronicon Angliae de Regnis . . . Henrici IV, Henrici V, et Henrici VI, ed. J. A. Giles (1848).

JEAYES, I. H., *Descriptive Catalogue of the Charters and Muniments of the Gresley Family* (1895).

KINGSFORD, C. L., *English Historical Literature in the Fifteenth Century* (Oxford, 1913).

—— 'An Historical Collection of the Fifteenth Century', *English Historical Review*, 29 (1914) 505–15.

LASCELLES, R., *Liber Munerum Publicorum Hibernia* (1824).

Letters and Papers Illustrative of the Wars of the English in France During the Reign of Henry the Sixth, ed. J. Stevenson, Rolls Series (1864).

Letters of Queen Margaret of Anjou, ed. C. Munro, Camden Society, OS, 86 (1863).

MARTIN, C. T., *Catalogue of the Archives in the Muniment Room of All Souls College* (1877).

Memoires pour servir de preuves à la histoire ecclesiastique et civile de Bretagne, ed. H. Morice (Paris, 1742–6).

MYERS, A. R., *The Household of Edward IV* (1959).

The Official Correspondence of Thomas Bekynton, ed. G. Williams, Rolls Series (1872).

NORTIER, M., *Les sources de l'histoire de Normandie au département des manuscrits de la Bibliothèque Nationale: Fonds latines* (Nogent-sur-Marne, 1959).

Original Letters Illustrative of English History, ed. H. Ellis, 3rd ser. (1846).

PALGRAVE, F., *The Antient Kalendars and Inventories of the Treasury of His Majesty's Exchequer*, Record Commission (1836).

Paston Letters and Papers of the Fifteenth Century, ed. N. Davis (Oxford, 1971–6).

The Paston Letters, 1422–1509, ed. J. Gairdner, (1904).

Proceedings and Ordinances of the Privy Council of England, ed. N. H. Nicolas, Record Commission (1834–7).

REANEY, P. H., and FITCH, M., *Feet of Fines for Essex* (Colchester, 1964).

The Register of Henry Chichele, archbishop of Canterbury, 1414–43, ed. E. F. Jacob, Canterbury and York Society (1937–47).

Registrum Abbatiae Johannis Whethamstede, ed. H. T. Riley, Rolls Series (1872).

Registrium Iohannis Mey, ed. W. G. H. Quigley and E. F. D. Roberts (Belfast, 1972).

Registrum Johannis Stanbury, episcopi Herefordensis 1453–74, ed. A. T. Bannister, Canterbury and York Society, 25 (1919).

Registrum Reginaldi Boulers, episcopi Herefordensis 1450–3, ed. A. T. Bannister, Canterbury and York Society, 25 (1919).

Registrum Thome Bourgchier, Cantuariensis Archiepiscopi, AD 1454–1486, ed. F. R. H. Du Boulay, Canterbury and York Society, 54 (1956).

Registrum Thome Spofford, episcopi Herefordensis 1422–48, ed. A. T. Bannister, Canterbury and York Society, 23 (1919).

Report of the Deputy Keeper of the Public Records, 34 (1873); 37 (1876).

Report of the Deputy Keeper of the Public Records of Ireland: Appendix viii: Calendar of Christ Church Deeds (Dublin, 1888–92).

Report of the Royal Commission on the Historical Manuscripts of Ireland (1810–15).

Reports from the Lords' Committees Touching the Dignity of a Peer of the Realm (1829).

Rerum Anglicarum Scriptores Veterum, ed. W. Fulman (Oxford, 1648).

Rotuli Parliamentorum, ed. J. Strachey, 6 vols. (1767–77).

Rotulorum Patentium et Clausorum Cancellariae Hiberniae Calendarium, i/1., ed. E. Tresham, Irish Record Commission (Dublin, 1828).

RYMER, T., *Foedera, Conventiones, Litterae, et Cuiuscunque Generis Acta Publica* (1704–35).

SHARPE, R. R., *Calendar of Letter Books Preserved among the Archives of the Corporation of the City of London: Letter Book K* (1911).

Six Town Chronicles of England, ed. R. Flenley (Oxford, 1911).

SMYTH, J., *Lives of the Berkeleys*, ed. J. Maclean (Gloucester, 1883).

Statutes at Large Passed in the Parliaments Held in Ireland (Dublin 1786).

STOW, J., *Annales, or a General Chronicle of England*, ed. E. Howes (1631).

Testamenta Eboracensia, ed. J. Raine, Surtees Society (1855).

Testamenta Vetusta, ed. N. H. Nicolas (1826).

THOMPSON, A. H., 'The Statutes of the College of St Mary and All Saints Fotheringhay', *Archaeological Journal*, 75 (1918), 241–309.

Three Fifteenth-Century Chronicles, ed. J. Gairdner, Camden Society, 2nd ser., 28 (1880).

VIRGOE, R., 'Some Ancient Indictments in the King's Bench Referring to Kent, 1450–52', in *Kent Records: Documents Illustrative of Mediaeval Kentish Society*, ed. F. R. H. Du Boulay, Kent Record Society, 18 (1964), 214–65.

WAURIN, Jean de, *Receuil des Croniques et Anchiennes Istories de la Grant Bretaigne*, ed. W. and E. L. C. P. Hardy, Rolls Series (1864–91).

WILLIAM WORCESTER, *Itineraries*, ed. J. Harvey (Oxford, 1969).

Wills and Inventories Illustrative of the History, Manners, Language, Statistics, etc., of the Northern Counties of England, from the Eleventh Century Downwards, Surtees Society (1835).

WRIGHT, T., *A Collection of Political Poems and Songs Relating to English History, from the Accession of Edward III to the Reign of Henry VIII*, Rolls Series (1859–61).

WROTTESLEY, G., *Extracts from the Plea Rolls of the Reigns of Henry V and Henry VI*, William Salt Archaeological Society, 17 (1896).

Wrottesley, G., *Early Chancery Proceedings*, William Salt Archaeological Society Collections, NS, 7 (1904).

Secondary Authorities

Allmand, C. T., 'Some Effects of the Last Phase of the Hundred Years War upon the Maintenance of the Clergy', in G. J. Cuming (ed.), *Studies in Church History*, 3 (1966), 179–90.
—— *Lancastrian Normandy, 1415–1450: The History of a Medieval Occupation* (Oxford, 1983).
Armstrong, C. J., 'Politics and the Battle of St Albans, 1455', *Bulletin of the Institute of Historical Research*, 33 (1960), 1–72.
Atkyns, R., *Ancient Gloucestershire*, 2nd edn. (1768).
Barron, C. M., 'London and the Crown, 1451–61', in J. R. L. Highfield and R. Jeffs (eds.), *The Crown and Local Communities in England and France in the Fifteenth Century* (Gloucester, 1981).
Bean, J. M. W., *The Estates of the Percy Family, 1416–1537* (Oxford, 1958).
—— 'The Financial Position of Richard, Duke of York', in J. Gillingham and J. C. Holt (eds.), *War and Government in the Middle Ages: Essays in Honour of J. O. Prestwich* (Cambridge, 1984).
de Beaucourt, G. du Fresne, *Histoire de Charles VII* (Paris, 1881–91).
Bellamy, J. G., *The Law of Treason in the Later Middle Ages* (Cambridge, 1970).
Bossuat, A., *Perrinet Gressart et François de Surienne, agents d'Angleterre* (Paris, 1936).
Butler, R., *Some Notices of the Castle of Trim* (Trim, 1840).
Carpenter, C., 'Sir Thomas Malory and Fifteenth-Century Local Politics', *Bulletin of the Institute of Historical Research*, 53 (1980), 31–43.
Carus-Wilson, E. M., 'The Iceland Trade', in E. Power and M. M. Postan (eds.), *Studies in English Trade in the Fifteenth Century* (1933).
—— 'Evidences of Industrial Growth on Some Fifteenth-Century Manors', *Economic History Review*, 2nd ser., 12 (1959–60), 190–205.
—— and Coleman, O., *England's Export Trade: 1275–1547*, (1963).
Chaplais, P., 'The Chancery of Guyenne, 1289–1453', in J. Conway Davies (ed.), *Studies Presented to Sir Hilary Jenkinson* (1957), 61–89.
Chrimes, S. B., *English Constitutional Ideas in the Fifteenth Century* (1936).
Cockayne, G. E. C., *The Complete Peerage of England, Scotland, Ireland*, ed. Vicary Gibbs, H. A. Doubleday, G. H. White, and R. S. Lea (1910–59).
Comber, J., *Sussex Genealogies* (1931).

COSGROVE, A., *Late Medieval Ireland, 1370–1541* (Dublin, 1981).

—— 'Parliament and the Anglo–Irish Community: The Declaration of 1460', *Historical Studies*, 14 (Belfast, 1983).

CRAWFORD, A., 'The King's Burden?: the Consequences of a Royal Marriage in Fifteenth-Century England', in R. A. Griffiths (ed.), *Patronage, the Crown, and the Provinces in Later Medieval England* (Gloucester, 1981).

CURRY, A. E., 'The First English Standing Army?: Military Organisation in Lancastrian Normandy, 1420–50', in C. D. Ross (ed.), *Patronage Pedigree and Power in Later Medieval England* (Gloucester, 1979).

CURTIS, E., 'The Bonnaght of Ulster', *Hermathena*, 46 (1931), 87–91.

—— 'Richard Duke of York as Viceroy of Ireland, 1447–1460', *Journal of the Royal Society of Antiquaries of Ireland*, 62 (1932), 157–86.

CUSSENS, J. E., *History of Hertfordshire* (1870–81).

DAVIES, R. R., 'Baronial Accounts, Incomes and Arrears in the Later Middle Ages', *Economic History Review*, 2nd ser., 2 (1968), 211–29.

Dictionary of National Biography, 63 vols. (1885–1900).

DOBSON, R. B. (ed.), *The Church, Politics, and Patronage in the Fifteenth Century* (Gloucester, 1984).

DOLLEY, R. H. M., 'Anglo–Irish monetary Policies', in J. C. Beckett (ed.), *Historical Studies*, 7 (1969).

DUGDALE, W., *The Baronage of England* (1675–6).

DUNLOP, A., *The Life and Times of James Kennedy, Bishop of St Andrews* (1950).

EDWARDS, R. D., 'The Kings of England and Papal Provisions to Irish Bishoprics, 1449–54', in J. A. Watts, J. B. Morrall, and F. X. Martin. (eds.), *Medieval Studies Presented to Aubrey Gwynn* (Dublin, 1961).

EMDEN, A. B., *A Biographical Register of the University of Oxford* (Oxford, 1957–9).

—— *A Biographical Register of the University of Cambridge to 1500* (Cambridge, 1963).

EUBEL, C., *Hierarchica Catholica Medii Aevi* (Regensburg, 1901).

FERGUSON, J., *English Diplomacy, 1422–61* (Oxford, 1972).

FIELD, P. J. C., 'Sir Thomas Mallory M.P.', *Bulletin of the Institute of Historical Research*, 47 (1974), 24–35.

FITZMAURICE, E. B., and LITTLE, A. G., *Materials for the History of the Franciscan Province of Ireland, 1230–1450*, British Society of Franciscan Studies (1920).

DE FRONDEVILLE, H., *La Vicomté d'Orbec pendant l'occupation anglaise 1417–49* (Paris, 1936).

GILSON, J. P., 'A Defence of the Proscription of the Yorkists in 1459', *EHR*, 26 (1911), 512–25.

GOODMAN, A., *The Wars of the Roses: Military Activity and English Society, 1452–97* (1981).

—— and MORGAN, D., 'The Yorkist Claim to the Throne of Castile', *Journal of Medieval History*, 11 (1985), 61–71.

GOTTFRIED, R. S., *Epidemic Disease in Fifteenth-Century England* (1978).

GRAY, H. L., 'Incomes from Land in 1436', *English Historical Review*, 49 (1934), 607–39.

GRIFFITH, M. C., 'The Talbot–Ormond Struggle for the Control of Anglo–Irish Government, 1441–7', *Irish Historical Studies*, 2 (1940–1), 376–97.

GRIFFITHS, R. A., 'Gruffydd ap Nicholas and the Fall of the House of Lancaster', *Welsh History Review*, 2 (1965), 213–31.

—— 'Local Rivalries and National Politics: The Percies, the Nevilles, and the Duke of Exeter, 1452–55', *Speculum*, 43 (1968), 589–632.

—— 'Duke Richard of York's Intentions in 1450 and the Origins of the Wars of the Roses', *Journal of Medieval History*, 1 (1975), 187–209.

—— 'Richard Duke of York and the Royal Household in Wales, 1449–50', *Welsh History Review*, 8 (1976–7).

—— 'The Sense of Dynasty in the Reign of Henry VI', in C. D. Ross (ed.), *Patronage, Pedigree, and Power in Later Medieval England* (Gloucester, 1979).

—— 'Public and Private Bureaucracies in England and Wales in the Fifteenth Century', *Transactions of the Royal Historical Society*, 5th ser., 30 (1980), 109–130.

—— *The Reign of King Henry VI: The Exercise of Royal Authority, 1422–61* (1981).

—— 'The King's Council and the First Protectorate of the Duke of York, 1453–54', *English Historical Review*, 99 (1984), 67–82.

HARE, J. N., 'The Wiltshire Risings of 1450: Political and Economic Discontent in Mid-Fifteenth Century England', *Southern History*, 4 (1982), 13–31.

HARRIS, W., *The Whole Works of Sir James Ware Concerning Ireland* (Dublin, 1764).

HARRISS, G. L., 'The Struggle for Calais: An Aspect of the Rivalry Between Lancaster and York', *English Historical Review*, 75 (1960), 30–53.

—— 'Marmaduke Lumley and the Exchequer Crisis of 1446–9', in J. G. Rowe (ed.), *Aspects of Late Medieval Government* (1986).

HEAD, C., 'Pius II and the Wars of the Roses', *Archivum Historiae Pontificiae*, 8 (1970), 139–78.

HICKS, M., 'The Changing Role of the Wydevilles in Yorkist Politics to 1483', in C. D. Ross (ed.), *Patronage Pedigree and Power in Later Medieval England* (Gloucester, 1979).

HOLMES, G. A., *The Estates of the Higher Nobility in XIV Century England* (Cambridge, 1957).

—— 'The "Libel of English Policy"', *English Historical Review*, 76 (1961), 193–216.

HUNGER, V., *Le Siège et Prise de Caen* (Paris, 1912).

HUNTER BLAIR, C. H., 'Members of Parliament for Northumberland, 1399–1558', *Archaeologia Aeliana*, 4th ser., 12 (1935), 82–132.

JACOB, E. F., *The Fifteenth Century* (Oxford, 1961).

JEFFS, R. M., 'The Poynings–Percy Dispute: An Example of the Interplay of Open Strife and Legal Action in the Fifteenth Century', *Bulletin of the Institute of Historical Research*, 24 (1961), 148–64.

JONES, M. D., 'John Beaufort Duke of Somerset and the French Expedition of 1443', in R. A. Griffiths (ed.), *Patronage, the Crown, and the Provinces in Later Medieval England* (Gloucester, 1981).

JOUET, R., *La Résistance à l'occupation anglaise en Basse-Normandie, 1418–1450* (Caen, 1969).

KEEN, M. H., and DANIEL, M. J., 'English Diplomacy and the Sack of Fougères in 1449', *History*, 49 (1974), 375–91.

KEKEWICK M., 'The Attainder of the Yorkists in 1459: Two Contemporary Accounts', *Bulletin of the Institute of Historical Research*, 55 (1982), 25–34.

KEMPE, A. J., *Historical Notices of the Collegiate Church or Royal Free Chapel and Sanctuary of St Martin-le-Grand, London* (1825).

KINGSFORD, C. L., *Prejudice and Promise in Fifteenth-Century England* (1925).

KIRBY, J. L., 'The Rise of the Under-Treasurer of the Exchequer, 1412–83', *English Historical Review*, 72 (1957), 666–7.

KNOWLSON, G. A., *Jean V, duc de Bretagne et l'Angleterre, 1399–1442* (Cambridge/Rennes, 1964).

LANDER, J. R., 'Henry VI and the Duke of York's Second Protectorate, 1455–6', *Bulletin of the John Rylands Library*, 43 (1960–1), 46–69.

—— 'Marriage and Politics in the Fifteenth Century: The Nevilles and the Wydevilles', *Bulletin of the Institute of Historical Research*, 36 (1963), 119–152.

—— *Conflict and Stability in Fifteenth-Century England* (1969).

LE CACHEUX, P., *Rouen au temps de Jeanne d'Arc et pendant l'occupation anglaise 1419–1449*, Société d'Histoire de Normandie, Paris (1931).

LEWIS, P. S., 'Sir John Fastolf's Lawsuit over Tithwell, 1448–1455', *Historical Journal*, 1 (1958), 1–20.

LLOYD, T. H., *The English Wool Trade in the Middle Ages* (Cambridge, 1977).

LOBEL, M. D., *The Borough of Bury St Edmunds* (Oxford, 1935).

LOVATT, R., 'A Collector of Apocryphal Anecdotes: John Blacman Revisited', in A. J. Pollard (ed.), *Property and Politics: Essays in Later Medieval English History* (Gloucester, 1984).

LYDON, J. F., *The Lordship of Ireland in the Middle Ages* (Dublin, 1972).

LYSONS, S., *A Collection of Gloucestershire Antiquities* (1804).

MACDOUGALL, N., *James III: A Political Study* (Edingburgh, 1982).

McFARLANE, K. B., 'Loans to Lancastrian Kings, the Problem of Inducement', *Cambridge Historical Journal*, 9 (1947), 51–68.

—— 'At the Deathbed of Cardinal Beaufort', in R. W. Hunt, W. A. Pantin and R. W. Southern (eds.), *Studies in Medieval History Presented to Frederick M. Powicke* (Oxford, 1948).

—— 'The Wars of the Roses', *Proceedings of the British Academy*, 50 (1964), 87–1119.

—— *The Nobility of Later Medieval England* (1973).

—— *England in the Fifteenth Century* (1981).

MATTHEW, E., 'The Financing of the Lordship of Ireland Under Henry V and Henry VI', in A. J. Pollard (ed.), *Property and Politics: Essays in Later Medieval English History* (Gloucester, 1984).

MAXWELL LYTE, H. C., *A History of Dunster* (1909).

MUNRO, J. H., *Wool, Cloth, and Gold* (Toronto, 1972).

MYERS, A. R., 'The Household of Queen Margaret of Anjou, 1452–3', *Bulletin of the John Rylands Library*, 40 (1957–8), 79–113, 391–431.

—— *The Household of Edward IV* (Manchester, 1959).

—— 'The Jewels of Queen Margaret of Anjou', *Bulletin of the John Rylands Library*, 42 (1959–60), 113–31.

NEALE, J. E., 'The Commons Privilege of Free Speech in Parliament', in R. W. Seton-Watson (ed.), *Tudor Studies* (1924).

NEWHALL, R. A., *Muster and Review* (Cambridge, Mass., 1940).

NICHOLS, J. G. (ed.), *Collectanea Topographica et Genealogica* (1834–43).

OTWAY-RUTHVEN, A. J., *A History of Medieval Ireland* (1968).

OWEN, H., and BLAKEWAY, J. B., *A History of Shrewsbury* (1825).

PLUCKNETT, T. F. T., *A Concise History of the Common Law* (1940).

POLLARD, A. J., *John Talbot and War in France, 1427–1453*, Royal Historical Society (1983).

POSTAN, M. M., 'The Economic and Political Relations of the Hanse from 1400 to 1475', in E. Power and M. M. Postan (eds.), *Studies in English Trade in the Fifteenth Century* (1933).

POULSON, G., *Beverlac* (1829).

POWELL, E., 'The Restoration of Law and Order', in G. L. Harriss (ed.), *Henry V* (Oxford, 1985).

POWICKE, F. M. (ed.), *Oxford Essays in Medieval History Presented to H. E. Salter* (Oxford, 1934).

POWICKE, F. M., and FRYDE, E. B., *Handbook of British Chronology*, 2nd edn. (1961).

POWICKE, M. R., 'Lancastrian Captains', in T. A. Sandquist and M. R.

Powicke (eds.), *Essays in Medieval History Presented to Bertie Wilkinson* (Toronto, 1969).

PUGH, T. B. (ed.), *Glamorgan County History*, 3 (Cardiff, 1971).

—— 'Richard Plantagenet (1411–60), Duke of York, as the King's Lieutenant in France and Ireland', in J. G. Rowe (ed.), *Aspects of Late Medieval Government and Society* (1986).

RADFORD, G., 'Nicholas Radford, 1385?–1455', *Report of the Transactions of the Devonshire Association for the Advancement of Science, Literature, and Art*, 63 (1931), 251–78.

RAMSAY, J. H., *Lancaster and York* (Oxford, 1892).

RAWCLIFFE, C., *The Staffords, Earls of Stafford and Dukes of Buckingham, 1394–1521* (Cambridge, 1978).

—— 'Baronial Councils in the Later Middle Ages', in C. D. Ross (ed.), *Patronage, Pedigree, and Power in Later Medieval England* (Gloucester, 1979).

REEVES, A. C., *Lancastrian Englishmen* (Washington, 1981).

RICHARDSON, H. G., and SAYLES, G. O., *The Irish Parliament in the Middle Ages* (Philadelphia, 1952).

RICHMOND, C. F., 'The War at Sea', in K. Fowler (ed.), *The Hundred Years War* (1971).

ROBINSON, W. R. B., 'An Analysis of a minister's accounts for the Borough of Swansea for 1449', *Bulletin of the Board of Celtic Studies*, 22 (1966), 169–98.

ROSENTHAL, J. T., 'Fifteenth-Century Baronial Incomes and Richard, Duke of York', *Bulletin of the Institute of Historical Research*, 37 (1964), 233–40.

—— 'The Estates and Finances of Richard, Duke of York, 1411–60', in W. M. Bowsky (ed.), *Studies in Medieval and Renaissance History* 2 (Nebraska, 1965).

—— 'Richard, Duke of York: A Fifteenth-Century Layman and the Church', *Catholic History Review*, 50 (1964–5), 171–87.

ROSKELL, J. S., 'The Knights of the Shire for the County Palatine of Lancaster, 1377–1460', *Chetham Society*, NS, 96 (1937), App. B.

—— 'The Office and Dignity of Protector of England with Special Reference to its Origins', *English Historical Review*, 68 (1953), 193–231.

—— *The Commons in the Parliament of 1422* (Manchester, 1954).

—— 'William Tresham of Sywell, Speaker for the Commons under Henry VI', *Northamptonshire Past and Present*, 2 (1954–9), 189–203.

—— 'Sir John Popham, Knight Banneret of Charlford, Speaker-elect in the Parliament of 1449–50', *Proceedings of the Hampshire Field Club and Archaeological Society*, 21 (1958), 43–55.

—— 'William Burley of Broncroft, Speaker for the Commons in 1437 and

1445–6', *Transactions of the Shropshire Archaeological Society*, 56 (1960), 263–72.

ROSENTHAL, J. S., 'Thomas Thorpe, Speaker in the Parliament of 1453–4', *Nottingham Medieval Studies*, 5 (1963), 79–105.

—— *The Commons and their Speakers in English Parliaments 1376–1523* (Manchester, 1965).

—— *Parliament and Politics in Late Medieval England* (1981–3).

ROSS, C. D., 'The Estates and Finances of Richard, Duke of York', *Welsh History Review*, 3 (1967), 299–302.

—— *Edward IV* (1974).

—— *The Wars of the Roses* (1976).

—— and PUGH, T. B., 'The English Baronage and the Income Tax of 1436', *Bulletin of the Institute of Historical Research*, 25 (1953).

ROWE, B. J. H., 'The *Grand Conseil* under the Duke of Bedford, 1422–35', in F. M. Powicke (ed.), *Oxford Essays in Medieval History Presented to H. E. Salter* (Oxford, 1934).

SCOFIELD, C. L., *The Life and Reign of Edward IV* (1923).

SETON-WATSON, R. W. (ed.), *Tudor Studies* (1924).

SHAW, S., *The History and Antiquities of Staffordshire* (1798–1801).

SIMMS, K., 'The King's Friend: O'Neill', in J. Lydon (ed.), *England and Ireland in the Later Middle Ages* (Dublin, 1981).

SOMERVILLE, R., *A History of the Duchy of Lancaster* (1953).

STEEL, A., *The Receipt of the Exchequer, 1377–1485* (Cambridge, 1954).

STOREY, R. L., 'The Wardens of the Marches of England towards Scotland, 1377–1489', *English Historical Review*, 72 (1957), 593–615.

—— *The End of the House of Lancaster* (1966).

—— 'Episcopal King-Makers in the Fifteenth Century', in R. B. Dobson (ed.), *The Church, Politics, and Patronage in the Fifteenth Century* (Gloucester, 1984).

THIELEMANS, M-R., *Bourgogne et Angleterre: rélations politiques et économiques entre les Pays-Bas Bourguignons et l'Angleterre, 1435–1467* (Brussels, 1966).

VALE, M. G. A., 'The Last Years of English Gascony, 1451–1453', *Transactions of the Royal Historical Society*, 5th ser., 19 (1969), 119–38.

—— *English Gascony, 1399–1453* (Oxford, 1970).

—— *War and Chivalry* (1981).

VAUGHAN, R., *Philip the Good* (1970).

VICKERS, K. H., *Humphrey Duke of Gloucester* (1907).

Victoria County History of Shropshire viii (1978).

Victoria County History of Suffolk ii (1907).

VIRGOE, R., 'The Composition of the King's Council 1437–61', *Bulletin of the Institute of Historical Research*, 43 (1970), 134–60.

—— 'William Tailboys and Lord Cromwell: Crime and Politics in

Lancastrian England', *Bulletin of the John Rylands Library*, 55 (1973), 459–82.

WATT, J. A., 'The Papacy and Ireland in the Fifteenth Century', in R. B. Dobson (ed.), *The Church, Politics, and Patronage in the Fifteenth Century* (Gloucester, 1984).

WEDGWOOD, J. C., *History of Parliament: Biographies of the Members of the House of Commons, 1439–1509* (1936).

WILKINSON, B. *The Constitutional History of England in the Fifteenth Century* (1964).

WOLFFE, B. P., 'Acts of Resumption in the Lancastrian Parliaments, 1399–1456', *English Historical Review*, 73 (1958), 583–613.

—— *The Royal Demesne in English History* (1971).

—— *Henry VI* (1981).

WOOD, H., 'Two Chief Governors of Ireland at the Same Time', *Journal of the Royal Society of Antiquaries of Ireland*, 58 (1928), 270–1.

WYLIE, J. H., and WAUGH, W. T., *The Reign of Henry V* (Cambridge 1914–29)

DISSERTATIONS

BURNEY, E. M., 'The English Rule of Normandy, 1435–50' (Univ. of Oxford B.Litt. thesis, 1958).

JONES, M. D., 'The Beaufort Family and the War in France, 1421–1450' (Univ. of Bristol Ph.D. thesis, 1983).

MARSHALL, A. E., 'The Role of English War Captains in England and Normandy, 1436–1461' (Univ. of Wales, Swansea, MA thesis, 1975).

RICHMOND, C. F., 'Royal Administration and the Keeping of the Seas, 1422–85' (Univ. of Oxford D.Phil. thesis, 1963).

WOODGER, L. S., 'Henry Bourchier, Earl of Essex, and His Family' (Univ. of Oxford D.Phil. thesis, 1974).

INDEX

The following abbreviations have been adopted: abp. archbishop; bp. bishop; c. count, countess; clk. clerk; d. duke, duchess; da. daughter; e. earl; ld. lord; m. marquis; s. son; w. wife